STIRRING UP SHEFFIELD

STIRRING UP SHEFFIELD

An insider's account of the battle
to build the Crucible Theatre

BY COLIN GEORGE & TEDD GEORGE

Foreword by Ian McKellen

© 2021 Colin George & Tedd George
ISBN: 978-1-8384036-2-1

First edition
All rights reserved

The rights of Colin George and Tedd George to be identified as the authors of this work have been asserted in accordance with the Copyright, Designs & Patents Act 1988.
No part of this book may be reproduced or transmitted in any form or by any means without the written permission of Wordville.

Cover design by Rozalia Sherwood
Front cover image: Sir Tyrone Guthrie, Colin George & Frank Hatherley survey the shell of the Crucible auditorium under construction, January 1971.
The back cover design of the Crucible Theatre auditorium is reproduced with permission from Anne Minors and Susanne Bochmann of Sound Space Vision.
Typeset by Paul Medcalf, Avocet Typeset
Proofread by Oliver Schick
Font: 12 on 14.75pt Goudy Old Style

Wordville

Wordville
www.wordville.net
info@wordville.net

Colin George

Colin George was the founding Artistic Director of the Crucible Theatre. Born in Pembroke Dock, Wales, in 1929, Colin read English at University College, Oxford, and was a founding member of the Oxford and Cambridge Players. After acting in the repertory companies of Coventry and Birmingham, Colin joined the Nottingham Playhouse in 1958 as Assistant Director to Val May. In 1962, he was appointed Assistant Director at the Sheffield Playhouse, becoming Artistic Director in 1965. Colin played a leading role in the creation of the Crucible Theatre, which opened in November 1971, and was the Crucible's Artistic Director from 1971 to 1974.

Colin was Artistic Director of the Adelaide State Theatre Company (1976-80) and of the Anglo-Chinese Chung Ying Theatre Company (1983-1985) and was Head of Drama at the Hong Kong Academy for Performing Arts (1985-1993). Colin joined the Royal Shakespeare Company as an actor for two seasons (1994-96 and 1997-99).

In 2011 Colin was invited by the Crucible's Artistic Director, Daniel Evans, to join the Company for the 40th anniversary production of *Othello*. This was to be his last theatrical performance and, fittingly, it took place on the thrust stage he had created. Following *Othello*, Colin produced the first draft of this book, before his death in October 2016.

Tedd George

Tedd George (aka Dr Edward George) is Colin George's son. Tedd is an economist, broadcaster and writer. He has a PhD in political science from the University of Bristol. His book—*The Cuban intervention in Angola, 1965-1991: from Che Guevara to Cuito Cuanavale*—was published by Routledge in 2005.

From 2005 to 2011, Tedd worked in the Africa Department of the Economist Intelligence Unit (EIU), focusing on Lusophone and Francophone Africa. From 2011 to 2019, Tedd worked as Head of Research and Head of the UK for pan-African bank, Ecobank, before setting up his own company, Kleos Advisory Ltd, which provides thought leadership and strategic advisory on African markets and fintech. Tedd regularly appears as chairman, speaker and moderator on the world conference and webinar circuit, and as a commentator in the media.

To David Brayshaw & Tony Hampton,
steadfast allies in the battle for the Crucible

TABLE OF CONTENTS

Foreword by Ian McKellen — xi
Prologue by Colin George — xiii
Editor's note by Tedd George — xvi
List of illustrations — xxv
List of plates — xxxi

Part I: The New Sheffield Playhouse
Chapter 1 — 3
Chapter 2 — 16
Chapter 3 — 30
Chapter 4 — 38

Part II: Guthrie & the Thrust Stage
Chapter 5 — 51
Chapter 6 — 60
Chapter 7 — 72
Chapter 8 — 87

Part III: Designing the Crucible
Chapter 9 — 99
Chapter 10 — 114
Chapter 11 — 127
Chapter 12 — 145

Part IV: The Three Knights
Chapter 13 — 159
Chapter 14 — 175
Chapter 15 — 188
Chapter 16 — 199

Part V: Battling for the Crucible

Chapter 17	209
Chapter 18	225
Chapter 19	235
Chapter 20	246

Part VI: Lights Up

Chapter 21	257
Chapter 22	273
Chapter 23	285
Chapter 24	297

Epilogue by Tedd George	314
Dramatis Personae	324
Bibliography	326
Six thrust theatres: 1948 to 1976, by Iain Mackintosh	330
Architectural plan of the Crucible Theatre, 1971	333
Ground plans of productions at the Crucible, 1971-72	336
Main auditorium productions at the Crucible, 1971-74	338
Contemporary & influential theatres	340
Index	341

FOREWORD by Ian McKellen

This is an adventure book. It's the story of how, against the odds, a new theatre was designed and built in Sheffield, where it is now, fifty years on, established as the city's glory. Adventures need heroes, and here its principal one is Colin George, the first artistic director of the Crucible Theatre, who in this memoir recalls in fascinating detail how, aided by others locally and internationally, a dream came true. Here, too, there are troublesome villains who failed to share our hero's imagination and determination.

The tale begins with another majestic man of the theatre, Tyrone Guthrie, the director whose passion for the thrust stage, opposed to one encased by a proscenium arch, inspired Colin George and his Yorkshire allies. In Minneapolis, Guthrie had overseen the erection of a thrust stage, with the constant aid of his designer Tanya Moiseiwitsch.

In Sheffield, where she was Design Consultant, Tanya devised a revolutionary auditorium with a stage closely surrounded by the audience. When I was cast as the old Russian actor in Chekhov's *Swan Song* (part of *Fanfare* which opened the Crucible), she lent me her father's shirt to wear. This maternal act was typical of the family atmosphere pervading the new theatre backstage.

My ex-National Theatre colleague Edward Petherbridge was the other half in Chekhov's double act. During our rehearsals with the director David William, we talked about and planned an Actors' Company of equals who would manage themselves, an experiment in theatre democracy which was inspired by the daring determination which got the Crucible built.

It's true that these days the Crucible is internationally best known as hosting the annually televised World Snooker Championship. *The Nap*, one of my favourite plays by Richard Bean, had its première there, a comedy set in a snooker hall. The opening line, as the players arrived onstage, dominated by a full-size green baize table, was the witty: 'Well, it's not exactly the Crucible.'

Sheffield has learnt to love its new playhouse and can be proud that the Crucible has not been surpassed by newer regional theatres in either design or prestige. Under the guidance of a series of renowned directors, the work onstage in Sheffield and around the city makes the initial disapproval of its architecture seem more misguided than ever.

So, the adventure has continued, and this personal report of its origins is a fascinating and authoritative introduction to all the subsequent achievements.

Ian McKellen

London
2021

PROLOGUE by Colin George

I describe this book as a biography. But it is not just a biography about my own creative journey as Artistic Director over the 12 years I spent in Sheffield. It is a biography of the Sheffield Playhouse and of the extraordinary efforts by the people who worked there to create what became the Crucible Theatre. It was a daring venture in the late 1960s for a city the size of Sheffield—not just in building a hugely expensive new theatre, but one which had a controversial stage design. Our vision for the new theatre would stir up bitter opposition both in Sheffield and nationally and would spark a debate which dragged in many of the leading actors, directors, playwrights, and designers of that era.

In this sense, the book could be said to be a biography of theatre itself—of the relationship between audience and actor, of the very different kind of theatrical experience we wanted to achieve at the Crucible. In those heady years I would become part of a remarkable period of change, one which transformed a locally funded repertory Company into a subsidised regional theatre performing in one of the most modern and radical auditoria in the country.

This book is based on numerous sources. I have at least two dozen huge box files that I assembled when I was working as Artistic Director at the Sheffield Playhouse and the Crucible (1962-1974). These include papers, letters, memoranda, and minutes relating to the design and building of the new theatre, some of which exist nowhere else. I also have my notebooks from the period and personal correspondence with the leading players in this story, as well as newspaper cuttings and articles in favour of and against our controversial stage design.

As I wrote this book, I realised that so many of the characters with whom I 'performed' have left the stage, making their final exit. Back then, members of the Sheffield City Council and the Playhouse Theatre Trust were all in their sixties or seventies, and I was a relative youngster in my early forties. Were they with us now, they would all be well into their hundreds; Sir Tyrone Guthrie and Tanya Moiseiwitsch would be among them.

I make no apology that this account of building the Crucible, and my working as its first Artistic Director, is coloured throughout by my imperfect memories of the time. Looking back at the whirlwind of productions, meetings and debates over twelve years, I am struck by how closely the history of the theatre resembles a kaleidoscope. A pattern is formed: for innumerable and diverse reasons, that particular image is shattered; a period of disintegration follows, until another seemingly different pattern emerges—though the elements remain the same. My old friend Kenneth Griffith, who was an actor, a documentary producer and director, used to say of his work that it was unashamedly subjective on the grounds that 'objective is boring'. That is where I come from.

However, there is a danger to such an approach. It might appear that I imagine the Crucible Theatre to be largely my own creation. Nothing could be further from the truth. Without the inspiration of Sir Tyrone Guthrie, there would have been no thrust stage. Lacking the genius of Tanya Moiseiwitsch, the precise design, shape and feel of the auditorium would not be, as Guthrie himself declared, 'the best thrust stage yet designed'. And then there was the army of those involved in building the Crucible: the City Council and the citizens of Sheffield, theatre personalities and performers, designers, experts in lighting, sound, or costuming, and so on. Where does one stop? Nor must one forget the architects who brought this vision to life.

As the story unfolds, I hope I have paid tribute to all of those without whose imagination and courage in the face of much opposition to the whole concept of a thrust stage, the building would never have risen from the ground. The greatest endorsement of their commitment is the fact that the theatre has proved to be a success and enhanced the profile of Sheffield, which, for all its size and activity, was often derided as 'England's biggest village'.

I received two grants which helped me research and write this book—an original grant of £500 in 1974 from the Arts Council (my apologies it has taken nearly 50 years to complete the book!) and a further grant from the Society for Theatre Research (STR) which enabled me to complete the first manuscript in 2012.

When it comes to expressing my gratitude to individuals, the cast list is long. My sincere thanks go to Ian McKellen, Daniel Evans, Rodney Ford, Iain Mackintosh, my agent Caroline de Wolfe, Sue Fulton, John Punshon, Paul Iles, Kath Jeffery, Jackie Pass and the Crucible Theatre staff.

And finally my family: my son, Tedd, who took on the task of completing the book for me, my daughters Gwendolyn, Caroline and Lucy, whose advice has given a tremendous boost to my efforts, my granddaughter Katie for help organising my materials, and my wife, Sue, without whose encouragement and understanding I would never have got beyond the first chapter.

Colin George

London
2012

EDITOR'S NOTE by Tedd George

Like the Crucible Theatre, this book has a long and complex history. When I promised my father I would complete his manuscript and get it published, I had no idea that he had been writing this book almost my entire life.

Shortly after leaving the Crucible in July 1974, my father received a grant from the Arts Council to write a book about his experience building the new theatre; this helps explain why he assembled such a rich archive of material on this period. But—as often happens with actor-directors—the book was barely started before he plunged into his next theatrical venture. Over the years he made various attempts to write an account of his time in Sheffield, often in articles in the press or for anniversaries of the Crucible, but they were never more than sketches.

In part this was because writing a book on such a wide-ranging subject was a Herculean task—one I am only too aware of, having gone through all the material myself while editing the manuscript. But I believe the delay in writing also reflected a reluctance on his part to return to a period of great strife in his life in which were buried many painful unresolved issues. The breakthrough came in May 2010, when he was invited by the Artistic Director of the Crucible, Daniel Evans, to take part in an event discussing the history of the theatre.

The talk he gave that day on the Lyceum stage astonished me, revealing so many details of the Crucible story I did not know. It laid the groundwork for the book that he started writing shortly afterwards. The following year, my father was invited to join the Crucible Company for a production of *Othello*, and while there he carried out extensive research, helped enormously by Jackie Pass and the Crucible staff.

In the months after *Othello*, he worked furiously on the book, supported by a grant from the Society for Theatre Research (STR), and by his wife, Sue. The first full draft was completed in 2012. It was a manuscript full of ideas, anecdotes and positivity, but it was difficult to follow and needed substantial revision. He was in the process of editing it when he developed Alzheimer's and, eventually, he was forced to give up. It was then I made the solemn promise to edit the manuscript for him and get it published.

But it was not until 2018—two years after he died—that I finally had the time to properly study the manuscript. I was left inspired by the determination of my father and his collaborators to make their vision of the Crucible a reality, but I was also intrigued by many unanswered questions about the design process and the conflicts it stirred up. Contemplating the vast amount of material to review for the edit— including over 20 boxes of documents, diaries, notebooks, letters, books, photos and designs—I despaired that I would ever find the time to do it properly. Then along came COVID-19 and I seized the opportunity, working through successive lockdowns to rewrite the manuscript.

My challenge has been to create a coherent narrative out of the multiple and often conflicting accounts of the battle to build the Crucible Theatre. Throughout, I have tried to keep my father's voice intact, maintaining the first-person narrative of his original manuscript. My own additions have mostly been in tying the story together, adding background (who today knows of Sir Bernard Miles?) and sorting out the numbers. (I am, after all, an economist.) But as the edit progressed, it proved increasingly difficult to say which parts were my father's and which were my own. Often phrases would tumble onto the page as if from his own pen. If I was indeed ghost-writing my father's book, then his ghost was writing through me.

The end result is neither an academic tract nor a personal memoir, but rather the story of an extraordinary theatrical journey and the many characters and arguments that shaped the theatre that was built in Sheffield. It is a story to be savoured by anyone who loves the theatre and is fascinated by the actor-audience relationship and the theatrical possibilities of the thrust stage.

I owe thanks to many people for their help as I prepared this book for publication. Special thanks go to Ian McKellen for writing the Foreword, to Anne Minors and Susanne Bochmann of Sound Space Vision for allowing me to reproduce their designs of open stage theatres in this book, and to Iain Mackintosh for writing an extended note about them and for sharing many insights on stage design.

During the edit, I carried out numerous interviews with those who are still alive from the era of the Crucible's creation. Looking back, I am struck by how young many of them were at the time: My father was 36 when the proposal for a new theatre was first mooted; the architect, Nick Thompson, was just 32 when he took over the design process, and his right-hand man, Robin Beynon, was in his late 20s. And many of the actors and technicians involved in the Crucible were in the early stages of their careers. Their accounts have helped enrich the story of the Crucible's creation, even if some of their memories needed a little dusting off.

I am especially grateful to Nick Thompson, with whom I have spent many delightful hours reconstructing the process of the theatre's design, and who has shared designs, photos and articles with me. I am also grateful to the following people for giving me detailed interviews, full of fascinating and amusing anecdotes, and for setting me straight on many details: Richard Pilbrow, Clare Ferraby, Robin Beynon, Anthony Naylor, Daniel Evans, Rodney Ford, Edward Petherbridge, Mike Harley, James Smith, Robin Cave, David Collison and Frank Hatherley.

I would like to offer special thanks to Rob Hastie, Artistic Director of the Crucible, and Jackie Pass, for their warm support for the book, and for sharing photos and designs from the Crucible archive. I am also grateful to John Bates (Operations Manager), Gary Longfield (Head of Lighting), and Andrew Wilcox (Company Manager), for giving me a tour of the theatre from top to bottom. Thanks also to Ben Geering and Will McGovern for giving me a tour of the Chichester Festival Theatre in April 2021.

For their work in preparing the book for publication, I am immensely grateful to my sister Lucy—who is my publisher, the book's publicist and a constant source of inspiration—and to Polly Bull, also at Wordville Press, for their help in securing rights for the dozens of images reproduced in this book. Thanks also to my sister Gwendolyn for helpful feedback, Mariano Capezzani for help photographing the images, our meticulous proof reader Oliver Schick, our front cover designer Rozalia Sherwood, and our layout designer Paul Medcalf of Avocet Typeset.

Finally, I would like to thank my stepmother, Sue, whose work with my father on the original manuscript made this book possible, and my wife Karina and our daughters, Isabella and Sofía, for putting up with me as I laboured to complete it.

One of the tasks my father did not complete was writing an account of his career before he came to Sheffield in 1962. By that time, he already had more than a decade of experience acting, directing and touring shows, all of which laid the groundwork for his Crucible journey. I have included a short biography here, based on personal memories and documents, among them my father's 'Faith in Practice', which he wrote for the Quakers in 2001.

Colin George was born in Pembroke Dock, Wales, on 20th September 1929. His father was a Congregational minister from a coalmining family in the Rhondda Valley; his mother was the star of Tenby's local amateur operatic society. At the age of eight, Colin was sent to boarding school at Caterham, Surrey, and three years later his father died while on service as an Army Chaplain. Although Colin never spoke about how this sudden loss affected him emotionally, it stayed with him throughout his life. He often remarked on how many of the young actors he worked with had lost their fathers when they were very young. 'By choosing the theatre, we were all searching for our fathers', he would say.

Colin was inspired to become a professional actor after seeing his hero Laurence Olivier playing Richard III at the New Theatre in 1944 (as well as Henry V on the silver screen), but he was persuaded by his mother to get a degree first. So after leaving school in 1947, Colin carried out two years' national service before going up to University College Oxford in 1949 to read English. However, to judge from the number of plays, poetry readings and reviews he was involved in during his three years there, most of his energies went into acting and directing.

It was while at Oxford that Colin and his friend, Paul Almond, decided to form a touring Company, inspired by the exploits of Frank Benson and Donald Wolfit.[1] On completing their degrees in 1952 they teamed up with a group of aspiring actors from Cambridge

---

[1] Frank Benson (1858-1939) was a legendary actor/producer who toured productions of Shakespeare around the country (he performed all but three of Shakespeare's canon). Donald Wolfit (1902-68) was known for his wartime tours of Shakespeare productions.

Acting for the Oxford & Cambridge Players as (Left) Henry V at the Edinburgh Festival, August 1953, and (Right) as Petruchio, August 1952

University—among them John Barton, Toby Robertson and Peter Hall—to create the Oxford and Cambridge Players (this later became the Elizabethan Theatre Company). Colin toured England with the Company for three years, acting and directing in numerous Shakespeare plays. His roles included Petruchio, Romeo, Cassius, Bassanio and Henry V, the latter being performed at the Old Vic and recorded in a live performance for the BBC in 1953.

In 1955, the Company disbanded, and Colin acted in a number of theatres, including a season at the Coventry Rep, before joining the Birmingham Rep in April 1956, the same day as another young actor, Albert Finney, with whom he was to perform in a number of shows.

After two years at Birmingham, Colin decided to move into directing. In 1958, he joined the Nottingham Playhouse as Assistant Director to Val May, where he acted in and directed numerous shows, at one stage performing as Hamlet in the evening while rehearsing *Reluctant Heroes* in the daytime. He was a driving force in bringing new writers to the theatre, some of whom were controversial at the time. He directed the Rep's first production of Arnold Wesker's *Roots* and played Jimmy Porter in John Osborne's *Look Back in Anger* and Mick in Harold Pinter's *The*

Left: Playing the Prince in Val May's production of Hamlet, 1959; Right: Discussing a production with Val May and Tony Church

Caretaker. All three plays sparked walkouts from conservative members of the audience, but also made an impact in the press. It was a pattern that he was to repeat throughout his directorial career.[2]

Aside from his responsibilities at the Nottingham Playhouse, Colin directed productions outside the city. In late 1959 he took *Peer Gynt* on an Arts Council tour of Wales and the North of England, and in 1961 he took productions of *A Man for All Seasons* and *Macbeth* with John Neville in both lead roles to the Manoel Theatre in Malta. He also worked in London, in 1961 creating the role of Jack Lucas in Keith Waterhouse & Willis Hall's *Celebration* at the Duchess Theatre, and in 1962 he was invited to direct a production of *Richard III* at the Old Vic with Paul Daneman in the lead role. It was shortly after this that he applied to the Sheffield Playhouse for the role of Assistant Director, where our story starts.

---

[2] The actor James Smith, who joined the Crucible in its first season in 1971/72, was given this cryptic advice before his audition: 'If you walk into a Colin George interview, he throws a rugby ball at you. If you catch it, you're in the Company. If you throw it back, you get one of the leads!' Tedd George's interview with James Smith, April 2020.

A few final notes, the first on stage terminology. The terms 'forestage', 'promontory stage', 'thrust stage' and 'open stage' are used throughout the book and can cause confusion. Indeed, the designer of the Crucible's thrust stage, Tanya Moiseiwitsch, always referred to her creation as an 'open stage', when this term is nowadays used for stages such as that of the Olivier Theatre, which is very different in design. A detailed analysis of the differences between stage designs is beyond the scope of this book and would be open to debate. But to give some context, in Chapter 6 there is discussion of the evolution of stage design, and in the Appendix, there are designs of six contemporary thrust and open stage theatres, with an extended footnote about them by theatre producer, designer and scholar, Iain Mackintosh, as well as a list of theatres that influenced the Crucible Theatre or were contemporary with it.

For those unfamiliar with theatre design, here are some simple definitions (see diagram). The proscenium is the frame or arch

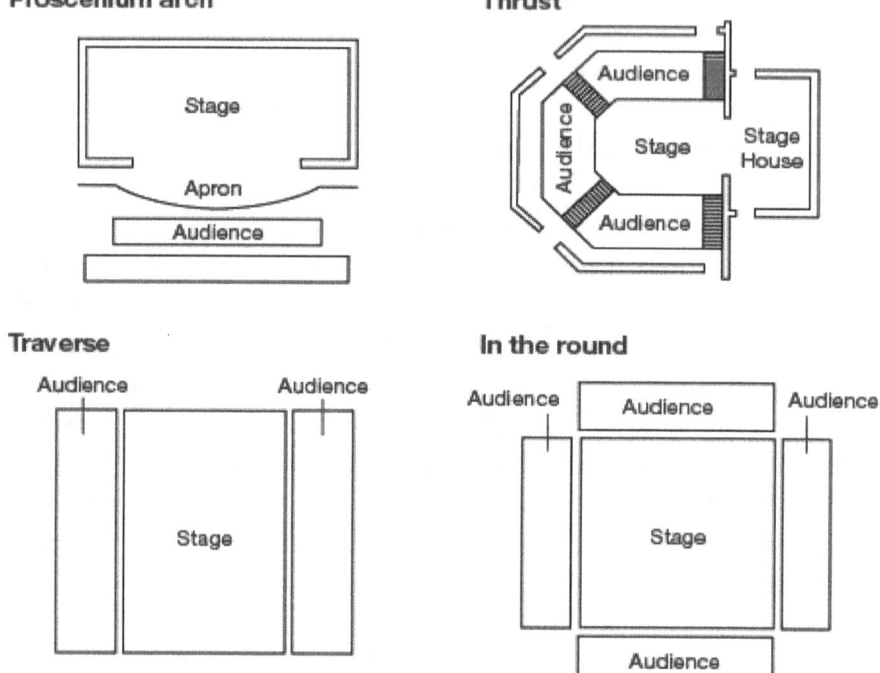

Four types of stage design

separating the stage from the auditorium, through which the action of a play is viewed. A forestage or 'apron stage' is a narrow stage area that juts out in front of the proscenium; a promontory stage goes further, pushing the acting area out towards (and often into) the audience; and a thrust stage removes the proscenium altogether and places the stage at the centre of the audience, which surrounds it on three sides. The 'Guthrie thrust stage' is the purest form of thrust stage and is discussed in this book. The term 'open stage' is more general and is commonly used to describe any acting space that is surrounded by the audience on at least three sides. Finally, traverse describes an acting area surrounded by two banks of seating facing each other, and theatre-in-the-round describes a central acting area that is surrounded by the audience on four sides, with entrances at the corners. Most modern theatres are convertible to different kinds of staging, which further complicates definitions of their stage designs.

Another potential cause of confusion are the terms 'repertory' and 'repertoire'. At the time my father started working in English theatre in the 1950s, 'repertory' theatres—'reps'—had resident companies of professional actors performing new shows every few weeks. This was not 'true repertoire', where companies alternated between different shows during the week; for example, running one show for two nights, switching to another for the next two nights, and then going back to the first show for the Friday and Saturday performances. The most successful shows could be kept in a company's 'repertoire' and staged at short notice for revivals or to fill gaps in the programme. The high cost and complexity of programming repertoire made it prohibitive for most regional reps, and it was only thanks to funding from the Arts Council that the Sheffield Rep was able to start performing in true repertoire in 1965 (see Chapter 2).

A final note on the value of money. The Crucible was built during one of the periods of highest inflation in Britain's history, and in the fifty years since its completion the figures have lost meaning. To put them in context, I have included estimates of values in today's money, using average CPI inflation rates. Although this is a crude measure, as the costs for construction, materials and equipment have changed dramatically since 1971, it is a useful benchmark for judging how expensive (or cheap) things were at the time. Knowing that the highest-priced ticket at the Playhouse in 1967 would cost just £5.78 today, or that a pair of soundproof auditorium doors would cost £75,000, helps put prices in perspective.

Tedd George

London
2021

LIST OF ILLUSTRATIONS

1. Colin George as Petruchio in *The Taming of the Shrew*, The Oxford & Cambridge Players, August 1952, and as Henry V at the Edinburgh Festival, August 1953
2. Colin George as The Prince in Val May's production of *Hamlet*, 1959, and discussing a production with Val May & Tony Church, Nottingham Rep, c.1960
3. Four types of stage design
4. Geoffrey Ost, Producer of the Sheffield Playhouse from 1938 to 1965
5. The Sheffield Playhouse after its refurbishment in 1954
6. Colin George directing a production at the Sheffield Playhouse, c.1964
7. Colourful fliers for the Pegasus Theatre Club, c.1963
8. Colin George directing the action during a Saturday morning session at the Sheffield Playhouse, July 1963
9. The opening of *Hamlet* on the stage at Ludlow Castle, 1965, and Colin George and Kenneth Griffith during rehearsals for *The Merchant of Venice*, Ludlow Festival, 1964
10. The Sheffield Playhouse Company, August 1965
11. Full house at the Sheffield Playhouse, 1966
12. Regular theatregoers crowding the Circle Foyer at the Sheffield Playhouse, 1966
13. Two very different plays in the Sheffield Playhouse's first season of true repertoire (1965-66): Roderick Horn plays the leads in *Charley's Aunt* and *The Chairs*
14. Theatre Vanguard in action, February 1967: Dorothy Vernon plays guitar with the children; Robin Hirsch directs a scene at Shooters Grove School, Sheffield
15. Alan Cullen and Roderick Horn, late 1960s
16. The cast of *Stirrings* during rehearsals, 1966

17. Dorothy Vernon & Veronica Lang in the first *Stirrings* revival, November 1968
18. Programme covers for the first two *Stirrings* in 1966 and 1968
19. Grace Tebbutt in full regalia as Lord Mayor of Sheffield, 1949
20. Tony Hampton, Chairman of the Playhouse Board and David Brayshaw, future Administrator of the Crucible Theatre
21. Regulars going into the Playhouse to see *It Happened in Irkutsk*, June 1967
22. Poster for the inaugural Stratford Shakespeare Festival season, 1953
23. Theatre Designs: Ancient Greek, Shakespearean, Restoration and Modern 'Picture Box'
24. Sketches & notes of theatres visited by Colin George during his trip to Italy, 1960
25. Architectural design of the Teatro Sant'Erasmo, Milan, 1953-54
26. Design of thrust stage at the Ludlow Festival, 1966
27. Sketch of the thrust stage, with steps up and scenery, Ludlow Festival, 1966
28. The Chichester Festival Theatre auditorium in 1962
29. Colin George, Wilfred Harrison and Sir Tyrone Guthrie during his visit to Sheffield, October 1967
30. Exterior of the Guthrie Theater at night, Minneapolis, late 1960s
31. The Guthrie Theater auditorium as it looked in 1967
32. Colin George's notes and sketches from *Harpers Ferry* at the Guthrie Theater, November 1967
33. Orestes kneels before Athena and Apollo, *The House of Atreus*, Guthrie Theater, 1967
34. The Stratford, Ontario auditorium as it looked in 1967
35. Stratford, Ontario's auditorium from the centre back
36. Sketches by Colin George of auditorium shapes during discussions at the Guthrie Theater, November 1967
37. Notes from Colin George's diary on the ANTA Theatre, November 1967
38. Main auditorium at the Vivian Beaumont Theater in 2018
39. Draft Programme for the construction of the New Playhouse, December 1967
40. Tanya Moiseiwitsch, c.1971, and Patrick Ide, 1979

41. Tanya Moiseiwitsch's initial sketches of the thrust stage, dated 29 January 1968
42. Tanya Moiseiwitsch's initial sketch of the thrust stage, dated 29 January 1968
43. Tanya Moiseiwitsch's adjustments to the draft design of the auditorium, February 1968
44. The architects' early option for the thrust stage, January 1968
45. Tanya Moiseiwitsch's telegram from Stratford, Ontario, March 1968
46. Tanya Moiseiwitsch's first sketch for the revolve on the thrust stage, June 1968
47. Tanya Moiseiwitsch's second sketch for the revolve on the thrust stage, June 1968
48. *Oedipus* at the Sheffield Playhouse, April 1968
49. Architect Robin Beynon's cut-through of the Crucible auditorium showing the boxes behind the stage, 1968
50. Entrance to Agamemnon's Tomb in Mycenae and entrance to the Crucible auditorium in 1971
51. Clare Ferraby's original design for the upper foyer carpet, 1970
52. Front page of the architect's Final Design Scheme, July 1968
53. Plans of the ground floor and foyer level of the new theatre, July 1968
54. Andrew Renton's conceptual drawing of the foyer bar with panoramic views over Sheffield, July 1968
55. Andrew Renton's conceptual drawing of the auditorium, July 1968
56. Theatre Project's innovative lighting rig in action, 1971
57. Sound control desk designed for the Crucible, 1971, and Q-File lighting control desk, 1970s
58. Back cover of pamphlet produced by the New Sheffield Theatre Trust, June 1969
59. Architects' model of the new theatre in cherry wood, 1969
60. Scene from *The Caucasian Chalk Circle* at the Sheffield Playhouse, July 1969, with Julian Forbes, Wilfred Harrison and Michael St. John
61. Tanya Moiseiwitsch and Elaine Garrard working on costumes for *The Caucasian Chalk Circle* at the Playhouse, June 1969
62. L. du Garde Peach, 1960s

63. Emlyn Williams and Keith Waterhouse
64. Flier from the New Sheffield Theatre open forum on 28th September 1969
65. 'Sir Bernard raps new Sheffield theatre plans' headline, *The Star*, 6 October 1969
66. The Three Knights: Sir Bernard Miles, Sir Laurence Olivier and Sir John Clements
67. Sir Alec Guinness, 1970s
68. Peter Cheeseman and Michael Elliot
69. David Campton and Henry Livings
70. Alan Plater and David Rudkin
71. Alan Ayckbourn and Peter Terson
72. Director Alfred Emmet, architect Norman Branson, actor Marius Goring and Questors designer Graham Heywood, examining plans for the Questors Theatre, 1955 (with permission of The Questors Theatre Archive)
73. The Crucible Theatre under construction, with the Victoria Hall visible behind, February 1970
74. Technical drawing of the auditorium and surrounding foyer
75. Cut-through of the auditorium, January 1970
76. Technical drawing of side view of the Crucible Theatre, January 1970
77. Technical drawing of ground floor of the Crucible Theatre, January 1970
78. Jozef Szajna in his studio, early 1960s
79. Scene from *Macbeth* at the Sheffield Playhouse, September 1970
80. Szajna's central design for *Macbeth* and Nigel Hawthorne's skinhead Macbeth, 1970
81. Josef Szajna chatting with Colin George & Madge d'Alroy during rehearsals for *Macbeth*, 1970
82. Brochures for the newly named Crucible Theatre, October 1970
83. Two views of the main auditorium & the Studio Theatre under construction, early 1971
84. Rodney Ford (Head of Design), Keith Green (Production Manager) and David Harvey Jones (Head of Wardrobe)
85. The roof of the Crucible under construction, February 1971

86. The closed Sheffield Playhouse announcing its successor, The Crucible, July 1971
87. The Crucible auditorium seating costs, November 1971
88. Colin George contemplating the Crucible Theatre as it nears completion, September 1971
89. West view of the Crucible with the entrance to the Studio Theatre and the main entrance to the building complex, 1971
90. The Austin Seven on stage during rehearsal for *Fanfare*, October 1971
91. Bill poster for *Fanfare*, November 1971
92. The full Company and staff of The Crucible Theatre, November 1971
93. First rehearsal on the thrust stage, 13th October 1971
94. The ground floor foyer with the 'Enchanter' watching over, November 1971
95. The audience gathers by the monumental entrance doors to the auditorium, November 1971
96. Young actors take the Crucible stage on opening night, November 1971
97. Ian McKellen and Edward Petherbridge in *Swan Song*, November 1971
98. Dorothy Vernon sings the Finale with the full Company on Gala Night, November 1971
99. The Aztecs and the Conquistadors come to blows on the Crucible stage, November 1971
100. Colin George directing young actors on the Crucible thrust stage, November 1971
101. Bill from the Crucible's opening season, 1971
102. Rodney Ford's design for the Button Maker in *Peer Gynt*, October 1971
103. Scene from *Peer Gynt* with the scene-stealing belly dancer, November 1971
104. Tanya Moiseiwitsch's designs for the Lord Mayor & Hans Meulter in *The Shoemaker's Holiday*, November 1971
105. Elaine Garrard's poster design for *Treasure Island*, December 1971
106. Councillor Michael Swain and Alderman Ron Ironmonger, 1971

107. Caroline Smith, Director of the Studio Theatre, January 1972
108. The Studio in performance, c.1971
109. Baby Edward's theatre christening on the Crucible stage, August 1972
110. 'Crucible chiefs seek £117,000 to avert crisis' headline, *The Star*, 1 November 1972
111. 'Too many chiefs and not enough Indians' headline, *The Star*, 1 November 1972
112. Tanya Moiseiwitsch's design for *The Persians* at the Crucible Theatre, September 1972
113. Colin George with the Company of *The Duchess of Malfi* and Jozef Szajna on stage in Warsaw, June 1973
114. Colin George playing Astrov in *Uncle Vanya* at the Crucible Theatre, November 1973
115. Flier for 'Col's Last Round-Up' and certificate granting Colin George Honorary Life Membership of the Crucible Club, June/July 1974
116. David Brayshaw and Colin George watch the Crucible rise out the ground, July 1970
117. The Crucible Theatre, with its new entrance, and the restored Lyceum, 2020
118. The Crucible auditorium during a technical rehearsal of Victoria Wood's *Talent*, June 2021
119. The Studio Theatre, June 2021
120. The Lyceum Theatre auditorium, 2014
121. Colin George as Jimmy Graham playing his final scene with Rita Littlewood (Barbara Knox) in the Rovers Return, *Coronation Street*, August 1974
122. Colin George playing the Porter in *Macbeth*, Chung Ying Theatre Company, Hong Kong, March 1982
123. Colin George next to a photograph of himself playing Begriffenfeldt in the RSC production of *Peer Gynt* at The Young Vic, 1995; Colin George as John Shakespeare in his one-man show *My Son Will!*, 1999
124. Colin George & Daniel Evans on the opening night of *Othello*, September 2011

LIST OF PLATES

i. Colin George, early 1960s.
ii. Colin George & Geoffrey Ost directing *King Lear* at the Sheffield Playhouse, 1963.
iii. Colin George (centre stage) playing Con in Gwyn Thomas's *The Keep* at the Sheffield Playhouse, a typical 'picture box' production of the era, March 1963.
iv. Sheffield's first Brecht: Colin George's controversial production of *The Good Woman of Setzuan*, September 1963.
v. Colin George having a drink with Sir Laurence Olivier at the Sheffield Playhouse, April 1966.
vi. Glen Walford with the Theatre Vanguard troupe and van, December 1968.
vii. Dorothy Vernon, Colin George, Allan Cullen & Roderick Horn during recording of songs from *John Willy and the Bee People*, 1967.
viii. Christopher Wilkinson, Myra Frances & Barrie Smith, June 1968.
ix. Barrie Smith & Myra Frances in *A Lily in Little India* at the Sheffield Playhouse, June 1968.
x. David Bradley & Dorothy Vernon in Alan Cullen's *The Life and Times of Charlie Peace* at the Sheffield Playhouse, July 1969.
xi. Colin George, Roderick Horn & Alan Cullen during their visit to Eyam to research *Ring o' Roses*, July 1967.
xii. Colin George's valedictory production at the Sheffield Playhouse: *Britannia's Boys*, May 1971.
xiii. Sir Tyrone Guthrie, 1950s.
xiv. Tanya Moiseiwitsch, 1949.
xv. Sir Tyrone Guthrie with the God Apollo during rehearsals for *The House of Atreus*, Guthrie Theater, Minneapolis, 1967.
xvi. Nick Thompson & Clare Ferraby, mid-1970s.

xvii. Peter Rice and Robin Beynon, 1970s.
xviii. Richard Pilbrow in front of the light board at the Littleton Theatre, 1976.
xix. David Brayshaw, Tony Hampton and Sir Tyrone Guthrie inspecting the Crucible auditorium under construction, January 1971.
xx. The engineers take a break in the half-built Crucible auditorium, 1971.
xxi. Tanya Moiseiwitsch and Colin George view the Crucible auditorium as construction nears completion, 1971.
xxii. The Company and staff of the Sheffield Playhouse at the start of our last season (1970-71).
xxiii. The Crucible main auditorium, and the ground floor bar, 1971.
xxiv. The foyers and upper floor bar at the Crucible Theatre, 1971.
xxv. Douglas Campbell chairing the Music Hall in *Fanfare* at the Crucible Theatre, November 1971.
xxvi. Ian McKellen as Hamlet, 1971.
xxvii. Niall Buggy & Fanny Carby in *The Birthday Party* at the Crucible Theatre, May 1972.
xxviii. Ann Casson as Kate & Paul Angelis as Petruchio in *The Taming of the Shrew* at the Crucible Theatre, October 1972.
xxix. Lynda Marchal & Paul Angelis in *Alpha Beta* at the Crucible, February 1973.
xxx. Colin George playing the title roles in *Dr Jekyll & Mr Hyde* during his final season at the Crucible, February 1974.
xxxi. Scene from *Calamity Jane* with Lynda Marchal playing the lead, The Crucible Theatre, July 1974.
xxxii. Tanya Moiseiwitsch and Colin George in her home, May 2001.
xxxiii. Colin George with the Company and stage crew of *Othello* on the Crucible thrust stage on his 82nd birthday, 20th September 2011.

Editor's note on image rights

We have made strenuous efforts to secure permission to reproduce the images, designs and drawings in this book. Most are from more than 50 years ago, some discovered as random cuttings or loose photos in my father's archives, and many involve people, publications and companies that have long ceased to exist. For this reason, I am extremely grateful to the Crucible Theatre for giving permission to use images from the Sheffield Playhouse and Crucible Theatre. Newspaper cuttings and press photos are reproduced with permission from Sheffield Newspapers and the Sheffield City Archive. All designs from the architects, Renton Howard Wood, are reproduced with permission from one of the practice's last surviving members, Nick Thompson. Where required, permission rights are included in each listing. All other images are from the George family archive or are reproduced with permission from those interviewed for this book.

Part I

The New Sheffield Playhouse

CHAPTER ONE

There is a tide in the affairs of men, which, taken at the flood, leads on to fortune.[†]

In the spring of 1962, Shakespeare's 'tide in the affairs of men' carried me to the shores of Sheffield. The reason? To interview for the role of Assistant Director at the Sheffield Playhouse. It was my first time in Sheffield, and although I knew of the Playhouse and had worked with actors and directors who had been in the Company, I knew little about the theatre or its history. What I could not have realised was that I was arriving at a moment of profound change, one which would transform the Playhouse from a self-funded rep into a subsidised regional theatre. And I was to play a key role in that transformation.

The Playhouse Theatre began its life just after the First World War. On 1st May 1919, an amateur performance of Tolstoy's *Where Love Is, God Is* was held at the Oxford Street Settlement in Shipton Street, Sheffield. From such humble beginnings was the Crucible Theatre born. In November 1919, Herbert 'Pip' Prentice, an instinctive theatre enthusiast, directed ('produced' was the terminology of that time) John Galsworthy's *The Silver Box* for five performances. Prentice quickly took the helm, and the following summer the amateurs confidently renamed themselves 'The Sheffield Repertory Company'. In 1924, they moved to a hall in South Street and then, in 1928, into the Temperance Hall on Townhead Street, which was to be their home for the next forty-three years.

The Sheffield Rep was one of a number of regional repertory companies that sprang up across the UK in the early 20th century. But Sheffield did not have access to the considerable resources of other pioneers, such as the Gaiety Theatre in Manchester or the purpose-

---

[†] William Shakespeare, *Julius Caesar*, Act IV, Scene 3. When my father went to Sheffield to interview for the role of Assistant Director in 1962, he was playing the role of Brutus—who speaks these very lines—in a production of *Julius Caesar* at the Nottingham Playhouse.

built Birmingham Repertory Theatre. As Alec Seed later wrote: 'The history of the Sheffield Repertory Company was one of long struggle against poverty. Inadequate premises, makeshift scenery, lack of equipment and lack of support were as nothing compared with the lack of capital.'[3] When I worked with my great friend Kenneth Griffith—actor, writer and polemicist—at the Ludlow Festival in 1964, he told me: 'You haven't the slightest idea, Colin, of what it was like before the war working as an actor or director in the profession. A ruthless business. You've got it cushy.'

That the Sheffield Rep survived at all was due to two factors: first, the unflagging and unselfish labour of an army of part-time and unpaid performers, backstage, front of house staff and administrators. And second, strong support from a loyal Sheffield theatregoing public and local businesses who regularly raised money to fund productions, pay off debts and make repairs to the theatre. Herbert Prentice left the Sheffield Rep in 1926, and in the following years the Company brought in its first professional actors, among them Donald Wolfit, which significantly boosted the box office. Another theatre professional engaged first as a designer and scene painter, and who ended up as an actor, was Bernard Miles. He makes a melodramatic entrance later in our Crucible drama.

In 1938, a new era began when Geoffrey Ost took the helm of the renamed Sheffield Playhouse; he was still the Producer when I arrived in Sheffield 24 years later. But his tenure got off to an uneven start. The year after he arrived, the War broke out, and as the Steel City was an easy target for German bombers, the Company moved to the Little Theatre in Southport, Lancashire. There they slowly began to build an audience, and over six years they presented over 240 plays.

When Geoffrey was called up in 1942, who should make his entrance again but Herbert Prentice, who returned as caretaker Producer. It was during his final tenure that the adventurous decision was made to move to fortnightly rep. Until then, each play ran for just one week; this meant that every week actors had to rehearse and learn a new show during the daytime while performing a different show at night (which they had only learnt the week before!). The

---

[3] Alec Seed, *The Sheffield Repertory Theatre: A History*, The Sheffield Repertory Company, 1959, p.3.

move to a two-weekly cycle, which doubled the rehearsal time, was perhaps the most important development in the early history of the Company. It made it possible for the Playhouse to join the elite of leading fortnightly reps: a Premier League club.

Geoffrey was demobbed in 1946 and brought the Company back to Sheffield the following year. Like all repertory theatres, the Playhouse rode on a tide of enthusiasm undiluted by the lure of television immediately after the War, but it did so by relying on a loyal audience who stood by the theatre in more difficult times.[4] By 1951,

Geoffrey Ost, Producer of the Sheffield Playhouse from 1938 to 1965

---

[4] At a time when provincial theatres were playing to business that would have been ruinous without Arts Council support, the Sheffield Playhouse was boasting regular permanent bookings of up to 80% capacity before each fortnightly show opened.

the Company had never seen better days—it was well patronised and offered work of a high standard. This success encouraged the Board, with support from local industrialists, to transform the Temperance Hall on Townhead Street into a modern 547-seat proscenium theatre with amenities to match—bar, café, and new box office.[5] The transformed theatre reopened in 1954 and now matched any theatre of its type in the provinces.

Geoffrey continued to run the Playhouse successfully through the 1950s to the early 1960s, maintaining an exemplary standard of presentation. Both as a designer and director he guided a superbly drilled organisation, one that for backstage efficiency could rival many more well-known theatres. Productions included a mix of West End successes, well known classics, the annual Shakespeare—for which some

The Sheffield Playhouse after its refurbishment in 1954

---

[5] The full cost of the refurbishment—£41,000—was raised by public donations and retained profits. This budget would be worth the equivalent of £850,000 in 2021.

regular patrons cancelled their seats—and an occasional glance at the new writing of the late 1950s. Most repertory theatres did the same.

Then fate took a hand. In 1960, when Geoffrey was directing the Christmas show, he suffered a minor heart attack. David Paul, who had previously stage-managed at The Playhouse, acted as temporary director until Geoffrey returned to direct in the spring of 1961. But given Geoffrey's age and the pressure of his job, the Board felt that the appointment of a permanent assistant should be considered. They debated this throughout the autumn of 1961, and in the spring of 1962 I was invited to Sheffield to interview for the role.

Although it was my first trip to Sheffield, I had worked for some years in repertory at Birmingham and Nottingham, so the territory I was applying for was not undiscovered country. I ended up arriving two hours late for my interview, but I had a stroke of good fortune. I had recently directed *Richard III* at the Old Vic which had received poor notices, except for one by Walter Kerr in *The Daily Telegraph*. This was the one review they had read! Coupled with my record at Nottingham and a recommendation from the Arts Council, it was enough to secure me the job.

In the summer of 1962, I moved to Sheffield with my first wife, Patricia Voysey—who was a designer and would also work on productions at the Playhouse—and our baby daughter Gwendolyn. We arrived at a difficult time for Sheffield's theatres. The Royal had burnt down, the old Empire and the Palace Theatre in Attercliffe had recently closed, leaving just the Lyceum and the Playhouse still in operation. I was arriving at a time of change for the Playhouse which was stirring up tensions in the theatre's management.

This became apparent at my first meeting of the Playhouse Theatre Board on 4th October 1962. Present were the twelve board members, including the Chairman, Tony Hampton, and the Chairman of the Executive Committee, David Brayshaw. Both Anthony and David were to become key allies in the battles ahead. In attendance from the Company were Geoffrey Ost (Producer), Bill Butler (Company Manager) and myself. Representing the Arts Council was Mr N V Linklater, Assistant Director of the Drama Department.

Two items on the agenda signalled the transformation that was underway. First was a proposal to move from two-weekly to three-weekly rep, which aroused opposition from three board members, including the local playwright Mr L. du Garde Peach. Mr Linklater of the Arts Council supported the change, arguing that the old pattern of rep had gone, that neither the plays nor the actors were available for such a rapid turnover of shows, and that most repertory companies of our standing had seen a fall in permanent bookings: patrons had become more selective. Ten years before, there had been no television as a counterattraction and the current young theatregoers were not permanent bookers like their parents' generation. In the end, three-weekly rep was adopted to begin at the start of the spring 1963 season.

The other item regarded extending the stage into the auditorium. After much discussion, and on the encouragement of Mr Linklater, it was agreed that the Playhouse should apply to the Arts Council for a capital grant of £10,000 for the stage extension work, and an income grant of £7,500 to widen our scope and improve the standard of production.[6] This decision was to prove a watershed moment, opening the door to Arts Council funding and driving the professionalisation of the Playhouse.[7] But it proved a step too far for Mr du Garde Peach who sensed that this move threatened the board's absolute authority, and he resigned shortly afterwards. He will reappear later in our story.

My arrival at the Sheffield Playhouse coincided with the departure of several long-standing actors and the emergence of a new generation of talent. Denys Corrigan reported that during the 1962-63 season, a total of 61 different actors appeared in 17 productions, compared with just 29 actors in 20 productions in the 1959-60 season.[8] Among the newcomers were actors Barrie Smith, Roderick Horn and Dorothy Vernon; the gifted actor/writer Alan Cullen with whom I would collaborate extensively over the coming decade;[9] and theatre

---

[6] The total grant (£17,500) would be the equivalent of £320,000 in 2021.

[7] In April 1963, the Sheffield Playhouse became one of only eight theatres outside London to be taken into formal association with the Arts Council.

[8] Denys Corrigan, *The Stirrings in Sheffield*, Sheffield Repertory Company, 1971, p.16.

[9] In the eight years they were both at the Sheffield Playhouse, my father directed nine shows written by Alan Cullen, as well as three revivals. They included *The Stirrings in Sheffield on Saturday Night* (1966-73), *John Willy and the Bee People* (1966) and *The Enchanted Lake* (1968, which ran for over 100 performances). They also scored a hit with *Treasure Island* (1971), the first Christmas show at the Crucible Theatre.

technicians such as Robin Cave (who went on to become our Master Carpenter).

As a newcomer to the Playhouse, I was incredibly fortunate to be the assistant to such an experienced and generous man as Geoffrey Ost. I found him to be a meticulous director, persuasive rather than dictatorial with the actors, and an extremely talented artist and watercolourist. He designed his own sets and lit them. When years later I mentioned to him that we were to use a lighting designer at our new theatre, he was astonished: 'The lighting is your signature on the production!' he commented. He had 24 years of experience guiding the artistic fortunes of the Playhouse. I learnt so much from him—indeed all I know about lighting I learnt from Geoffrey.[10] I cannot speak too highly of him.

Directing a production at the Sheffield Playhouse, c.1964

---

[10] Geoffrey Ost's book, *Stage Lighting*, was the standard text for directors and theatre technicians throughout my father's career. Even though lighting design and equipment has evolved hugely in the years since this book was first published, Geoffrey's clear and uncomplicated explanation of how to light actors on the stage has probably never been bettered.

I arrived at the Playhouse half-way through the 1962-63 season and threw myself into my work. With the shift to three-weekly rep, I was able to direct nine plays in six months, as well as play the part of Con in *The Keep* by Gwyn Thomas. My productions included a few 'pot-boilers', a critically acclaimed *King Lear* with Michael Turner in the title role, and the Playhouse's first full-blown musical, Sandy Wilson's *The Boy Friend*, which packed out houses at the end of the season.

I also worked hard to introduce new playwrights to the Playhouse audience. However, my choice of Sheffield's first Harold Pinter play—*The Caretaker*—proved controversial. I knew Harold Pinter from his time as an actor when he used the stage name David Baron, and I had played Mick in *The Caretaker* at Birmingham two years previously.[11] The play was, to be sure, an adventurous choice for the audience of the time and was noted by Denys Corrigan both 'for the high quality of its presentation and [for] the number of people who walked out on it'.[12] In my second season (1963-64), I staged the Playhouse's first production by Bertolt Brecht, *The Good Woman of Setzuan*, which also sparked a number of walk-outs, as well as considerable interest in the press.

Some patrons did not like having their routine of a fortnightly visit to the rep being disrupted by a play as profound and disturbing as *The Caretaker* or as raw and experimental as *The Good Woman of Setzuan*. Some critics went further, dismissing our choice of plays as unsuitable for Sheffield audiences who, they claimed, wanted everyday popular plays and not 'arty type' theatre.[13] But the box office told another story. When the numbers were tallied, to everyone's surprise *The Caretaker* was the only production in my first season to make a profit. Even allowing for the small cast and inexpensive setting (junk is always to hand in the environs of a theatre), this fact became a banner to wave

---

[11] Pinter saw my father in the Birmingham Rep production of *The Iron Harp* with Albert Finney and afterwards they discussed a love scene my father had played with a girl (just sitting on a sofa, nothing racy). Pinter said to him: 'People don't talk like that.' My father replied: 'Well, you should write your own play' to which Pinter retorted: 'I have done, it's being done at Bristol.' He was referring to his first play, *The Room*, which was first performed at the Drama Studio of the University of Bristol in May 1957.
[12] Corrigan, *The Stirrings in Sheffield*, p.13.
[13] For example, Cyril Lowe in *The Stage*, July 1964.

Colourful fliers for the Pegasus Theatre Club, c.1963

in the face of all the pessimists from then on. We were beginning to acquire a new audience.[14]

It was during this season that I started to expand my interest in theatre for young people, which was to become central to the work of the Playhouse and its successor, the Crucible. My interest was sparked by the Pegasus Theatre Club, which had been created in January 1963 by a local teacher, Dorothy Vernon, for children aged up to 13. Working with other city teachers (all of them amateur actors), Pegasus brought theatre to the children of Sheffield. However, at the age of 14, unless their parents were theatregoers, the children's interest in theatre was lost.

So, in May 1963, in association with Pegasus, a children's theatre club for 14- to 18-year-olds was formed at the Playhouse. On Saturday mornings, club members came to the Playhouse not to see a play as an audience, but to be involved in performing a scene on stage. As

---

[14] The Playhouse's conviction that there was a young audience for new and experimental work was confirmed when Samuel Becket's *Waiting for Godot* played to a 73% house in our 1966-67 season.

Assistant Director, running these mornings became my responsibility. Some of the children preferred to watch the proceedings, but an enthusiastic group would always leap on the stage. I would light the scene beforehand and add some sound effects. We explored episodes from our current repertoire, as well as excerpts from plays like *Oh! What a Lovely War*. I remember that the rattling of machine guns led to some very convincing deaths on stage.

The Saturday morning theatre club grew to 330 members by the end of 1963 and to over 500 by 1967. We even held a competition to write a scene based on a Wild West scenario I had created. On 9 November 1963, the winning submission by schoolgirl Lyndsay Stanworth was performed on the Playhouse stage to a raucous audience of 300 children. Little did I imagine that such amateur young performers would be the very first actors to grace the stage of the future Crucible Theatre.

Directing the action during a Saturday morning session, July 1963

While at the Playhouse, I also worked as an associate or guest director at other theatres, bringing some of their shows back to the Playhouse. From 1964 to 1966 I was Artistic Director of the Ludlow Festival, held each summer in the spectacular grounds of the castle. In June 1964, I directed *The Merchant of Venice* there, forming a life-long friendship with the actor playing Shylock, Kenneth Griffith. I returned the following summer with *Hamlet*, with Emrys Jones in the lead role, and completed my hat-trick in the summer of 1966 with a production of *Much Ado About Nothing*. Directing actors on an open stage, with an upper level behind and the audience surrounding the action on three sides, was a major influence on my thinking about the acting space and the restrictions of the conventional theatre.

During this period, I also worked as Associate Producer to John Neville at the new Nottingham Playhouse, whose revolutionary auditorium—a mix of open and proscenium stage—had opened in December 1963. In August 1964, I brought my production of *The Merchant of Venice* there, with Alasdair Sim as Shylock, and that October I directed John Neville in *Oedipus*. The experience of working on the semi-open stage at Nottingham would prove crucial years later when we were designing the stage for our new theatre.

My third season at the Playhouse in 1964-65 was to prove pivotal. It again started controversially with my production of a new play by

Left: The opening of Hamlet *on the stage at Ludlow Castle, 1965; Right: With Kenneth Griffith during rehearsals for* The Merchant of Venice, *1964*

Madeleine Bingham, *The Real McCoy*, which prompted the Vicar of Tinsley to walk out in protest and demand the play be censored. Quite why the play so offended this cleric is hard to say. There was some swearing, a scene of women in underwear and discussion of prostitution, but these were hardly new. Perhaps it was a sign of how tastes were changing, and how some members of our audience did not want to change with the times.

Then, in October, Geoffrey dropped the bombshell, announcing he would retire at the end of the 1964-65 season. As the title Producer had been hijacked by the film industry to describe whoever subsidised the enterprise, I was interviewed with the prospect of succeeding him with the more contemporary title of Artistic Director. Geoffrey would remain at the Playhouse as Director of Productions.[15]

The appointment of Geoffrey's successor was not without its own drama. The Board of Governors had for years run the theatre efficiently, but as the first Board meeting I attended in October 1962 had demonstrated, times were changing. At my interview, I made a condition of my appointment as Artistic Director that I should decide the programme we presented. Up until then, this had been decided by a play reading committee of which the Director was a member. I said I would of course refer to this committee, but the final decision on our programme must be mine.

The Board couldn't agree to this and asked me to wait outside. After about 15 minutes, they called me back in and said that they couldn't grant my request solely to be responsible for the programme. In that case, I replied, I couldn't accept their offer of the artistic directorship. I was asked to wait outside again for a bit longer. Eventually they called me back in and offered me the post on my terms.

To put all this in perspective, my request was not unusual—it reflected the way the organisation of regional theatres like The Playhouse was changing. Although there was an 'amateur' Board to whom the director was responsible, companies were run professionally in all departments, and most important of all: they were now

---

[15] In the 27 years he was Producer at the Sheffield Playhouse, Geoffrey directed over 400 productions. After my father took over his role in 1965, Geoffrey remained at the Playhouse and went on to direct a further 29 productions, concluding with Strindberg's *The Father* in the last season in the building in 1971.

subsidised by the Arts Council. The director's responsibility, given government funding, was no longer just to the Board but also to the Arts Council and the City—that is to the whole city of Sheffield. While I owe a considerable debt to the Board for their support in the extremely difficult times that lay ahead for us, had I not challenged their authority at the start and left it as absolute as in the past, I feel the Crucible and its revolutionary stage design might never have been considered.

CHAPTER TWO

Ideologies separate us. Dreams and anguish bring us together.†

The Sheffield Playhouse Company, August 1965

When I became Artistic Director of the Sheffield Playhouse in January 1965, I felt it would be valuable to have a survey of our audience. The Arts Council annual grant had risen from £18,000 to £38,000 that year and we needed to know which public we were serving. Moreover, it was clear to even the most partisan observer that our audience was growing older and that the 'regular rep audience' was disappearing. We needed to innovate to survive.

I approached the University of Sheffield, and the survey was undertaken by Dr Peter Mann, Senior Lecturer in Sociology,

---

† Eugène Ionesco.

Full house at the Sheffield Playhouse, 1966

supported by his second-year sociology students. Questionnaires were given away with a free programme. This triggered an inborn Northern conservatism that resulted in some patrons insisting: 'I have paid for my programme for the last twenty-five years and I am not going to be given it free now!'

Two productions, each playing for three weeks, were selected—*Rodney Stone*, an adaption by Alan Cullen of Sir Arthur Conan Doyle's novel, with a young audience in mind, and Anton Chekhov's *Uncle Vanya*, aimed at our more traditional 'regulars'. The university students expected a response rate of around 70%, but the result was remarkable—5,584 for *Rodney Stone* (91%) and 5,367 for *Uncle Vanya* (92.5%). Back then, the repertory audience was a solid one.

So what did the survey reveal about the make-up of our audience? Well, the bedrock was made up of 'highly-educated females'. Two thirds of the audience were women, evenly split between married and single, and there was a high proportion of non-graduate teachers and teacher trainees. Couples made up around half of the audience. As we suspected, the 25-44 year-olds were 'the missing generation', making up just 25% of the audience versus 45% for the over 45s. We needed to reach out to a younger audience.

Age Group (% of total)	Rodney Stone	Uncle Vanya
Under 11	4	-
11–14	8	1
15–18	9	11
19–24	12	18
25–34	11	14
35–44	13	11
45–54	18	18
55–64	17	18
65 or over	8	9

Social class defined the audience the most. Back then, you could divide Sheffield into two halves—the eastern city with its industry and poorer housing and the plusher residential suburbs to the west. Sheffield had 14 postal districts at that time, and in our survey over 40% of the audience came from three western districts: Nether Edge (District 10), Hathersage (7) and Totley (11). Few people from the east side came to the Playhouse. Moreover, half of our audience came from social classes A and B (professional & semi-professional) and one third from C1 (clerical and technical). This was far higher than the national average and meant that semi-skilled, unskilled or casual workers (D & E) formed almost no part of our audience.

Following the survey, we made two important changes in Playhouse policy. The first was to start playing in true repertoire. Rather than

Social class	National ave %	Rodney Stone %	Uncle Vanya %
A	3	21	18
B	9	29	32
C1	17	33	39
C2	38	14	9
D	12	3	2
E	2	0	0

running new productions for three weeks, each would have an initial two-week run after which we could either extend it (if the show was popular) or give it a few additional nights and fill the gaps with more popular shows in our repertoire. At that time, apart from the world of opera and ballet, playing in repertoire was practised only during the Shakespeare season in Stratford-upon-Avon and at a handful of theatres, such as the Old Vic and the Nottingham Playhouse. So my suggestion was radical.

There were huge advantages to the repertoire model. Instead of having to endure prolonged and tiresome breaks between productions (when they had to be at the Playhouse to rehearse but not to perform), actors would have perhaps only one night off per week. Repertoire would also enable us to attract leading actors from the West End, film and television, who would balk at a three-week run but might be persuaded to play a number of performances over a three-month period which they could fit around other commitments.

But the key advantage of repertoire was the flexibility it gave us with programming. Under our three-weekly cycle, popular plays could take a while to catch on, resulting in half-empty houses in the first week and turning patrons away in the third; conversely, less popular plays could struggle to fill the theatre for more than 14 performances. Repertoire would enable us to mix well-tried classics and revivals with new or experimental work, exploiting our successes and cutting back on the failures. The aim was to settle down to a three-weekly rhythm, but to plan around eight weeks ahead, as after the second or third week of a show you knew which to extend a little and which to drop.

We were careful how we rolled out this change to our conservative audience. First, we ensured that every play would run initially for seven performances. This meant that our regular patrons, who made up one third of our audience, could maintain their fortnightly ritual of going to the Playhouse one week and to the Hallé Orchestra at the City Hall the next. We also tempted these regulars by offering two seats for the price of one to those who booked for the first four performances.

The introduction of playing in repertoire at the start of the 1965-66 season was like freeing the Playhouse from a straitjacket. We had the freedom to run a popular piece like *Charley's Aunt* (which

Regular theatregoers crowding the Circle Foyer, 1966

opened the season) for 25 performances instead of the usual 14, but also to run controversial pieces and new plays for a handful of performances after their initial week run. These included Pinter's *The Birthday Party*, the first stage adaptation of Stan Barstow's 1960 novel *A Kind of Loving*, and a double bill of Eugène Ionesco's *The Bald Prima Donna* and *The Chairs*. Some of our regulars—who did not like their routines disturbed—were sceptical of the change, but they embraced it once they realised that they got fresher shows, cheaper seats and the prospect of visits by leading companies and actors to the Playhouse.[16] This change in creative direction was supported by my new Associate Director, Wilfred Harrison, and by our new designer, Edward Furby, who both joined the Playhouse at the start of the 1965-66 season.[17]

---

[16] My father also introduced two-year contracts for actors at the start of this season, which was unheard-of for regional theatres and was a major incentive in keeping actors in the Company.

[17] My father knew Wilfred having directed him as Lord Stanley in *Richard III* at the Old Vic in 1962. In 1965, my father invited Wilfred to play Prospero in *The Tempest*, his first production as Artistic Director of the Playhouse. Later that season, Wilfred directed *Uncle Vanya* and my father asked him—literally half an hour before the production opened—to become his Associate Director. He accepted and went on to direct 18 productions and play numerous parts over the next five seasons.

Two very different plays in our first season of true repertoire (1965-66): Roderick Horn plays the leads in Charley's Aunt *and* The Chairs

The second major innovation concerned theatre for young people. I have already recounted the Saturday morning theatre club for 14- to 18-year-olds I was running at the Playhouse with the Pegasus Theatre Club. This proved a springboard for our youth theatre ambitions. The first Repertory Company to employ a professional group of actors to visit schools was The Belgrade Theatre in Coventry. During my first year as Artistic Director at Sheffield, I went to see their Theatre in Education (TIE) team in action. I was picked up at the stage door by the Belgrade Company van and driven to a school where the actors were already at work. There were six actors who performed short plays and improvised with the students, working with them on scenes from plays they were studying and also on scenes they had encouraged the youngsters to write themselves. The actors were on Equity contracts, earning about as much as they would in the regular Company.

On my return to Sheffield, I reported to the staff and the Board about what I had seen, and with their enthusiastic support an approach was made to the Arts Council for a grant to form a children's theatre company. Several members of our regular Company were interested

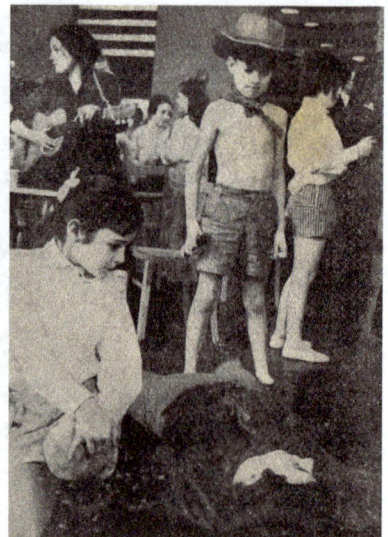

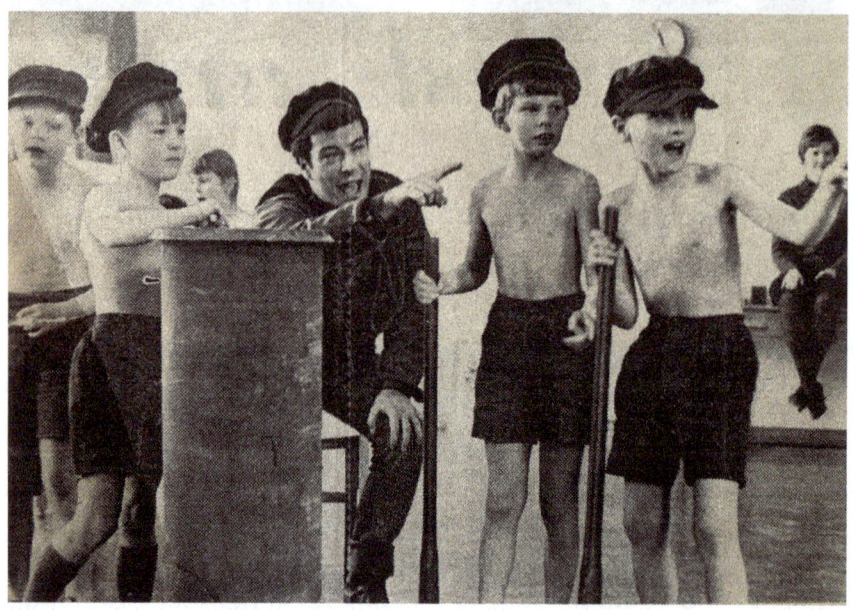

Theatre Vanguard in action, February 1967. Top: Dorothy Vernon plays guitar with the children; Bottom: Robin Hirsch directs a scene at Shooters Grove School, Sheffield

in this kind of work, and after funding was secured from the Arts Council, in February 1967 a group we christened 'Theatre Vanguard' took to the road in a hired van.[18]

The qualifications of the five actors who made up the first Theatre Vanguard troupe were impressive. Dorothy Vernon, founder of the Pegasus Theatre Club, was a teacher who had taught drama at two Sheffield schools for five years. Dorothy was on sabbatical to work with Vanguard, but her talent soon emerged, and she went on to become a leading performer both at the Playhouse and in West End musicals. (She later became my second wife.) The other four actors—Glen Walford, Christopher Wilkinson, Robin Hirsch and John Pickles—had university degrees and a wide range of experience teaching drama at schools and universities. We could not be accused of offering the difficult and important work in schools to actors unqualified for such a challenge!

Theatre Vanguard performed with no charge to as many schools as we could fit in during the school year. I directed the first play, written by our resident playwright, Alan Cullen, entitled *The Bear Who Liked Geraniums* for the youngest audience, which involved considerable audience participation. For the older pupils, Christopher Wilkinson devised an improvised scene based on the Loving-Richardson gunfight at the Long Branch Saloon, Dodge City, in 1879. For sixth form students, I directed extracts from *Edward II* by Christopher Marlowe, *The Birthday Party* by Harold Pinter, *Richard III* by William Shakespeare and *Look back in Anger* by John Osborne, juxtaposing similar dramatic situations from classical and modern authors.[19]

Glen Walford eventually became the Director of Theatre Vanguard, other actors were engaged (notably Alun Armstrong), and the team's engagement with young people grew in all directions, beyond performing plays to encouraging them with improvisation to write and share their experiences.[20] We believed that drama had an

---

[18] It was Geoff Hook, a Sheffield head teacher, who came up with our children's company name.
[19] In Vanguard's first autumn season, the troupe gave 51 performances attended by 5,202 children.
[20] One of Theatre Vanguard's original troupe members, Robin Hirsch, went on to found the Cornelia Street Café in New York's Greenwich Village in 1977. The café's downstairs performance space became a hub for up-and-coming musicians, poets, writers & dancers, among them Suzanne Vega and Eve Ensler (author of *The Vagina Monologues*).

educational as well as a therapeutic value, especially if children were making their own drama. We discovered that it was the students who were not academically brilliant who gained the most through building self-confidence, self-control and an awareness of one's fellow human beings and our relationship to them.

After Coventry, Sheffield and Watford were the first companies to deploy TIE teams. At the time I was asked to explain what Vanguard believed the theatre exists for and I wrote: 'It is there to celebrate life. We all have a feeling of responding to a ritual. This needs to be developed so that our imagination, our compassion is awakened. If this process starts as a child, then as an adult our awareness, our theatrical appreciation is that much more keen and alive. A demanding, cultivated audience begets an imaginative exciting theatre. That is what all of us here want at the Playhouse Theatre.'

In May 1967, in support of Vanguard's work, I made a month-long trip to Eastern Europe to study children's theatre at the Boško Buha Theatre (Belgrade) and the Jiří Wolker Theatre (Prague). While impressed by the quality of their work, I was surprised that neither theatre company worked in schools and that many of the actors were against the idea of children performing on stage. Not so with Vanguard! Children's theatre was central to the work of the Playhouse and influenced our move towards a more open and interactive form of engaging our audience.[21]

Another Playhouse initiative was the introduction of Sunday night readings and entertainments. These included a poetry and music evening given by six actors from the Company, a professional singer and a pianist who had written music for Playhouse productions, and *Feast of Fools*, an illustrated lecture to celebrate Shakespeare's quatercentenary. But it was not all highbrow. There were jazz evenings, readings of plays not in the usual repertoire, and some new work. Occasionally, there were performances by distinguished actors; for example, Micheál Mac Liammóir brought *The Importance of Being Oscar* to the Playhouse.

Looking back now, none of this looks very innovative. But for the Sheffield of that time it was, and those of us working at the

---

[21] Thanks to the Playhouse's work with children's theatre, my father was appointed as one of the original members of the Arts Council Panel for Young People's Theatre.

Playhouse were determined to widen the audience if we could, and to some extent we succeeded. When I was interviewed in 1971, I noted that the average age of our audience had dropped by ten years. This undoubtedly had an influence on the decision by the City Council when the time came to replace the Playhouse with a new theatre. But there was one production in my first season as Artistic Director which stands out, capturing the spirit of change, creativity, and experimentation at the Playhouse at that time, and which came to define it: *The Stirrings in Sheffield on Saturday Night*.

The inspiration for *Stirrings* came in the summer of 1965, when I made a trip over the Pennines to the Victoria Theatre in Stoke-on-Trent. This revolutionary theatre-in-the-round under the direction of Peter Cheeseman had put on a lively production—*The Jolly Potters*—which explored the history of the district and came up with a show that spoke to those living in the locality. The show had that rare quality of saying something significant in a thoroughly entertaining manner. Given that our older regular audiences were getting frustrated by changes in theatrical taste and our need to attract a younger audience, I thought a *Jolly Cutlers* might be a useful addition to our repertoire.

So I put the idea of a musical about Sheffield to Alan Cullen and Roderick Horn. They had collaborated on our Christmas play for

Alan Cullen (Left) and Roderick Horn (Right), late 1960s

children, *Trudi and the Minstrel*, which had demonstrated the powerful combination of Alan's words and Roderick's music. John Hainsworth, a keen supporter of the Playhouse working at the University of Sheffield, offered some research he had carried out on a local trade union leader of the 1860s: William Broadhead. Alan produced a series of scenes which Rod set to music with contemporary ballads. The links between Alan's sharp and effective episodes gave plenty of scope for the Company and director to shape and give life to the production in rehearsal. *Stirrings* (as it became known) owes much to the inspiration and ingenuity of the actors, designers, and staff who were involved in the production from the outset.

We described the results of this collaboration as a 'tragical-comical-historical-industrial' evening with 'skulduggery in the back streets interwoven with a farcical sub-plot about a local gas company and laced with folk songs of the period'.

There are two stories in the play. The first deals with William Broadhead, leader of the saw-grinders in the 1860s. At that time the

The cast of Stirrings *during rehearsals, 1966*

unions were not recognised in law and the only way they could coerce their members into paying their dues was by intimidation or physical violence. Automation was raising its head in the cutlery trade: a machine could do the work of a roomful of men, and some employers (the 'little mesters') unscrupulously took on too many apprentices to do the work of fully-fledged union members. Broadhead, with the connivance of the union committee, used his own methods to discipline the grinders and the small employers.

The second story concerns Isaac Ironside, who formed the Consumers' Gas Company to compete with the United Gas Company which, in his opinion, was overcharging its customers. His struggle ended with the amalgamation of both companies by order of the

Dorothy Vernon and Veronica Lang in the first Stirrings *revival, November 1968*

government. Ultimately, the Amalgamated Gas Company did lower its prices and Ironside threw his enthusiasm into other aspects of civic endeavour, such as sewerage.

Given the show's subject matter, the Playhouse Board was nervous at how it would be received by the Sheffield public, with one Board member predicting any show about trade unions would empty the theatre. Undeterred, we opened *Stirrings* on 31st May 1966 and it was a massive success.[22] Wilfred Harrison's performance as Broadhead and the singing of Dorothy Vernon and Roderick Horn won widespread praise. Describing the show as an 'irresistible *tour de force*', Denys Corrigan recalled: 'I have never heard acclamation to surpass that accorded it by the first-night audience; and, ever after, the 'House Full' notices were standing by whenever it played... [The

Programme covers for the first two Stirrings *in 1966 and 1968*

---

[22] Years later, my father was given a leather-bound copy of *Stirrings* with messages from the Company inside. David Brayshaw wrote: 'I too doubted—a little; but it didn't empty the theatre—it helped to build one.' Alan Cullen wrote: 'Many thanks for lighting the fire and stirring the pot.'

Playhouse] has never done anything which so completely captured the audience's hearts and imaginations and set them humming so irresistibly.'[23]

Some theatregoers saw *Stirrings* seven or eight times and, more important still, large numbers returned to the Playhouse who had ceased their theatregoing with the demise of the local variety house. A reliable source even told me that a programme for *Stirrings* found its way onto a workbench in the local steel mills!

The overwhelming success of *Stirrings* led to two revivals—the first in November 1968 (to coincide with the centenary of the TUC) and the second at the Crucible Theatre in 1973. All three productions were sell-outs and had extended runs.

There is something about the sheer theatrical impact of *Stirrings* which is indestructible. It has survived innumerable changes of cast and even weathered the sea change from a small proscenium theatre to the thrust stage. I believe the show owes its lasting popularity not to its political themes, but to its infectious and diverting mixture of 'popular' entertainment: the variety sketch, the monologue and Music Hall. The show has since become a part of local history: there was even a restaurant, 'The Stirrings', named in its honour.

There is one memory from our first run of *Stirrings* that I particularly savour. Towards the end of the play, the disgraced hero William Broadhead justifies himself by saying: '[My] only wish and object has been to protect and defend the labour of thousands of workmen.' At that moment, a formidable Sheffield lady on the back row raised her arms aloft and shouted out in ringing tones: 'Well said, lad!'

The creative forces of the Playhouse had stirred up Sheffield and put our theatre back on the map. The timing could not have been better, as our Company was about to experience an extraordinary turn in its fortunes.

---

[23] Corrigan, *The Stirrings in Sheffield*, p.26.

CHAPTER THREE

Don't trust tomorrow's bow for fruit. Pluck this here now.[†]

The Crucible adventure started one sunny August day in 1966. I had recently finished directing *Much Ado About Nothing* at the Ludlow Festival. That summer would turn out to be anything but, both for England's World Cup-winning football team and also for the Sheffield Playhouse.

That day I was walking to the Town Hall as part of a large delegation from the Playhouse. Among us were three members of the Playhouse Board—Tony Hampton (Chairman), David Brayshaw (Chairman of the Executive Committee) and Dr Maisie Glass, as well as a troupe from the Playhouse Company, including myself, Bill Butler (Company Manager), Geoffrey Ost (former Producer of the Playhouse) and Wilfred Harrison (my Assistant Director). Why were we on our way to the Town Hall? To ask the Council for a grant of money to assist in running the theatre.

My arrival as Assistant Director at the Playhouse in late 1962 had coincided with a first grant from the Arts Council of £5,000. Within three years, this had grown to £38,000, including a grant for improvements to the Temperance Hall building.[24] Imaginative as the 1954 re-build had been in redesigning the auditorium and the front of house areas, there had not been enough money to improve the backstage facilities. When I first arrived and acted myself, the men all shared one communal dressing room and the women another. One lavatory served both sexes.

As we were reaching out to a new audience, had created Theatre Vanguard as a full-time children's theatre company and were offering Sunday night programmes in cooperation with the University of

---

[†] Horace, *Ode II*.
[24] In 2021, the increased grant would have been worth the equivalent of £635,000.

Sheffield, we felt we could ask the City Council to support a local theatre which demonstrably served the community. We already had an annual grant from the Arts Council to help run the theatre and pay for our children's work in schools, and we were hopeful that the City Council could be persuaded to match it. So when we were summoned to the Town Hall, I was expecting to hear whether our grant had been approved.

We arrived at the Town Hall and were ushered into the main Council Chamber—a long room with a polished table and chairs either side. At one end, on what might be described as a throne, sat a formidable Northern lady. This was Alderman Grace Tebbutt, former Lord Mayor of Sheffield and the first female Leader of Sheffield City Council. We sat in front of her like naughty schoolchildren in front of

Grace Tebbutt in full regalia as Lord Mayor of Sheffield, 1949

the headmistress. She looked us over for a minute and then dropped her bombshell.

'Nah then—where do you want your new theatre?' To those of us working at the Playhouse it was a bolt from the blue. 'You probably want an island site', she continued forcefully, and with a wave of her hand effortlessly destroyed Norfolk Street. Over the next breathless minutes, we discovered that the Council had decided that as the citizens of Nottingham, Coventry and other cities had benefited from the post-war theatre-building boom, so should their Sheffielders. Stunned as I was, my wits did not desert me completely and I had enough adrenaline racing to reply that we really needed two theatres, a studio as well as a large auditorium.

Tony Hampton and Bill Butler stepped in and engaged the Lord Mayor in conversation—after all, they knew the city much better than I did. I merely looked on approvingly. I remember some talk of the theatre being placed opposite the Lyceum, a Victorian theatre then reduced to housing bingo.[25] There was also discussion of the Adelphi Hotel on the corner of the proposed site, at the end of Norfolk Street, in whose pub the Yorkshire County Cricket Club and both of Sheffield's football teams had been founded. As it happened, our new theatre won that particular match.

As I left the Council Chamber, the thrilling prospect opened up for me to be involved in designing a theatre from the ground up. It seemed like a gilt-edged opportunity. I would have been utterly astonished if you had told me that the deliberations over the design of this new theatre would take me to North America and unleash some of the most turbulent and hard-fought years I have ever experienced in the theatre.

I later learned of the chain of events that led to that momentous meeting in Sheffield Town Hall. Among various urban improvement schemes during this period was an inner ring-road: the so-called 'Civic Circle'. Under the plan drawn up in 1965, the new road would cut through Townhead Street, demolishing everything in its path, including

---

[25] In his initial discussions with Tony Hampton and the City Council, the Chairman of the Finance Committee, Alderman Isador Lewis, had offered the site of an old tram office near Fitzallan Square. But this was turned down in favour of the larger site available on Arundel Gate.

the Playhouse.[26] News of the plan leaked to the press, and in August 1965 the Playhouse Board started discussions with the Arts Council and Sheffield City Council on finding a new site for the Playhouse. The timing was good as that year the 'Housing the Arts' scheme had been launched. This empowered the Arts Council to rehouse repertory companies when their theatre facilities were inadequate.

Sheffield Council had other reasons for wanting a new theatre. The facilities of the Playhouse were rapidly becoming inadequate, and with new repertory theatres being built or planned in nearby Nottingham, Leeds, and Birmingham, the City of Sheffield, which boasted one of the most thriving regional theatres in the country, needed a custom-built drama venue. But it was never intended to be a 'civic theatre' playing host to a variety of touring entertainment and amateur dramatics. Much of the subsequent criticism of the new theatre's design failed to recognise this.

For me personally, what was so stunning about their decision was their commitment to me as Artistic Director of the new theatre. It would have been understandable if those responsible for providing the city with a new theatre had looked elsewhere for a new Artistic Director. London and Stratford throw a long shadow over the theatre scene and the Council would have been forgiven for seducing someone with a metropolitan CV and a reputation to their new building. But I guess they felt I had been working in Sheffield long enough to win their loyalty—not least with several successful seasons, including the indomitable *Stirrings*.[27]

On 24th August 1966, the Playhouse announced that a new theatre would be built to house the Company. At a press conference that day, attended by the Playhouse Board and the Leader of the City Council, Sir Ron Ironmonger, I described the decision as 'a wonderful justification of all we have been trying to do at the theatre recently, to make the Playhouse a real part of the community.

'Architecturally, this is the most exciting time to contemplate putting up a new theatre building. It would have been tragic had

---

[26] As it turned out, the Civic Circle scheme was only partly completed and Townhead Street was saved.
[27] When *Stirrings* was revived by popular demand in December 1968, my father invited to the production, on consecutive nights, the Town Clerk, the Conservative Leader of the City Council and the Labour Leader of the City Council, Alderman Ironmonger.

this decision been taken 15 or perhaps 10 years ago. We have seen a revolution in the theatre since the war, and we should be, when planning the new Sheffield Playhouse, in a position to reap the benefit of experimental work already done in this country, on the Continent, and in America.

'What is so important about this decision is that the city appears to have accepted that a theatre is a necessary—and one of the most vital—amenities which it has a duty to provide for its citizens. Drama is already playing an increasingly important part in education and to build a Playhouse providing the best in classical and contemporary theatre is the logical culmination of this. A new Playhouse will surely bring prestige, and focus attention, on a city which is already well-known for its imaginative new buildings.'[28]

Before any decision was taken on the location of the new theatre, there was considerable discussion about what sort of theatre it should be. That September, I pulled together the collective thoughts of the Playhouse Company and produced a four-page document—'Notes on The New Sheffield Playhouse'—which outlined our collective vision for the new theatre.

Our first thought was that any new building should reflect the best new ideas in theatre design. The theatre should be modern and inspire pride, both within and without, and should be designed with a view to how we would use it in five, ten or even twenty years' time. We outlined the new theatre's priorities as:

(a) to provide a varied repertoire of plays in true repertoire;
(b) to house visiting companies such as the National Theatre;
(c) to mount and send out tours both in this country and abroad;
(d) to be the base for a company visiting schools and theatre clubs in the region;
(e) to provide theatregoers with 'club activities' such as poetry readings, lectures, intimate concerts, films, and exhibitions.

To achieve these aims, we would need two auditoria: a large auditorium for the main productions and a small experimental studio

---

[28] *The Star*, 25 August 1966.

which would also function as the headquarters for educational and club work.

First, the large auditorium. We thought hard about the impression we wanted the auditorium to make on spectators. Right from the start, we wanted a different kind of stage which could free us from the constrictions of the proscenium arch. We liked the idea of spectators being aware of their fellow spectators, as they might be in a football crowd, to see the stage as a stage and to have the feeling that something was about to be demanded of them.

When it came to stage itself, I proposed a number of options, all based on the idea of a forestage that was adaptable to a proscenium theatre, rather than vice versa. One option involved adding a permanent small forestage, possibly with an entrance on the side, and in front of this a large adaptable forestage. This could sink to provide an orchestra pit or could be raised to the level of the seating, adding an extra 60 seats for a proscenium production. Another option involved combining the stage and forestage into a space that fanned out into a wider, more open look, connected by a ramp to the back of the auditorium, either from one side (as in the Japanese Noh theatre) or up the central gangway. This ramp would enable entrances to be made through the audience, which could be most effective if the auditorium were steeply raked.

The layout of the seating was also crucial for this new kind of theatre. I wrote: 'Unless the theatre is particularly small (for example, The Georgian Theatre in Richmond), the circle are not going to see the actors' eyes as well as those sitting in the stalls. From the back of the "gods" in Victorian theatres you literally see the top of the actors' heads. Nevertheless, the feeling of the spectators toppling onto the stage from the tiered galleries in some of the old theatres like the Royal at Margate or Bristol is theatrically right: whereas the high characterless bank of seats facing the actor, as in the new Southampton Theatre is clinical, lecture-dominated, and inhuman. I would therefore suggest an auditorium with one bank of seats, possibly with two gangways, raked reasonably steeply, and possibly curving at the sides.

'The general colour of the auditorium should be warm, with the lighting and decorations such as to set the blood racing. The texture should be natural and not synthetic—wood rather than anything shiny and manufactured—giving a feeling of life and vulnerability rather than being calculatedly scientific and rigid. Finally, the auditorium should be of a sufficient size to ensure a reasonable financial return. Nottingham is already finding its 700 capacity too small. For a community the size of Sheffield a capacity of 900 would be needed.'

Next, the Studio Theatre. We wanted a permanent theatre that was adaptable, seating about 250 people in one permanent bank of seats. With extra seating, the space should be adaptable to theatre-in-the-round and I mooted adding a small open-ended stage for film shows, concerts, and readings. The Studio Theatre would need ancillary workshops and administrative rooms for Theatre Vanguard.

And finally, the theatre complex itself. We wanted a visually exciting structure with a bright and spacious foyer—visible from the outside—which could be used for drinks, exhibitions, and events. There should be a buffet restaurant and a bar which opened directly on to the street and which was open full-time to the public. For the backstage staff, there should be plenty of space for the theatre administration, wardrobe, workshops, and dressing rooms.

Regarding the size of the Company and staff, there would need to be a substantial increase on the 36 employed by the Playhouse. The acting Company would have 36 members, two Artistic Directors and six musicians, supported by 74 administrative, design, and technical staff. This was perhaps 'blue sky thinking', but I noted that the Guthrie Theater in Minneapolis employed 110 staff and that this reflected the level of staff needed to run this kind of theatre.[29]

Looking back at this document more than 50 years after it was written, much of it seems rather predictable. But in the years after the Second World War, those of us working in the theatre—especially in the provinces—were used to performing in city halls, town halls, school halls, church halls and, as at Sheffield—Temperance Halls; that is, in buildings not erected solely as theatres. In the early days of the Sheffield Repertory Company, stages on which they performed had inadequate wing space and lacked flying facilities. In one venue, The

---

[29] When the Crucible Theatre finally opened in November 1971, the Company and backstage staff totalled 73 people, double its size at the Playhouse.

Little Theatre, an actor entering stage right had to do so by climbing through a window![30] The jump from the Sheffield Playhouse to our new theatre would be a leap worthy of an Olympic athlete.

---

[30] Alec Seed recalls that on one occasion at the Little Theatre 'they had a piano "in the wings" for music "off", turned on its side and the players had to clamber over it to get on and off stage.' *The Sheffield Repertory Theatre*, p.3.

CHAPTER FOUR

When we mean to build, We first survey the plot, then draw the model.[†]

Following our report, in September 1966 the New Sheffield Theatre Trust was created to manage the financial planning and construction of the new theatre. The Trust consisted of fifteen members who were an imaginative cross-section of leading and influential citizens. Four company chairmen represented the steel and local industry. From local politics we had the leaders of the Conservative and Labour groups, as well as the Trades and Labour Council. Two solicitors and the Chairman of the Magistrates represented the Law, while the Vice-Chancellor and Senior Pro-Chancellor of the University of Sheffield sat in for academia.

The Trust was charged with building an entirely new theatre at a total cost of £500,000-600,000.[31] Sheffield Corporation would fund 50% of the cost, the Arts Council 33.5%, with a public appeal covering the remaining 16.5%. The theatre would have a main auditorium seating around 950 and a 250-seat studio for youth theatre work. It was appreciated that the budget would not necessarily be enough to build the main theatre and the studio, but we decided to include the studio in our plans anyway and worry later about getting the money to build, equip, and run it.

A Building Committee was also created, and I have the minutes of the first meeting in December 1966. The Chairman was Dr Gerard Young: he was a steel manufacturer but, as Senior Pro-Chancellor of the University of Sheffield, he had also been responsible for overseeing considerable new building over the preceding ten years. Having served on numerous committees myself, I was always impressed by the

---

[†] William Shakespeare, *Henry IV, Part II*, Act 1, Scene 3.
[31] This would be the equivalent of £8 million to £9.6 million in 2021. The budget for the Crucible grew almost from the first discussions and would eventually reach £884,000.

Left: Tony Hampton, Chairman of the Playhouse Board; Right: David Brayshaw, future Administrator of the Crucible Theatre

way Dr Young kept the balance between those of us working in the theatre and the other Committee members. While always aware of the financial implications of what was discussed and how it related to Sheffield's resources, he displayed a genuine respect for those whose commitment was to the arts.

The Vice-Chairman of the Building Committee came from the Playhouse Board—Chairman, Tony Hampton. Anthony had grown up immersed in theatre through the passion of his mother and as a young man had been an amateur actor. He was invited to become Chairman of the Playhouse Board when Alec Seed retired, but he continued his activities as a local businessman and in 1966 served as the City's prestigious Master Cutler. Anthony's connections to Sheffield's business community were to prove critical in our fundraising efforts, and throughout the controversies that lay ahead he would remain a staunch supporter of our creative efforts.

The other Board member, David Brayshaw, was an old comrade of Anthony's. David had also been an amateur actor in his youth before setting up his own law practice, and he had been invited by Anthony to join the Board as the Chairman of the Executive

Committee. David would go on to become the first Administrator of the Crucible Theatre, and a dear friend and ally.[32] Also present at this meeting were Roy Johnson, the Planning Officer of the University of Sheffield, myself, Wilfred Harrison, and the Hon. Secretary, Mr D Harrison.

At its first meeting, the Building Committee made a number of critical decisions. These included starting the search for an architect; agreeing a basic schedule of requirements and estimated building costs; sketch plans of the new theatre; a tender for the erection of the building; and the timetable for the hand-over of the completed building. A draft programme was adopted which envisioned completion of the building in October 1970. A shortlist of architects was also submitted. The Committee requested that I and Roy Johnson visit London to interview the architects and report back urgently.

Looking back on that first meeting of the Building Committee, I realise the importance of the support of the University of Sheffield. Dr Gerard Young was a commanding figure who understood how to get buildings built and the Planning Officer Roy Johnson had a very down-to-earth, pragmatic character. Both had been involved in considerable new building at the University and would bring their knowledge and expertise to bear on the construction of the new theatre. Roy and I quickly became a double act, being tasked to investigate and report on a number of questions regarding the dimensions of the stage and storage areas.

Following our report to the Trustees, the City Engineer recommended a site for the new theatre near the corner of Norfolk Street. The City Surveyor ascertained that the cost of the site would be around £200,000, a much larger proportion of the funds than originally envisaged. This was one of the factors that started to increase the budget. An initial programme was laid out for the work:

---

[32] Tedd's Note: David also became godfather to my sister Lucy.

- February 1967: Appointment of architects, schedule of accommodation
- October/November 1967: sketch plans in final form, along with the architects' report and cost estimate
- November 1968: acceptance of the tender and placing of contract for construction of the building
- September 1970: completion

This early programme was a realistic one, and in the form the theatre was envisaged, this timeline was entirely feasible. It was only our subsequent decision to take the stage design in a radically different direction that delayed completion of the building until 1971.

A list of twelve architects was circulated, including those who had been involved in buildings such as the National Theatre, the Nottingham Playhouse and the Belgrade Coventry. The Building Committee settled on a shortlist of four: Ove Arup Associates; Renton Howard Wood Associates; Denys Lasdun (who immediately said he would be unable to undertake the project owing to his commitment to the ongoing National Theatre project), and William Whitfield. On 3rd February 1967, Roy Johnson and I visited the three remaining architects on the shortlist.

Ove Arup Associates had famously been the design engineer of the Sydney Opera House in Australia. I recall the firm's office building and the ambience of the whole interview was, as we expected, high profile. We outlined our thoughts about the stage and the accommodation we envisaged for the new theatre. Their response was friendly and professionally thorough.

Renton Howard Wood, however, were much more approachable. Created in 1961 by Andrew Renton with his associates Peter Howard & Humphrey Wood, the practice had been involved in a wide range of projects, including the design of offices for the Port of London Authority in the St Katharine Docks area. Andrew Renton and Humphrey Wood knew Dr Gerard Young and Mr Johnson well, having worked on a project at the University of Sheffield, and they leapt at the opportunity to be involved in designing a new theatre.

The final Architect, William Whitfield, was working on the Geography & Planning Building of the University of Sheffield, but his firm was not as experienced as the other two candidates and he was dropped from the process. Our instinctive choice was for Renton Howard Wood.

On 14th February 1967, the Building Committee met in the Town Hall to interview Renton Howard Wood, Ove Arup Associates and in addition Bob Adams of Hadfield Cawkwell Davidson, who had worked on the rebuilding of the Playhouse. Those of us at the Playhouse knew Bob's work on the old Temperance Hall, but we felt his firm lacked the staff and expertise to cope with the demands of such a huge enterprise. The Committee came to the same conclusion and appointed Renton Howard Wood. We had our architects.[33]

If I had to say what swayed the opinions of those on the Committee, it was quite simply the enthusiasm of Andrew Renton and his associates. One member of his team was Nick Thompson who was to become central to the design of the new theatre. Aged just 31 at the time, Nick had worked on a number of school halls and had a keen interest in theatre. Years later, when he was working on a new theatre for Warwick University, I asked him how it was going. 'Oh, we're enjoying it', he said, adding 'but there is nothing like your first theatre!' And, looking back at how things developed, I can see that Sheffield would have been a remarkable opportunity for any architect.

Several other important appointments were made that day. These included the structural engineers, Ove Arup & Partners,[34] whose brilliant engineer Peter Rice had worked on the Sydney Opera House and who was at the time developing the Beaubourg project (this became the Pompidou Centre); Mechanical Engineers, Dale & Benham, whose services engineer Peter Goldfinger, son of the Hungarian Modernist architect, Ernö Goldfinger, would design our new theatre's innovative ventilation and air-conditioning system; Acoustics, Hugh Creighton; and Quantity Surveyors, Gleeds, whose partner John Bensley would keep a tight control over building costs.

---

[33] Nick Thompson later recalled: 'We got the job because we'd never done a theatre before! I think that says a lot for Colin's set-up: they had a pretty clear idea of what they wanted and they didn't want an architect who thought he knew it all telling them what to do.' Tedd George's interview with Nick Thompson, October 2020.

[34] Ove Arup Associates and Ove Arup & Partners were two different entities, the former focused on architectural design and the latter on structural engineering.

After a tender, the builders would be a local firm, Gleesons, whose regional director Sean Fahy, one of the last great building contractors, would oversee construction on site. More about them later.

The architects set to work, and by the end of February 1967 they had prepared a costed outline schedule of accommodation for the new Playhouse, which matched the brief we had prepared for the Trust the previous October. The new theatre would start construction in December 1968 and open in October 1970. Most important was the design for the stage, which was a thrust forward-style that could be adapted to proscenium performance. There would also be a small, fixed forestage and a larger forestage adjustable to three levels—up for open stage productions, floor level for proscenium productions and sunk for an orchestra pit.[35]

However, almost immediately disagreement arose over the site of the new theatre. The City Engineer felt the building should only extend part of the way up Norfolk Street, dismissing the architects' suggestion that it should spread down the whole of Norfolk Street as too complicated and expensive. Looking at the structure of the building today, it is clear that the architects' vision was the right one. But the enlargement of the site would increase the construction costs to £640,000, above the top range of the agreed budget.[36]

The final minute of the Building Committee's report to the Trustees read: 'If a larger sum of money than that at first envisaged is not forthcoming, one would have to scale down the whole project to the size of the present Playhouse with very restricted objectives.' Given the considerable publicity around Sheffield's wonderful new theatre, this was a neat way of encouraging the Trustees not to be fainthearted. But it would be several months before additional funding was agreed.

During this hiatus, those of us in the theatre struck up a friendly and positive relationship with the architects. I shared a number of articles about theatre design with them, including pieces by the director Sir Tyrone Guthrie and the theatre designer Richard Southern. In an enclosed note, I wrote: 'These are extremist ideas, you appreciate, the first two personalities are highly idiosyncratic workers, and you would

---

[35] Nick later recalled: 'The early concept was something fairly close to the Nottingham Playhouse.'

[36] In 2021 this budget would be the equivalent of £9.9 million.

certainly get a different theatre from them than you would from me.' Given what was to happen a few months later, this remark was ironic in the extreme.

I also sent to Andrew Renton diagrams with notes on how we felt the design might progress, and some material about the remarkable Malmö Municipal Theatre in Sweden of which Ingmar Bergman had been Director. Built in 1944, it could offer not just plays but opera, ballet, and experimental theatre. He replied: 'Fascinating cuttings of the Malmö theatre... audience of 2,000... 4 rising stages... black marble... stainless steel (Sheffield?)... marble paved piazza... bronze fountains... spacious foyers. However, although the Playhouse cannot be too expensive, I feel sure we can still produce something exciting and provocative.'

He went on: 'We are at present working on the functional solution in diagrammatic form—though we always have the architectural solution in mind—and once we are all absolutely certain of the functional solution we then have to launch our architectural attack.'

While the Architects got on with the functional design, I reached out to the Playhouse Company to get their views on the dressing rooms. It was clear that actors needed somewhere for more than just putting on a costume. They needed somewhere to prepare for the show, to retire any time of the day, with the space and length to lie down on a couch. The dressing rooms needed to be soundproofed so they could play guitar or shout out lines without disturbing other actors—or as our own avant-garde playwright/actor, Christopher Wilkinson, put it: 'a room to go mad in!' And most of all, the dressing rooms needed windows!

From this discussion came the idea of a number of 'cells' for, say, six performers opening onto a central dressing room. The 'cells' would be soundproof and include a couch, outside window and personal wardrobe. Make-up, costume and hand basins would be in the communal dressing room in order to save space. The architects' brief had outlined 10 dressing rooms for three actors and two large chorus rooms for ten performers each. We proposed to have more individual dressing rooms incorporating as many ideas as possible from the actors' requests, while retaining two large chorus dressing rooms on the conventional pattern, plus rooms for the assistant stage managers and a room for them to study and rest. I agreed to present these proposals to the architects at our next meeting.

Another issue on which the Company had an important input concerned the stage at the new theatre, a topic we were to debate intensely over the coming months. Our work both in the Playhouse and in schools, and for a short experimental season in South Street, was confirming our desire to reach out to the audience from the constrictions of the proscenium arch. Hardly a production passed without someone entering through the audience, or the house curtains being banished to the fly tower. A brief I drew up with the cooperation of all the staff expressed our desire for the new stage to jut out towards the spectator.

In our original design concept, there would be an unobtrusive proscenium, in front of which sat the forestage. This would be a 'tongue' 20 feet wide that reached into the auditorium, with the main stage action focussed in a 9-foot circle in the centre—the so-called 'Magic Circle'. The front could be splayed or shaped so as not to interfere with this circle. To describe this acting space, we needed to use new terms. We turned to the medieval castle: a 'moat' surrounded the wide forestage, with steps down from the stage; actors entered from two 'sally ports' set in the raked seating and wide enough to take a chariot. (On a thrust stage these would be called vomitories). The stage floor would be polished wood and would have trapdoors where actors could make dramatic entrances and exits, as well as a large, medium, and small revolve for moving scenery during a performance.

The debates over the stage over the coming months revealed how the disciplines of the theatre designer and the architect differ fundamentally. To a designer or director in the theatre, the stage space is clearly defined. You use it as space for the actor or to furnish this basic area in different ways. It is confusing to an architect that a theatre director or designer can completely change the use of the stage and even the auditorium as the production develops in rehearsal.

The director emerges from an early run-through and tells the designer: 'I think the main entrance is more effective stage right than up centre and the arrival of the police might be more threatening if they come through the auditorium.' The architect, who is dealing in bricks and mortar, not wood and canvas flats, finds this approach unsettling. He needs his client to be precise and committed to an idea, not constantly changing his mind—as we did frequently.

Nick Thompson later recalled: 'Mr Johnson said to me: "You need to understand this—theatre people will be constantly having new ideas, changing their minds. You can listen to them as much as you like, but you are not to do anything without my approval because it's money, and I handle the money!" It was the best advice I've ever been given. Because it meant that I could really enjoy listening to Colin and the others and forming new ideas, knowing that I had to get back to the budget all the time and control it.'[37]

In a letter to Roy Johnson that summer, I suggested a combination of stage and forestage: 'a reasonable, practicable scenic space fanning out into the wider, more open look.' We were moving beyond the proscenium arch into the darkness of the auditorium, fumbling

Regulars going into the Playhouse to see It Happened in Irkutsk, *June 1967*

---

[37] Tedd George's interview with Nick Thompson, October 2020.

towards a different kind of actor-audience relationship. But as my correspondence from the time shows, we were unsure of exactly what we wanted. It would take the intervention of someone extraordinary to inspire us to embrace a radical design for our stage.

We continued to discuss our ideas with the architects when I invited them to see our work at the Playhouse. In June 1967, Humphrey Wood, Peter Howard, and Nick Thompson came to see my production of *It Happened in Irkutsk* by the Soviet writer Aleksei Arbuzov. They sat in different parts of the auditorium—the stalls and circle, front and back—to give them a complete perspective on the theatrical space.

They returned in July to see *Ring o' Roses*, Alan Cullen's follow-up to *Stirrings* set in the village of Eyam during the Plague of 1665. They spent their time in the wings watching what is involved in the work of actors and technicians—things like quick changes of costume in the wings, collecting of props, setting or striking scenery and furniture, and the value of having extensive wing space. It was the last night of the production, and the architects stayed into the early hours of the morning making notes on the strike of the production they had just seen and on the set-up of scenery and lighting for the following production.

Looking back, I realise how important it was for the architects to see the limitations of the old Temperance Hall proscenium arch in order to fully appreciate why we needed an open stage and a building that was fit for purpose, especially for our legion of backstage staff. Their visits were a most useful bonding experience both for those who would work in the new theatre and for those designing it.

That summer of 1967 I was tied up with personal affairs, with my marriage to my second wife, Dorothy Vernon, and the birth of our daughter Caroline. In the space of one month my personal life changed dramatically. I had no idea how plans for the new theatre would change in equally dramatic fashion.

Part II

Guthrie & the Thrust Stage

CHAPTER FIVE

Two roads diverged in a wood, and I–
I took the one less travelled by,
And that has made all the difference.[†]

In the autumn of 1967 two events, one day apart, were to radically alter our plans for the new theatre. On the first date—Saturday 14th October 1967—I went to Nottingham Playhouse with the three architects and their junior associate, Nick Thompson. As I had previously been Assistant Director to John Neville there—directing him as Oedipus on the large, adaptable and occasionally-used forestage—and had worked with children in that format during Saturday morning sessions, I thought that our new Sheffield theatre might relate, without banal imitation, to Nottingham's actor-audience relationship.

When we arrived at the Playhouse, I pulled rank with the Company Manager and as the theatre's current production was using the forestage, the architects and I were given forty-five minutes between shows to explore the space. These proved to be crucial minutes. We examined the stage and backstage first—roomy but conventional. The auditorium had stalls and a circle, so the four architects sat in different places to judge the sightlines. Then came the moment of truth.

I told them I would start delivering a speech from the back of the stage and walk through the proscenium to the very front, where there would normally be footlights. 'You should find that when I get below the proscenium arch we are in the same room: audience and actor sharing the same space. That is the advantage of the large forestage we are planning'. I stood well upstage and began the opening chorus from *Henry V*—'Oh for a muse of fire that would ascend the brightest heaven of invention!....'—and made my way to the front of the stage, finishing with a theatrical bow: '[...] Gently to hear, kindly to judge our play'. I did not receive the accustomed

---

[†] Robert Frost, 'The Road Not Taken'.

applause but something more disturbing: poor feedback about the forestage.

'You are never in the same room or space as us, even on the forestage', they told me. 'You remain in a proscenium theatre. Only when you stand on the very tip of the forestage do we feel we are near you and sharing your space.'

'We must think further, then', I replied.

Driving back to Sheffield, I began to have doubts about the plans we had made so far. It was clear to me that a forestage did not provide that magic contact which the spectators in Sophocles' Athens or Shakespeare's London felt with their performers, that feeling of being in the same space. There was no point spending time and money making a life-size mock-up of our proposed forestage, even allowing for it being bigger than Nottingham's. We needed to go back to the drawing board.

The very next day, Sunday October 15th, a giant walked on stage at the Sheffield Playhouse. A *Jack and the Beanstalk* production? No, I refer to Sir Tyrone Guthrie. He was indeed a dominating figure, not just in stature (he was six foot six) but in his conviction that the theatre had an important contribution to make to the life of the community. My Associate Director, Wilfred Harrison, who knew Guthrie, had invited him to give a public address to help raise funds for the new Sheffield theatre. It proved to be a most fortunate invitation.

By 1967 Sir Tyrone Guthrie was a towering figure of international theatre, with a boundless energy and a sharp intelligence to match. Guthrie was at heart an innovator and he was passionate about the thrust stage, which harked back to the times of Shakespeare and the Greek Classics, with the actors playing in the middle of the audience who surrounded them on three sides.

In his autobiography, *A Life in the Theatre*, Guthrie describes the 'tipping point' when he became convinced of the power and effectiveness of the thrust stage. His momentous discovery happened quite by chance. In 1937, at the invitation of the Danish state, Guthrie took a production of *Hamlet* with Laurence Olivier and Vivien Leigh to Elsinore to be performed spectacularly in the courtyard of Kronborg Castle. The day dawned and Lear's 'cataracts and hurricanoes' spouted, threatening to drown both performers and audience.

Guthrie decided to move the production into the hotel ballroom with the audience sitting in 870 basket chairs on three sides of the action. A rapid rehearsal—exits and entrances—and suddenly it was 'Who's there?'—'Nay, answer me: stand, and unfold yourself'. Needless to say, the spectators were swept up in it all, although, after two hours of improvisation the actors grew exhausted, and Guthrie described the finale as 'a shambles, but not quite in the way the author intended.' Nonetheless, the experience strengthened his conviction that for Shakespeare the proscenium stage was unsatisfactory.

He later wrote: 'I should never have suggested staging this rather impromptu occasion as we did if I had not already had a strong hunch that it would work. At its best moments that performance related the audience to a Shakespeare play in a different, and, I thought, more logical, satisfactory and effective way than can ever be achieved in a theatre of what is still regarded as orthodox design.' The great director had turned his back on the proscenium arch.

Inspired by his Danish experience, Guthrie tried out this stage design for a production of Sir David Lindsay's 16th-century morality play *The Thrie Estaits* at the second Edinburgh Festival in 1948. The venue Guthrie chose—the 19th-century General Assembly Hall of the Church of Scotland, seating 1,300 spectators on three sides—was adapted to a thrust stage, with steps leading up to it and a small upper stage above. The production was to prove a decisive turning point in his career.

Guthrie later wrote: '[the Assembly Hall] threw a new light for me on the whole meaning of theatrical performance. One of the most pleasing effects of the performance was the physical relation of the audience to the stage. The audience did not look at the actors against a background of pictorial and illusionary scenery. Seated around three sides of the stage, they focused upon the actors in the brightly lit acting area, but the background was of the dimly lit rows of people similarly focused on the actors. All the time, but unemphatically and by inference, each member of the audience was being ceaselessly reminded that he was not lost in an illusion but was in fact a member of a large audience, taking part, "assisting" as the French very properly express it, in a performance, a participant in a ritual.'[38]

---

[38] Tyrone Guthrie, *A Life in Theatre*, Hamish Hamilton, 1959.

Encouraged by the production's success, four years later Guthrie collaborated with the gifted designer Tanya Moiseiwitsch in designing a thrust stage for the inaugural festival in Stratford, Ontario. Tanya had designed sets for Guthrie at the Old Vic, the Theatre Royal, Drury Lane and the Festival Theatre in Stratford-upon-Avon, and she was developing a flexible model of stage design that fitted with his vision for the new theatre. Years later, I interviewed Tanya and asked her how she started working with Guthrie in Canada.[39] She recounted:

'Guthrie invited me to go to Canada with him and some other people and start a theatre. They didn't have anything at the time, it was just a hole in the ground. His idea was to reproduce the best qualities of the Assembly Hall, which was adapted for the production that he did, but which I never saw. Guthrie had a way of making things happen like they never happened before. Well, I fell for that!'

But Tanya had never seen a thrust stage and Guthrie talked her through the improvements he wanted to make to the stage they had built in Edinburgh:

'Guthrie showed me how the steps there were very steep because they had to build the stage over the moderator's throne, which they weren't allowed to stick things into. And, therefore, to get from the stage level down to the floor level and whiz off up the aisles—the steps were very high and the women in the Company complained a lot. So, he said: "Now we're starting from scratch, we can do what we like. Just see to it that the steps are much shallower, but they mustn't be so shallow that they aren't useful for people to be masked and unmasked." You see, if you want to get rid of someone, get them down a step or two, you don't want them to sit down or crouch, but they should leave the eyeline clear. And I got all of these instructions more or less on the back of an envelope—and off we went!'

Tanya always referred to their creation as an open stage, and it brought with it a different series of challenges for the actor, director and designer. Take scenery: 'You didn't have to have any scenery, as it were, and certainly not painted scenery. It was this kind of 'Wooden O' which had entrances and exits galore, you could change the shape of it just by moving your actors around. If you needed to seat your

---

[39] The following excerpts are taken from Colin George's interview with Tanya Moiseiwitsch in May 2001.

actors, somebody might bring on a stool or a chair, but nothing elaborate. Nothing that got in the way of a quick change from one scene to another.

'Scenes would run into each other—indeed sometimes overlap, the next one would start before the present one had finished—and that meant you got through the plays rather more quickly. Not perhaps "two hours' traffic", as Shakespeare told us, but it was a speedy arrangement, and they came and went at the double. Most of them were young enough to do that. The older ones of necessity went off or came on in a more dignified way.'

The rapid changes of action on the stage were enabled by something they had not been able to construct in the Assembly Hall: tunnels under the audience through which actors could enter and exit quickly. The technical term for these tunnels is vomitories, a Latin word harking back to the days of amphitheatres when gladiators and wild animals 'spewed forth' from these tunnels. Tanya (who disliked the word) described them simply as a means of 'getting rid of people very quickly. With luck nobody stumbled or fell or screamed: "I'm in the wrong tunnel!" That once happened, but it wasn't a performance it was a rehearsal, and an actor had to be rescued and pushed into the right tunnel!'

Surrounding the thrust stage was the gutter, an undefined space between the bottom of the stage and the first row of seats. Tanya described it as 'a kind of No-Man's-Land and no scenes were played there. With luck the actors had it their way, and not the audience putting their coats, or their box of chocolates, or their feet even, in the gutter. That was rather awkward. They had to be told not to do that.' I was later to discover that defining this area would be key to the audience's reaction to the actors on stage. Come too close and a psychological barrier is crossed and it becomes awkward and even embarrassing for the spectator.

Behind the triangular thrust stage, jutting out into the audience, was a fixed upper stage, enabling the playing of scenes on a higher level, or from one to the other (as in the famous balcony scene from *Romeo and Juliet*). Guthrie had built one at the Assembly Hall which was narrower because of the measurements of the hall. But, as Tanya explained: 'When we had nothing to stop us, we decided that the point of the upper stage should jut out—rather than running flat

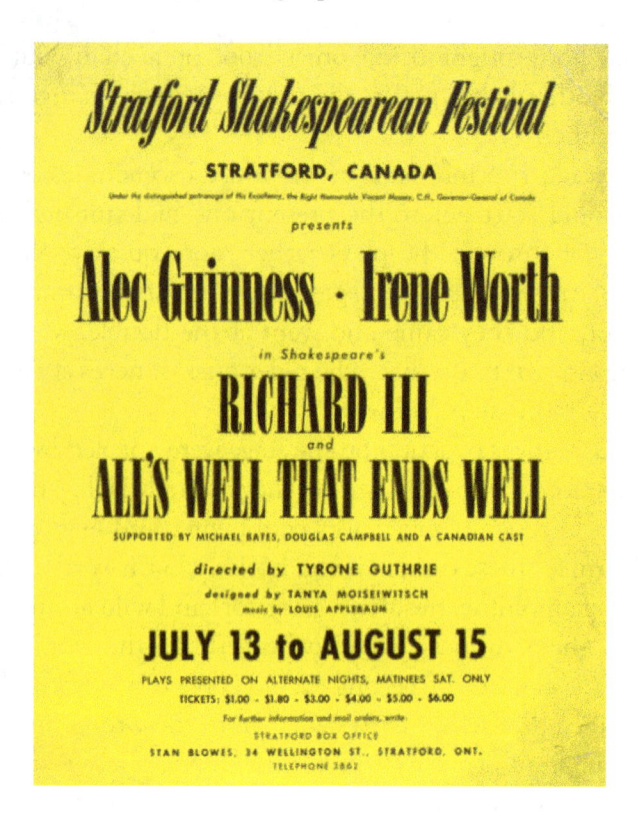

Poster for the inaugural Stratford Shakespeare Festival season, 1953

straight across, which might look like a little proscenium on its own. If you sat or stood on the jutting-out bit you could be seen by every seat in the house. Sometimes actors stood further back and were not visible to absolutely everybody—you might hear them shrieking or see a hat or something. But the main thing was the line of sight. And the architects played along wonderfully with that concept.'

But Tanya and her design team had little time to contemplate what they were building at Stratford. 'I didn't go to rehearsals because we were always having either fittings or just making things. All of our hands were very active and our poor little brains were being overworked. Two plays—*Richard III* and *All's Well That Ends Well*—going on back-to-back. Very different staging and modern dress—Guthrie's idea of "modern dress" was rather Edwardian, you realise.'

The first season in 1953 opened with Alec Guinness playing Richard III and was a huge success. The American theatre critic and playwright, Walter Kerr, saw the production and wrote a vivid description of the intimacy that the thrust stage created between the actors, the audience and each other: 'The auditorium [...] was brazenly original. One entered, in 1953, to look down steeply-banked aisles toward a three-sided arena [...] which fed its actors onto an open platform from passageways directly beneath the audience. [...] Seated, one looked at the fluid, swift, uncluttered performance with some astonishment.

'Though the actors were below us rather than above us, they seemed larger. Though they have no scenery to provide them with a literal environment, they seemed to be their own environment, to carry a world with them, and to be the fatter for it. Though our eyes never quite met, they were speaking to us, or at least to the man seated directly behind us. Though we were perfectly aware of a vast blur of faces across the platform from us, the presence of our fellow men was not so much distracting as enlivening.

'We were, all of us, players and playgoers alike, at last in the same building. The actors were doing most of the work, as usual, but we were engaged in a communal and reciprocal experience. [...] Being thoroughly present and not merely eavesdropping, we longed to participate, and savoured the sense of being permitted to'.[40]

Stratford's second season opened with James Mason playing the lead in perhaps Guthrie and Tanya's most celebrated collaboration, *Oedipus Rex* (which was later made into a film with Douglas Campbell in the title role). In 1957, after four seasons in 'The Tent', a new 2,300-seat Festival Theatre was built in its place, with a thrust stage designed by Tanya (and modified by her in 1962). Then, in 1963, Guthrie founded what became the Guthrie Theater in Minneapolis, Minnesota, a 1,400-seat auditorium which also had a thrust stage designed by Tanya, and he served as the theatre's Artistic Director until 1966.

When Guthrie came to the Sheffield Playhouse the following year, it was to be my first meeting with him. I had listened to him talking at the old Nottingham Playhouse years before and knew his style—a forthright commitment to the important role the theatre had to play

---

[40] Walter Kerr, 'The theater breaks out of Belasco's Box', *Horizon Magazine*, July 1959.

in society, and often delivered with a knife-edged, unexpected and irresistible sense of humour. His enthusiasm was infectious, linked as it was to a lifetime's experience.

His talk at the packed Playhouse that Sunday evening was entitled 'What's a Theatre for?' I remember one comment that caused a stir. Guthrie suggested that once the new theatre was open, we should raise the seat prices because, he declared, if prices are low the public assumes that what is on offer isn't very good. Seat prices at that time *were* ridiculously low—seven shillings and sixpence was the top price on a Saturday night.[41] There were loud objections from the audience and Guthrie said: 'I am going to take my coat off to answer that!' I suspect his enthusiasm was making him hot, but in a typically theatrical gesture he threw his coat over a chair and proceeded to challenge the questioner. 'How much are you prepared to spend on an evening out—dining at a restaurant with your wife?' Needless to say, it was considerably more than two seven and sixes.

Guthrie was also insistent that the director of a publicly supported theatre like the Playhouse should be artistically independent of the councillors and committee men who paid him. In his view, there was never a sillier idea than 'he who pays the piper calls the tune'. The tune should be called by the most musical person, and the people who pay the piper are rarely very musical. Guthrie did not pull his punches when it came to programming; he felt that a serious theatre should lean heavily towards the classics. As he described it, a great classic tragedy should be a purgative similar to five sets of tennis, a game of rugby or a cross-country run—you should be glad when it is over![42]

During drinks in the bar afterwards Guthrie asked me what kind of theatre we were planning to build. I explained that we felt the need to embrace the audience more enthusiastically than was possible with the traditional proscenium arch. I noted that our children's work in schools had never used the school stage but instead improvised with whatever large space was available. The resulting 'performance' with the audience sitting almost on three sides involved the children not just as passive spectators but as contributors to the event.

'You should see some of the open stage theatres in the States and

---

[41] This would be the equivalent of just £5.78 in 2021.
[42] *Morning Telegraph*, 16 October 1967.

Canada', Guthrie replied.[43] It was a comment that caught my interest as, by then, I was not only harbouring doubts about our plans for the forestage, but I was open to the concept of the thrust stage. To explain this, I should give some background.

---

[43] Like Tanya, Guthrie usually referred to the thrust stage as 'the open stage'.

CHAPTER SIX

Study is like the heaven's glorious sun.†

I had been interested in theatre design since my earliest days as an actor. When touring with the Oxford and Cambridge Players, we had improvised performances in all kinds of venues, from school and town halls to traditional proscenium arch theatres. Many of these productions were on open stages or extended forestages, which permitted a more intimate relationship with the audience. When I started working in repertory theatre, all of the auditoria were proscenium theatres. Over time, I grew frustrated with the limitations imposed by the 'picture box' frame and became interested in the potential of the open stage.

At that time, open stages—either thrust stages with the audience on three sides, or in-the-round stages, with the audience on four sides—were considered a radical departure from traditional theatre. What I discovered was that, in reality, the opposite was true, and the proscenium arch was itself the aberration. The article I quoted in the previous chapter by the American theatre critic and playwright, Walter Kerr, explains how theatre design lost its way when the proscenium took over from the circular performing area of Ancient Greek theatre.[44]

'The Romans were the first to dilute the design. Seduced by the back wall and decorating it extravagantly, they pushed it forward to cut off half of the magic acting circle. The drama of the Medieval theatre

---

† William Shakespeare, *Love's Labour's Lost*, Act I, Scene 1.
[44] The article's title, 'The theater breaks out of Belasco's Box', refers to David Belasco, one of New York's most successful theatre impresarios and directors. Belasco used the proscenium arch to frame his completely naturalistic setting. To achieve this level of reality, he once went to a doss house and paid to have one of the rooms brought lock, stock and barrel to the theatre and installed on the stage, removing the wall facing the audience so the action could be seen. It would be difficult to find a greater contrast to the open stage.

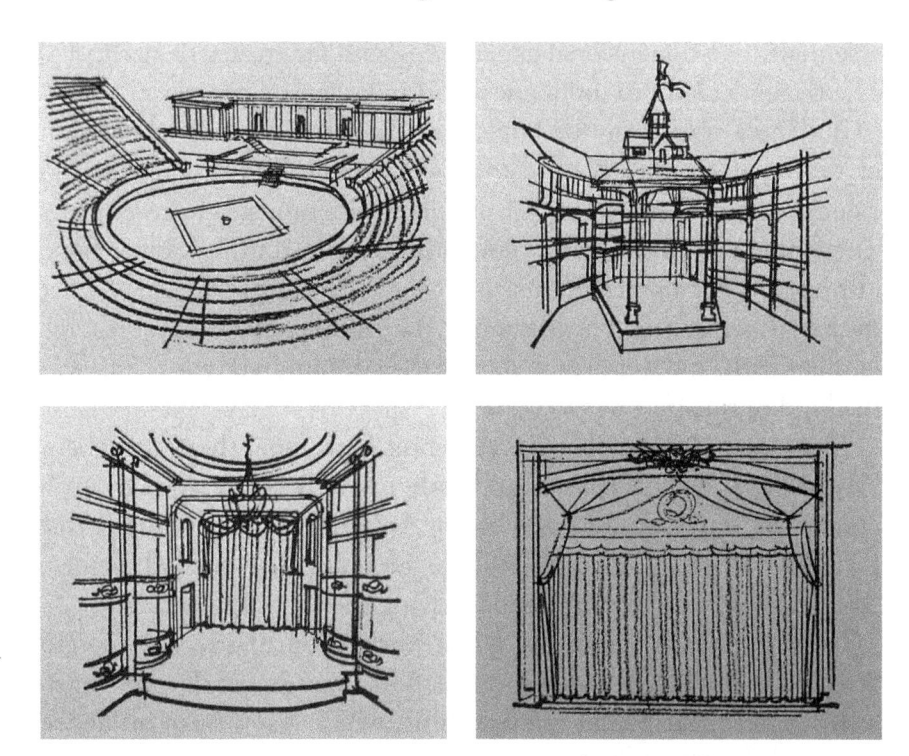

Theatre Designs: Ancient Greek (top left), Shakespearean (top right), Restoration (bottom left) and Modern 'Picture Box' (bottom right)

took place in the town square on travelling carts, and Shakespeare's Globe was a mixture of the pageant wagon and the inn yard.'

During the Renaissance, the Roman Façade re-emerged, and as Kerr puts it: 'Given fresh interest by the discovery of perspective painting, it made its first conquest in Italy, and found its way to post-Shakespearean England by courtesy of the court masque, the love of tableau, and Inigo Jones's passion for paint. Court circles became interested in pictures. If actors do not need a frame, pictures do—and our proscenium arch was born [...] It is an intelligible form designed to produce one kind of experience—that of viewing an isolated world in a spirit of detachment.'

Kerr's final comment is irrefutable: 'By the beginning of the twentieth century we had perfected the box image. At the same time, a succession of scientifically devised box images—the motion picture and later television—came along to duplicate the pictorial and essentially two-dimensional experiences with far greater flexibility [...] The theater's claim to uniqueness had in large part been lost.'

But there was cause for hope. Kerr noted that a new generation of off-Broadway theatre directors, who could have worked in old cinemas closed down by the advent of television, instead chose spaces where they could present productions in the round. 'Somewhere, just beyond our immediate reach, hovers a tantalizing image of what theater *is*—what it is that is *not* like the experience we have become familiar with, and wearied of, during the last hundred years.' This was the kind of theatre I was looking for.

In January 1960, while I was Assistant Director at the Nottingham Playhouse, I made a trip around Italy to study theatre design on a grant from the International Theatre Association. Over two months, I visited theatres in Rome, Naples, Florence, Milan, and Venice, sketching their auditoriums and studying their productions.

I remember being impressed by the work of Italian director, Giorgio Strehler, at the Piccolo Teatro in Milan. He was one of the great postwar directors and Brecht was his thing, which had a huge influence on me. Even though it was a proscenium theatre, he would break out of the picture box—putting a chair on the side of the stage to create a separate area—and he had a remarkable ability to move people about the stage and give meaning to the production.

Looking through my notebook, I am struck by what I wrote about another theatre I visited in Milan, the Teatro Sant'Erasmo, designed by the Italian modernist, Carlo de Carli. Situated under a block of

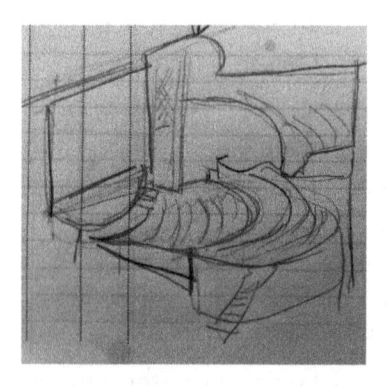

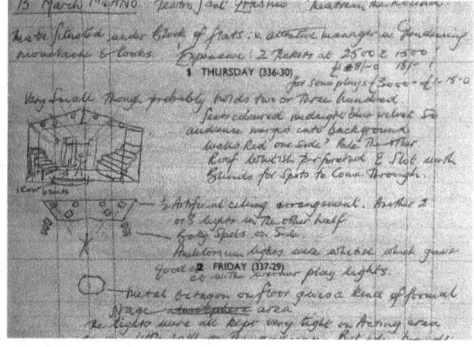

Sketches & notes of theatres I visited during my trip to Italy, 1960

flats on Via dei Giardini, the theatre seated up to 300 people in two banks facing each other around a metal octagon stage area. The lighting was kept very tight on the acting area so there was very little spill on the audience, who tended to blend into the background of blue velvet seats.

But there were two things that didn't work about the space. First, owing to the theatre's traverse seating arrangement—with two banks of the audience facing each other and the actors down below them—the actors did not really play the show in the round. Instead, they played against one wall and acted to two sides, which greatly limited the staging possibilities. And second, having the actors enter and exit through the auditorium broke the audience/actor relationship: I noted that the actors needed 'definitively separate' entrances/exits. Without realising it, I was referring to vomitories, a key feature of Guthrie thrust stage theatres.[45]

My search for a new kind of acting space continued during three seasons as Artistic Director of the Ludlow Festival in 1964-66, which I discussed in Chapter 1. Ludlow had an open stage, set in the middle of a spectacular courtyard facing the imposing walls of the castle, with the focus of action on the 'Sacred Circle' near the front of the stage.

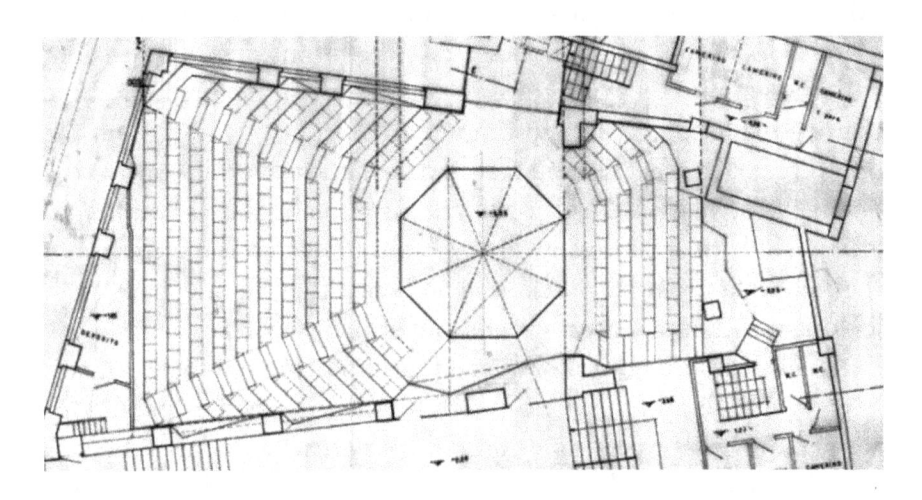

Architectural design of the Teatro Sant'Erasmo, Milan

---

[45] Sadly, the Teatro Sant' Erasmo was demolished in 1969.

But it was not a pure thrust stage, as the audience did not surround it in a full arc and were mostly to the front, looking up at the actors (see designs on next page). Directing on the open stage brought us closer to the audience and gave me huge freedom to move actors around and make quick scene changes. I had just finished my last season at Ludlow when the decision was taken to build a new theatre in Sheffield, and I would bring the spirit of Ludlow with me into our first discussions on the stage design.

During this period, I was also influenced by English theatres I visited that were trying to break out of the proscenium. These included Peter Cheeseman's in-the-round Victoria Theatre in Stoke-on-Trent, where I saw *The Jolly Potters*, the inspiration for *Stirrings*, and Sir Bernard Miles's Mermaid Theatre in London. But my only experience of working on an adaptable stage was at the new Nottingham Playhouse where I directed *The Merchant of Venice* and *Oedipus* in 1964. The theatre had a large forestage that could be extended into the auditorium, effectively turning the proscenium into the back wall. Indeed, Guthrie had opened the theatre in 1963 with a production of *Coriolanus* that was played on the forestage.

But the design of the auditorium was problematic, as the Artistic Director, John Neville—who had worked on the thrust stage at the Edinburgh Assembly Hall—explained in an interview with TABS in March 1965: 'To be quite honest [the stage] is an extension. It is not true adaptability... I don't think it was meant to be anything more than an extension of the proscenium arch. In fact, I think I am the only director that has worked here and used the full extension.' At the Sheffield Playhouse we had tried building a small forestage but found it impossible to advance any distance into the auditorium because of the sightlines from the circle; the audience there would have been looking down on the actor's heads, not at their faces.

Neville was also critical of the auditorium being split between two levels, the stalls and the circle, which he felt were too far apart. 'This is something that worries me constantly as an actor and as a director here. I have to remember as an actor that my line of sight, of playing, has to be pitched somewhere between these two levels, and they are very wide apart. You feel as an actor that you're playing in a theatre that has stalls and a gallery with no circle, and one has to learn to play

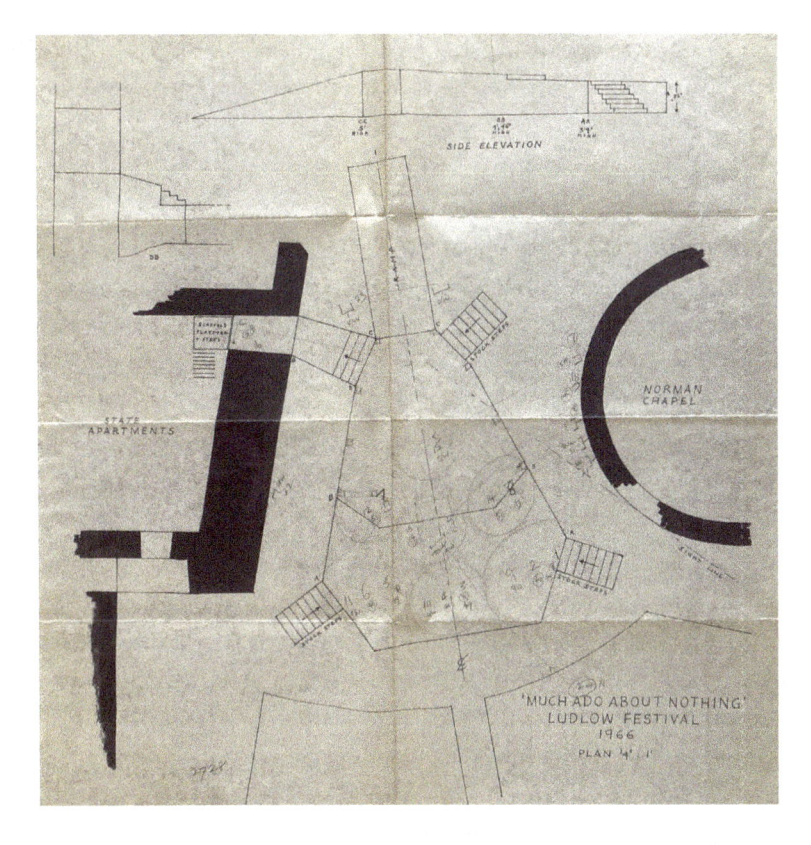

Top: Design of thrust stage at the Ludlow Festival, 1966; Bottom: Sketch of the stage, with steps up and scenery, 1966

to this.' Moreover, the drum shape of the auditorium caused sightline problems for anyone sitting on the sides, especially for proscenium productions.

But Neville's most striking criticism was reserved for the backstage facilities. There was an acute lack of storage space, which made it hard to run in repertoire where costumes and scenery are needed for up to six productions at one time. For budgetary reasons, the fly tower did not go back far enough, so you could not fly anything in the upstage area, and they often struggled to get the sky cloth far enough upstage. In addition, the workshops were not large enough, there was far too little office space for the administration, the rehearsal room in no way resembled the size of the stage and the dressing-rooms had no windows!

On this final point Neville did not hold back his exasperation: 'We are civilised human beings just like everyone, even though we are actors. You know, a lot of belly-aching went on in the old theatre about us taking our clothes off in dungeons and in cells, which were next to the boiler room, and you come into a brand new theatre and find that the dressing-rooms haven't got windows. It's absolutely stupid. I mean, one floor of dressing-rooms is above ground and it is simply an architect's whim that there are no windows on that particular wall'.

These were sobering lessons for us as we designed our new theatre and we would ensure that the backstage facilities were as much a focus of the design brief as the auditoria and the foyers.

But there was another English theatre that caught my imagination in this period: the Chichester Festival Theatre, which opened in July 1962, shortly before I came to Sheffield. Chichester is a thrust stage theatre, with the audience surrounding the stage on three sides. In its design and concept, the theatre has many similarities to what became the Crucible Theatre in Sheffield, and after the Crucible was built it was assumed (and often said) that we simply copied Chichester's stage. The truth is quite different.

What is certain is that both Chichester and the Crucible had difficult openings. It was unfortunate for Chichester's first Artistic Director, Sir Laurence Olivier, that his first two productions were not tried-and-tested masterpieces. (I was accused of making the same mistake in 1971.) John Fletcher's *The Chances* opened the season, its first performance for three hundred years. The next play was not such a rarity—John Ford's *The Broken Heart*—but it was followed by *Uncle Vanya*, which was the sort of play that cried out for a proscenium theatre. Disaster threatened.

The leading theatre critic of the era, Kenneth Tynan, was scathing about the choice of opening plays, which infuriated Olivier as it was Tynan who had recommended *The Chances* to him in the first place. But Tynan also took issue with the thrust stage auditorium itself.[46] Reading his opinions many years later, with the benefit of having been involved in the design of a thrust stage theatre and of having worked on it as both director and actor, I would challenge him on several points.

For example, he wrote: 'Nothing so quickly dispels one's sense of reality as a daubed and bedizened actor standing four feet from one's face and declaiming right over one's head.' But this was not true. The actors on open stages rarely indulged in 'daubing on make-up', as they were too near the audience. When Tynan was writing, heavy make-up was going out of use, anyway. The harsh, unrelenting footlights—which demanded the strong black lines I used to put under my eyes when I began as an actor in the 1950s— were being replaced by follow spots and distant, softer focused front of house lighting. Added to which, in a properly-designed, thrust stage auditorium, the very steep rake of the seating means that the audience look down on the actor, not up at him. (Unfortunately, this was not the case at Chichester.)

Tynan also wrote: 'The picture frame stage was invented in the seventeenth century to give all the spectators the same sightlines and the same viewpoint.' Not so. The proscenium was built to give the Lord and Lady in the centre box at the back of the auditorium the best view, together with their friends in the centre stalls. Sightlines got progressively worse for those less fortunate friends sitting in the side seats, more so for the wretched plebeians watching the action in 'the gods'. When opera became popular, the proscenium stage also acquired an orchestra pit to accommodate a conductor with his

---

[46] 'Open letter to an open stager', *The Observer*, 15 July 1962.

musicians, which pushed the action and performer even further away from the spectator.

I also take issue with another point Tynan made: 'In the last 50 years we have been urged to revive the projecting stage, ostensibly for artistic reasons but actually because it cuts the scenic costs to a minimum.' This was also untrue. It was not the money men who were trying to revitalise the actor-audience relationship. It was the artists of the theatre—the adventurous writers, directors, designers, actors, and stage managers who yearned for a different way of connecting with the audience.

As it turned out, the naysayers were proved wrong and Olivier's production of *Uncle Vanya* was a triumph. It was revived for the second season and seats were almost impossible to come by. Fortunately, I knew a member of the Chichester Company, Robert Lang, with whom I had worked at the old Nottingham Playhouse, and he got me a ticket. The cast was superb—Michael Redgrave as Vanya and Olivier as Astrov, Fay Compton as Vanya's mother and Joan Plowright as Sonya.

The use of the thrust stage during one moment of that production stood out for me. The Second Act concluded with Redgrave as Vanya trying to shoot the Professor (played by Max Adrian). The professor ran on and across the stage as Redgrave shouted at him off-stage. The professor doubled back as Vanya entered. Terrified, he turned and escaped down a tunnel as Vanya fired at him. Left alone onstage, Redgrave flung his revolver down with a tortured 'Missed!' The stage lights quickly faded to black out—End of Act Two. The whole episode took hardly any time at all, but the audience was transfixed and burst into wholehearted applause.

Aside from the initially negative reaction from the critics, the other thing Chichester had in common with the Crucible was the source of inspiration for its thrust stage: Tyrone Guthrie. The man he inspired in Chichester was a local optician, councillor and theatre impresario, Leslie Evershed-Martin. He had founded the Chichester Players in 1933, and his indefatigable devotion to create a theatre festival in Chichester, build a thrust stage to house it, and raise the money to do it, are remarkable.

His conversion to the concept of the thrust stage came about when he was watching TV one Sunday evening in 1959. Guthrie was being interviewed and passionately described the potential of the thrust stage of which he had been the Director in Stratford, Ontario. Evershed-Martin thought the comparatively small town of Stratford, Ontario was similar to Chichester in England. Why not have a similar festival stage and, as in Canada, set it in a park? Forty-three acres of parkland had just been acquired by Chichester Council and they were near the town centre. A wonderful site for the new theatre.

But here the similarities with the Crucible end, because Chichester and the Crucible had very different budgets and—as a result of this— very different designs. Chichester's architects—Philip Powell (a local man, his father was Canon of the Cathedral) and Hidalgo Moya—had previously designed the Skylon, symbol of the 1951 Festival of Britain, but they had no experience in constructing theatres and had mainly worked on hospitals. They got their brief from Evershed-Martin himself—an amphitheatre seating at least 1,400 on three sides of a thrust stage, and building costs kept to a minimum. In comparison, when we built the Crucible we spent over two years developing the design of the theatre, involving world experts on the thrust stage.

But the key difference between the two theatres was their budgets. Chichester had an initial budget of £70,000 which eventually rose to £105,000. In comparison the Crucible's starting budget was £500,000-600,000 and it eventually rose to £884,000.[47] Even adjusting for inflation in the decade separating their construction, the budget for the Crucible was six times higher than Chichester's.[48] By the 21st century, building costs had escalated even further: the refurbishment of the Chichester Festival Theatre in 2012-14 cost £22 million, more than ten times the inflation-adjusted cost of the original theatre!

Chichester's tight budget had a huge impact on the kind of thrust stage auditorium that could be built. As Guthrie described it in his very last interview, Chichester 'was put up on half a shoestring, and this isn't always conducive to the best results'.[49] Indeed, the whole cost of the theatre was less than the heating and cooling system at either of the Guthrie theatres in North America!

---

[47] In 2021 these budgets would be the equivalent of £1.9 million and £11.1 million, respectively.
[48] In terms of cost per seat in the auditorium, the Chichester Festival Theatre is probably the cheapest theatre built in post-war Britain.
[49] Keith Slade's interview with Guthrie on Radio Brighton, May 1971.

One consequence of the lack of funds was the design of the two vomitories through which actors enter the thrust stage. These tunnels are important for keeping the actor's imaginary world separate from the spectators; but at Chichester the actors must use the same entrances as the audience. This is because the first architect approached to build the theatre, Harry Sherwood, concluded that separate vomitories would be impossible to build as the site was waterlogged and at the bottom of a steep slope. He withdrew from the project and the final architects went their own way with the stage and auditorium design.

The design of the vomitories sparked a heated stand-off with Sir Laurence when he learnt that actors and audiences were to share the same entrances and exits. But he had little choice other than to accept the theatre he was given. Of the thrust stage theatres Guthrie inspired, only Stratford, Ontario and the Crucible have separate vomitories for the actors.

Chichester Festival Theatre auditorium in 1962

The design of Chichester's thrust stage auditorium was also less than ideal. In July 1971, a few months before the Crucible opened, David Brayshaw and I visited Chichester to get a fresh view of the auditorium. We immediately noted that the enormous roof was not over the centre of the stage, but half-way back over the audience. As David sat in the auditorium, he said: 'I can't make out where I am in relation to the circle.' He was not referring to the Dress Circle or Upper Circle, but the nine-foot 'Magic Circle' in the centre of the auditorium where the main stage action takes place. We also noted that the arrangement of the seating meant that 80% of the audience was still to the front: not much of an improvement on the proscenium arch.

However, criticism of Chichester's design should not take away from the enormous success that the Festival has enjoyed since the theatre's opening in 1962. The theatre sits in superb surroundings and was enhanced by the addition of a studio theatre, the Minerva, in 1989. A major re-build in 2012-14 by architects Haworth Tompkins also addressed many of the shortcomings of the original design, notably regarding the seating, sightlines, back- and under-stage areas, and the adaptability of the stage.[50]

But as the Chichester Festival Theatre was originally built in 1962, it fell far short of what we wanted to achieve in Sheffield. And we had the backing of a large industrial city that was prepared to put up the money to realise our dream on a more complete scale.

---

[50] Tedd's note: I am grateful to Ben Geering and Will McGovern for giving me a tour of the Chichester Festival Theatre in April 2021 and for showing me the changes that were made during the 2012-14 refurbishment. These included the addition of a large stage dock, a fully demountable stage sitting over an expanded under stage area, adjustments to the vomitories and seating aisles, increasing the rake of the upper level, and expansion of backstage and dressing room facilities.

CHAPTER SEVEN

People cannot discover new lands until they have the courage to lose sight of the shore.[†]

Myself (sporting a goatee), Wilfred Harrison and Guthrie during his visit to Sheffield, October 1967

The day after Guthrie gave his Sheffield talk, he met with the Chairman of the Trust, the Playhouse Board, and Dr Gerard Young of the Building

---

[†] André Gide, '*The Counterfeiters*'.

Committee. Tyrone's advice was, as always, direct and uncompromising. Dr Young's notes from the meeting summarise it succinctly:

a) Design the theatre for your own local Company; not for visiting players like the National Theatre.
b) 900 seats minimum, preferably 1,200. The more seats available, the higher your average takings, because more seats are sold for successes.
c) An open stage is essential. The proscenium is 'old hat' and too reminiscent of the TV screen. Also, you can fit more seats round an open stage and there are many dramatic advantages.
d) Choose a dramatic site away from the city where you can create a 'pleasure dome' with its own restaurants and other services. Nottingham Playhouse is 'too safe', too much like every other town theatre. Sheffield has the opportunity to do something much more interesting and enduring. Make the Arts Council find the extra quarter or half million pounds required. This should be a national breakthrough, not only Sheffield's.
e) Visits by more than one of your team to other modern theatres are essential before you re-write your brief to the architects. Britain and Europe have nothing relevant to see. You must visit open stage theatres at Stratford, Ontario (2,300 seats), Minneapolis (1,400+ seats), and the Vivian Beaumont Theatre, New York (1,100 seats).

His advice given, Guthrie departed. Eight days later, the Trustees held a special meeting attended not only by the Playhouse administration, but also senior members of Sheffield City Council: Aldermen Hebblethwaite, Ironmonger and Lewis. The City of Sheffield was going to be involved in whatever decisions were made!

The Trustees agreed to consider Guthrie's recommendation of an open stage and a site away from the city centre for the new theatre. To determine whether a thrust stage was preferable to a proscenium, the Trust agreed to send me and David Brayshaw to visit open stage theatres in North America. We were tasked with reporting back to the Trustees at their next meeting on 7th December, to which Sir Tyrone Guthrie and the architects would be invited. In the meantime, Dr

Young, Mr Johnson, and the Hon. Secretary would explore potential out-of-town sites with the City Engineer and Surveyor and report back.

Planning for our trip began immediately, and Guthrie was immensely helpful in arranging the itinerary and connecting us to the right people. They included his trusted 'path smoother' in New York, theatrical agent Charlie Baker, and the key people involved in running the theatres in Stratford, Ontario, and Minneapolis. Guthrie confirmed that he would attend our post-trip meeting with the Trustees on 7th December, adding with characteristic frankness: 'Unless, after you've all spent a fortune going to the USA and back, and HATED what you see, you decide you'd rather put me off.' He needn't have worried.

On 10th November 1967, David and I set off for North America, unsure of what we would find. We were searching for a new kind of stage that could restore the relationship between the actors and the audience and we needed hard evidence to take back to the Board. But, in truth, neither of us knew much about the thrust stage, nor did we have any idea of the conversion to its cause we would undergo.

We arrived in Minneapolis on 11th November 1967 and visited the Guthrie Theater that very evening. The theatre stood in the outskirts of a small park on rising ground, flanked on one side by the Walker Arts Center, and on the other by a block of modern flats. Our first impressions of the theatre from the outside were disappointing. The

Exterior of the Guthrie Theater at night, late 1960s

basic structure with large windows revealing staircases, encased in a white concrete jigsaw framework reminiscent of 1930s architecture, was to me unsuccessful. The building looked cramped—a large square art gallery dominated it on the right and made the entrance look poky and unimportant. After dark, with all the lights on and theatregoers circulating, the building looked more attractive, the 'pierced outer shell' breaking up into a series of smaller pictures.

The main entrance lobby was also poorly realised. Three pairs of solid swing doors were shut during the day, forcing the would-be visitor to try all of them to find which one to enter by. Once inside, there was no sense of space in the entrance foyer—with bookstall, postcard counter, and box office cubicles cutting circulation to a minimum. The practice of not letting theatregoers into the auditorium until after 7.30pm compounded the impression that we were being 'kept out'. David put these failures down not to the architects, but to the theatre management.

The interior decoration was, as at the Nottingham Playhouse, all white, grey, and black. Whilst this preserved the visual kick of the auditorium and the play itself, we both felt this was too high a price to pay for this effect. Colour and a sense of emotional entanglement should inform the foyer and all the circulation areas rather than a drab uniform monochrome.

Once inside the auditorium, it was a different story. I collected our tickets from the box office and led the way into the auditorium down a narrow tunnel. And suddenly there it was, through a doorway at the end: the stage. Gleaming polished wood, a narrow promontory jutting out into space, inviting the actor to stand on it and 'ascend the brightest heaven of invention.' I cannot describe my feelings without waxing lyrical. It was the 'tipping point' for me—a phrase that in hindsight defines the moment a revolution suddenly catches fire, or a battle is won or lost.

It was quite the most exciting modern interior I had ever seen. Only an opera house such as La Fenice in Venice could equal the effect. This may be because the modern proscenium theatre, shorn of its Victorian side boxes, presents a drab aspect as the eye approaches the stage. At the Guthrie Theater, the eye was continually excited. The roof was alive with suspended irregular shapes, light grey acoustic

The Guthrie Theater auditorium as it looked in 1967

panels; some masked the lights, others completed the decoration. The seats were in different 'harlequin' colours—reds, yellows, greens, and blues. Contrasting the black and grey walls and ceilings of the auditorium, the impact was quite intoxicating. If the audience was thin, there were no accusing areas of red plush to greet one. The auditorium looked just as attractive half-full as full.

One notable characteristic of the auditorium was the interplay between the stage and the seating. Although the seating embraced the stage in a semi-circular sweep, the stage jutted asymmetrically to the audience's right, where a bank of seats rose steeply from the ground level to the back wall for one third of the semi-circle (they called this 'the ski slope'). This gave the impression of pitching the audience forward onto the stage in a marvellous manner and broke up the 'bisected' view you get on entering a conventional theatre at either the stalls or circle level. Whichever door you entered the Guthrie auditorium through, you felt you could see the *whole* theatre at first sight.

It is worth noting that subsequently we heard much criticism about the harlequin seats and the asymmetrical auditorium. Many felt that these elements were exciting at first but, after working in the theatre for some time, they found the mixed colour feverish and the broken balcony distracting. The general view was that it was better to opt either for an arena-type theatre or the traditional circle than trying to mix the two.

To announce the performance, instead of barbells there was a flourish of live trumpets and drums in the foyer. Not having heard this before, for me that moment was the most thrilling of the whole evening. The source of this golden sound was only diminished a little by turning round to see the musicians in modern evening dress rather than Elizabethan tabards.

That evening we saw *The Thieves' Carnival* by Jean Anouilh. Like the more familiar *Ring Round the Moon*, Christopher Fry's adaptation of Anouilh's *Invitation to the Castle*, the play was light romantic entertainment for all its disillusioned undertones. Oliver Messel's enchanting set contributed to an atmosphere of elegant make-believe, but something was not right. It was as if the relationship between the audience and actors was too significant for the lightweight material presented. The scenery, music, and costume were four-square, forthright and unsubtle. The eye was never enraptured by the stage picture—the lighting was never evocative. Make-up varied from the stylised to the naturalistic and I was reminded of how the spectator is very aware of make-up on a thrust stage.

David, who described himself as a 'man-in-the-street member of the audience', noted his reaction to seeing actors perform on a thrust stage for the first time: 'I very rarely felt frustrated at not being able to see actor's faces. I very soon learned to watch the faces of other actors who were being spoken to as one would in normal life, and I could hear the actor perfectly. By reason of the artificiality inherent in it (*Thieves' Carnival* is not a naturalistic play taking place in "natural" surroundings) I did not have to stretch myself to accept it.'

One notable difference with the thrust stage was how it affected laughter from the audience. Laughter in a proscenium theatre is instantaneous and somehow builds throughout the performance. In contrast, laughter rarely enveloped the house in this production. This might be because in a proscenium theatre every member of the audience gets the same visual clue for the laugh at the same time, whereas on a thrust stage they might be looking at the back of the actor delivering the punchline. We would later discover how to play comedy and farce on a thrust stage which requires careful blocking and timing for the delivery of key lines.

The next day, we went to see a production of Edward Albee's *Tiny Alice* at the student theatre of the University of Minneapolis. It would have been difficult to find a bigger contrast to the Guthrie auditorium. Scott Hall was a typical college hall with a heavily defined square proscenium. There was a platform stage at one end, stalls, and a balcony on the other. One was aware of the easy focus of attention the proscenium provides. Although the actors were students, the standard of performance and presentation were excellent. Three settings—garden, library, and sitting room—immediately provided a change of atmosphere.

By the end of the performance, however, the limitations of the proscenium were becoming irritating. Actors constantly moved to present profile or full face to the spectator and some groupings were contrived. This created a very definite sense of detachment in the auditorium rather than involvement in what was happening on stage. One sat back, mentally commenting on the technical facility and was quite unaware of the other spectators. David was also disappointed with the theatrical experience, noting that although the performances were technically efficient, he did not feel the personalities of the actors. He wondered if the sense of detachment he felt came from the type of stage and whether the production would have been more exciting on a thrust stage.

We returned that evening to the Guthrie Theater to see Friedrich Dürrenmatt's *The Visit*. Being a much heavier piece, it flourished on the open stage. I had seen a superb production of this play in Milan—entitled *La Visita della Vecchia Signora*—directed by Giorgio Strehler. The old lady of the title—a millionairess—returns from abroad to her impoverished hometown. She offers a million dollars to the town and its citizens. Then she demands in return the death of the man who seduced her as a young girl. In this production, the news of the money was greeted with jubilation, the citizens cavorting over the stage to the sound of the town brass band in jubilation. Then they froze in horror on learning they had to kill one of their own to earn the money. There was a deathly silence on stage and the crowd melted away through the upstage entrances and under the audience through the tunnels. This was electrifying and showed how the stage could be used.

David was seeing the play for the first time and thought the crowd scenes, interspersed with intimate dialogue, worked well on the thrust stage. In one scene, a brass band stood in the 'gutter' which surrounds the stage while the main action played out above them. This meant that those in the front rows had to watch the action over the band's shoulders, just as they would if they were standing in a crowd. There was also a lively scene with dignitaries speaking into microphones and members of the company scattered round the audience shouting and applauding, which reminded David of the Music Hall scene in *Stirrings*.

But when we discussed this afterwards, we agreed that bringing the actors into the audience broke the convention more than the *Stirrings* scene—one sensed the audience was embarrassed at being involved and did not know whether to join in or not. David also noted that the scene changes were distracting, especially when scenery was visibly flown in and out in a manner that 'looked rather Heath Robinson-ish'.[51] We needed to carefully consider how to use scenery on the thrust stage.

That night after the production, as midnight drew near, as part of an invited audience we saw a workshop production of Luigi Pirandello's *The Man with a Flower in his Mouth*. This had been put together by the actors and their friends, just for their own interest. A brilliantly written essay in the macabre, this duologue showed that 'chamber theatre' could be performed effectively on this stage. Even though the two actors played to a central segment of the audience, there was a sense of the theatre being 'in the round'. A couple of chairs and a table, and we were soon believing we were all sitting in a draughty waiting room.

In the theatre club afterwards we met several actors, including Robin Gammell, a former Sheffield Playhouse player, Douglas Campbell, the Guthrie Theater's senior actor and director of several plays, and his wife and fellow actor, Ann Casson (daughter of Sybil

---

[51] A Heath Robinson contraption is any invention or machine that is simultaneously ingenious, overly complicated, and makeshift.

Thorndike). Four years later, all three would play leading roles in the opening productions of our new theatre. They told us they enjoyed playing on a thrust stage because whatever your position, you were always acting to someone. You literally could not turn your back on the audience. Robin Gammell described the sense of release he experienced acting on the thrust stage: 'As soon as you realise you can't direct your performance to any one bank of spectators and that someone is bound to see your back, you relax and play for the scene.'

We spent the next morning being taken around the Guthrie Theater, visiting all the departments. We met with the Managing Director, Peter Zeisler, and lunched with him and the Chairman of the Board, Philip Von Blon. We had a wide-ranging discussion which helped focus our thoughts on a number of key decisions relating to the design of the auditorium and stage. In his report to the Trustees, David condensed the conclusions of our discussions into these key points:

a) You can't (without unlimited money) build a 'flexible theatre'. You must decide on either a thrust or a proscenium stage and stick to it.
b) It is a false economy to cut back on the space backstage. They did this owing to budgetary constraints and now they can't store scenery by flying it and have very cramped storage space.
c) They have no facility for flying scenery onto the stage. This is a mistake.
d) One doesn't use 'scenery' on a thrust stage. The proscenium stage meaning of the word is to 'dress the stage'. On a thrust stage one uses costumes and props to dress the scene.
e) Both had criticisms of the theatre as it now is (but who is ever satisfied with any theatre?), but both were convinced that the thrust stage is the right one.
f) Both felt that the two Guthrie-inspired theatres in North America were too big (the Guthrie seated 1,400 and Stratford, Ontario seated almost 2,300). They suggested a theatre of 950-1,000 would be better.[52] (The previous night Douglas Campbell had suggested an auditorium bigger than the Guthrie.)

---

[52] This is exactly the size of audience they settled on for the Crucible.

g) They agreed with criticism of the asymmetrical stage and recommended it should be built symmetrical and then adapted if need be.

We were to continually debate these issues over the rest of our trip, but some of them were undeniable and would become part of the concept for our new theatre.

The following day we finally got to see two productions directed by Guthrie himself. We started with a children's matinee of *Harpers Ferry* by Barrie Stavis, the story of John Brown's body and how his spirit went marching on, told in a simple, pedestrian text. The stage was used as it should be by the Master himself. A simple scenic statement: a flight of stairs up the back wall to a loft door; in the centre a table, chairs, and benches: we were in a farmhouse. In the second act, a skeleton building frame dressed with barrels, a cart, and farm implements suggested a front porch. Later the veranda swung

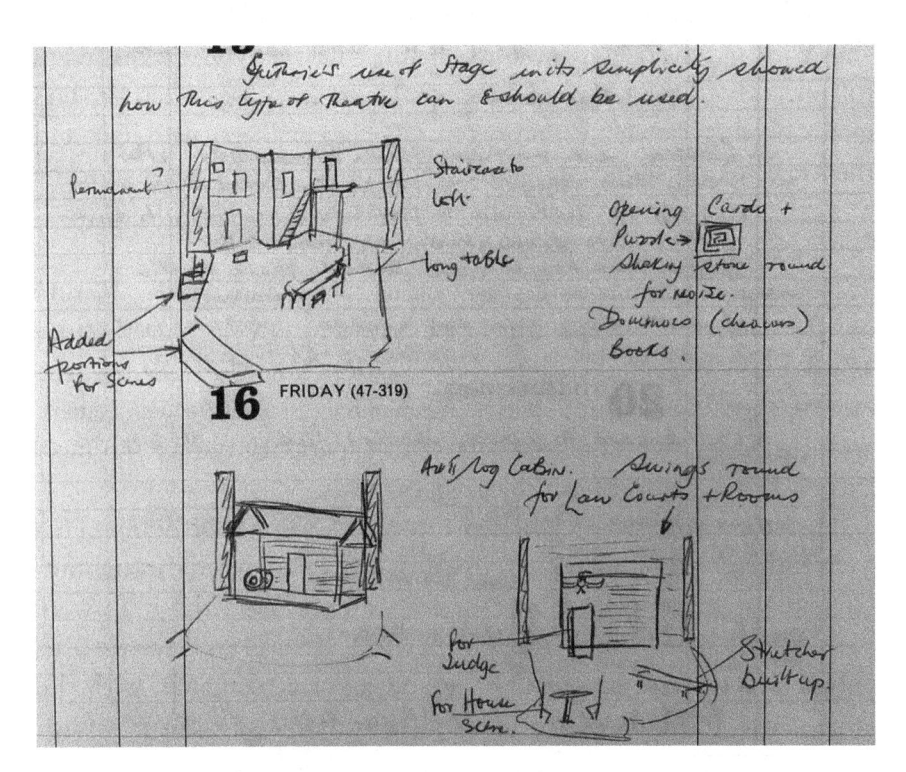

My notes and sketches from the performance of Harpers Ferry

round to become a courthouse. The mise-en-scène was convincing and continually interesting.

David was also seeing his first Guthrie-directed production and he wrote later that 'the full implication of this stage hits you at once. *Carnival* and *Visit* were puny by comparison, not only because of the type of play but by reason of the way the stage was handled'. Scenes were played on all parts of the stage, but also at the front of the stage, in the gutter, or looking down into one of the vomitories. David noted the easy way in which the actors—who were accustomed to working on the thrust stage—never faced in one direction for more than a short time. There were many occasions when the principal character was screened from him by others, but he could always hear the actor and found satisfaction from the reaction of the other characters—even their backs.

There were several 'Guthrie moments'. My favourite came as a dozen black slaves were relaxing in Brown's house; someone rushed in to say the Sheriff was coming. The slaves ran desperately up the stairs to the loft and were out of sight by the time the Sheriff and his men entered. The space and the height of the area behind the open stage were used to full effect. For David, the most memorable moment was when Brown's men looked off down a vomitory towards Harpers Ferry with light and the sound of gunshots coming from the tunnel. 'The change of scene was achieved perfectly—"naturally" is the only word I can find; I was never conscious of it as I was irritated by *The Visit*.'

However, the climax of our visit was to come: Guthrie's production of *The House of Atreus*, which we saw on our last evening in Minneapolis. Adapted by John Lewin from Aeschylus' *Oresteia*, the evening combined three plays: *Agamemnon*, *The Libation Bearers*, and *The Furies*. We were both about to experience one of the most extraordinary nights of our theatregoing lives.

The story unfolded—with two intervals—over three hours. This was Guthrie's threatened purgative, but I was captivated throughout. Clytemnestra was played by Douglas Campbell (all the roles were played by men as in the Athenian theatre). He was an actor with an extremely powerful stage presence and a voice to match, with the appearance and bulk of a wonderful Falstaff.[53] The Chorus was on

---

[53] Douglas Campbell gave an extraordinary performance as the lead in the film version of Guthrie's *Oedipus* in 1957 and was a seasoned player in Guthrie's style of Greek Classics.

Orestes kneels before Athena and Apollo, The House of Atreus

stage having described Agamemnon's approach, when Clytemnestra entered in a magnificent costume and mask from the palace at the back, with a looping feminine walk. The Chorus scattered to the exits like frightened chickens. Having slowly circled the stage, the Queen surveyed the oncoming army (and us) without a word being spoken. She then re-entered her palace and the huge doors were swung shut by her slaves. No words were necessary to build up the tension.

As the doors closed, there was a flourish of live trumpets and drums, and up one of the tunnels appeared Agamemnon in a four-wheeled chariot with Cassandra by his side. At the conclusion of the first scene, he entered his palace for the last time on a red carpet rolled out by slaves. He had divested himself of his armour and walked to his death in a white robe. Later the dead bodies of the murdered Agamemnon and Cassandra—two larger-than-life figures sculpted in all their blood and agony—were wheeled out on an *eccyclema* (a large four-wheeled rostrum). This was the climax to the Messenger's speech which had described their death: the sculpture visually echoing its horror.

One effect in the final scene startled me. Orestes is tried for the murder of his mother before the goddess Athena. Following the placing of two huge bowls of incense and in a storm of smoke, the goddess entered, carried on a vast throne by slaves. This was Douglas Campbell again, this time inside the body of the statue but with his masked features, padded shoulders, and arms visible. The towering god Apollo who championed Orestes stood next to Athena, with Orestes standing below him. Orestes knelt before Athena and, to my amazement, the eyes of the goddess looked down from above on the suppliant. They actually moved.

The final image was of the Chorus singing its way off stage as Athena disappeared into smoke. One solitary citizen from the crowd remained on stage. A humble figure in contrast to all the splendour we had seen, he stood in a single spotlight and took a bow for the whole Company. It would have been blasphemous to applaud Athena.

After the performance, I spoke to Douglas Campbell in the bar and mentioned the effect of Athena's eyes moving downwards to look at Orestes in the trial scene. I asked how this technical effect had been achieved by the mask maker. 'You'd like to see?' he asked. 'Well, come with me,' and he led me under the stage. And there they were—all the masks from this colossal drama placed on stands. In the half-light of a couple of overhead fluorescent tubes, the heads looked frighteningly real.

I went up to the mask of Athena on its stand. And the eyes? They were painted on the surface of the face. They could no more have moved than the eyelids fluttered. It was the skill of the actor and more important, my own belief in that theatrical moment that had blessed Athena with human eyes. In later years, I directed Greek drama with an all-male cast performing in masks. On more than one occasion, an actor sitting in the auditorium, who had been watching a scene in which he did not appear, would come round afterwards and say: 'I saw the eyes move today.' It was a measure of his involvement in the performance.

The impact this production had on me—both in terms of demonstrating what could be done on the thrust stage, but also of the design, lighting, and acting style—was immense and could be seen in my work over the coming years. That night I wrote in my diary:

'For the first time Greek Tragedy made sense! I shall never see this play again without thinking of it in these terms. This was a great production, definitive as far as recreating Greek Tragedy is concerned. I gave myself up to it. This was the thrust stage recreating the essence of amphitheatre performance. The scale of the production matched the stature of the playwright's conception. Gods stalking the stage twelve-foot high on stilts, heroes on six-inch lifts, ordinary mortals in bare feet, and all the performers in masks.

'As an arena for acting and speaking on the scale of Greek Tragedy, the thrust stage proved itself perfect. The heightened atmosphere was akin to the Japanese Noh theatre—the sense of ritual performed on polished wood. The sheer classical beauty of the choreography, the visual impact dwarfing the spectator and at the same time uplifting him, all these elements of Greek Tragedy which one felt were antithetical to modern theatre were present, completely acceptable, and utterly moving. To talk of technicalities like audibility and lighting is as puny as brandishing a plumb line in front of the Parthenon. As for the stage itself—it works!'

My exuberance at that evening's show was matched by David. In his report, he wrote: 'I thank heaven that we did not see this as our first production on Saturday; I should have been too stunned to form a proper appreciation of anything else afterwards. It is one of the greatest productions I have ever experienced, if not the greatest. I say "experienced" advisedly—one did not "see" or "watch" this play. I am persuaded that, produced by Guthrie on a proscenium stage, different though it would have been, it would not have affected me to the same extent.

'The technicalities are much more Colin's province than mine, but the settings by Tanya Moiseiwitsch were exquisite, the costumes, with mortals on built-up boots, and the Gods, on stilt boots, giving them figures 12 feet high, were tremendous, and marvellous performances by Douglas Campbell as Clytemnestra and Athena were unforgettable. I think, however, that the chorus work, moving, speaking, singing, will stay longest with me; and largely because it was in the middle of us—the audience.

'For the first time, I was aware of part of the audience across the auditorium caught in the spill from a spotlight on the chorus and—as Guthrie says—this heightened my participation in what was happening on stage; it did not destroy the illusion. It does seem the final justification for the thrust stage. I know that one cannot serve up Greek drama for 48 weeks per annum in Sheffield, but the sort of programme we present is, obviously, perfectly capable of going on a thrust stage.'

CHAPTER EIGHT

Travellers never did lie, though fools at home condemn them.[†]

The next day, we came back to Earth. We returned to the Guthrie Theater to see *The Visit* again, this time to watch with a more critical eye on both the production and the auditorium. During the performance, we sat on the back row of the balcony, on the front row right at the side, and on the front row of one of the box sections of the balcony. We both felt the production had been directed for a proscenium stage. Too much of it played straight out front, which seemed to miss the whole point of the thrust stage. The only area of seating that disappointed us was the front row of the balcony, where we felt cut off from the action on the stage and, in fact, from sight, by the rail of the balcony which blocked a small section of the stage and the whole of the gutter on one side.

During the afternoon, we had the opportunity of watching Douglas Campbell rehearsing *She Stoops to Conquer* in the rehearsal room. He was blocking out the moves and it was interesting to watch how, on a thrust stage, the actors could turn and move 'naturally' without the conventional necessity of turning via the audience. Even in the bareness of the rehearsal room, one could accept, quite easily, a garden where the scene was set with thickets, brambles, and horse ponds. The story and the actors conjured up the scenery before us.

During our time in Minneapolis we also met with Alan Schneider, a well-known theatre director on both sides of the Atlantic who was connected with a new thrust stage theatre that was going to be built in Ithaca, New York. Our discussions with him helped confirm two key points: first, that we must decide on either a proscenium or a thrust stage and build it. At current prices and with current techniques,

---

[†] William Shakespeare, *The Tempest*, Act III, Scene 2.

there was no 'flexible' stage. And second, having built one type, we must accept its discipline, and this applied particularly to a thrust stage. One fails on a thrust stage if one tries to direct in 'picture' style—from the back wall forwards. This might be why both David and I found *The Visit* unsatisfactory.

While at the Guthrie Theater, we also met with the talented scenic designer Robert Mitchell, who had long experience of working on the thrust stage and a philosophical concept of its use. Robert described the proscenium arch as a 'nuisance invention', presenting 'the action of the actor to the universe'. In contrast, the thrust stage placed the actor at the heart of the theatre, creating a 'soft edge' to reality, like Leonardo's *sfumato* technique. But he warned that an architect inevitably divides the theatrical space into two parts and, even when designing a thrust stage auditorium, creates a 'psychic proscenium'.

Robert believed in a new type of theatre where the stage was a battleground, where everything was used on it and anything could happen. As it was more embracing, the thrust stage enabled a return to the Greek idea of action, where the gesture is primal and there is an expressiveness exceeding thought. For him, the bugbear of the Guthrie Theater was literal thinking—he found *Harpers Ferry* far too literal and compared it with the *Oresteia* where the audience lost the literal effect but could more clearly see the play's themes relating to all of mankind. And when it came to scenery and props, he believed that they grew directly out of the action. Insensitive directors cluttered the stage; selectivity was the key.

The next day we drove from Minneapolis over the border to Stratford, Ontario. During our drive, we had a very interesting chat with our taxi driver, a Mr Fin Diehl. He had never seen much theatre beyond Music Hall and had gone to the opening production of *Richard III* in 1953, not expecting to enjoy it. But ever since he had been a devotee of thrust stage productions.

That evening we dined with Mr and Mrs Alfred Bell, two dedicated lovers of the theatre who had been involved since the very beginning with the Stratford Festival Theatre. Also at the dinner were Victor Polly (the Theatre Administrator) and his wife, and Desmond Heeley, the resident designer. Desmond was the first to raise a dislike for the multi-coloured seats and ski slope in the Guthrie Theater, but this did not affect his dedication to the thrust stage.

The next morning, we visited the 'mother theatre' at Stratford, Ontario. As it was outside of festival season, we were unable to see a production, but we were shown round the theatre and introduced to the staff by the Artistic Director, Jean Gascon, accompanied by Victor and Desmond. There was a sense of loyalty to the theatre from all those connected to the Festival, and this included the townsfolk who knew how much the theatre had boosted Stratford's fortunes.

So what were our impressions of the Festival Theatre? From the outside, it had the organic unity of the circus tent from which it sprang. The outside silhouette and the circular building were at once eye-catching and satisfying. Inside, the experience was much better than at Minneapolis: there was so much light in the building, the foyers were uncluttered and clear and the whole theatre was air-conditioned.

The auditorium was positive and forthright. The roof, in blue, reminiscent of the former tent, was attractive in colour and line. You could see why Stratfordians did not approve of the Minneapolis roof. There were straightforward stalls and a balcony in one simple attractive semi-circular sweep, and good views from every part of the

The Stratford, Ontario auditorium as it was in 1967

auditorium, although the sightlines were extremely acute on the side. We felt that the concrete-stepped auditorium with the seats attached to the risers was a good model.

The stage had been deliberately built for Shakespeare and had a permanent balcony and stairs which precluded productions of other types of plays without expensive scenery being built. This had been done because Stratford, like Minneapolis, was a Festival Theatre with a limited twelve-week season during the summer only. Although Jean Gascon expressed horror at having to produce plays for 48 to 50 weeks in a year (as we did in Sheffield), there was no suggestion that this would be impossible on a thrust stage.

In our discussions that day, Jean, Victor and Desmond emphasised that the thrust stage is a very definite form and worked best at Stratford when directors worked in harmony with the positive stage there. The fact that at Stratford the 'scenery' is permanent meant that all the emphasis was on costume and props which must be highly detailed. The walk-ons are nearest to the audience and as much care must be

Stratford, Ontario's auditorium from the centre back

taken with their costumes as with those of the stars. All three shared a dislike of the Guthrie Theater's steep rake on one side, the multi-coloured seats and the fussy ceiling which became irritating after a while.

Desmond Heeley also showed us drawings he was preparing for the new theatre at Ithaca, which seemed to me to provide the most flexible design for a thrust stage, giving scope for all types of play, from the spectacular to the intimate. He recommended adding a grid over the back part of the stage to fly scenery in and out and suggested that the arc of seating need not be as wide as at Stratford. Regarding the size of the auditorium, he echoed the advice we had been given in Minneapolis to go for a smaller house than Stratford's 2,300—he suggested 1,000 spectators—which he felt would ensure greater vocal flexibility.

On leaving Stratford, en route to Toronto, we called at the University of Waterloo to see the theatre which several people had recommended as a good example of a smaller theatre. In fact, we felt that it was a good example of how <u>not</u> to build a theatre: a classic case

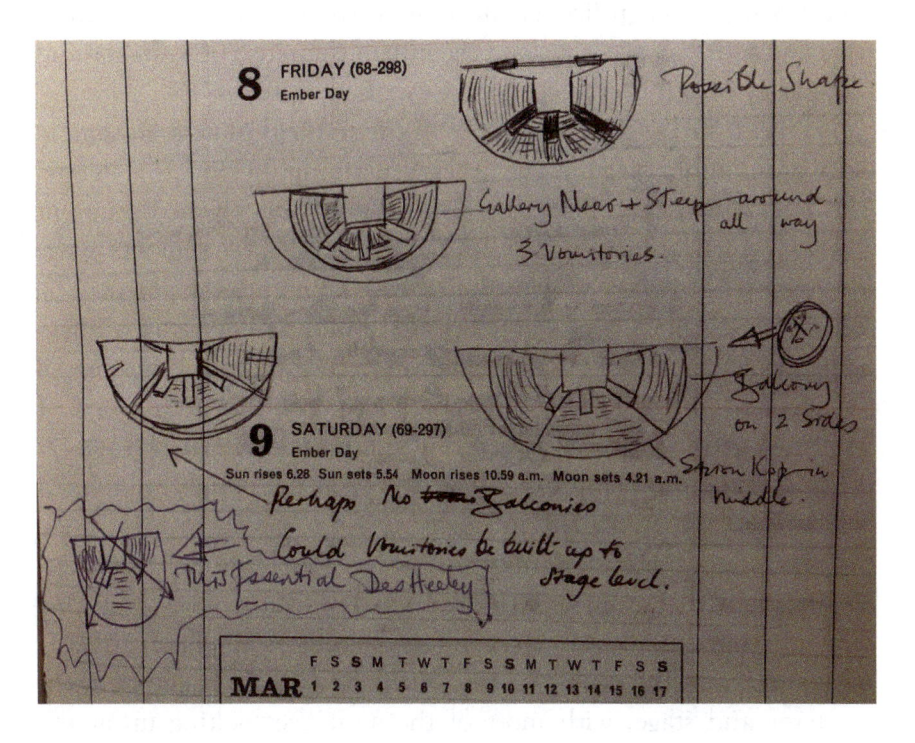

Sketches I made of auditorium shapes during our discussions that day

of failed compromise. The building had originally been designed for the Engineering Department but then switched to Creative Arts, its lecture hall format 'fiddled' into a theatre. The thrust stage had been built with sliding doors along the back which could be opened to convert into a proscenium stage with forestage.

The result was—tragically—neither one thing nor the other and merely reconfirmed what we had repeatedly been told: you must commit yourself to one type of stage and stick with it. One final point: the theatre had one central vomitory which was quite obviously wrong. This dictated a single central axis running straight out from the back wall which negated the whole principle of 'in the round.' This confirmed Desmond Heeley's point that the vomitories must form crossed axes with the back entrances onto the stage.

We rounded off our trip with a two-day visit to New York. We were unable to get theatre tickets our first evening (it was a Saturday) but were given two tickets for a Symphony Concert in Carnegie Hall. Although this theatre had no direct relevance to our research, experiencing its magnificent auditorium with proscenium stage, 2,760 seats and four balconies, helped reconfirm the sense of intimacy and immediacy we felt on the open stages we had visited so far.

The next day, we saw a matinee of the musical *Man of la Mancha* on a promontory stage at the ANTA Washington Square Theatre. The ANTA had been built as a prototype for the Vivian Beaumont Theater, which opened in 1965, and was scheduled for demolition the following year to make way for the Lincoln Center development. The fact that the ANTA was a prefabricated building put up in a hurry helped the atmosphere. Lights hanging from girders and a sense of the circus having come to town seemed more relevant to this form of staging. A great effect was achieved when, for the overture, panels at the side of the proscenium slid back to reveal the orchestra grouped behind the stage on the left and right.

Otherwise, we both felt this was how NOT to build a thrust stage. At first sight the auditorium looked ideal—1,130 people, all in one slope, surrounding a wide proscenium opening from which a thrust stage jutted out. But there was too great a division in height between spectator and stage, with most of the audience looking up at the actors. This, in principle, was wrong. We were also surprised that the auditorium did not seat more, given its size. We felt that if the slope had been pitched more steeply, and if the back section behind the gangway had been hung as a balcony and brought forward over the stalls, the auditorium could have been reduced in size without reducing the number of seats.

The production itself was a curious mixture of styles. A good deal of the show was sickly sentimental and the proximity of the actors and the stage itself exacerbated this. It would have been more acceptable had it retreated behind a proscenium arch. A further irritation was that the production was played persistently out front, reducing the spectators on the side to second-class citizens. I felt that the fact the seats were not carried round in a full sweep of 180 degrees had tempted the director and cast him into this trap.

That afternoon, we met with director Michael Lessac, who shared some crucial advice on the theatre we were planning to build. Michael felt the back wall behind the thrust stage should be constructed with

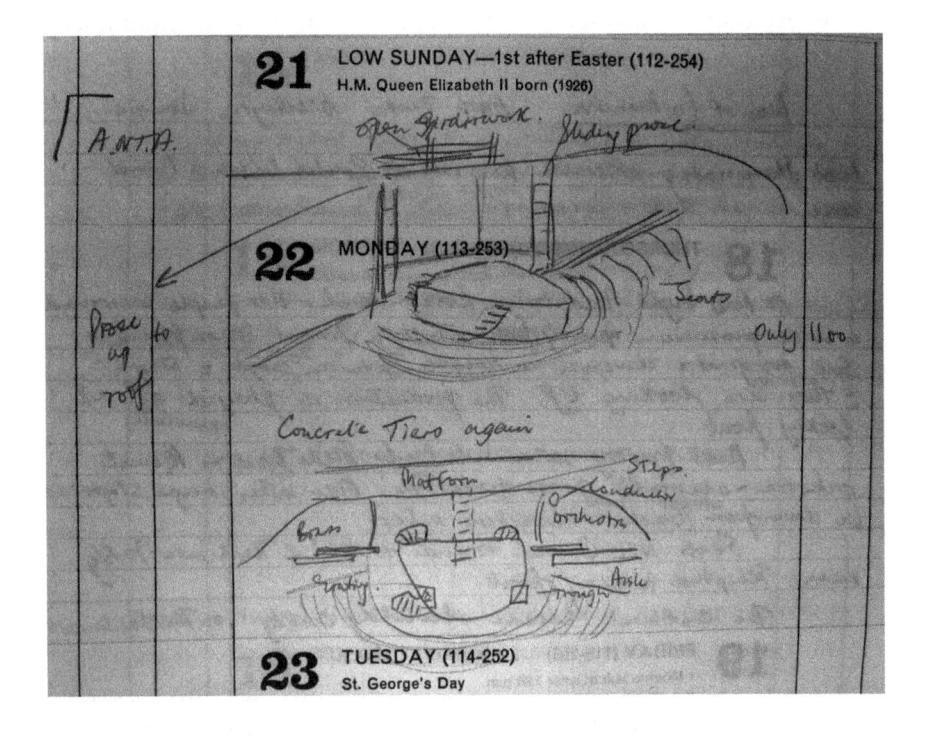

Notes from my diary on the ANTA Theatre

the idea of using a variety of levels. We should consider all forms of basic set design and incorporate features such as windows and doors from the start. That said, the dressing of the stage should primarily be with props and furniture. He warned us that acoustics are the most important feature to watch in building this type of theatre and that the sound system is very important. And he advised us to build a Studio Theatre in which all types of staging are possible and to explore front and rear projection.

On the final day of our trip, we visited the ANTA's successor: the Vivian Beaumont Theater at the Lincoln Center. We were immediately reminded how important the interior decoration of a theatre is. It was clear that a lot of money had been spent on this theatre—and in David's opinion, most of it had been misspent.

The décor was lush to the point of being completely repellent. There were vast lobbies, glass walls, dark red carpet, and black everywhere. This gave an opulent south-coast resort theatre feel. The lack of daylight and saturation lighting inside meant the theatre had none of the excitement, intimacy or atmosphere that we had experienced in Minneapolis or Stratford. And the ubiquity of nylon carpeting supercharged the building with static electricity so that whenever you touched a metal door handle or handrail (and they were all metal) you received a painful shock. Hardly an inviting space for a theatregoer.

We were unable to see a show, as they did not play on Mondays, but we were given the run of the auditorium. It seated 1,100 in stalls and balcony and although no seat was more than 64 feet from the stage, the auditorium gave the impression of vastness and (for those in the balcony) of being cut off from the performance and looking down on the actors' heads. There was no central focal point. We noted that just as in the ANTA Theatre, the seats did not come round the full 180 degrees. For this show, the vomitories were filled with seats, which gave the space a further proscenium effect. The stage was set for *The Little Foxes*, which was to be transferred to a Broadway theatre shortly. It was clear that the production was going to be played out front in proscenium style.

The theatre could be adapted from proscenium to thrust stage—which was large and lavishly equipped—by mechanically operated turntables. But the guide told us that, after the opening thrust stage production, not a single production had used the thrust stage in the

Main auditorium of the Vivian Beaumont Theater in 2018

three years which followed. This confirmed David's impression that the theatre was 'a good example of having enough money to try to do everything and failing dismally to do anything decisively'.

Having been underwhelmed by the main auditorium, David and I were much more taken with the studio theatre in the basement, which seated 400. The Forum Theater was unequivocally a thrust stage, the back wall about ten feet behind the thrust, two vomitories in the usual place and the seating on a single slope. It was interesting that both actors and audience preferred this theatre to the larger one. Our guide explained that should there not be a full house, spectators sitting on the side seats preferred to remain there rather than transferring to equally priced seats facing the stage. This would indicate that the theatre was being used properly.

That evening, we finished our North American trip with a good old-fashioned proscenium stage production of *Henry, Sweet Henry* at the Palace Theatre. Even here, it was interesting to see that they had built flats out onto the proscenium in front of the curtain, but the design of the flats—a spidery outline drawing effect—contrasted oddly with the gold carvings and red plush of the auditorium. It was an attempt to burst out of the picture stage which wasn't really needed. The production was a first-class example of how this type of show 'goes' on a proscenium stage: witty, colourful, alive with movement and ingenuity, but detached.

And so ended our marathon trip to North America. Over ten days, we had visited eight theatres, watched nine plays and spoken with administrators, governors, artistic directors, designers, actors, and members of the audience. It was clear that if we wanted to reach beyond the proscenium and restore our contact with the audience, we would have to be bold. There could be no half-measures: we would propose a thrust stage for our new theatre. Everything we had seen on this remarkable trip had cemented this belief in us. Without that conviction, we would never have survived the onslaught that fell upon us.

David perhaps had an inkling of what lay ahead when he wrote: 'I began this trip with a question in my mind whether a thrust stage might be more readily acceptable in North America than in Sheffield, where our audience has had no experience other than the proscenium stage. I think there may well be a truth in this, and, no doubt, if we build a thrust stage, not a few of our older patrons may not be able to follow us. But, remembering the lowering of the average age of our audience in recent years, and the work of Vanguard and listening to the children's reaction this afternoon, both during the play and in the intervals, I am certain that the audience of the future will accept the thrust stage as a perfectly normal medium for dramatic communication.' This was an assumption that would be tested to its limits.

My own moment of truth was my first glimpse of that polished wood—the Minneapolis stage gleaming in anticipation of the forthcoming performance. Paul Allen, a Sheffield newspaper critic and a supporter of what we were trying to achieve, was interviewed thirty-two years after the Crucible opened about my decision to opt for a thrust stage and said: 'Colin was an Evangelist. He'd had a "Road to Damascus" conversion to the thrust stage following his first visit to such stages in America.' Looking back, I can see that's exactly what it was. But the Board of the New Sheffield Theatre Trust had to be convinced of my, and indeed David Brayshaw's, conversion. We could not count on them travelling to Damascus with us.

i. Colin George, *early 1960s*.

ii. Colin George & Geoffrey Ost directing King Lear *at the Sheffield Playhouse, 1963.*

iii. *Colin George (centre stage) playing Con in Gwyn Thomas's* The Keep *at the Sheffield Playhouse, a typical 'picture box' production of the era, March 1963.*

iv. *Sheffield's first Brecht: Colin George's controversial production of* The Good Woman of Setzuan, *September 1963.*

v. Colin George having a drink with Sir Laurence Olivier at the Sheffield Playhouse, April 1966.

vi. Glen Walford with the Theatre Vanguard troupe and van, December 1968.

vii. *Dorothy Vernon, Colin George, Allan Cullen & Roderick Horn during recording of songs from* John Willy and the Bee People, *1967.*

viii. *Christopher Wilkinson, Myra Frances & Barrie Smith, June 1968.*

ix. *Barrie Smith & Myra Frances in* A Lily in Little India *at the Sheffield Playhouse, June 1968.*

x. *David Bradley & Dorothy Vernon in Alan Cullen's* The Life and Times of Charlie Peace *at the Sheffield Playhouse, July 1969.*

xi. Colin George, Roderick Horn & Alan Cullen during their visit to Eyam to research Ring o' Roses, July 1967.

xii. Colin George's valedictory production at the Sheffield Playhouse: Britannia's Boys, May 1971.

xiii. *Sir Tyrone Guthrie, 1950s.*

xiv. *Tanya Moiseiwitsch, 1949.*

xv. *Sir Tyrone Guthrie (who was six foot six) with the God Apollo during rehearsals for* The House of Atreus, *Guthrie Theater, Minneapolis, 1967.*

xvi. *Nick Thompson & Clare Ferraby, mid-1970s.*

xvii. Left: Peter Rice; Right: Robin Beynon, 1970s.

xviii. Richard Pilbrow in front of the light board at the Littleton Theatre, 1976.

Part III

Designing the Crucible

CHAPTER NINE

What do we then but draw anew the model?†

Following our return to Sheffield, David Brayshaw and I wrote two reports which we submitted to the Trustees. Condensing all the ideas and advice we had debated over our ten-day trip, we made the following joint recommendations:

1) That the Trust instruct the Building Committee to reconsider the brief for the new Playhouse with a view to building a thrust stage theatre.
2) That the Building Committee should (granted the willingness and availability of the persons concerned) refer to Sir Tyrone Guthrie and Miss Tanya Moiseiwitsch in so doing.
3) The following conclusions and impressions emerge from the theatres and productions we have seen:
    (i)   Do not build an adaptable theatre—settle for a thrust stage theatre.
    (ii) The audience should wrap around the stage in a semi-circle of 180 degrees. Taking out side-seats in an effort to improve sightlines vitiates the conception of a thrust stage.
    (iii) In addition to traps and vomitories there should be facilities to fly scenery and equipment both over the stage area for visual effect and behind the stage area for storage.
    (iv) The auditorium capacity needs considerable thought. One of the advantages of a thrust stage is that by bringing the audience around the acting area a large number of spectators can be comfortably contained in what would be a small proscenium auditorium. Stratford, Ontario

---
† William Shakespeare, *Henry IV, Part II*, Act I, Scene 3.

is 2,300, Minneapolis is 1,400, Vivian Beaumont (New York) is 1,100. We offer 1,000 as a figure and suggest this might assist the director or actor to scale his work with the greatest flexibility.

(v) While the theatre interior should be warm and inviting, the theatre atmosphere we most responded to was light and airy. This principle should inform both the front of house and backstage area.

(vi) The nature of the thrust stage invites the audience to complete the performance; in designing the auditorium, the architect should keep this in mind—particularly the area surrounding the stage which should be capable of exposing the mechanics of lighting, etc.

(vii) With a 1,000 capacity (not large by thrust stage standards) it may be possible to do away with a balcony. This was much favoured by the practitioners we met.

We also raised two other points for consideration:

(a) Building a thrust stage would mean that we could explore the possibility of inviting theatre companies with similar facilities to visit us (Chichester, Minneapolis, Vivian Beaumont, the National Theatre and RSC) and our Company could possibly visit their theatres.

(b) Open stage work is in line with our children's theatre work in schools (which, incidentally, seems much more advanced than anything we encountered in the States).

We had put everything on the line, advocating a no-compromise thrust stage design for our new theatre. Had the Trustees not been convinced by those 24 sheets of paper, then Sheffield might well have had not the Crucible, but instead have been stuck with a proscenium theatre with a large forestage. It is easy to forget, many years later, that to build a thrust stage was an adventurous choice for a leading regional city. At that time, the only other theatre in the city, the Lyceum, which had an excellent proscenium stage, was reduced to offering bingo, and before our new theatre opened, the Lyceum had closed down.[54]

I have often been asked how the City Fathers were persuaded to sail into such dangerous waters. The simple answer is that the detail of the reports proved convincing. Although personally I was able to offer the opinion of someone who had worked in the theatre for over twenty years, mine was the passionate outpouring of a fervent, visionary Welshman. I feel sure that the observations and reactions of David Brayshaw—a local solicitor and someone who represented the audience we were hoping to attract—might well have tipped the scale.

There was one issue, however, where David and I were not in agreement with Guthrie: his suggestion that the theatre should be sited outside the city centre in parkland. After presenting our reports and recommendations to the Trustees, I wrote to Dr Young, noting: 'We say nothing about the site, but I can see, following our visit to America, why Guthrie would like to put us in a dramatic Festival surround. Nevertheless, in this country, apart from Chichester and Glyndebourne, our theatres are, as I think they should be, very much in the centre of communities and performing all the year round.'

On 7th December 1967, the Trustees met to give their response to our report. Those of us involved from the theatre were present, together with the architect Andrew Renton, all in our formal suits and ties. Sir Tyrone arrived from a rehearsal in London and was dressed casually wearing a polo neck jumper.

He was informed that, subject to further detailed discussion, Sheffield was to have a thrust stage. What had not been decided was his suggestion that the site be moved into the Derbyshire countryside. He pleaded his cause and I recall Dr Gerard Young glancing in my direction; but I chickened out. This was not the moment to disagree with the man who had opened a magic casement for me in Minneapolis. Besides, I knew that the Trustees were unlikely to erect a theatre in the Derbyshire hills, and one which only functioned for a

---

[54] The Lyceum closed in 1969 and, despite being granted Grade II listed status in 1972, the theatre only narrowly survived demolition in 1975. Its subsequent fate is recounted in the Epilogue.

limited festival season. I kept quiet and no decision about the site was taken, and the meeting finished in good spirits.

As it turned out, Guthrie's suggestion about the site was never taken up. But when he came to Sheffield in the years that followed to see how construction was progressing, the Festival Theatre on the Moors was never mentioned. He was delighted to see his thrust stage becoming reality in Norfolk Street.

Not long after our meeting with the Trustees, David and I met with the architects in a pub near their office in Queen Anne Street to talk through our ideas. Nick Thompson later recalled: 'Colin and David came to see us and said: "We've got good news and bad news. The good news is we've found the £640,000. The bad news is we've met this man Tyrone Guthrie, he sent us to see some theatres in North America and we now want a completely different kind of stage!" It was almost like starting from scratch. There was nothing normal about the Crucible, that was what was so exciting about it. We really had to use ingenuity to achieve it.'[55]

But the architects rose to the challenge and on 14th December 1967, barely a week after the Trustees had agreed to adopt a thrust stage, they presented a revised Draft Programme for building the new Playhouse, adjusted to accommodate the new thrust stage design:

- Draft sketch design & cost estimate — 26 January 1968
- Submission of final sketch design and cost outline — 21 June 1968
- Final sketch design approval by client — 6 July 1968
- Planning and other approvals obtained — 2 August 1968
- Start of working drawings — 5 August 1968
- Bills of quantities — 4 April 1969
- Tenders out — 30 May 1969
- Tenders in — 11 July 1969
- Start of work on site — 28 July 1969
- Handover — 10 June 1971
- Completion of fitting out — 5 August 1971
- Curtain up — 2 September 1971

---

[55] Tedd George's interview with Nick Thompson, October 2020.

Given the notorious delays in completing new buildings on time, especially a theatre of this size and complexity, this was a remarkable forecast. Its accuracy says a lot not only for the experience and skill of the architects, but also for the commitment of the local building firm Gleesons.

On my wall at the old Playhouse was a chart outlining the schedule of work up to the opening night. The time span was two years, and we kept to it to the week. We did indeed start rehearsing in September 1971 and opened in November. (Although I do remember that just before the first public dress rehearsal, workmen were still fitting carpets in the foyer.) The only error might be the phrase 'Curtain up'. For an open stage, perhaps 'Lights up' would have been more apt?

The next day, December 15th, the Building Committee met to reconsider the schedule of accommodation for the new Playhouse. They agreed to adopt a thrust stage for the new theatre and instructed the architects to prepare an updated brief. It was also at this meeting that I was able to press another urgent issue—the appointment of Tanya Moiseiwitsch to consult on the thrust stage design.

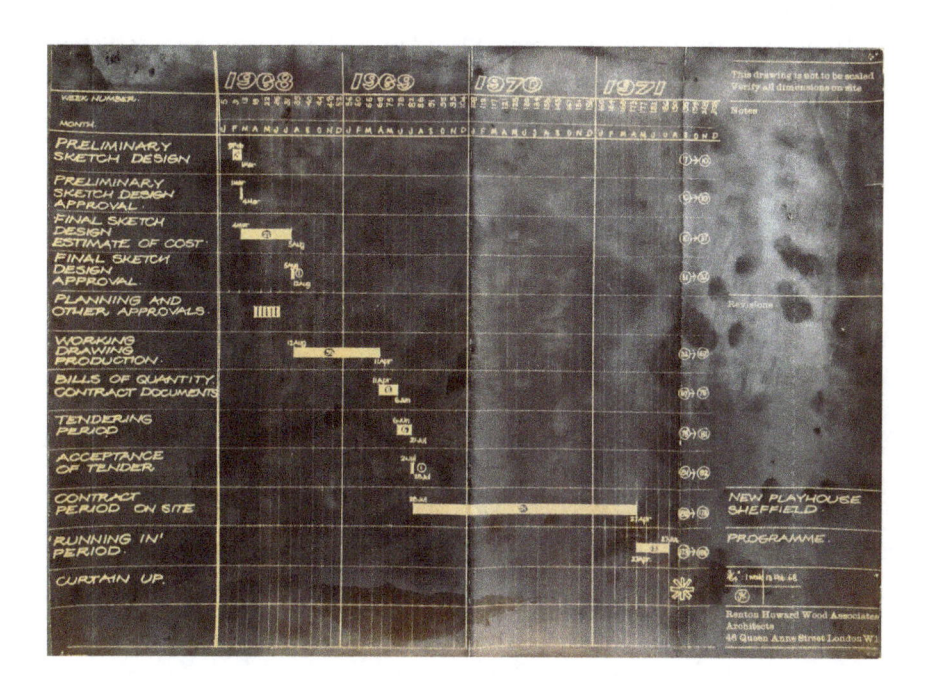

Draft Programme for the construction of the New Playhouse, December 1967

David and I had experienced Tanya's work close-up when we saw the breath-taking *House of Atreus* in Minneapolis. Not only did this production demonstrate the power of the thrust stage she had designed, but it also showed us how this kind of stage worked in tandem with the elaborate costumes and props used by the actors on it. Even then, before I knew Tanya, I was aware of the crucial role she had played in designing the thrust stages for Guthrie's theatres.

Tanya's stage was stripped bare of all pretention—an open space of polished wood set in the middle of the audience. This exposed the actor unlike any other stage—there was literally nowhere to hide, no sightline that was not met by a member of the audience. Tanya's open stage also exposed the other elements of the performance, notably the costumes and props which had to be of the highest quality as the actors were so close to the audience. But the thrust stage also liberated the lighting, opening up a world of possibilities for setting the scene and mood with light (as opposed to scenery on the proscenium stage). It was clear that if we were to adopt a thrust stage and change the way we acted, directed and designed productions on it, then we would need Tanya's expertise.

In our reports to the Trustees, David and I had recommended that, if we were to go for a thrust stage, then it was imperative that Tanya

Left: Tanya Moiseiwitsch, c.1971; Right: Patrick Ide, 1979

Moiseiwitsch should be involved. At the meeting of the Building Committee on 15th December, it was agreed that she should be approached as a potential consultant on the thrust stage. This was arguably one of the most important decisions made by the Committee regarding the new theatre. But it would take some time to close the deal.

A few days after this meeting, I finally met Tanya in person in London. She was accompanied by a great friend of hers—Patrick Ide. Pat was a West End producer with considerable experience in theatre management. He had been the publicity manager at the Old Vic for 11 years, where he had worked with Tanya, and two years in administration at the Mermaid Theatre, so he was no stranger to controversial stage design. Tanya and Pat were to play pivotal roles in the design of the thrust stage, the Studio Theatre and the wider theatre complex.

Tanya, Pat and I met in a deliberately modest environment—the Pizza Hut in Cambridge Circus. We talked about the reports David and I had made to the Trustees, which she found most interesting. I described the work we had been doing at the Playhouse and developments like Theatre Vanguard. Then I suggested that it would be a good idea if we did a production together at the Playhouse Theatre. She could meet the staff—some of whom would be members of the new Playhouse theatre—and we could discuss how the design of the stage itself was progressing. She expressed interest in the idea and said she would think about it. It would take me eighteen months of asking until we finally produced a show together in Sheffield.

On 19 January 1968, the architects presented us with a preliminary investigation for a thrust stage, based on the brief given them in December. They had examined a number of open and thrust stage designs, including the Barbican, Chichester, Stratford, Ontario, the proposed National Theatre and the Tyrone Guthrie in Minneapolis. They had also consulted with Denys Lasdun (designer of the National Theatre), Peter Chamberlain (designer of the Barbican Theatre) and Norman Branson, whose Questors Theatre they had visited.

Keen to get Tanya's views, I met her at her home in Chelsea at the end of the month. We talked about the new theatre and I still have the pencil sketches Tanya drew of the stage and a fearsome outline of what it could look like with a revolve.

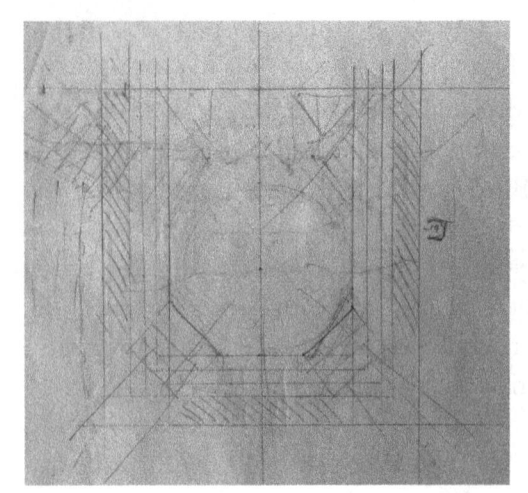

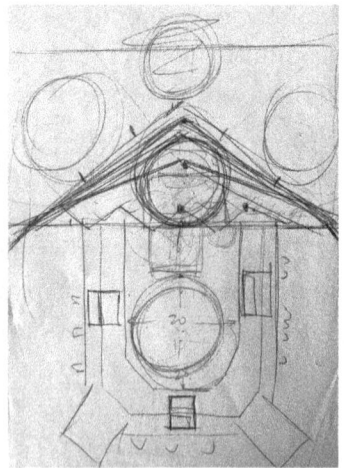

Tanya's initial sketches of the thrust stage, dated 29 January 1968

There were to be many discussions about the concept of the thrust stage, but these sketches would define the acting area of the new theatre. The stage would be 20 feet wide, barely half the width of Chichester, but as deep, with steps leading up from the moat. The focus would be on the 'Magic Circle'—clearly marked in her sketch—near the front of the stage. Twin vomitories (or tunnels, as Tanya preferred to call them) would come in at the front corners of the stage. The back wall of the stage would be adjustable, giving the possibility of creating a hidden rear stage area through which actors could dramatically emerge. Looking back at these sketches, it is astonishing how close they are to the final design of the stage and auditorium.

Tanya was on board. Even though it would not be until March that both she and Pat Ide were formally appointed by the Trustees, they both agreed to offer informal advisory. This was to prove invaluable when they attended a pivotal meeting with the architects and the Building Committee on 9th February 1968. We reviewed the architects' report, as well as a quarter-inch scale model of their three-dimensional interpretation of the auditorium. Their report laid out a series of variations on four auditorium models and highlighted the tension created by the conflicting requirements of the thrust and proscenium stages. They wrote:

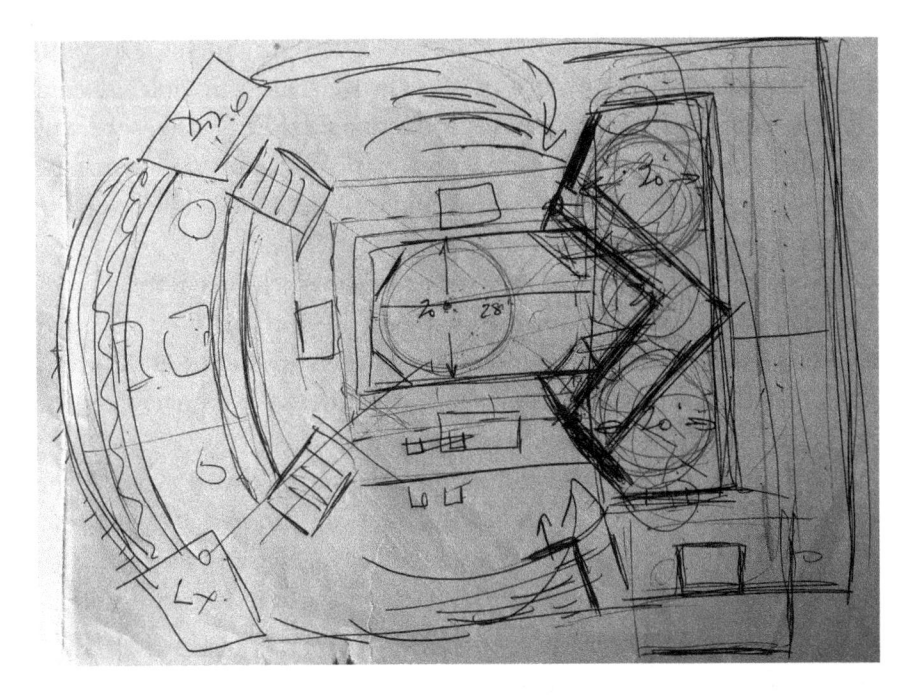

Tanya's initial sketch of the thrust stage, dated 29 January 1968

'The problem hinges on the provision of major items of scenery and the proscenium. Both the National Theatre and the Royal Shakespeare intend to use scenery and, for a number of productions, a proscenium presentation. To this end, they have been forced to sacrifice the majority of the 'thrust and wrap round' principle. Conversely, the Tyrone Guthrie auditorium wraps around to such an extent (over 180 degrees) that some of the audience cannot see the rear part of the stage on which is the majority of the set, but only the 'tongue' of the thrust. The exact 180-degree arrangement is in this respect an improvement on Minneapolis, but still cannot make use of the 'back wall' as a setting.

'Reducing the auditorium fan, whilst maintaining the penetration of the stage into the audience, seems to offer some advantage. Better sightlines allow a depth of stage behind the 'back wall' in which large sets could be provided through which actors could approach the thrust proper and against which the main action would be seen. Such scenery could of course be "flown" or wagoned unseen.

But the report ended with a clear warning that there would be no turning back from a purely thrust stage design: 'Such a proposal, although allowing better use of the thrust stage principle, should NOT accommodate proscenium productions. If the Trustees were at any time to decide that a proportion of proscenium work must be possible, it is our opinion that this could only be achieved by reverting to an auditorium similar to the new National Theatre.'

We started by looking at the 'suggested Sheffield Playhouse form'. Tanya was concerned about the shape of the auditorium and asked whether it was possible to round off the corners where the auditorium shell met the back wall. After she made a few adjustments to the design in pencil, the architects concurred.

We then examined the cardboard model of the thrust stage. After what David and I had seen in North America, I immediately felt that it lacked the strong clarity of Tanya's thrust stage vision. I repeated to the Committee one of the key findings of our visit to North America,

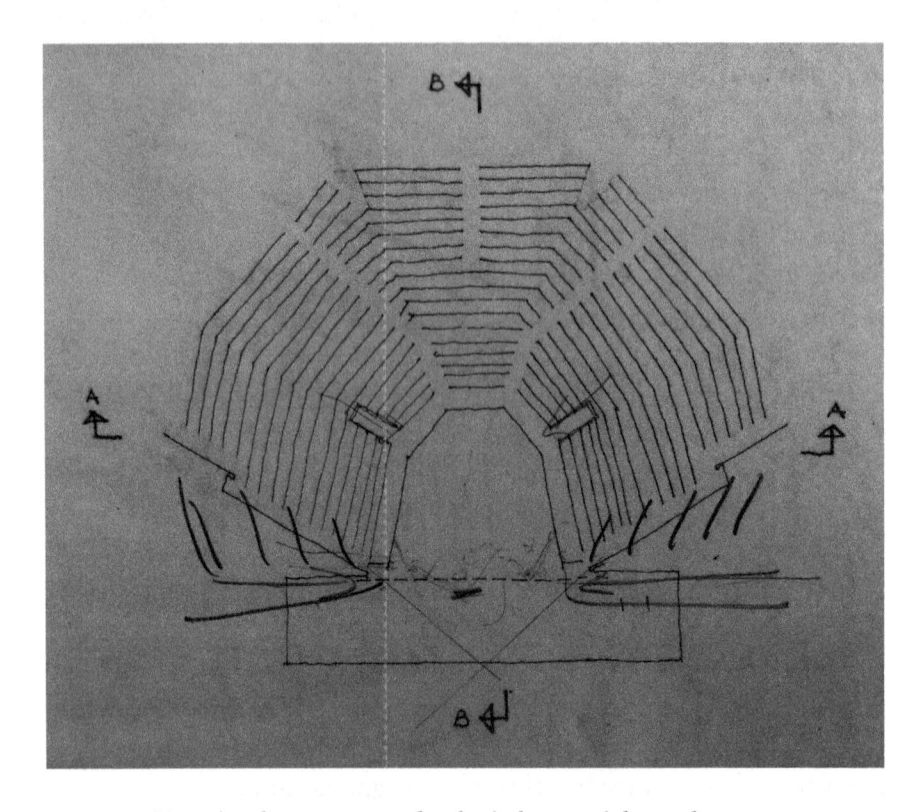

Tanya's adjustments to the draft design of the auditorium

The architects' early option for the thrust stage

namely that the design of the stage should not be a compromise, and that proscenium productions were not a consideration.

Next it was time for the dimensions of the thrust stage and surrounding area, and here Tanya demonstrated her remarkable precision. Having designed and adapted numerous thrust stages in her career, she knew what worked and what didn't, and she laid out for us a series of golden measurements:

- The eye level of the actor on the stage should be approximately at the height of the centre of gravity of the whole audience;
- The moat surrounding the thrust stage should be four feet wide and fifteen inches below the floor of the first row of seats;
- The vomitories should be 6 feet wide and a minimum of 8 feet 6 inches in height;
- The head room under the stage should be no less than ten feet; and,
- The height of the ceiling above the stage should be 'domestic in scale' (the architects eventually settled on 25 feet).

As for the tunnels, the architects had spaced them relating to the gangway exits. I suggested that the axes of the tunnels should be at

45 degrees to the centre of the stage itself (as advised by Desmond Heeley). And on no account should they be used by the public, even as an emergency exit. While no scenery would be flown over the stage, small pieces of furniture (chandeliers) or possibly an actor could be lowered onto the acting area. I also suggested that three turntables or revolves of various sizes could be laid on the stage floor and designed to match the stage finish. (I later changed my mind about this.)

In the space of a few hours, we had reached agreement on all key issues, and now the architects got on with the job of turning our ideas into a working design. The theatre would be, as Michael Elliot later described it, 'a fourth-generation Tyrone Guthrie auditorium', learning the lessons from previous attempts to build a thrust stage auditorium whilst pushing the boundaries of its theatrical potential.

From this point onwards, Nick Thompson became the Lead Architect on the project, under the oversight of his mentor Peter Howard. Nick was assisted by his right-hand man Robin Beynon, who drafted many of the architectural drawings and who regularly drove Nick up to Sheffield in his Austin Healey 3000. When it came to the thrust stage and auditorium, it was back to the drawing board, as Nick later recalled:[56]

'I began by sitting down with Tanya. It was a remarkable experience—she was quite phenomenal, patient and delightful, but very clear. And she said: "Where do we begin?" and I said: "Don't we begin with the stage?" And so Tanya explained how you could use a thrust stage to build up the actors in three dimensions: placing them in the moat, on the steps and on the stage, with the figures on top in more heroic poses. So I made a simple model of card, based on the dimensions she gave me, and I put a red circle on the stage which became the base for everything.' The 'Red Dot', as it became known, marked the centre of the 'Magic Circle'.

Tanya wanted the stage to be adjustable, so directors could change its shape. To achieve this, the architects settled on a series of demountable panels made of stained birch plywood which could be lowered in increments or removed altogether. Tanya also had a radical idea for where she wanted backstage: in order to allow large groups of actors to assemble in their own space before surging out through the vomitories,

---

[56] Tedd George's interview with Nick Thompson, October 2020.

'backstage' would be under the stage. Theatre Projects' engineer, Dick Brett, came up with a solution, as Nick Thompson explains:

'Dick had the idea of having a hole the width of the stage and moat inside the concrete and filling it with a steel frame up to the level of the moat. On top of this there would be a secondary steel structure, smaller and lighter in scale, which was removable in any part. Although we didn't realise at the time, this meant you could take the stage down to the lower level, with the audience looking down on the performers, which was ideal for snooker!'[57]

Discussion of the stage moved to the auditorium itself, its shape defined by the geometry of the thrust stage. Tanya and Nick developed the idea of throwing a pebble in a pond and following the ripples as they spread out. In this way, the stage influenced the octagonal shape not only of the auditorium, but also of the entire theatre complex, as Nick Thompson explains:

'The octagon shape came from the stage itself. I don't think Tanya said: "We've got to have an octagon-shaped stage." But in this kind of auditorium the focus was on the stage. So, you had to wrap the seating round and I didn't want to use a circle, because it's too expensive. Building materials are not curved, they're flat. If you made circular rows, every row would have a different radius, which meant that every row would need a separate mould.

'Therefore, the octagon became a very simple, all-encompassing solution. In fact, because we had the very defined geometry of the octagon, it meant things either worked easily or they didn't work at all. So, bringing the vomitories in at right angles to the corners of the octagons was very easy. It's interesting that Chichester is a hexagon, which doesn't work as easily as an octagon.

Nick continued the feel of the octagon beyond the auditorium, influencing the design of the entire theatre complex, as he explains: 'I became obsessed by this idea of putting a 135-degree angle against a 45-degree angle. The 135-degree angle gives you a sense of movement, a sense of drift, whereas the 45-degree angle is abrupt, you've got a point digging right into you and you've got to make a decision: do you go upstairs or round to the right? One angle is a drifting, the

---

[57] See the Epilogue for discussion of how snooker came to be played in the Crucible auditorium.

Tanya's telegram from Stratford, Ontario, March 1968

other is a finite decision. And I really enjoyed that geometry. It set up the movement of people that drifted around and was a strong determining factor for change of direction—it was all about the flow of people'.

Throughout this process, Tanya was as precise as Nick with her measurements. Among my papers, I have a telegram sent to her from Stratford, Ontario which reads: 'GRADE TWENTYFOUR DEGREES HEIGHT SEVENTYFIVE AND HALF INCHES'. Next to the second measurement Tanya scribbled in pencil: 6' 3 ½". These measurements referred to, respectively, the angle of the raked seating and the height of the vomitory entrances (which was based on the clearance needed for a soldier wearing a helmet and carrying a spear). In the end, the architects opted for a rake of 21 to 28 degrees, which was substantially more pronounced than Chichester's rake of 13 to 19 degrees (the result of the council limiting the height of the building).

On 1st March 1968, the architects presented their revised Schedule of Accommodation to the Building Committee, distilling all of our discussions over the previous year. Although there would be further alterations to the design, this document recorded in black and white just what those of us in Sheffield, from the Playhouse to the local

Trustees, were offering to the city as their new theatre. Although it had been inspired by the vision of Tyrone Guthrie and the skill of Tanya Moiseiwitsch, it was very much a Sheffield adventure. There were of course smaller experimental theatres playing in the round or on three sides, and outdoor festival venues, but no one had attempted to build a thrust stage theatre on this scale before. We were pioneering as far as English theatre was concerned.

CHAPTER TEN

The details are not the details. They make the design.[†]

On 15th March 1968, the Trust formally appointed Tanya Moiseiwitsch and Patrick Ide as advisers to the Building Committee. Tanya could still work internationally but her professional commitment would be to the new theatre in Sheffield. One of the first subjects we focused on was finalising the exact dimensions of the thrust stage. When I asked Tanya how they had settled on the length of the stage at Stratford, Ontario, she told me a story from her first season in 1953. At the close of the season, Alec Guinness, who had played Richard III, was asked if he had any ideas or criticism about the stage, and he replied: 'When I was on the flat stage, I always wanted to take one more step on that level before I went down, but it wasn't to be'. And so the next year, when they rebuilt the stage, they added 'Guinness's Yard' to it.

This gave me an idea regarding Sheffield's thrust stage. I went to the University of Sheffield with my Associate Director, Wilfred Harrison, and into a large lecture hall. Wilfred stood at one end and I at the other as if it were the back of the stage. I began my usual *Henry V* Chorus speech and slowly walked forward, finishing the speech at the point where I felt the front row should be. We measured this length and noted it down. Then I went to one side of the stage, playing Iago, while Wilfred went to the other as Cassio talking to Desdemona. I began Iago's speech: 'He takes her by the palm. Ay, well said, whisper! With as little a web as this will I ensnare as great a fly as Cassio.' I felt I was sufficiently apart to be credibly out of Cassio's earshot. We measured the width and noted it down.

That evening, we telegraphed Stratford, Ontario for their stage's length and width and we discovered that our measurements were

---

[†] Charles Eames.

within six inches of the length and one foot of the width. When I told this story to an interviewer from an architectural journal, he said: 'Oh, you built an anthropomorphic theatre!' In the end, the measurements we settled on for the thrust stage were 18 feet wide, 28 feet deep, 2 foot 6 inches above the surrounding moat and 2 foot 9 inches below the eyeline of the front of the audience, with a stage focus 9 feet from the front edge.

The other key issue relating to the stage was the revolve. In our earliest discussions about the stage—before David and I visited America—we considered building two concentric revolves on the stage, but not to cut into the 'Magic Circle' of the downstage area. These revolves were in the architects' original Schedule of Accommodation. But after our research trip I started to feel that the revolves were too complicated: they needed a demountable structure behind the platform and a number of uprights slotted into the revolves to provide an upper level. Struck by the simplicity of the staging we had seen at the Guthrie in the opening scene of *Agamemnon*—the soldier on the roof of Clytemnestra's palace merely squatting on the floor and the lighting, the text and the acting creating the illusion of him looking from a height into the distant horizon—I had a gut feeling against this idea.

So, on 6th June 1968, I wrote to Tanya: 'With regard to the revolve, onto which the back wall of our open stage is attached, there have been suggestions this should be brought down as far onto the tongue as possible. You could then swing furniture and the like down onto the acting area. I immediately feel this is dangerous but can't offer anything except an emotional reaction. What is your feeling?'

Two days later, Tanya replied: 'Your emotional reaction, strange to relate, was precisely my own—BUT on mature thought it boiled down to a prejudicial fear of the revolve being used in a Brechtian way. A ridiculous and ignorant prejudice which I must suppress in favour of the usefulness in whirling furniture and objects into the visible-to-all area of the stage, though not necessarily into orbit—I mean onto the Magic Circle itself.' She then sketched the thrust stage with two suggestions for the revolve—the first just cutting the Magic Circle (see next page).

She continued: 'There is an aesthetic bother which is almost too trivial to mention—but I'll mention it. The arc (caused by the revolve) on the floorboards, interrupts that continuous movement which the

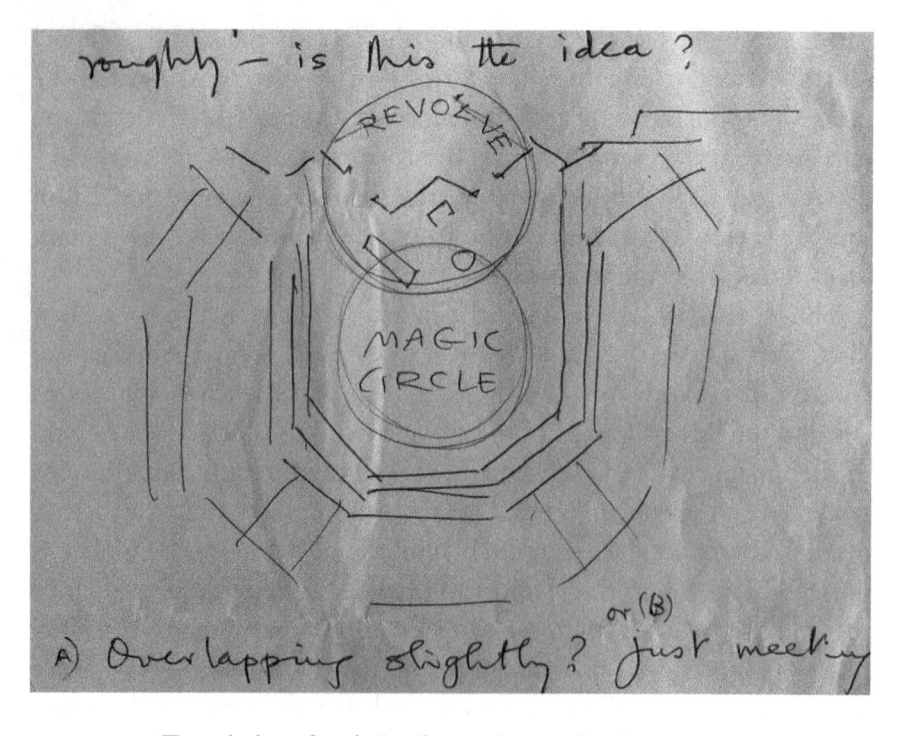

Tanya's first sketch for the revolve on the thrust stage

floorboards suggest—but one could argue, so would any rostra or other additions to the stage interrupt the flow.'

She then drew the second sketch (opposite), adding underneath: 'I know this looks like a child's garment (pin-striped), but do you see what I mean? Or do you agree that it couldn't matter less? The cuts in the floor by traps could also be said to interrupt, but the arc of the revolve would be much more noticed, though not if there are scattered pieces of furniture, rugs and so on—let alone ACTORS! Perhaps this can come up at the next meeting if you think it is of any importance.'

As it turned out, we abandoned the idea of using revolves later in the design process. But I have included these sketches to counter subsequent suggestions that Tanya had simply copied the design of similar theatres in America; nothing could be further from the truth. It was a new creation and Tanya started the design with a blank sheet of paper. So personal was her involvement that when it came to painting the stage, which she wanted to look old and used, Tanya got down on her hands and knees and painted it herself! I was always amazed

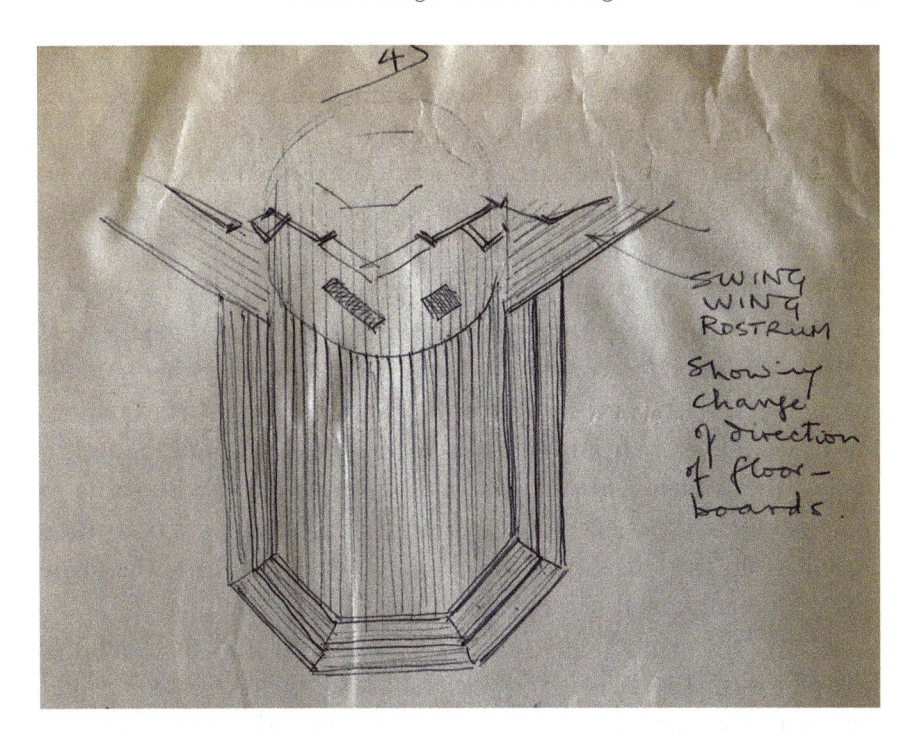

Tanya's second sketch for the revolve on the thrust stage

at Tanya's humility as shown in this letter of hers—never dogmatic but feeling her way towards what she felt was the right answer to a problem. And when the sticking-point came, she had her own brand of ruthlessness if she felt that something was done for superficial effect contrary to the integrity of the open stage.

With Tanya now officially involved in the new theatre, I invited her to see our production of *Oedipus* that April. I had directed the play before at the Nottingham Playhouse with John Neville in the lead, but—after seeing *The House of Atreus* in Minneapolis—this production would be radically different. Before we started rehearsing, I wrote to Guthrie to tell him how his production had inspired me to direct *Oedipus* at the Playhouse. He offered to send me an essay he and Tanya had written about their production, modestly insisting that he wouldn't be at all wounded if I didn't want to read it. I, of course, asked him to send me a copy.[58]

---

[58] The original typed copy of this essay is in the George Archive. It was subsequently reprinted in the book *Thrice the Brinded Cat Hath Mewed* (see Bibliography).

It is one of the most brilliant essays I have ever read about the theatre and the collaborative process involved in creating a very different kind of performance. The essay is far too long to quote in full, but there were three areas which were influential not only on what would be the Playhouse's first ever Sophocles, but also on the evolving design of our new theatre.

First, the ritualistic aspect of the performance: '[We were] not aiming to persuade the audience that the goings-on on the stage were really happening, nor to attempt to induce illusion, but rather to make the audience participate in a ritual [...] The intention was to remove the play completely from the arena of theatrical naturalism, and to compel the audience to relate what they were seeing and hearing to their religious experiences [...] Above all, the attempt was to raise tragedy from the triviality of detail and particularity, onto the plane where it belongs, of abstracted and removed grandeur.'

Second, the symbolic nature of the characters and their actions. The play was written for a very different audience, one which would have read the symbols as easily as we understand ironic jokes. But they would have interpreted the tragedy differently. Guthrie gives the example of the last scene, when Oedipus gives a long lament, listing all of his crimes in front of his children. To modern audiences, this could appear self-pitying, even melodramatic, given that both his children could start a new life in a different kingdom under the protection of their doting aunt.

'But all such ideas are trivial and irrelevant and provincial. They assume that Greek manners are, or ought to be, the same as our own. They fail to assume the preconceptions of the audience for whom the play was written. This family, to the Athenian audience, was clearly and irrevocably doomed and polluted. There was absolutely no possibility for a new and happier life for Ismene and Antigone. Their fate was part of the symbolic curse hanging over their symbolically polluted house.'

And third, the use of masks, which would be my first time in a professional production. The symbolism of the play dictates the need for the actors to wear masks which are a deliberate attempt to cut off the actor's face, obscuring any individual features. This gives a universality to all the characters and enables the audience to see how their actions and plights relate to all of humanity.

Guthrie summed up his creative approach in this magnificent passage: 'The performance of a tragedy must aim higher than at an audience's susceptibility to pathos. An audience will cry readily; the death of Little Willie or a pretty girl singing the sorriest rubbish will melt to tender tears the hardest-bitten men and the hardest-biting women. The emotion aroused by even a half-decent performance of great tragedy cannot be measured in terms of chewed hankies and misted specs. The full impact of great tragedy is not immediate: it takes effect slowly. It lies in wait on the fringe of dreams. It wakes one with a start in the small hours. It can shake the confident and strengthen the weak, stop the clock, roll back the seas. It can give a new meaning to life, and an old meaning to death.'

Inspired by Guthrie's vision, we opened *Oedipus* on 9th April 1968 with an all-male cast. The 'heroes' wore high boots and all the actors wore masks designed by Edward Furby. Wilfred Harrison played Oedipus, the versatile Barrie Smith played three parts (Tiresias, the Shepherd and the Second Messenger), while Mike Harley led the Chorus. The Sheffield critics had never seen anything like it.

Oedipus *at the Sheffield Playhouse, April 1968*

The *Morning Telegraph* wrote: 'Colin George's production sucks you up, swallows you alive, whirls you through a succession of near-religious experiences with a bold harshness you do not often see in the theatre and finally spits you out, bemused and shocked.'[59] Some years later, Denys Corrigan wrote: 'Night after night, at the final curtain, audiences sat in stunned, awed silence, then subscribed, few by few, to an inexorable crescendo of applause, which one felt would have continued for as long as the players were prepared to stand there and receive it.'[60]

Needless to say, Tanya was delighted to see that her work with Guthrie was the inspiration for our production. Guthrie was magnanimous in his response to my homage to his work, writing: 'I have always taken literally and seriously the proverb that imitation is the sincerest form of flattery!'

While I was focused on productions at the Playhouse, the architects and engineers worked on the design of the auditorium. In order to meet our requirements for an adaptable stage, raked seating and vomitories, they proposed building a concrete bowl to house the auditorium. This bowl could support pre-cast concrete steps and could be cut through for entrances and vomitories. On top of this bowl, supported by the outer walls, would be a roof made of steel trusses with a double skin of woodwool slabs for sound insulation. This design meant that the auditorium could have a span of 120 feet without the need for supporting columns.

Within this structure, Ove Arup's engineer, Peter Rice, and Dale & Benham's services engineer, Peter Goldfinger, developed modular units which could be fitted in sections onto the concrete bowl. These units were pre-cast in concrete, L-shaped and stepped. Each unit had a flat top, a vertical riser and a gap underneath. This design meant the auditorium could be constructed in modular fashion—rather like LEGO. But the gaps under each unit would also play a role in the air-circulation system. The engineers placed the air-circulation plant on the roof of the auditorium, fed in filtered cooled air from the roof and extracted stale air through the slots under the concrete seating and back up to the plant.

---

[59] The *Morning Telegraph* was a Sheffield daily newspaper that published until 1986. It was relaunched as the *Sheffield Telegraph* in 1989.
[60] Corrigan, *The Stirrings in Sheffield*, p.33.

The concrete bowl design also enabled the architects to fit 1,000 seats in the auditorium whilst ensuring the entire audience was physically close to the focus of action. This was achieved in accordance with health and safety restrictions (which at that time limited row sizes to 22 seats) and without the need for curved seating (which was expensive), as Nick later explained:

'It's all about scale and groupings of audiences—you don't want to be sitting like in a stadium, on the back row of a huge ring. But if we could bring in the entrances two thirds of the way up the auditorium, anyone sitting in the top third of the rake could enter, turn around and walk up to the back rows. This meant no seat was far from an exit, so we could get away with three principal entrances and two on the edges. The back rows were made up of four groupings of 22 seats, focused by the walls of the entrance lobbies, with no seat further than 59 feet from the centre of the stage.[61] It was not about packing in more seats; it was more about avoiding a monumental back row all the way round. But this design also meant that the audience entered into the heart of the auditorium, right into the melting pot, which was one of the great unintentional successes of the design.'[62]

The concrete units fitted well with Nick's concept of a minimalist auditorium, focusing all attention on the thrust stage: 'It seemed to me that the whole interior had to be non-architectural. We were not going for decorative objects or pronounced materials—it was all about 'THE STAGE'. What was fundamental to me, when considering the difference with a proscenium theatre, like Sprague's Lyceum next door, was that when you came in you saw nothing—a bare stage waiting for something to happen. This was an utterly different world from the decorative auditorium the public was used to.'[63]

In line with this vision, the materials and fittings of the auditorium would be functional rather than ornate. For the seating, the architects sourced seats from a company, Race, which produced them for greyhound stadiums. These seats were on cantilevered aluminium

---

[61] This is little more than halfway back in the stalls of a proscenium theatre of comparable size.
[62] According to Nick Thompson, Dr Gerard Young, who was a tall man, asked for some of the rows to have more legroom, and in the final design rows D and E were slightly wider than the other rows.
[63] Tedd George's interview with Nick Thompson, October 2020.

brackets, with an upholstered plywood base and back, that were screwed into the upstand of the concrete units. This meant that when the audience left, the seats would flip up and the floorspace could be cleaned quickly. The colour scheme was also neutral, although Tanya was insistent on not using black paint for the walls, as it would give off reflections. Instead, she wanted a dark brown that created an indefinite boundary between the stage and walls. When it proved difficult to source the right colour, the ICI rep was called in, and Tanya simply pointed at his trilby hat and said: 'That colour!'

The magical twinkling lights above the stage were also deliberately non-obtrusive, as Nick explains: 'I wanted the sense that there's an indeterminate space up there but you're not quite sure where it is or what's in it. We did not want the audience to be distracted by the lights, the catwalks and the ventilation units above. So when they came in and the house lights were up and twinkling, they were not going to try to see beyond them.' Robin Beynon, the Job Architect, drew up a complex design of over 1,000 lights scattered at random above the stage, but installing the bulbs would prove a huge challenge. They were wired in series of eleven bulbs, which meant that if one bulb went out, so did the other ten. As a result, the wiring had to be spread all over the ceiling to avoid distracting dark patches if one series went out.

But there was a problem with the overall auditorium design: it created a large bare back wall behind the stage, facing half the audience. The challenge of how to join the stage and the back wall was characteristic of Guthrie thrust stages, as Michael Elliot later explained in an article published in *The Architectural Review*:

'There is no satisfactory way of making the two meet. I would suggest the reason is profound, not practical. The semi-circle of the auditorium belongs clearly to the world of the audience, and the stage to the world of the actor, with the moat between them emphasising the distinction, but to which world does the wall behind the stage belong? It is certainly part of the main auditorium structure, as the architecture makes clear, but it physically meets the stage, and the world of the stage makes demands on it. In the evolved Guthrie theatre it tries to belong to neither and both. It is in constant conflict, softened during the performance by blurring its relationship to the auditorium.

'The truth is that all lasting theatre design must express not two worlds, but three. The world off-stage, the world of the audience, and where the two meet, the stage [...] The problem with Guthrie theatres is that the auditorium back wall cannot easily be evocative of worlds beyond, it can have no melting, suggestive depth—if it could, it would be beyond the sightlines. In short, it can have no visual mystery.'[64]

To lessen the impact, the architects introduced 'boxes' on the left and right of the stage, which visually softened the break between the dark and level stage and the lighter vertical auditorium wall. These boxes could theoretically be used for audience seating, but they were primarily a device for use by musicians or groups of actors in order to amalgamate the stage and auditorium.

A further solution proposed by Tanya was to use periactoids. Modelled on the *periaktos* used in ancient Greek theatre, the

Architect Robin Beynon's cut-through of the auditorium showing the boxes behind the stage

---

[64] Michael Elliot, 'A director's view of the Crucible', *The Architectural Review*, February 1972.

periactoid was a scaffolding structure with a triangular base. It ranged in height from 16 to 24 feet, with a floor every 8 feet, and ladders down one corner. Periactoids could be used as a kind of adaptable wall, by attaching panels painted the same colour as the auditorium, or as scenic elements, such as brickwork, balconies or even Guthrie's dramatic palace doors in *The House of Atreus*. Periactoids were a way of filling the space between the stage and the boxes without the need to build heavy scenery or hang a cloth. They also created a large rear-stage area behind which, out of sight of the audience but still audible, an army of actors or a band of musicians could assemble, building tension before their entrance.[65]

In tandem with work on the stage and auditorium, Pat Ide developed the brief for the Studio Theatre. Coming from the rigours of commercial theatre, Pat's contributions to the development of the new theatre design, the building's operation and in due course fundraising, were invaluable.

Drawing on the basic outline of the Studio Theatre in the architects' revised Schedule of Accommodation from March 1968, Pat fleshed out the ideas in a brief to the Trustees. The architects envisioned a building shell some 50 feet square by 20 feet high with a level floor, no windows, mechanical ventilation, and an exposed lighting grid. The Studio Theatre would seat 200 and have a demountable stage adjustable to open stage production, theatre-in-the-round, concert, and films. It would have adequate rooms for acting, technical, and administrative staff.

Pat made a number of recommendations. First, the Studio Theatre should be acoustically independent of the main theatre and insulated from the street. It should have the finish of a workshop, with recessed holes in the walls so that battens could be screwed in vertically or horizontally. Actors should have four entrances to the Studio theatre—from the dressing rooms, the workshop, the foyer and a trap at the centre of the floor with a tunnel underneath. Pat noted that a further public exit into Norfolk Street might be needed to meet fire regulations.

---

[65] The fate of Tanya's periactoids remains unclear. They are visible in photographs prior to the Crucible's opening and are in Tanya's ground plan for the first production she designed there, *The Shoemaker's Holiday* (see Appendix). However, I am told that the periactoids were not popular with other designers and they appear to have been abandoned by the time she left the theatre.

Next, Pat suggested expanding the number of seats from 200 to 250. These should be tiered arena-type seating and utilitarian rather than sophisticated. The seats should have detachable backs (and possibly no armrests) so that they could be easily subdivided into units to seat the audience in the round, on either side or facing one way. Seating could also be removed altogether for exhibitions or conferences, in which case adequate storage was required. The proposed single-row gallery around the Studio would add 100 seats.

Regarding the technical requirements of the Studio Theatre, there would need to be lighting units, a switchboard and a 16mm projection facility. Pat also suggested we explore using the space as a television studio. This would require installing in the exterior wall a small trap about 8 feet above ground for television cables. The Studio floor would also need to be made of a stable material suitable for the 'dollies' used by television cameras.

I forwarded Pat's report to Tanya, who wrote back: 'The Studio summed up by Pat. It's so vivid and thorough that I can't think of a thing to add except praise. Will the acoustic considerations be left for the acoustic consultant?' Pat would return to this issue in depth in his next submission to the Building Committee.

During this crucial phase of planning the new theatre, the contribution of the University of Sheffield was important. We were indebted to Dr Gerard Young, Chairman of the Building Committee, whose experience and knowledge of erecting new buildings was to prove crucial to promoting the cause of the thrust stage. In May 1968, while on a trip to America, Dr Young visited the Guthrie Theater in Minneapolis and sent the Trustees a full report on his return.

Dr Young saw a technical rehearsal of *Twelfth Night* and visited the theatre's backstage facilities. His findings were broadly in line with our own, but with some useful observations. Like us, he had found little to commend the building from the outside, but once inside the auditorium he pronounced it a success. Dr Young liked the variegated colouring of the seating and found the acoustics remarkably good in the entire house. This he put down to the 'liberal, sound-proof and light-proof double doors with a big area of trap between them'.

But he was critical of the roof, which was completely obscured by 'clouds'—panels to obscure lighting equipment. He noted: 'They are effective if sitting centrally but on the side seats I was horribly conscious of the huge variety of lights, many of which got into one's eyes.' Like us, he disliked the balcony because the front barrier obscured the vision of the front of the stage, but he approved of the 'ski slope' of steeply raked seats on one side of the auditorium.

Perhaps the key finding of his visit was the need for adequate space backstage. A staff of over 200 people worked backstage at the Guthrie and they were terribly cramped, often having to pass through sewing rooms, canteens and rest rooms to get from one side of backstage to the other. There should be toilets, a lounge and a cafeteria backstage, and the floor area of any rehearsal room should be at least as big as the stage plus the steps to the moat. Dr Young also touched on an issue that irked both David and me—the lack of natural daylight. None of the backstage offices or dressing rooms had windows, which, in his opinion, was 'a grievous mistake'.

One sobering detail Dr Young included towards the end of his report was that the Guthrie Theater ran an annual deficit of $350,000.[66] This issue would confront us at the end of our very first season in our new theatre.

Dr Young's report gave a boost to the credibility of our plans for the thrust stage in Sheffield and, I believe, reassured the Trust and Building Committee that the theatre project was going in the right direction. His findings would also prove helpful in countering the criticism of the thrust stage that was to follow.

---

[66] This would be the equivalent of $2.7 million in 2021, around £2 million.

CHAPTER ELEVEN

*Perfection is achieved not when there is nothing more to add,
but when there is nothing left to take away.*[†]

Following the architects' revised Schedule of Accommodation in March, the next four months were spent ironing out kinks in the design before it was locked down. While Guthrie had influenced Sheffield's decision to build a thrust stage theatre, it was a team of disparate members—from the University of Sheffield, the local Council and theatre staff—who took the design of the whole building forward. I was heavily involved in this process and reduced my directing duties at the Playhouse, letting Wilfred Harrison and his assistant, Frank Hatherley, take up the slack.[67]

The first matter I took the lead on was the appointment of a lighting consultant for the new theatre. Having studied the thrust stages at Minneapolis and Stratford, Ontario I was aware of how radically different a space we would be working in. The thrust stage presented a daunting set of challenges—and opportunities—for a lighting designer. Although the Building Committee had already appointed Electrical Engineers, if we were to exploit the full potential of the thrust stage, then I felt we needed an expert to advise on lighting it.

My thoughts turned to Richard Pilbrow, a highly successful lighting designer who ran his own firm called Theatre Projects. Richard had previously worked with Michael Elliot at the experimental Manchester 69, Sir Laurence Olivier at Chichester and Tanya Moiseiwitsch at the Old Vic, and he was at the time a lighting consultant at the National Theatre. Richard has, of course,

---
[†] Antoine de Saint-Exupéry.
[67] Frank Hatherley joined the company in December 1966 on an ABC Television trainee director scholarship and the following year became a full-time Assistant Producer. Between *Oedipus* in April 1968 and the inevitable *Stirrings* revival that December, my father directed just one production at the Playhouse that year, *A Lily in Little India* with Barrie Smith in the lead role of Alvin.

since become one of the most successful lighting designers of the twentieth century.

Although I had not worked with Richard, I had seen his work at the National Theatre and at Drury Lane where he lit *Camelot*. I first met him after a production of *Mister* he had directed, with my wife Dorothy playing the role of Ella, and we discussed the challenge of lighting a production on the open stage. I felt he would be ideal to advise on lighting at the new theatre, so in February 1968, I arranged to meet him at the National Theatre. Richard expressed interest in being lighting consultant for the new theatre and introduced me to the latest in lighting technology, the Computer Memory Control (CMC) system.

Following our meeting, Richard drew up notes from our discussions which demonstrated his deep understanding of how to light the thrust stage and the technical requirements required to achieve this. He summarised his thoughts thus:

'An open stage production is three-dimensional, as opposed to a proscenium presentation where the action and the actor are viewed against a scenic background. One therefore relies on lighting, instead of scenery, to provide mood and atmosphere. The proximity of the spectator to the performer is one of the virtues of the open stage—and the better and more imaginatively lit the actor, the more effective the performance—and the more this form of theatre is exploited.

'On the open stage where an actor is visible to the audience from three sides, he has to be lit with a minimum of three lanterns. The actor must stand in a circle of light, in order to be isolated on the open stage which is one of the principal ways of achieving variety and dramatic effect in such a theatre. The smaller the circle of light in which the actor stands, the greater the isolation. The greater the number of lanterns that cover the stage, the smaller the circle of light thrown and the greater the dramatic effect.

'With these two factors in mind, open stage lighting demands three times the lamps used in a proscenium stage of equivalent size. The present Sheffield Playhouse proscenium has 72 lanterns. York—a more recent installation—100. The electrical consultants recommend for the new Playhouse, as an absolute minimum, 200 lanterns—probably a working minimum of 250. In practice it has been found impracticable for one operator to control more that 100 lanterns by manual control. Covent Garden Opera House has over 200 lanterns, which requires two electricians to set the cues and another to control each cue change. Moreover, there are three lighting consoles which take up three times the space required for the proposed CMC system.

'The CMC system magnetically records any setting of the 200 or more lanterns available and has a capacity of 250 cues. The alternative is for the electrician to write down the cues and set them manually as the production proceeds. The sum of £1,300 which this system costs would be an extravagance were it a sophistication;[68] in fact it is a practicable solution to a very complex question of lighting control. There is a further refinement, 'automatic programming', which requires a standard 8-hole computer tape machine, which will automatically make a permanent recording of any production. As it currently stands, to record a production permanently you have to write out cues by hand.'

Looking back many years later, lighting equipment has become much more sophisticated and automated. To suggest that recording the lighting design of a production was a matter of someone laboriously writing cues on a piece of paper would be regarded as laughable. But CMC was cutting-edge for the time and would be essential if we were to get the most out of the acting space we were creating.

I was determined to get Richard on board and immediately sought the approval of the Building Committee, which they gave readily after I secured a ringing endorsement from Sir Laurence Olivier, with whom Richard was working at the National Theatre. We had our man, but, as occurred with Tanya and Pat, it would take several months before his official appointment was made.

It was not until July 1968 that Renton Howard Wood decided to split the electrical work between Theatre Projects and the Electrical Engineers appointed the previous year, Dale & Benham.[69] Theatre Projects would specify the electrical, sound and communication equipment, provide the wiring diagrams and technical equipment. Dale & Benham would incorporate all of this into an engineering contract

---

[68] This is the equivalent of £20,000 in 2021.
[69] Dale & Benham acquired a new partner during the project, becoming Dale & Ewbank by the time the Crucible opened, and subsequently Dale & Goldfinger.

and supervise the installation on the advice of Theatre Projects. This seemed to me a great compromise, enabling me to bring on board a lighting designer whose experience was proven on the thrust stage.

Following their submission of the revised Schedule of Accommodation in March, one of the most important alterations the architects now made was how to fit the theatre building on the site. Originally the foyers and main theatre entrance were to be built on Norfolk Street facing north into the town. But at that time the area was very run down, with the backs of bombed-out buildings and the new Arundel Gate road under construction. So, instead, the architects swung the whole design around to face south so that the public areas, the main foyer and the bars afforded much larger and panoramic views across Sheaf Valley. They also re-orientated the auditorium so that its centre line bisected the site on a diagonal axis, increasing the available depth from 150 feet to 240 feet.

Pat Ide had been concerned that the public grill bar was too remote from the entrance foyer and now it was to be sited directly off the main entrance. There, it would be sure to attract more custom whilst not violating licensing laws (young people could take their seats without passing closely to areas serving alcohol). Thanks to these adjustments, the usable space in the foyers and circulation areas increased by a further 9,000 square feet—but so had the cost of the theatre, to an estimated £740,000.[70] Thinking back to the first impressions David and I had of the Guthrie Theater in Minneapolis and how cramped the whole front of house area had been, we felt that the architects' revised scheme was absolutely right.

For the design of the foyers and public areas, Nick Thompson worked closely with Pat, as he later explained:[71] 'Right at the start Pat said to me: "We don't want one of these bloody stockbroker-belt theatres. We're up North, we need plenty of brass and Indian restaurant wallpaper." So, we distinctly didn't go for a grand building; there was no monumental entrance. It wasn't a place you arrived at the front door and had to be allowed in—it was meant to be low-key, accessible and always open.

---

[70] In 2021 with would be the equivalent of £11.1 million.
[71] All quotes from Nick Thompson in this section come from Tedd George's interviews with him in October 2020 and early 2021.

'People were coming up from the train and bus station down in the valley, up an escalator and through a subway under Arundel Gate and the idea was that they should be able to drift in and out. Colin wanted it to be a thoroughfare and his view was that it didn't matter if people just came in to buy a newspaper or have a drink in the bar—one day they would buy a ticket for a show. That's why the paving in the terrazzo came about—we wanted an almost street surface, you didn't want to come in onto carpet. The carpet only went upstairs, the bottom level was hard.

'On the ground floor were the Green Room and the Rehearsal Room, which were semi-public spaces. There was a lot of work going on with children and they would hold events in the rehearsal room, entering through the foyer rather than the stage door. The Green Room enabled people to meet actors from that side of the building, or the management to come out into the foyers for meetings, because there weren't many offices.'

When it came to the foyers upstairs, the contrast with the austere interior of the auditorium was deliberate. Nick explains: 'When I began designing the foyers I thought of the Aldwych [Theatre in London]. They have that open circle above the entrance foyer with the ring around, where you can see everyone's faces. And I realised it was all about seeing and being seen. You need to build an audience before you let them into the auditorium. You've got to get their pulse up.

'I think it was Peter Rice, the engineer, who said we want the auditorium to be an object in its own right, we don't want it just to be a wall. So we pitched the design so that the audience entered two thirds of the way up the rake, which exposed the bottom of the shell to the foyers. What I wanted was a huge object that stood there like a sort of sanctum. You're going from the real world of the foyers—the people, the noise—into somewhere you don't know what's going to happen.

'But how do you get into that space? I thought back to my visit to the Tomb of Agamemnon [in Mycenae] and that amazing diminishing route in through the walls, and finally the door. And I realised I need to create something that is not just a door in a wall: it's a mighty entrance because you're going into a totally different, unknown, world. It's the world of make-believe, it's not reality in there. You're leaving one set

Left: Entrance to Agamemnon's Tomb, Mycenae; Right: Entrance to the Crucible auditorium in 1971

of senses behind and taking on a fresh lot. But getting those doors made was a nightmare. Because no one had any hinges for doors of this shape, scale and weight, so we had to design them ourselves.'

Nick wanted to have a lot of colour in the foyers and turned to his wife, Clare Ferraby, who was a textile designer. Taking his initial design for the doors, Clare developed a colour scheme that was both theatrical and practical. There would be a separate colour for each of the five entrances to the auditorium—blue, orange, red, purple, and green—with all signage and tickets marked in the same colours.[72] This avoided the need for graphics, which they both found distracting. But there was a problem with this approach, as Nick explains: 'There were very few materials available at that time. Paint manufacturers only made pillar box red, Thames green, cream, and various shades of mud and coffee—and that was about it. We had to get them to mix new colours for us—so it was quite an experimental period.'

Clare also designed the striking carpet in the foyer. The carpet, which was made by Brintons of Kidderminster, was in fact two

---

[72] Unfortunately, owing to budgetary constraints the Crucible was unable to produce coloured tickets during the opening season, which rather undermined this whole approach.

Clare Ferraby's original design for the upper foyer carpet

separate carpets of similar size and patterns, one with red, purple, and brown stripes, the other with red, brown, and purple stripes. These were stuck together and spread across the floor in a varied and uneven pattern.[73]

The architects also experimented with new materials for the finishing. Nick wanted polished concrete on the structural bridges around the foyer, but as this technology was still very new, Gleeson's contractor, Sean Fahy, experimented with varnishing plywood which gave the same effect. For the cladding of the building, the architects had wanted bronze, but this was far too expensive. Instead, they went to a local fibre plaster manufacturer—Hodkin & Jones of Dronfield—and experimented with moulds to create non-reflective penny bronze fibreglass panels.

The combination of these design elements created a spectacular variation of sightlines, colours, textures, and shapes as the audience

---

[73] Sadly, Nick and Clare's colour scheme did not survive various refurbishments of the Crucible, and today the only surviving fragment is the original sample in their possession. Nick later said: 'I find it very sad that most of the colour has been taken out of the building. I think the colour was fundamental to the design—because I loved the contrast of this rich vibrant foyer with the absolutely neutral auditorium'. Tedd George's interview with Nick Thompson, October 2020.

made their way up the stairs, through the foyers and towards the grand doors into the auditorium. The different levels, the steps and the sense of a constantly unfolding landscape as you moved towards a destination was, Nick later said, inspired by his love of Italian hill towns.

While Pat and the architects developed the foyers, I became personally involved in a second area of the theatre's design: the actors' dressing rooms. Shortly after we first heard we would have a new theatre, I had met with the Playhouse actors and discussed what sort of dressing rooms were needed in the new theatre. The least expected suggestion was that as many actors as possible should have a solo dressing room. 'A room to go mad in!' was the phrase Christopher Wilkinson used.

So, when we read in the architects' revised Schedule of Accommodation that there were to be twelve dressing rooms for three actors each and two for choruses of 15 each, we were disappointed. Although each room had basic amenities, the dimensions had not been outlined in detail and we felt that the architects had not considered the actors' inputs that I had passed to the Building Committee.

I called a meeting with the senior members of the Company and we marshalled our arguments. There were huge advantages to having solo dressing rooms, even if the size was moderate. In a solo dressing room an actor could make up, dress, shave or wash, write letters, even stretch out full length on the couch or on the floor. To prepare a characterisation, actors need to be away from distracting noise, and this didn't mean isolated in a public library but somewhere where the atmosphere of the production prevailed. It is also easier to learn lines if you can say them out loud, encouraging the physical as well as the mental memory.

Although the actors preferred solo dressing rooms, they also enjoyed visiting each other—the feeling backstage was one of community, not solitary confinement. They suggested giving the dressing rooms sliding doors which opened onto a furnished corridor, allowing actors to shut themselves off if they wished or join with other Company members socially. In order to create the space, the showers and lavatories would be communal and not in the solo dressing rooms. And one issue on which we all agreed: all the dressing rooms must have windows. After what David, Dr Young and I had seen at Stratford, Ontario and the Vivian Beaumont, we would not make the same mistake.

At a meeting in May 1968, the architects presented detailed plans of the new theatre foyers and dressing rooms. I raised the concerns of the actors and, there and then in ink, we radically altered the design. There would be six solo dressing rooms on the ground floor, with an office for the stage director and stage manager, and a further six solo dressing rooms on the first floor, next to two chorus dressing rooms. Communal showers would now be placed on the landing outside the dressing rooms to make room for the new design. The dressing rooms would be numbered A, B, C, and not in numerals that would have implied a hierarchy.

Years later, when my successor at the Crucible, Peter James, was being shown around the building, he was amazed by the dozen solo dressing rooms. 'You looked after your actors well, didn't you?' he remarked. In fact, they had looked after themselves; and the architects, I should add, had willingly gone along with our ideas. I believe those hours the architects had spent backstage at the old Playhouse during performance, as well as front of house, had helped them appreciate how apart from a commitment to the performance on stage, an actor must also prepare for this long before the curtain rises. Having somewhere to retreat during rehearsal or performance with an outside window and a couch on which to relax would greatly contribute to the Company's feel-good factor backstage.

Another issue we needed to address in these crucial months was fire regulations. When we had proposed building a thrust stage, we never envisaged the problems it would pose for the architects in terms of fire safety. It quickly became clear that the proscenium arch stage had dominated theatre building for so long less for artistic reasons and more for those relating to the safety of the audience.

In the early days, theatres were lit partially from the front of the stage by candles or wicks, floating in oil, which were trimmed and the oil replenished. In time electricity took over, but even when I began acting, the footlights were still referred to as 'the floats'. With this fire hazard, and with candelabras illuminating the stage, auditorium and backstage, it was no surprise when theatres burnt down. When the Drury Lane Theatre caught fire in February 1809, Richard Brinsley

Sheridan—who owned the theatre—was seen sipping a glass of wine as he nonchalantly watched his theatre in flames. Noticing his companions' looks of surprise, he remarked: 'A man may surely be allowed to take a glass of wine by his own fireside.'

Around this time, attempts were made to confine any fire to the stage where it began, rather than let it envelop the whole building, with the introduction of iron safety curtains. Fire safety tests were also introduced, but they tended to focus on the safety of the public rather than of the actors. In 1911, the Empire Palace Theatre in Edinburgh burnt down, but an audience of 3,000 got out of the building in just two and a half minutes while the orchestra belted out the national anthem. Tragically, ten actors and stage management died, caught behind the iron safety curtain.

It was with this history of theatre disasters that in early 1968 we sat down with Inspector Brannan of the Sheffield Fire Brigade to discuss the new theatre's construction. The challenge posed by the thrust stage was immediately apparent. To his first question: 'Where is your safety curtain?' We replied: 'We haven't got one!' To his second: 'So where are you placing the combustible material—the scenery, furniture, properties and so on?' We replied: 'In the middle of the audience!'

Fortunately, the meeting proved to be very positive and we were able to convince the authorities that our radical auditorium design required a different approach. Unlike a proscenium theatre, the stage would be in the middle, surrounded by the audience on three sides. There were would be little scenery and few props used on stage in order to allow adequate 'sighting' by the audience. This meant that the standard fire safety requirements of a proscenium wall, a safety curtain and stage sprinklers would not be practical.

A number of design possibilities were discussed, but it was accepted that some quantities of combustible props would have to be exposed on the auditorium side. Restricting the amount of material would be very difficult to control and would vary depending on the nature of each production. One way of mitigating these risks would be to ensure that the width of the emergency exits was generous. We also discussed the possibility of installing automatic sprinklers, but the low height of the roof above the stage would likely reduce their effectiveness.

We were able to resolve outstanding fire safety issues at a second meeting in June 1968 with the Divisional Officer of the Sheffield Fire Brigade. He agreed that access to the building was adequate and he accepted the principle of fire separation provided by the wall around the auditorium which acted as a fire break. It was agreed that the emergency exits and public lift doors should be wide enough to allow two wheelchairs to pass. Considering the widths of the main stairwell and the two subsidiary stairwells, the fire officer estimated that 1,200 people would be able to escape in three minutes. I believe that this is probably less time than it would take to clear a West End proscenium theatre auditorium of equal size.

At the start of July, we entered the final month of the design phase during which time the input of Pat Ide was again to prove invaluable. Pat had a very human and hands-on style based on his years working his way up in the profession, which differed from the 'academic' approach we had heard in some of our Committee meetings. On 17th July 1968, he produced a report for the Trustees on the theatre design that revealed his commercial and practical insights.

When it came to the building itself, Pat stressed the importance of making the public spaces inviting and spacious. He warned: 'We compete for the public's attention against cinemas and concert halls, restaurants and stores which are daily attaining higher standards of comfort. This is a major issue which must not be shirked.' The building should look attractive from the outside, especially 'the north-east front which is seen a very great deal by the lower part of the town looking up Norfolk Street and Arundel Gate'. He felt there should be a completely open feeling between the entrance foyer and the grill bar, which would reveal the entrance foyer and box office more clearly to passers-by.

The audience should feel comfortable in the auditorium. Seats should not be made of PVC, which is hot to sit on and apt to get tacky. Adequate ventilation was essential. David and I had sweltered in the auditorium of the Guthrie Theater during the interval and Pat warned: 'The foyers will be fullest (and smelliest) at Christmas. Can they be ventilated without creating a howling draught?'

Pat attached great importance to completing the Studio at the same time as the main theatre. He recommended making the Studio theatre the subject of a separate financial appeal, emphasising the children's theatre connection, for which special sources of money might be available. This suggestion would eventually lead us to the Gulbenkian Foundation.

But the key focus of Pat's report was acoustics, which Tanya had raised with me in her letter earlier that year. Regarding the auditorium, Pat warned that installing soundproof doors on the auditorium needed careful study. In another theatre he had seen such a door that was installed at a cost, he was told, of £5,000, but proved totally ineffective.[74] We also needed to consider how to keep the noise created by the ventilation system to a minimum, not only so as not to disturb the actors' speeches, but also to allow uninterrupted periods of silence on stage when the concentration of the audience is undisturbed. But he warned that acoustics in the Studio might be a more critical problem than in the main theatre.

In the public areas, Pat warned that there would be a great deal of traffic between the cellar, kitchen and the main foyer bar, and he suggested installing a service lift instead of a hoist and extending the internal communication system to the administrative staff. When it came to the lobbies between the foyer and the auditorium, Pat noted that it was impossible to introduce large numbers of people into the auditorium without some noise, which could disturb productions in the adjacent Studio Theatre. But he suggested that if the lobbies were large enough it would encourage people to use them as a waiting area rather than remaining in the foyer, somewhat reducing the noise.

On 31st July 1968, the cut-off point finally came at a meeting in London at the offices of the architects. There they presented us with the 'Final Design Scheme', a 29-page report with numerous designs and drawings which condensed all of our thinking and deliberations in the two years since Alderman Grace Tebbutt had first asked us: 'Where do you want your new theatre?'

Reading through this document more than fifty years later, I am struck by how central the architects made the thrust stage to their design. The shape of the auditorium was dictated by the central octagon of the stage, as they explained in their report: 'From studies of 180° seating patterns suitable for an open stage, an octagonal form

---

[74] This would be the equivalent of £75,000 in 2021.

developed which was to become the dominant motif of the design, giving unity to the complex forms resulting from the irregular shape of the site and the requirements of the brief. The building is low in proportion to its spread and the geometry deriving from the octagon is used consistently to give unity to the continuing elevations from every viewpoint.'

The theatre complex would sit at the centre of a new Civic Square, covering an area of 57,780 square feet. There would be three public entrances to the complex—the main entrance on the forecourt facing Tudor Square, a smaller one from Arundel Gate and a third for the Studio. This meant you could have just the Studio operating and close off the rest of the theatre if you wanted. The Norfolk Street side of the building would have the Stage Door, with a large reception area inside (no more hiding the stage doorman in a hole under the stairs), and the 'get-in' for deliveries into the loading bay.

Making the most of the site's position on a hill, the foyers would be glazed along their entire length, giving views over the Sheaf Valley

Front page of the Final Design Scheme with the 'Red Dot' in the middle

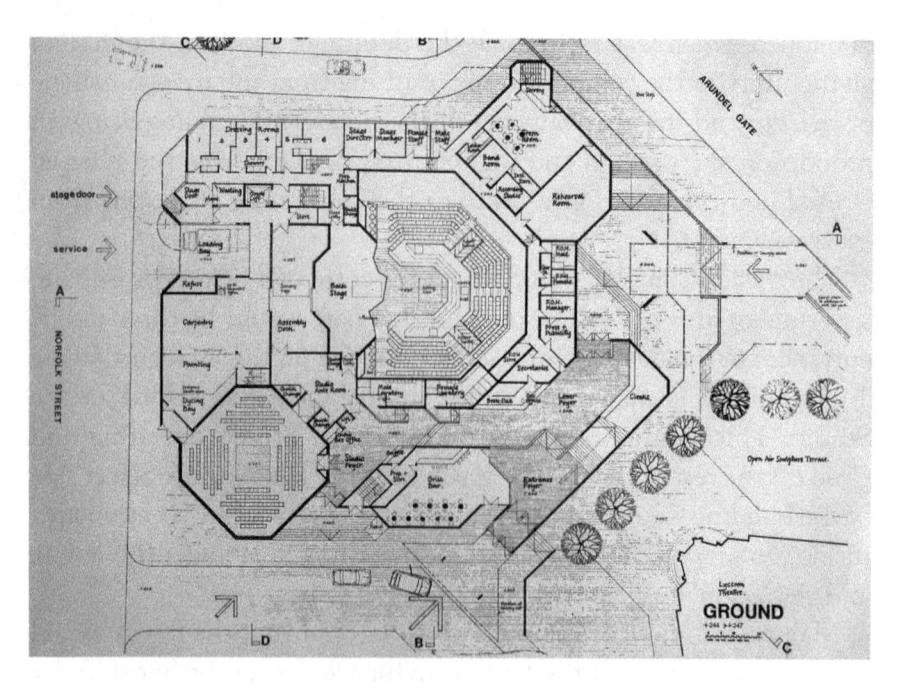

Plan of the ground floor of the new theatre (above) and the foyer level (below), with the main auditorium and Studio Theatre clearly visible. The funnel-shaped design for the main entrance (bottom middle) was later changed.

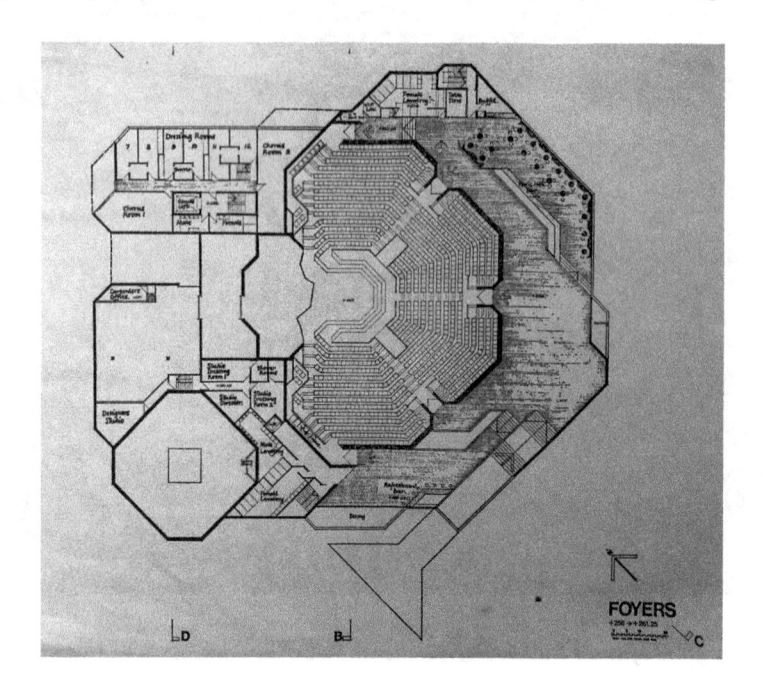

to Park Hill and Skye Edge. The entrance area and adjacent grill bar would be connected to the other public entrances of the lower foyer, which would act as an internal thoroughfare and contain the box office, kiosks, cloakrooms, exhibition area, and entrance to the Studio Theatre and buffet. The foyers could be divided up and used for receptions, poetry reading, and catering. The octagonal motif would be mirrored throughout the building in moulded fibreglass honeycomb shapes in the ceilings. (This concept was later abandoned when an architectural lighting designer was hired.)

The auditorium would be 120 feet wide and seat up to 1,000 people in a 180° arc, with the furthest seat 59 feet from the central point of the acting area.[75] The stage would be 18 feet wide and 28 feet long, with three steps down into a 4-foot-wide surrounding moat into which actors would enter via the vomitories. A range of octagons

Conceptual drawing of the foyer bar with panoramic views over Sheffield, by Architect Andrew Renton

---

[75] As part of the design process for the National Theatre, Theatre Projects conducted tests on a number of West End stages with actors, among them Sir Laurence Olivier himself. He concluded that no one could adequately watch him perform from more than 65 feet away. This became the benchmark for the furthest seat from the centre of the stage—six feet further than the Crucible.

Conceptual drawing of the auditorium, by Architect Andrew Renton

could be hung over the stage which could be raised or lowered to alter the volume above the stage from a maximum clear height of 23 feet down to 15 feet. With money lacking for the full Studio Theatre, the architects would provide the structural shell only, with heating, ventilation, and acoustic treatment.

Backstage facilities had been well thought out. Not only were there 12 solo and 2 chorus dressing rooms, but also a private staircase for actors to the stage, a Green Room, a canteen and a large rehearsal room. There were substantial backstage workshops (all soundproofed), storage areas and plenty of clearance for moving scenery. Reflecting the demands of the thrust stage, the carpentry workshop would be small (there would be no sets), but the wardrobe and props workshops would take up most of the lower level. Taking advantage of the fall in the ground to the north of the site, this level would be fully glazed. No more hiding our staff underground!

The architects' 'Final Design Scheme' also included detailed reports from experts on various technical aspects. Theatre Projects gave an overview of the lighting, sound and intercommunication requirements. Discussions over what this would involve would dominate the early part of 1969.

Acoustics expert Hugh Creighton provided a report on the acoustics. Given the theatre's location in the city centre, it was exposed to traffic noise on all sides, so he recommended the insulation of the roof be no less than 47dB. He noted that the shape of the theatre was naturally soundproof against echoes and other disturbances and he recommended we adopt the NR 20 standard, which was suitable for theatres seating more than 400 people.[76] The new Nottingham Playhouse had NR 25, which in his view was too high, resulting in obtrusive ventilation noise. Like Pat, he expected the acoustical challenges of the Studio to be more difficult and suggested NR 25 would be acceptable, but he warned that 'the regular shape of the room means that fairly extensive diffusing and absorbing treatment will be needed on the walls.'

Dale & Benham provided a report on the mechanical and electrical services. They would ensure the building had adequate ventilation using, where possible, natural ventilation through openings in the building cladding. Air conditioning for the auditorium would be essential, as the space was sealed from the outside, with high occupancy and a large amount of heat generated by the stage lighting. They outlined a complex air supply and exhaust system, plus ventilated areas around the building complex. They also recommended air conditioning for the rehearsal room, which would be sealed and likely to have high occupancy.

Ove Arup provided the structural report, which revealed some startling facts about what lay under the site of the new theatre. The theatre would sit upon a layer of Silkstone rock (a type of sandstone), but they noted: 'It is likely that coal has been worked in the Silkstone seam under the site. The recorded level of the seam is approximately 130 feet below the site surface.' This was not judged to offer any risk of subsidence to the site.[77] Ove Arup were also responsible for the

---

[76] The Noise Rating (NR) curve runs from 0 to 130, comparing the sound pressure level (dB) with the frequency (Hz). NR 20 is just audible, but it does not interfere with the hearing of speech.

[77] One anomaly that had not been picked up by the City Surveyor was discovered when builders broke ground on the new theatre the following year. They found a huge water tank dating back to the Second World War which was underneath the site of the main courtyard and part of the Studio. There wasn't time to cast concrete, so it was decided to fill it with rubble and construct a steel grillage over the hole. Unfortunately, Sheffield's steel industry was on strike at the time, so the steel had to be imported from Belgium! Tedd George's interview with Nick Thompson, October 2020.

superstructure and proposed that the roof of the auditorium should be of double-skin construction, containing the steel supporting structure within the sealed air space, which would reduce the weight.

And finally, Gleeds provided the quantity surveyors' report, which laid out the first detailed cost analysis of the project. This factored in expected inflation during the construction period and was based on the costs of the Nottingham Playhouse, which was viewed as a good benchmark, although that theatre did not have air-conditioning. Gleeds estimated a total construction cost of £660,000, which was £20,000 above the agreed budget.[78] This cost broke down into £560,000 for the theatre complex, including air conditioning of the auditorium, seating, stage lighting, stage and sound equipment, Studio and ancillaries; £80,000 for the fees and expenses of the architects, structural and services engineers and quantity surveyors; and £20,000 for loose furniture, furnishing and workshop machinery.

Gleeds put the £20,000 cost overrun down to the sophisticated services that were envisaged and recommended reducing the scope of these works if we wanted to get back to budget. Gleeds also warned of several costs that were not in the budget, including the demolition of existing buildings on the site, the construction of pavements and steps around the new buildings, furnishing for the grill bar and lighting, control and seating for the Studio. We were edging inexorably towards a total cost of £1 million for the entire theatre complex.

I remember that as Peter Howard shared this document with us, he said: 'The plans are now frozen, and no further alterations can be made without delaying the working drawings.' Although there were many more details to iron out, one sensed that the exploration phase was over. From now on, the architects would be hunched over their desks, and our enthusiastic dreams were to become cold, sober reality.

---

[78] In 2021 this would be the equivalent of being £300,000 over a £9.9 million budget.

CHAPTER TWELVE

Light is not so much something that reveals, as it is itself that revelation.†

That autumn, while the architects worked on the technical drawings, I visited Yugoslavia to study children's theatre. As Artistic Director of the Playhouse, I had been nurturing a connection with Eastern European theatre, supported by grants from the British Council. I made my first trip to Belgrade and Prague in May 1967, visiting the Boško Buha and Jiří Wolker children's theatres (as previously discussed). While in Belgrade I met the Yugoslav director, Arsenio Jovanovic, and invited him to direct a production at the Playhouse later that year. He duly came to Sheffield in October 1967 to direct Pirandello's *Six Characters in Search of an Author*.

In October 1968, I was invited back to Yugoslavia to continue my research on children's theatre. I saw performances of children's theatre in Ljubljana and Zagreb, and also visited the children's theatre in Celje, which, even though it was a small town, had a permanent Company of 20 actors. I spent my last three days in Belgrade where I saw several productions at the Boško Buha, including an adaptation by Arsenio Jovanovic of Alan Cullen's *John Willy and the Bee People*.[79] It was fascinating to reflect on the very different treatment of the Yugoslav production. The hero John Willy had become a heroine with the name Myra Frances, a former member of the Sheffield Company. The atmosphere, which had been in Sheffield jolly and colourful, had been transmuted to something mysterious and awe-inspiring. While in Belgrade, I also started planning for a production of *Romeo and Juliet* that I would direct at the Boško Buha the following April.

---

† American artist, James Turrell.
[79] This play was first performed at the Sheffield Playhouse in December 1966 and was so popular that a record was produced of songs from the show. A photo of the recording is in the plates section.

On my return to Sheffield, I started rehearsing the revival of *Stirrings* for that December and resumed my focus on the theatre project. With the basic design locked down, the next major decision concerned the material used for the main outer structure. The architects suggested forticrete building blocks. Forticrete, which could be dense or lightweight, had been used since the 1920s, mainly for domestic buildings and with different textured surfaces. Nick Thompson had seen forticrete used throughout the home of architect Sir Colin St John Wilson in Cambridge and he was excited by its potential.

Pat Ide had also seen buildings using forticrete and found it suited them admirably, but he feared that using this material on a large scale would give the building a mechanical feel. In a report to the Trustees, he concluded: 'I am against the use of the blocks because I feel they are too geometrical and insufficiently brutal, too light in colour, and do not express to me in any way the feeling of Sheffield.'

The look of the new theatre was critical, as it would stand opposite the Lyceum—and an impressive building it is. The designer was W G R Sprague, who trained under Frank Matcham, the leading theatre designer of the time, and went on to surpass his mentor. Among the London theatres Sprague designed were the Aldwych, the Gielgud, the New Ambassadors, the Noel Coward, the Novello, St Martin's and Wyndham's. The Lyceum in Sheffield, which he completed in 1897, was the only surviving Sprague design outside London.

One can appreciate the architects wanting to make a different statement with our new theatre, and one of the late 20th Century rather than harking tamely back to Victorian tradition. Pat's anti-forticrete views were not shared by others on the Building Committee, including myself. It was decided that the best way of making a decision on this matter was to have a wall built on the theatre site—half in brick and half in forticrete, so that we could compare the two materials.

On 26th December 1968, the Committee visited the site; the wall standing alone and isolated appeared quite forlorn and vulnerable. It was clear that the bricks looked far less impressive than the forticrete blocks, and someone commented that the architects had deliberately chosen rather 'tired' bricks. But at the Committee meeting which followed, it was decided to opt for forticrete masonry blocks for the external walls and some of the internal walls. This proved a sound choice. After the theatre opened, it won the British Architects award for Best New Building in Yorkshire and a certificate of high commendation from the Concrete Society.[80]

In January 1969, Richard Pilbrow was finally appointed as lighting consultant—having been informally consulting on the project for almost a year. As things turned out, his presence and advice were to prove invaluable in two meetings that month. At the first, Mr Johnson, Chairman of the Building Committee, wanted to explore ways of reducing costs without compromising the equipping of the theatre. Given the high cost of the CMC lighting control system, he suggested it might be hired rather than purchased. Richard thought this unlikely but promised to investigate. Mr Johnson also suggested hiring the lamps. Richard said this was short-sighted, as the cost of buying them would be the same as hiring them for 15 weeks. Moreover, having a large number of lamps allowed you to set more than one production at once and obviated the need to re-focus lamps between shows. In this way, 150 dimmers could serve far more than that number of lamps. Mr Johnson was persuaded and agreed that the installation should take the maximum number of lamps: 320.

When it came to lighting the foyers, Richard was not confident there was enough in the budget to do this properly. Pat stressed the importance of the foyer lighting; if they were under-lit, it could be disastrous. Richard promised to look into it and later came back with the recommendation that we hire Tony Corbett, whom he had appointed MD of a subsidiary in Theatre Projects called Light Limited. Using great ingenuity and on a tight budget, Tony would do a magnificent job on the foyer lighting and would be the first architectural lighting designer ever hired by a UK theatre. Regarding lighting of the auditorium, in Richard's view the best solution would be a grid and he undertook to produce a design for discussion with the architects and the committee.

---

[80] The forticrete used for the fabric of the building was truly built to last. When I was given a tour of the Crucible by the Operations Manager, John Bates, he showed me a cut-through of a floor slab which is reinforced in several layers. So resilient has this engineering proved that builders had great difficulty in demolishing the south wall to extend the foyer area during the refurbishment of 2007-10. Tedd George's interview with John Bates, June 2021.

At a second meeting a fortnight later, we discussed the mechanical and electrical services installation and the stage lighting equipment. Richard had contacted the two firms making the CMC lighting control system, Strand and Thorn, but neither were prepared to hire out this equipment which was experimental at the time. In the end Richard opted to purchase the Thorn Q-File system which had been designed for the BBC colour TV studios then being built and had been adapted for theatrical usage. The system could handle up to 1,000 channels from a single console, with 140 dimmer channels and the ability to memorise the intensity for each circuit of 100 different lighting cues.[81]

Richard also presented Theatre Projects' innovative design for lighting bridges over the stage. In those days, proscenium theatres had three rows of concentric rings of lighting bridges running round the auditorium. But with a thrust stage you needed to be able to light actors from multiple directions at once. It was while working on Chichester's thrust stage that Richard had developed the concept of three-dimensional lighting, with the actor on stage lit from at least

Theatre Project's innovative lighting rig in action, 1971

---
[81] Richard Pilbrow, A *Theatre Project*, PLASA Media, 2011, p.120.

four angles. As he later described it: 'The light creates the air the actor is breathing.'[82]

This resulted in Richard's 'inverted egg crate' lighting and suspension rig design which has become standard for thrust stages. Lighting would come from four intersecting lighting bridges which followed the shape of the stage and could be directed at 45, 135, 225 and 315 degrees to the centre line of the stage. This would enable low frontal lighting, down, side and back lighting, supplemented by lighting from the grid over the stage. There would also be four sets of counterweights, each of which operated a spotlight. The bridges would also a serve an acoustic purpose, by giving relatively early reflections from the stage down into the audience.

Theatre Projects also innovated when it came to the new theatre's sound and communications. The sound control room would have large windows that opened completely so that the operator could hear what was happening in the auditorium, something that was not standard practice at the time. More importantly, the sound engineer would be a trained professional and not, as was often the case back then, an Assistant Stage Manager (ASM) operating a tape recorder backstage. Our new auditorium would need surround speakers, faders, sound effects, and microphones. This would require a new breed of theatre professional—the Sound Designer—and we were fortunate to hire the first person to use such a title in the UK: David Collison.

David had worked with Michael Elliot and Tyrone Guthrie at the Old Vic and had recently designed the sound and communication system for the Thorndike Leatherhead on a budget of just £5,000.[83] As there were no affordable mixing desks available on the market, David worked with Theatre Projects to design a bespoke mixer for our new theatre. This would be able to mix eight microphone channels and tape machines through four input channels, a huge step up from the manual faders used at the time. There would also be a speaker above the stage, so that actors could be read lines if they dried on stage (a prompter could hardly huddle at the side of a thrust stage),

---

[82] Tedd George's interview with Richard Pilbrow, October 2020.
[83] This was around 1% of the theatre's total budget and would be worth the equivalent of £71,000 in 2021. Since then, sound budgets have soared and today they are typically bigger than lighting budgets, at over £1 million for a typical West End show.

(Left) Sound control desk designed for the Crucible Theatre, 1971; (Right) Q-File lighting control desk, 1970s

and a microphone in the sound control room so that the operator could talk directly to the director and actors during rehearsals.[84]

The next issue that needed deciding was seat prices in the new theatre. Having seen performances on proscenium and thrust stages, we adopted a simple principle: in a proscenium theatre, those sitting on the sides of the auditorium have an inferior view of the same picture, whereas in an open stage theatre everyone sitting around the action has a different and equally valid view of the performance. The open stage emphasises the awareness of the spectator not only to the performance but also to the reaction of the other members of the audience. In theory, the most satisfying seats are those on the side (but not acutely so), where you receive the performance, the architectural background and a view of the other spectators in equal proportion.

Taking these arguments into consideration, and based on the spectator's distance from the actor, we judged that the best seats were between a quarter to half-way back from the stage. Consequently, the moderately priced seats would be at the front, the expensive seats five or six rows back, and the cheapest right at the back. This would apply all the way around the auditorium. However, it was vital that the designer, the actors, and the director laid down the rule that the performance must be shared all around the auditorium. Any suggestion that the best seats were in the front or central rows negated this.

When as the Artistic Director I was later asked where I liked to sit in the auditorium, I admitted that I preferred the side of the auditorium

---

[84] David Collison, *The Sound of Theatre*, Entertainment Technology Press, 2020.

just beyond either vomitory. I explained my reasoning thus: 'If the particular quality of the open stage is to see the action against both a visual background and other spectators, rather than to see it against scenery as if one were peeping through a keyhole, the side seats seem an obvious choice. Sitting on the side usefully reminds one that the ritual of theatre is not to be confused with the chaos of everyday living.

'Seeing the action against a bank of spectators at first may appear to make it difficult to accept the action and become involved in it. As the director of two of the opening productions, and knowing each line before it came up, I never suspected that I would be "taken in" by a performance any more than I used to be sitting in front of my own productions at the old Playhouse. However, more than once, watching a Crucible performance from the side, I suddenly found myself totally involved in what was going on and only as the house lights came up and the applause roused me from my glimpse through the theatre's 'magic casement', was I aware that the indeterminate background which had been a wall of a house to me, was, in fact, a sea of faces. One had been focusing on the action and instead of an inanimate blur of painted canvas and wood in the background, there had been a living mass of humanity. Sitting immediately in front of the action, one can miss this.'

But I was realistic that this would be a difficult change for many theatregoers to accept: 'Like all artistic theories, those working in the theatre and the audiences attending the productions will confirm its validity or prove it academic speculation. I feel strongly that we should give the conception behind the design of the open stage—that the seats are equally satisfying all the way round the auditorium—an opportunity to prove itself. It is certainly going to take time before the audience, as much as the performer, get used to the auditorium.'

I got to test out this theory after the Crucible opened when we invited 30 supporters to watch a practical demonstration of the new open stage one Sunday evening. Two actors performed the same scene from *Mister* while, each time, the supporters shifted to a different part of the auditorium to watch. After three rotations I asked the spectators for their views and the first remark said it all: 'I saw three plays!' I would describe the experience as 'three productions of the same play', and all equally valid.

Another issue that was decided during this period was the catering brief. In his report in July 1968, Pat Ide had called on the Trustees to consider the catering facilities, and by early 1969 we had outlined a catering plan for the new theatre. It would be a considerable step up from the meagre and cramped facilities at the Playhouse. There would be a fully licensed grill bar on the ground floor, the Park Hill Buffet on the first floor of the foyer serving light refreshments, and the fully-licensed Park Hill Bar serving alcohol and cold shelves. Backstage, there would be a Green Room serving light refreshments all day as well as substantial meals at midday and between rehearsals and the evening performance.

There was some debate over whether the theatre should undertake all the catering itself or sub-contract it to an external service provider. The advantage of the latter approach is that they would find the staff, supply reliefs for special occasions and do all the accounting. Bass Charrington was approached, as were two local firms—Marsden's and Gardner Merchant Caterers. But, after much discussion, it was agreed that the advantages of keeping the catering in-house outweighed those of outsourcing it. The Playhouse Company Manager, Arnold Elliman, had wide experience in catering and was keen to take on that responsibility.[85]

In late July 1969, the first serious discussions on fundraising were held by the Trustees. From the theatre's inception, it had been envisaged that a large proportion of the cost would be raised by public appeal, and as the budget had steadily risen to £910,000 by that point, this meant we needed to raise £260,000 from the public. So a Fundraising Committee was formed, comprising myself, David Brayshaw, Pat Ide, Peter Bennett-Keenan (a local businessman), Arnold Elliman (Company Manager) and Hilary Young (the Publicity Officer).

Our first decision was to hold a fundraising lunch at the Top Rank Suite on 31st October 1969.[86] The 'come hither' for the occasion

---

[85] In the end, the Crucible was forced to outsource the catering to Gardner Merchant for the first year of the theatre's operation, when staff were too busy adapting to the new building to run the catering. This resulted in a loss of £3,609 during the first six months, but as the Crucible bar grew in popularity, catering started to run at a healthy profit, and in 1973 the theatre took it back under its own management.

[86] The Top Rank was a live music venue located just below the site of the new theatre. Opened in 1967, it has been described as 'a brutalist gem' and was a fitting venue from which to contemplate the modern theatre set to rise on the hill above it. It is now part of the O2 Academy network.

Finance
Current estimated cost of the project-site included–is £910,000; of which £650,000 will be contributed by Sheffield Corporation and the Arts Council, reducing the sum the Trust needs to raise by public subscription to just £260,000.

would be the presence of stage and television personalities, preferably known names associated with the Playhouse. Among those suggested were Patrick McGoohan, Margaret Tyzack, Peter Barkworth, Paul Eddington, Keith Barron, Alan MacNaughtan, and Angela Thorne. Pat Ide suggested that Geoffrey Ost be co-opted onto the Committee in order to 'exploit the sentimental angle all stops out'. Pat and Geoff even persuaded the landlord of a local pub to start a pillar of pennies to which they contributed the first 240.

As the summer approached, we felt we were ready to face the public, and on 3rd June 1969 Tony Hampton chaired the first press conference of the New Sheffield Theatre Trust. To a gathering of over 50 press and TV journalists, Anthony described how our original concept had evolved into a cultural and social centre which would be in constant use by the community. A pamphlet detailing the project was distributed, including the architects' design, models of the new theatre and information about the fundraising appeal (the back cover is reproduced above).

The press was delighted, and the next day the front page of the *Morning Telegraph* carried an artist's image of the new theatre and an imagined aerial view. The evening edition of *The Star* led with the

Architects' model of the new theatre in cherry wood

headline 'City Super Theatre'.[87] The theatre profession's newspaper *The Stage* lauded what it described as 'One of the world's finest stages in Sheffield' which it believed would 'place the city in the very forefront of theatrical endeavour'.[88]

The *Morning Telegraph* critic, Paul Allen, wrote an article highlighting the ground-breaking nature of the new theatre under the headline 'Unique Theatre for Sheffield by 1971'. He wrote: 'It will be the first-full scale theatre in this country committed to the concept of a deep thrust or promontory stage, with the audience seated on three sides. This arrangement means that, even in a full house, no-one will be more than 59 feet or 14 rows from the actors. Apart from the stage, the theatre is the first in the country to be fully air-conditioned and will far outstrip similar ones—such as the Chichester Festival Theatre—in its additional facilities, for audience and company.

---

[87] Tedd's note: *The Sheffield Star* is known in its mother city as *The Star* (which is how its name appears on the front page), so I have used *The Star* throughout this book.
[88] *The Stage*, 12 June 1969.

'Although it would be technically possible to stage opera and ballet, this is unlikely to happen in the event, but fears that other more traditional forms of drama might be shut out by the auditorium, a marriage of the Greek and Elizabethan stages, were allayed by Mr. Antony Hampton. Although farce and drawing room comedy might be more difficult than large-scale productions of Shakespeare, he was sure they could be done with maximum effect.

'Mr George held out hopes of visits from the National Theatre, and possibly exchange productions with Stratford, Chichester and other theatres. He also offered a concept of a theatre in almost continuous 24-hour use, with a children's show in the morning and psychedelic extravaganzas late at night to complement normal productions in the two auditoria during the day.'

The *Morning Telegraph* also ran an editorial that day entitled 'Curtain Call' which lauded the 'proud and brave plans' to build the new theatre in Sheffield. 'Proud, because the concept of the theatre will break new ground in design. And brave because courage is undoubtedly needed to launch such a magnificent project during a period of economic squeeze. There are plenty of good reasons, however, why the new theatre is unquestionably worthwhile and deserving general support. Certainly, the project will need the widest financial backing if is to achieve its public subscription target of £260,000.[89] Let us all hope this is attained.'[90]

In support of our endeavour, the *Morning Telegraph* launched a competition to come up with a name for the new theatre. This would provoke a deluge of suggestions from its readers—some brilliant, others tongue-in-cheek. But it would be more than a year before the Trust finally settled on our new theatre's name (about which more later).

Under the heading 'Public Patronage', *The Sun* also pledged its support to the new theatre: 'For the first time, [there will be] a reason for people from the great outside world to come to Sheffield for their entertainment and their cultural experience. This alone could transform the image of Sheffield—inward looking, England's biggest village—and not before time. It would ultimately help to increase the trade and commerce that passes through the city. But perhaps more

---

[89] This would be the equivalent of £3.7 million in 2021.
[90] *Morning Telegraph*, 4 June 1969.

importantly it will improve the quality of life for the people who live here and round about.'[91]

The positive and supportive response of the press to their first sight of the plans for the new theatre is worth recording, given what happened later. There was clear excitement at such a prestigious project for Sheffield, tinged perhaps with underlying resentment that such a formidable industrious town should be relegated to 'England's biggest village'. However, it only needed a small and turbulent minority to cast doubts on the adventurous design of the new theatre for the press to smell profitable copy.

---

[91] *The Sun*, 4 June 1969.

Part IV

The Three Knights

CHAPTER THIRTEEN

*Sound all the lofty instruments of war,
And by that music let us all embrace...*†

Hotspur's battle cry from *Henry IV* might seem out of place in Sheffield in the summer of 1969. But those of us involved in building the new theatre would feel the need to embrace each other as we were confronted by an enemy not wielding swords and lances, but columns of print in the local press. Until the announcement that Sheffield was to have a new thrust stage theatre, the provincial press had reserved their more sensational headlines for the activities of the Nottingham Playhouse. But once the ambition of the Sheffield project became public knowledge, it aroused opposition.

What we did not realise was that our press conference would unleash a bitter debate in the press, pitting the *Morning Telegraph* in our corner against *The Star* in the opposition's, while other newspapers, local and national, sniped from the sidelines. It would spark one of the richest theatrical debates in my career, as the cream of contemporary acting, directing and playwrighting talent argued the case for and against the thrust stage. The controversy would force us to confront the kind of beast we had decided to build in Sheffield and reaffirm our belief in the theatrical space we wanted to create.

The first serious salvo was fired by Mr L W Cotton, a keen theatregoer from Bakewell. Writing in *The Star* under the headline 'A Case of Stage Fright', Mr Cotton laid into the new theatre's design. While broadly supporting what he described as a 'desirable but controversial project', he argued that Sheffield's new theatre should be able to present a wide variety of performing arts and that this could not be achieved by the 'deep thrust stage'. Mr Cotton bolstered his argument by quoting from *Effective Theatre* by Professor John Russell

---

† William Shakespeare, *Henry IV, Part I*, Act V, Scene 2.

Brown of Birmingham University, who stated that on a thrust stage 'the actors become moving statues viewed from almost all sides and isolated from the setting.' This, of course, is exactly what a thrust stage is all about. There can be a scenic contribution to the production, but the audience's involvement relates primarily to the vitality of the performers on stage.

Then Mr Cotton played his trump card, and one has to admire his audacity, by writing to Sir Laurence Olivier to get his views. I don't think Mr Cotton knew about the difficulties Sir Laurence had had during the early days of the Chichester Festival Theatre, but the knight rose strongly to the defence of the open stage.

Sir Laurence wrote: 'I am much exercised by your letter and have been for some years now upon the subject. I think on the whole that you are wrong and the truth is that absolutely any kind of drama can be managed on the open stage. Of all the many genres which it concerns I would say, and I hope not sweepingly, that it is least contributory to quick-laugh comedy on account of the difficulties of multi-direction, and literary plays of the more discursive type (Shaw), though we must admit that St Joan was immensely successful at Chichester, and it seems that most comedy played nowadays at Chichester goes every bit as well in most other theatres.

'I don't know whether or not you have seen the designs for the new National Theatre, but therein I believe the audience/actor relationship to have achieved its most perfect design in an open stage theatre. The audience seem to take hold of the stage like a pair of pincers and yet do not seem to be blowing a draught from the port or the starboard quarters. I find as an actor that more than a quarter circle is a wee bit disconcerting, a full circle is a simpler exercise (than the 'all but' that is). If I were you, I should snaffle at any theatre in Sheffield rather than none. A theatre in a town is, after all, the primary outward and visible sign of an inward and possible culture.'[92]

David Brayshaw—who would become the new theatre's administrator—responded to Mr Cotton's article in a letter to *The Star*. He noted that if one was to admit that the thrust stage had limitations, then one should also admit that so did the proscenium stage. 'We are

---

[92] *The Star*, June 1969.

building a theatre for the future, and the changes taking place in human relationships, means of communication and social habits too numerous to mention, lead us to believe that the open stage type of theatre is the theatre of the future. I admit that some plays written in the first part of the 20th century will need adapting to the new stage, but the writers for television could respond to the challenge of a different space, and actors and directors are learning new techniques inspired by a more exciting relationship with the audience.'[93]

Mr Cotton responded more than once in the press, but always covering the same ground. He brandished the name of Sir Laurence Olivier and twisted the meaning of the knight's statement that 'any kind of drama can be managed on an open stage' to exclude what Mr Cotton termed the 'deep thrust stage' of Sheffield, a more frightening, sexually-provocative description for the uninitiated.

Dr Gerard Young, Chairman of the Building Committee, then entered the fray with a professional contribution to the *Morning Telegraph* on 29th August, based on his work as a supervisor of the design and construction of new buildings at the University. As his experience was not purely theatre-based, it was all the more telling.

'Sir, the camel has been described as a beast of burden invented by a committee; yet it works, economically, and endures. I hope the new Sheffield theatre will be just as satisfactory, but more pleasing to the eye. As a layman, may I dispel some anxieties aroused by the welcome debate by experts to whom you have opened your columns and add some inside information. There are six main elements to accomplish in any new building—the purpose, the timing, the finance, the site, the design, the construction. To neglect any one of these will fail the whole.

'A decade ago, the University wanted an all-purpose theatre—but successive Committees in four years recast the functional requirements so often that the grant which had been earmarked by the University Grants Committee for this project was withdrawn and spent elsewhere. My first task as a Trustee of the new theatre project was to collect the many ideas for it that had been independently noted by Sheffield's hard-working enthusiasts and professionals at the

---

[93] *The Star*, June 1969.

Playhouse and to assemble those with other technical information in a draft brief.

'The completed design has gone through many phases of evolution; but always related to one focal point in the centre of the stage, around which everything else has, literally at different moments, revolved. Any artistic production must evoke varying personal judgements of its value. El Greco was deemed obscene by his contemporaries; Shakespeare was not regarded with much enthusiasm in his day. Even those of us who enjoyed *Punch* before the war will admit that Bernard Partridge's cartoons would seem dull in 1969. Tastes are naturally various, and they change. But to our own and the next generation or two of theatregoers dwelling in a very wide area within and around this city, I believe that the New Sheffield Theatre will be a centre of great interest, attraction, and enjoyment.'

Who next joined the debate but Guthrie himself? In July 1969—one month after our press conference—we opened Brecht's *Caucasian Chalk Circle* with Tanya Moiseiwitsch designing. It was our first production together and Tanya had never worked on Brecht before

Scene from The Caucasian Chalk Circle *at the Sheffield Playhouse, July 1969, with Julian Forbes, Wilfred Harrison and Michael St John*

(and took some time to convince), but the influence of her work with Guthrie was everywhere, with the actors using masks and boots with lifts. The Governor, who represented inhuman authority, was an eleven-foot-tall figure played by three actors, one for the body and one for each arm. Those in or with power tended to be masked, but not Grusha (played by my wife, Dorothy Vernon) and the compassionate peasantry. Needless to say, Tanya's costumes and properties had the style and authority of a great designer. Guthrie came to see the opening night and approved without being pontifical in any way.

While in Sheffield, Guthrie was interviewed by the press on the qualities of the open stage and came out strongly in its defence: 'The theatre no longer treats the audience as if they had a mental age of

Tanya (right) and Elaine Garrard (left) working on costumes for The Caucasian Chalk Circle *at the Playhouse, June 1969*

eight and expects them to believe that what is going on stage is really happening. With one or two exceptions, anything that can be done on a proscenium stage can be done as well or better on an open stage. Shakespeare and the Greek tragedians wrote for this type of theatre, and modern playwrights are moving more and more towards the freedom of time and place which cinema and television have taught people to expect.'[94]

One month later, on 30th August 1969, I gave my own views on the thrust stage as the new theatre's future Artistic Director. The *Morning Telegraph* gave me a half-page spread—'Colin George Takes the Stage'—with Paul Allen interviewing. I was determined to get across that the thrust stage design was a conscious choice, not an accident. 'Theatre reacts to life around it as do all the arts, and as painting was influenced by the discovery of photography, so theatre has reacted to television and the cinema. It possesses a quality they lack—personal contact between actor and audience. It is three-dimensional in a way the others can never be. The audience sitting on three sides are aware both of the performance and the other spectators enjoying and being moved by it. A shared experience like being in a football crowd or at a revivalist church meeting.'

I also wanted to dispel the notion that this was an elitist project. 'The open stage is not the choice of an "intellectual coterie" as has been said. Our theatre design owes much to the Greek and Elizabethan theatre; even the Victorian Music Hall was not simply action at one end and the audience at the other. The audiences David Brayshaw and I saw in America were anything but a coterie of earnest long-haired students and long-faced professors. And writers now attracted by films and TV may well respond to the open stage as a springboard for their imagination'.

I disagreed with Paul's suggestion that a 1,000-seat capacity was too big: 'Ours is probably the smallest theatre of its type in the world. None of the audience will be more than 59 feet from the centre of the stage. Yet a success playing to 1,000 people will obviously bring you more money than a 750-seat proscenium house. Over a year's season this can make a big difference'.

---

[94] *Morning Telegraph*, July 1969.

During the interview we discussed how the thrust stage would provide a very different type of theatrical experience. 'All types of theatre have their limitations, and the proscenium theatre is probably the most limited of all. The interesting thing about the last decade has been the way directors have been trying to get over those disadvantages. The idea that spectacle must necessarily be paint and canvas is a mistake. To my mind the biggest spectacle around here is the Lord Mayor's Show. For that kind of pageantry our stage is a wonderful arena.'

The acting would be different too. 'The open stage encourages the actors to play to one another and off one another to the audience. It's difficult to "ham" on an open stage. The soliloquy reached its peak with Shakespeare, who wrote for an open stage. It will be easier for the actor to be heard which is essential and will be possible to hold interest without gambolling about the stage'.

To Paul's question of why we didn't choose an adaptable stage, I replied that we could have, if we were prepared to spend £8 million! But everyone we had met in America and Canada had advised us against it. The Vivian Beaumont Theater in New York only used the open stage once for its first production and then reverted to the proscenium version for the next four years. Directors were just not used to an open stage and played it safe.

Paul's final question of whether the new theatre would work prompted a bullish response from me: 'This is commercial theatre at its best and a direct answer to the challenge of colour television. I think many of the fears about the theatre are natural, but I am confident they will evaporate when people actually sit in front of an open-stage performance. For example: at the Theatre in the Round in Stoke-on-Trent, someone in the audience once told the director Peter Cheeseman how much he liked the light shining through a window in one production. Being in the round there was a light but of course there was no window. What people can imagine is much more powerful than anything you can show them.'

In the same edition was an interview with the architect of the new National Theatre, Denys Lasdun, who had been on our shortlist. His remarks—free of local passions, as it were—made great sense to me. Asked about the pros and cons of different types of stages, he replied: 'Forget the word open, thrust or proscenium. There are some types of play where the relationship between the actors and the audience is one of confrontation. Certain plays of the past and many plays of the future will still want this quality. A proscenium stage means you look directly at the action and the action looks directly at you. There are other sorts of productions where you want the feeling of being in one room with the actors, embraced by the action. The boundaries between these two are not hard and fast. Some plays can be done one way or another, some plays absolutely can't. I think to attempt to arrive at a perfect solution is a contradiction in terms.'

Mr Cotton penned a response to my interview which was published in the *Morning Telegraph* in September, mostly covering old ground. But one remark he made—that 'one would have liked to have had the opportunity for more public discussion' about the design—galvanised the Trust into action. It was decided that before the fundraising event in late October we would hold an open forum at the Playhouse to outline in detail the design and plans for those interested and to seek their feedback.

Shortly afterwards, a new opponent drew his sword and entered the fray. This was L. du Garde Peach. Born in Sheffield in 1890, he was a successful writer of children's books and between the wars was a prolific writer for the stage, radio and film. Many of his plays had been performed at the Sheffield Playhouse. He founded an amateur group close to his home in Derbyshire and built a theatre there, where I saw an impressive amateur production of *Macbeth* he had directed. He resigned from the Sheffield Playhouse Board shortly after I arrived in 1962, sensing that the theatre he knew and had supported was going to change, as indeed it did.

Mr du Garde Peach wrote to the *Morning Telegraph* with great panache: 'As an ex-member of the Board of Management of the Sheffield Repertory Theatre, I read with much disquiet the article "Colin George takes the Stage". I noted with interest and dismay that on an expensive and, to my mind, entirely unnecessary visit to America, Mr. David Brayshaw and Mr. Colin George talked with, I quote, "designers, directors, and actors, administrators, and members of theatre boards, both lay and expert". A number of well-known names were dropped, including Tyrone Guthrie and Tanya Moiseiwitsch; even lighting and acoustic experts are included. Apparently, these gentlemen did not consider it either necessary or desirable to waste any time talking to a dramatist; it would appear that in their view the opinion of the "onlie begetter" of the play is unimportant.

'This attitude might be variously attributed to lack of interest, lack of imagination, lack of intelligence, or sheer impertinence. What they do not appear to realise is that a dramatist writes his plays with a particular stage in mind, and he may be presumed to know what he wants. To produce it on any other type of stage is an assumption of knowledge which the designer, director, lighting expert, and the rest

L. du Garde Peach, 1960s

of the journeymen involved in a production, cannot possess; hence impertinence.

'Mr Brayshaw would, I hope, shudder if he were offered hock in a burgundy bottle, but he does not apparently mind seeing a Somerset Maugham play on the stage favoured by Aristophanes. Actually, Colin George supplies the evidence in support of this view when he says later in the interview, that Shakespeare wrote specifically for an open stage. Of course he did, but Noel Coward did not.

'It is charitable to attribute the attitude of the Board of Management of the Sheffield Repertory Theatre to a combination of woolly-mindedness and an inability to distinguish between a passing fashion and eternal realities.

'The proscenium or aptly-named picture frame stage is designed to present a picture, and the picture is important. The dramatist counts on it and relies on it to establish an atmosphere as well as to localise the action. Shakespeare did not. He relied on verbal suggestion and noises off, as did those of us who wrote hundreds of plays for sound radio before the advent of television. The sound radio play is still with us side by side with television, but the technique is different.

'I have written successful plays for every known medium of dramatic projection, from open air pageants to plays for puppets and I may be presumed to know what I am talking about. Where the visual impact is important, the dramatist must be able to rely on the producer to supply it, otherwise I hope the day will come when authors will refuse permission to people like Colin George to produce their plays on the wrong type of stage. And let him not forget that they would be within their legal rights, and there would be nothing he could do about it.

'The Board of Management of the Sheffield Repertory theatre may well live, some of them, to see their expensive open stage hopelessly outdated as well as black-listed by all reputable dramatists. They have been warned.'

I re-read this with great admiration for Mr du Garde Peach's commitment and turn of phrase. But his warning that no reputable dramatist would agree to have his play performed at the theatre he criticised, has become, to use his own phrase, 'hopelessly outdated'. In 2011, I saw an excellent production of *Racing Demon* on the open stage at the Crucible and talked afterwards with the reputable modern dramatist who was very appreciative of the production and the stage—David Hare.

By now, our allies were starting to emerge in the press, and Paul Allen from the *Morning Telegraph* led the way with an article entitled 'Playwrights greet open stage' which rebuffed Mr du Garde Peach's warnings. Paul had approached several playwrights for their views and cheekily wrote—'preliminary inquiries indicate that many of our current dramatists do not much mind being thought disreputable'.[95] Their comments reveal the appreciation that the new generation of writers had for different acting spaces.

William Douglas Home, the popular West End playwright, denied that his domestic comedies could not be presented on an open stage: 'Some entrances and exits are difficult. But I do not think these are insuperable problems—a good director should be able to manage them. Drawing room effects can be achieved quite simply just by having a chair or two around. Actors can be moved around so they don't have their backs to the same people all the time. I would certainly be happy for my plays to be put on there.'[96]

Actor, director and playwright Emlyn Williams wrote: 'This controversy in Sheffield seems to be a lot of fuss about something which is a most worthy move. People should give it a chance. There is a similar theatre in Chichester which has succeeded—Shakespeare, Chekhov, Pinero's *The Magistrate*, a real old-fashioned farce, have gone very well there. There would certainly not be any need to re-write my own plays.'

Keith Waterhouse, author of *Billy Liar*, wrote: 'I don't think the opponents of the Sheffield have much of a case.' He argued that the thrust stage would enhance, not inhibit the production of some plays. 'The proscenium arch certainly inhibits the production of a lot of plays and while you can dress up a thrust stage if necessary, the proscenium arch is something you are stuck with. The general ambience is important. The place should feel like a theatre. You get

---

[95] *Morning Telegraph*, 16 September 1969.
[96] In the Crucible's second season, Douglas Home's *Secretary Bird* was performed with great success with Hubert Greg starring. It was a touring proscenium production with a group of highly professional actors who, on the afternoon it opened, my father re-directed for the open stage. He recalled that one of the tunnels became the French windows to the garden. Hubert Greg was at home almost at once.

Emlyn Williams and Keith Waterhouse

this at Nottingham Playhouse and you can get it in a warehouse if necessary. Everything in the theatre is a matter of fashion and in ten or twenty years I suppose there might not be any stage at all.'

Henry Livings, actor and playwright wrote: 'Plays which I have thought were inevitably proscenium arch pieces have been done on other sorts of stages. "Eh?" for instance has been done in the round. God knows how they did it, but this is a director's problem rather than an author's – and if you set a play in a fish tank they come back and ask you to try something difficult. Noel Coward plays? You can still create a background. [...] Cut the audience off with lighting as effectively as with a curtain and no more artificially. The conjuror who really wants to impress you comes right down into the audience. A lot of playwrights are very interested in close audience contact now—the closer you can get to an audience, the better. When you have to stand up there behind the arch and blare away at them, they might as well just be snaffling chocolates for the contact you make with them.'

Ten days before the Open Forum was due to take place, two Conservative councillors, Martyn Atkinson and Michael Swain, appeared in *The Star* denouncing the 'wastage of public expenditure'. They urged the Council to withdraw the £300,000 it had promised towards the new theatre. Councillor Swain complained that the new Playhouse would be designed only for drama and warned: 'If the producer Colin George decides to go to Bournemouth and the whole thing collapses around our ears, we shall be left with half-empty houses and another white elephant like the City Hall.'

They claimed the city needed a proper theatre with a proscenium arch which could take touring companies. 'We are the fourth biggest city in the country and we are excluding every other type of stage presentation. If you have £300,000 to spend you have an obligation to distribute that money as fairly as possible among the ratepayers.'[97] They declared they would attend the forum and air their doubts about the design and cost of the theatre.

The *Morning Telegraph* responded on September 19th with an editorial under the headline '"Bingo" may be a saving cry', which pointed out that the new theatre was not, and was never intended to be, a civic theatre. 'The point ought to be obvious, but bears repeating, at least to councillors Martyn Atkinson and Michael Swain. They have pledged themselves to fight the new theatre plans to the bitter end only because it turns out to be what it was always intended to be.

'This is a repertory theatre with a permanent company. Such a project could never provide a home, save for limited periods, for touring companies, let alone amateur shows. Even if it had been designed with the most orthodox of proscenium stages, this fact would still have to be accepted. So the shape of the new stage is irrelevant to the fate of touring and amateur productions in Sheffield. And even if the two councillors fear the worst for British drama it is fair to say, in a town of Sheffield's size and geographical position, that the touring companies will fail the city before the local rep. Sharing the stage between a permanent Company and other productions would be an impossibility. You cannot forge an acting team of any value on seasonal terms. Nor, to be pedantic, can you produce opera properly in the sort of auditorium which a play can fill.'

On 28th September 1969, the Open Forum was held at the Playhouse, with 300 people in attendance. In the chair on stage was Tony Hampton, alongside David Brayshaw, myself, Pat Ide and

---

[97] *The Star*, 18 September 1969.

> **The New Sheffield Theatre**
> **First**
> **Open Forum**
>
> 8.00 p.m.
> Sunday
> 28 September 1969
> **Sheffield Playhouse**
> Townhead Street, Sheffield 1
>
> Speakers will include
> Antony Hampton
>   Chairman: New Theatre Trust
> Peter Howard, FRIBA
>   Architect: New Theatre
> David Brayshaw
>   Chairman: Playhouse Executive
> Patrick Ide
> Colin George
>   Advisers: New Theatre Trust
>
> **Admission Free**

Flier from the open forum on 28th September 1969

Peter Howard from the architects. I had also invited Trust members Alderman Hebblethwaite and Alderman Ironmonger (who had recently become Leader of the City Council) for moral support. While we had stated that we would listen to and answer questions from those opposed to the plans, we did not invite them to sit on the stage with us. They took offence at this.

After an introduction by Tony Hampton, I gave a presentation to the audience about the new building. With the help of slides, I took them around all four floors, from basement to the lighting galleries, describing every space and how it would be used. I described the demountable stage as 'a Meccano set you muck about with' and the huge loading bay 'through which even an elephant could walk straight onto the stage'. I confess I forgot about time and I went on for over two hours. This was followed by over half an hour of questions. Afterwards, several Trust members, including Anthony, told me that they had been surprised to learn in such detail just how meticulous the design of the theatre was and how it would operate.

And what of the threatened opposition to our plan? It fizzled out. One of the two Conservative councillors, Michael Swain, was unable to attend because of his wife's illness. His colleague, Martyn Atkinson, got a round of applause when he commented: 'Pantomime has as much right to be subsidised as Repertory', but he left shortly after. *The Star* later reported that he had dismissed the forum as 'a carve up', fuming that he had not been allowed on the platform, and declared it had 'reinforced our opinion that the whole thing is a waste of money and time'. The spokesman for the 'Save the Lyceum' campaign, who also attended, was more conciliatory: 'We entirely support the new Playhouse. Don't think we are trying to knock it. But we do feel Sheffield should have a theatre where we can see ballet, pantomime and opera.'[98]

Councillors Swain and Atkinson were not to be deterred, and a few days later at a meeting of the Town Council they tabled a motion—along with twelve fellow Conservative councillors—to revise the theatre design from a thrust to a proscenium stage.[99] They argued that this would enable productions of ballet, opera, pantomime and musical comedy, as well as touring productions which would balk at the expense of adapting their productions to the thrust stage.[100] Councillor Atkinson added for good measure that one of the most popular theatrical entertainments in Sheffield had been the Black and White Minstrel Show which could not be played on the thrust stage. This comment, which was uncontroversial at the time, illustrates how times and attitudes have changed since 1969.

The vote was defeated 44 to 14. Labour councillor Reg Munn, whose colleagues opposed the motion, pointed out that the Council was scarcely competent to judge the design of the theatre because its original motion had been to grant £300,000 to the new theatre with no say over programming policy. Moreover, the Conservative councillors' proposal would have involved building an expensive fly tower for scenery and reducing the number of seats (adding the proscenium arch would cut off the sightlines for a large section of the audience), which ultimately would force up seat prices.

Another attendee at our Open Forum was Mr Cotton, who wrote to the *Morning Telegraph*, insisting that opposition to the thrust stage had not been stronger because it was clear that the Trustees had no intention of changing their plans. 'What is the purpose of these open

---
[98] *The Star*, 29 September 1969.
[99] This vote split the Conservatives on the Council. Their leader, Alderman Hebblethwaite, refused to take part in the vote and waited outside the chamber.
[100] As it turned out, in the Crucible's first season the theatre hosted visiting productions of the Ballet Rambert and the Phoenix Opera and produced *Treasure Island* (which played for 53 performances) and the musical *Mister*.

forums? The truth is that this is a specious and grandiose name for a jolly exercise of the 'brand promotion' type; the stage that really thrusts! Deeper than deep! It is an attempt to create, if not a demand, the impression that a demand exists, to present as credibly as possible the fantasy of a theatregoing public suffering from deep thrust stage starvation.'

He concluded: 'This should not be a case of deep thrust versus proscenium stage—but a specialised building against a more adaptable one; of a stage which retains many of the qualities of the thrust stage, without losing all the advantages, real and nostalgic, of the proscenium stage.'[101] Those of us involved in designing the new theatre knew that this was not possible. It had to be one or the other. Any compromise on the stage would fail both theatrically and practically.

---

[101] *Morning Telegraph*, September 1969.

CHAPTER FOURTEEN

Once more unto the breach, dear friends, once more!†

In October 1969, the rousing battle call of Henry V seemed appropriate, as the public debate over the thrust stage design was about to go up a notch. It was time for another knight to enter the fray, one who would raise the drama of local antagonism towards our new theatre to the realms of melodrama.

In September, *The Star* had invited its readers to join the debate over the new theatre's thrust stage, arguing that if the so-called experts were in disagreement about its virtues and over £600,000 of public money was at stake, then all opinions should be aired. There followed a month of 'opinionation', as Denys Lasdun described it,[102] until on October 6th *The Star* really had something to brandish in its columns. Its lead editorial that day read: 'New theatre—The Knights say "caution"'.

'Only when it seems too late do we learn that there is really distinguished opposition to the stage and auditorium design of Sheffield's Playhouse replacement theatre. Not until a contract has been awarded and it is announced that work is to start "immediately" do we hear of the design reservations of Sir Laurence Olivier, Sir John Clements and Sir Bernard Miles.

'Sir Bernard Miles, founder of the Mermaid Theatre in London, is so opposed to the concept of a deep-thrust stage that he has refused to be a patron of the new theatre. Sir Laurence and Sir John, who is director of Chichester Festival Theatre, urged caution in adopting such a revolutionary stage design.'

---

† William Shakespeare, *Henry V*, Act III, Scene 1.
[102] *The Star*, 5 September 1969.

Sir Bernard raps new Sheffield theatre plans

The theatrical knight did not mince his words. 'I think this stage is a kind of freak. It is a retrograde thing, and it will be out of date in seven years' time.' He warned that it would be impossible to accommodate in the new theatre great prestige touring attractions in ballet, opera and musical comedy, which would have to be redesigned to fit the stage.

'A lot of devoted people, among them myself, have spent 20 years trying to demonstrate that the old three- or four-deck theatre is outmoded because it creates second- and third-class citizens. Now the Sheffield theatre simply finds a new way of creating second- and third-class citizens by putting them round the side of the stage. No one buys a side seat until they are forced round the side because all the front seats have been sold. Some members of the audience would be restricted to a "back view of Hamlet's legs".

'Acting is frontal activity, because the actor's means of expression, his eyes and his mouth, are in the front of his face. An actor can only control as many people as he can see—as he can hold with his eyes, and that as we know is no more than a 160-degree angle of audience.' Refusing an invitation to become a patron of the new theatre, Sir Bernard signed off with a stark warning: 'The Theatre Trust would do well to stop the plans now, even if it costs £50,000 to delay a year. They will never regret it if they do'.

Sir Bernard's criticism of the thrust stage was hugely damaging to our plans for the new theatre. As a veteran of the early years of the Sheffield Playhouse and the country's most recently anointed actor knight, Sir Bernard was a popular figure, known for his rambunctious performances as Long John Silver in *Treasure Island*. In 1959 he had opened the 600-seater Mermaid Theatre—the first to be built in the City of London since the 17th century—whose open stage design was widely lauded, and this gave his criticisms of our thrust stage

The Three Knights: Sir Bernard Miles, Sir Laurence Olivier and Sir John Clements

credibility. What made it worse was the pairing of Sir Bernard's name with two other luminaries of the stage, Sir Laurence Olivier and Sir John Clements.

Sir Laurence—a household name—had not only been the founding Artistic Director of the Chichester Festival Theatre, whose design concept echoed our own, but, as Artistic Director of the new National Theatre, he was overseeing a parallel project to build a large auditorium with an adaptable open stage (this became the Olivier Theatre). Sir John was the current Artistic Director of Chichester and a film star in his own right. It is important to remember that back then there were far fewer famous actors and celebrities and the 'Three Knights' were hugely popular and respected figures.

Councillors Michael Swain and Martyn Atkinson leapt on this opportunity and announced that they would invite the Three Knights to a public meeting in Sheffield to give their views on this type of stage. Needless to say, the Three Knights didn't ride into Sheffield, lances aloft, to join the jousting. But the perception that they viewed the thrust stage as 'a craze gimmick, a theatrical blind alley'—which in the case of Sir Laurence was untrue—could severely undermine our fundraising appeal.

I needed to respond and reached out to the man who had inspired our thrust stage, Tyrone Guthrie. He had written to me on 29th September accepting our invitation to become a patron of the new theatre, congratulating us for 'daring to build what seems a new-fangled stage to those who can only envisage the theatre or opera house as it has been fashionable for the last 300 years, and do not realise that the proposed design is merely a return to the principle where auditorium and actor were related for 2,000 years before the Italian opera house was ever envisaged.'

On 7th October, I wrote to him in Minneapolis where he had just opened *Uncle Vanya*, enclosing cuttings of Sir Bernard Miles's attack and adding that his onslaught might cause our appeal for public money to founder badly. 'This is tragic,' I wrote, 'as we had made a splendid start and had about £40,000/£50,000 in the kitty already.' But I concluded defiantly: 'Heads are being held high—"We shall delve one yard below their mines and blow them at the moon".'[103]

Two weeks later, I received a four-page hand-written reply from Guthrie, full of his brash humour, raw encouragement and critical eye. His opening was uncompromising: 'Dear Colin, Don't moult a feather on account of B Miles. His bark is a thousand times worse than his bite [...] Write him at once rather a jolly letter—but let on that you take him et al. seriously—asking him to state publicly what performances he has witnessed on a thrust stage. I *know* he's never been either to Minneapolis or Stratters Ont. He may have been to Chich. But I suspect he's talking without any first-hand knowledge at all.'

'And, of course, all that about the actors having to face *head-on* into the audience is just blethers. Ask him if actor A is *facing* the audience *squarely* (as he advocates) how does B (his interlocutor) face? Do they stand side by side, both facing [the audience], like a Minstrel Show? As a matter of strict (confidential) fact, in Bernard's own productions they *do* and it isn't a hot idea!

'As his experience of an open, thrust, promontory stage is negligible, he is in the absurd position of the person who says: "Such and such is a dirty book, picture, song, piece of sculpture". "Oh, then you've seen it?" "Well, no." "Oh, then how can you be so sure?" "Well, everybody says; and anyway, lots of my friends have seen it." Thereafter collapse of stout party is but a matter of pressing your advantage.

---

[103] This quote is from *Hamlet*, Act III, Scene 4.

'I think, perhaps, Bernard has rather a good point when he says Ballet and Opera won't be able to come to the Playhouse, but you answer that Ballet and Opera aren't the fish which the Playhouse exists to fry. When he goes on about our ideas being so "new-fangled", it might be worth pointing out that Stratford has been going for more than 16 years and that the success has never wavered, though the first gloss of newness has long faded. Further, the first successful experiment on a big scale was made with "Three Estates" at the Assembly Hall, Edinburgh in 1948. That, except to elderly gaffers like Bernard and myself, is NOT yesterday.

'I shall be home just before Christmas and if that's not too late, quite willing to plunge into the fray. Meantime, defend by attacking; put your enemies into the position of being fogies defending a Maginot Line which, to all intents, was stormed in 1947. Ever, T. G.'

At the bottom was a P.S.: 'Attack Bernard *at once*. If you hit him hard twice or thrice, then L.O. [Laurence Olivier], who doesn't like to be unpopular (who does?) will lay off damn quick.'

I did write to Sir Bernard immediately. I had met him when I visited the Mermaid with a view to doing a production there at his invitation, although this never materialised. While keeping a collegial manner, I took Sir Bernard to task on his criticism of the thrust stage, writing: 'I was of your opinion as to how an actor or director commands and moves his spectators, until I went to America. The theatre at Minneapolis changed all that. I was suddenly sitting in an auditorium in which phrases we have toyed with so often like "audience participation", "four boards and a passion", "the ritual of the theatre", suddenly began to have some meaning.

'I am astonished that you should have been left unmoved by promontory stage performances you have seen, and I should find it most helpful to compare notes. I don't think such a stage is new-fangled—after all, Sir Tyrone began rejuvenating this form of theatre in 1948. And didn't I hear about Max Reinhardt and Terence Gray?[104] If you claim to have lived through all that unmoved, I would refer you back in time to Shakespeare and Sophocles. And you're not telling me

---

[104] Max Reinhardt (1873-1943) was an Austrian-born theatrical producer who was renowned for his innovative stage productions. Terence Gray (1895-1986) was a theatre producer who created the experimental Cambridge Festival Theatre.

(or the Observer) that you were alive then! To return to the present day, Stratford, Ontario and Minneapolis have been packing them in for the last sixteen years.

'What has been particularly distressing for those of us in the theatre here has been the way that opposition to any form of subsidised regional theatre has been able to make use of your remarks to embellish their own philistinism. You are in most unusual company—if you are, as I think, interested in there being lively regional theatres outside London.'

I included a conciliatory olive branch: 'There are so many reasons why we chose a promontory stage for the new Sheffield theatre that I would much rather grab some plans, search you out at the Mermaid, and enjoy an impassioned artistic collision. And if a bottle of whisky were to hand, so much the better'.

Sir Bernard replied the next day: 'Dear Colin, the *Morning Telegraph* offered me 1,500 words with which I could have demolished the thrust stage, but I have declined because the last thing I would wish to do would be to embarrass your appeal. But really the whole thing is rubbish; you have to force people to buy seats round the sides and a theatre in which the public are under duress is not theatre at all, especially in these days when Jack is as good as his master. *You* are even having seats *behind* the performance. I fear you have all been led astray by the fact that Larry and Clements both worked at Chichester. Anyway, God bless you and your efforts, Yours ever, B. M.'

He added a P.S.: 'We built a promontory stage at the Royal Exchange in 1963 and couldn't sell the seats around the corners, just as they can't at Chichester—unless they have a smash hit on their hands. You have already got an experimental theatre down in the left-hand corner holding 250. That's the place for working out these very debatable physical relationships.'

I wrote back a polite letter, acknowledging that we would not be able to discuss the matter artistically. He responded on 5th November by sending me two cuttings. The first was his letter to *The Sunday Times* two years previously—in June 1967—in which he corrected an article that had suggested the Mermaid had a thrust stage. He wrote: 'I long ago abandoned the three-sided stage as an abortion born of street platforms set up inside bear- and bull-baiting rings and inn yards.

'The Mermaid stage is aggressively frontal, i.e. based upon the position of the actor's chief means of expression, eyes and mouth, in the front of his face; and upon the angle they can sweep (and thus control) with a single movement of the head from side to side, viz. about 120 degrees. I believe the three-sided stage results in bad-mannered theatre, the side seats only filling up when all the front seats have gone, and the actors being obliged to sell a large part of the audience short, either orally or visually, or both.'

The second cutting was an extract from a translation of *The Art of the Actor* (1894), by the 19th century French actor, Benoît-Constant Coquelin, which explained where Sir Bernard's belief that acting was 'a frontal business' came from. Coquelin wrote:

'It is the eye that sums it all up. It is the light, the transparency, the life of expression. There, the public watches you, and there it tries to read you [...] You have a story to tell, let your eye visualise the thing you speak. The public will see it reflected there [...] What you are about to say they see there, before you utter it, and speech does no more than drive home the impression which the glance has already fixed in the attention of the spectator. You will never be able to arrange for your back to express these shades of feeling with such mastery of resource as your eye, and the public who see only your back will be inclined to believe you are making game of Corneille or of your audience.'[105]

We never did get together to thrash our conflicting ideas. If we had, I would have emphasised that the discipline of the actor and director is very different on the open stage when it comes to lighting, designing and blocking. It becomes a three-dimensional challenge based on the two tunnels on the diagonal of the promontory. But while disagreeing with Sir Bernard, I did respond to his passion for the theatre.

I also wrote to Sir Laurence Olivier. As a young man, I was inspired to become a professional actor by his performances and had seen his marvellous production of *Uncle Vanya* on the Chichester thrust stage. I got to meet him in April 1966 when he brought his National Theatre production of Sean O'Casey's *Juno and the Paycock* to the Sheffield Lyceum. As we were opening our production of

---

[105] Typed excerpt sent with letter by Sir Bernard Miles, 5 November 1969.

John Arden's *Sergeant Musgrave's Dance* the very next day, I invited him to see it. He turned up unannounced, wearing dark glasses so as not to draw attention away from the production, and afterwards he came backstage and met the entire Company—the actors, the stage management, the technicians, the dressers—everyone. It meant a lot to the Company.

So, three years later, I wrote to Sir Laurence, enclosing cuttings of Sir Bernard's interview in *The Observer* and stating: 'I know you have been approached about the New Sheffield Theatre and offered a courteous word of restraint. This has now grown out of all proportions [...] Whatever your reservations about the design of our new theatre (I wonder if you have seen the detailed plans?), your name is being taken in vain here by so many people whose opinions and attitudes I suspect are diametrically opposed to your own.'

He wrote back, thanking me for bringing it to his attention. We spoke by telephone and although I knew he was not a believer in the thrust stage, he seemed very distressed that his name should have been linked with such a hysterical and abusive attack. It was only after the Crucible opened in 1971 that I discovered Sir Laurence had written a response to the editor of the *Observer*, which was published. He later shared a copy with me, which reads:

'Sir, I feel it is very wrong of you to lump Sir Bernard Miles, Sir John Clements and myself all together in denouncing the thrust stage of the Crucible, Sheffield, in such scathing terms as you quote. I think we all three had different things to say and these do not add up to a corporate or unanimous condemnation such as you describe. Yours sincerely, Laurence Olivier'

Reading this back years later, Sir Laurence's defence of the thrust stage feels lukewarm. Despite helping give birth to the Guthrie stage on that stormy night in Denmark in 1937, and three successful seasons at Chichester, he clearly didn't like the form. When designing what became the Olivier Theatre, he would pursue a very different concept of the open stage, proposing a stage that was 'in the audience's space, backed by infinity',[106] with the auditorium holding the stage 'like pincers'.

---

[106] Richard Pilbrow, *A Theatre Project*, pp.173-174.

John Bury, Theatre Design Consultant on the Barbican Theatre, which was being designed at the same time as the National and Crucible, later wrote: 'Olivier wanted an arc of command no greater than can be encompassed in a gesture, or, as Sir Laurence put it, the audience had to see both his eyes. So this was going to be very different from the then prevailing Guthrie open stage where the unfortunate actor had to keep on the trot, rationing out his words and gestures to the various seating areas. "I cannot make all the audience laugh at the same time", said a despairing Olivier at the Chichester Festival Theatre!'[107] It is a shame Sir Laurence never saw a production at the Crucible while I was Artistic Director. If he had seen the thrust stage concept fully realised, he might have changed his mind.

I also wrote to one of the most distinguished actors who had performed at Stratford, Ontario under Guthrie—Sir Alec Guinness, who opened the theatre in 1953 playing the lead in *Richard III*. I asked Sir Alec what his views on the thrust stage were and whether he would give his support for our theatre design. On 20th October I received a very straightforward reply which was not the least what I had expected.

He wrote: 'My first experience of acting in the round was in Denmark in, I think, 1926—and that was exciting. I was also very much in sympathy with the Stratford, Ontario venture, where I played for about three months in its opening season... [However,] visiting the kabuki and Noh theatres in Japan convinced me that the prototype of theatre established at Stratford was by no means the most admirable means of presenting a variety of plays.

'I think the open stage as exemplified so far, although giving the modern (or current) sort of director a field-day and allowing new playwrights to be loose in construction (and of course a certain freedom), is detrimental to both performer and audience. An audience in such theatres must miss at least three-quarters of a performance and the actor is aware of that. Playing and directing at Chichester last year—although personally a pleasurable experience—I found presented rigid and tiresome patterns and problems which could hardly ever arise in a conventional theatre. But I am not asking that more conventional theatres should be built, although there is need for them. If I were a

---

[107] Mulryne, Ronnie & Shewring, Margaret, *Making Space for Theatre: British Architecture and Theatre since 1958*, Mulryne & Shewring Ltd, 1995, p.122.

Sir Alec Guinness, 1970s

multi-millionaire, dilettante, dictator of such things I would explore—and I hope build—something on the lines of traverse theatre and seek to learn something from the Noh theatre of Japan into the bargain.

'Tyrone Guthrie is a dear and respected friend, and has genius, but I cannot keep feeling that this particular type of theatre is admirable for his own huge talents, less admirable for his imitators, disastrous for the untalented and is not a step forward. We will have the National Theatre on similar lines and by the time it is erected the whole thing may be dated and boring. I would beg you to think again rather more adventurously. I do sincerely hope that none of the above will read offensively—it is certainly not meant to be rude in any way. But you asked me what I think—or so I assumed. Whatever you do about it, you have my good wishes.'

One can challenge a good deal of what Sir Alec wrote—for example, that an audience misses three-quarters of a performance on an open stage (an even more sweeping statement than that of Sir Bernard Miles). And if he found the discipline of working on such a stage rigid and tiresome that was as much a criticism of his ability as an actor to explore the dynamic of a different space from the one to which he was accustomed. One might add that if Sir Tyrone Guthrie made it work at Stratford, Ontario, then so had many other directors for 14 years after the great man left.

It is also easy now to say with hindsight that the National Theatre and the Crucible have not become 'dated or boring'. When I returned to see productions on the Crucible stage forty years after Sir Alec's letter, I was astonished and delighted at the way the thrust stage has been used in ways those of us involved in the design could not have imagined at the time it was built. The stage acting area often projects towards the right or left bank of seats, not to the front. That would appear to make the front stalls—in what would be a proscenium theatre—the most disadvantaged. In fact, the performance involves all three banks of spectators. Directors, designers and actors have learnt to relate to the audience and the space just as they had to when they began working on a proscenium stage. And, technically, the use of lighting—to form a pattern directly under the acting area, for example, to assist a change of scene or atmosphere—is something we never fully explored.

However, life was not just a matter of responding to criticism of the theatre's design. There was still a hole in our finances. The Appeal Launch was held on 31st October 1969 in the Top Rank suite overlooking the site where the contractors were already at work. More than 200 people attended an informal buffet luncheon to mark the official launch of the appeal to raise the £260,000 required to complete the building. The deputy Lord Mayor, the Master Cutler and Mistress Cutler were among the local dignitaries, along with the Trust Chairman, Tony Hampton. A clutch of former Playhouse actors attended and there were recorded messages of support from James Mason and Albert Finney, whose photographs adorned the walls.

In the days before the digital world, I remember that when they played the first message—'This is James Mason speaking'—the sudden resonance of his voice was thrilling. He described the thrust stage he had performed on at Stratford, Ontario as 'the most exciting theatrical development of our day' and reminded us that he was a local man. 'As a Yorkshireman, it has pained me to note that Lancashire already boasts two excellent small thrust stages, the Manchester University and the Bolton Octagon, while Yorkshire lags. Let us therefore stick to what we believe is right and stimulation for today's theatregoers.' Albert Finney, who I knew from our days at the Birmingham Rep, sent a message of support, prompting laughter at his suggestion that the tape itself should be considered his first donation to the new theatre.

There was also an invitation to the public to join what we called The Collaboration: 'a growing, entirely independent, friendly band of people who arrange and run their own fundraising schemes for the new theatre'.[108] The first Chairman of this group, Jill Barton, declared they were looking for 'a broad cross-section of the Sheffield public, sceptics and devotees, young and old alike'.

The Collaboration's first fundraiser was a 'happening style' fashion show held at The Fiesta night club opposite the theatre in February 1971. Other events included an art auction held at the University of Sheffield, a gala ball, amateur musicals and the first-ever limbo dancing contest in the North of England. A derby match between Sheffield Wednesday and Sheffield United was proposed to raise funds for the appeal but, alas, it never took place. Instead, six local schools—Chaucer, Firth Park, High Storrs, Abbeydale, King Edward and King Ecgbert—organised a five-a-side football match over forty-eight hours, raising £130.[109] All this activity was a clear demonstration to critics of the theatre that Sheffield's citizens were not all opposed to the building that was shortly to rise in Norfolk Street.

One of the most effective means of raising civic awareness of the new theatre was placing a Portakabin opposite what was to be the Studio Theatre entrance. Run by The Collaboration's members, the Portakabin was open from 10am to 6pm most days of the week. On its walls were copies of the architects' designs and drawings of the new theatre, fundraising literature and photos of similar thrust stage theatres worldwide. When I first visited the Portakabin, my eye was caught by a photo of the thrust stage of the Octagon Theatre in Perth, Western Australia. The design was familiar but in a strange sort of way. Then I realised the photo had been displayed upside down! This was not an ironic comment that this theatre was 'Down Under' but

---

[108] The Collaboration would eventually become the Crucible Club.
[109] This would be worth £1,800 in 2021.

reflected the fact that most of our supporters had never been in a thrust stage auditorium, nor seen a production on a thrust stage.

The Company felt we should have a theatrical opening of the Portakabin, and I penned a few lines which one of the Playhouse actors delivered from the doorway, wearing a theatrical mask from one of our Greek productions:

> 'The theatre is dying', so they said
> When Father Time put Aeschylus to bed.
> No doubt they said the same that very year
> Stout Burbage hired as prentice young Shakespeare.
> The Puritan then drama did assail,
> But still it offered up its 'cakes and ale'.
> The secret weapons of the modern age,
> TV and Bingo to the wanton stage,
> Fierce blows may offer but no *coup de grâce* –
> The laughs still come when falling on its arse.
>
> So here in Sheffield, 'fore your very eyes,
> A theatre is rising to the skies.
> Once more a cheeky Thespian you will view,
> Not just his codpiece, but his backside, too.
> Gone is the arch proscenium's monotony.
> You'll find you're sitting round a promontory.
> You want to see the plans—a place to blab in?
> Well, here you are—a brand new Portakabin
> Which now we open—all for your delight,
> Giving you pleasure, taking your widow's mite.
>
> Anticipate that great and glorious day
> You'll gather here, good people, for the play!

CHAPTER FIFTEEN

Those friends thou hast, and their adoption tried,
Grapple them unto thy soul with hoops of steel...[†]

Not Henry V but Polonius introduces the next chapter of our story. We had to do a good deal of grappling with our friends over the coming months, and in a way Sir Bernard Miles's sweeping attack galvanised some of our most eloquent supporters who might not have roused themselves to write to the press as they did.

The day after Sir Bernard's outburst, Peter Cheeseman, Director of Stoke-on-Trent's Theatre in the Round—and a friend to be grappled indeed—wrote to me with heartening news. He had been in touch with the theatre critic of *The Observer*, Ronald Bryden, to suggest using the newspaper's Pendennis column to air views defending the thrust stage. Peter then arranged for some of Britain's leading playwrights to write to Mr Bryden with their opinions on the thrust stage.

He also told me that Bryden had attended a conference in Manchester organised by Theatre 69, and when Sir Bernard had raised his opinions, he had been shot down effectively by the theatre's director, Michael Elliot—'a good man for you to contact'. Michael Elliot quickly became another friend to be embraced. In fact, he had already written to Sir Bernard on October 10th to counter his claims that the actors of Ancient Greece did not perform in the chorus area almost surrounded by the audience, but were instead on a raised platform behind. Michael wrote:

'Dear Sir Bernard, in all friendliness I am afraid I must disagree with you entirely. Your arguments about the Greek theatre are very familiar to me from the time when I spent six months researching archaeologically in the theatres in Greece. There is no conclusive evidence anywhere that the main action of the Greek play was

---

[†] William Shakespeare, *Hamlet*, Act I, Scene 3.

separated from the area in which the Chorus worked, and I myself was convinced, after studying the question for some time, that in the great days of the Greek theatre much of the action took place in the orchestra.[110] To me it is illogical to build a circular theatre and then stand outside the circle. I feel myself that the retirement of the actor from the central point of control to a point outside and above the circumference of the orchestra happened at a date early in the 4th century and is typical of the continuous decline in theatre design throughout the Hellenistic phase, the Roman, the Renaissance and the Restoration to the Victorian.

'No one in his right mind could deny the power and effectiveness of proscenium arch production. I hope no one tries to. I am only disappointed that someone of your stature and understanding is so intolerant of a view of theatre which may be inappropriate or out of date but must have been held by Shakespeare. The only argument I have ever heard to suggest that the Globe Playhouse is of no significance in its ground plan is that "they knew no better at that time". It is an argument about a building which was purpose-built for Shakespeare's Company, which I find quite ridiculous.

'I know that you and many others dislike the thrust stage, and you have every right to do so. Perhaps it does not suit the kind of theatre and the kind of acting that you wish to see. However, you must recognise that there are an increasing number who do not share that view. I am one. I would not dream of going into print to prevent you building a proscenium arch theatre if that would be what you wish. Why should you try to prevent others in their equally sincerely and strongly held convictions? None of us has the right to forbid experiment in an attempt to discover the truth.'[111]

There then followed, at Peter Cheeseman's prompting, a flurry of letters to *The Observer* in defence of the thrust stage.[112] They

---

[110] In Ancient Greek theatre, the '*orchestra*' was the circular space in front of the stage which was surrounded on three sides by the audience. As such, it was the inspiration for the 'Magic Circle', which became central to the design of the Crucible's thrust stage auditorium.
[111] This missive, which Michael Elliot shared with my father, started a lengthy exchange of letters between him and Sir Bernard. Michael later wrote to my father: 'Glad to hear the effects of Sir Bernard's madness are lessening in Sheffield. He will not stop writing to me!'
[112] The following letters by playwrights were published in *The Observer* during October 1969.

Peter Cheeseman and Michael Elliot

demonstrated the breadth of views that existed about the thrust stage and exposed how ridiculous and short-sighted Sir Bernard's criticism had been. I have included excerpts from them as they capture so well what we were aspiring to achieve with our revolutionary stage.

First was David Campton, a prolific dramatist who had pioneered the Theatre of the Absurd in Britain. He wrote: 'It is a long time since I vowed never to write to a newspaper again. But the Miles outburst fills me with such horror that I have to write to someone. This sinister old gentleman, in declaiming against putting the theatre back for fifty years, is in fact advocating putting it back for a hundred and fifty.

'His argument about selling two thirds of the audience short in a theatre with a thrust stage only applies when an old-fashioned director tries to use the thrust stage as though it were behind a proscenium arch. Even the latest model Jaguar will appear at a disadvantage compared with an old-fashioned buggy if the driver insists on harnessing a horse to it. Nor does Sir Bernard's insistence on frontal acting hold much water. He may achieve his effects by holding an audience hypnotised with his beady eye: but an actor also possesses a back, shoulders, and bottom. He should be acting with this whole body, and not with a part of it. Before my writing expanded to take up all my time, I acted for ten years with Stephen Joseph's Theatre in the Round. I may not be as good an actor as the Grand Old Man of the Mermaid, but I managed to hold my audience.

'The occasional geyser spouting from the Mermaid is expected, and normally I would let even this one pass. However, the projected new theatre in Leicester is being subjected to the same attack as that at Sheffield, and in the main, from the same section of the community: local operatic societies. These people insist that any new theatre should be designed for their ritual annual production of The Mikado. The fact that drama will have to scrape along for the rest of the year on a stage not designed for it does not concern them—after all, it has scraped along for years now. They are concerned only that the new theatre should resemble as closely as possible the old theatres which are being scrapped as unworkable. This attitude might be expected of some amateurs who see no further than their next production of Lilac Time; but I am saddened that Sir Bernard (who was knighted for his services to the theatre!) should be adding his contribution to ill-informed and selfish prejudice.'

Peter Strick of the Evening Sentinel, the critic who regularly reviewed Cheeseman's productions in Stoke-on-Trent, was the next to pitch in, writing under the headline 'Argument comes into the open'. Dismissing Sir Bernard's claim that 'acting is a frontal business' as 'curiously old-fashioned', he noted that: 'We in Stoke-on-Trent know that people can act with their backs just as effectively, and most actors who have tried it like the greater freedom of movement that open and thrust stages offer. From an audience point of view, the initial strangeness is soon cancelled out by the advantage of closer proximity to the stage and the sense that we are indeed watching a three-dimensional performance. And what on Earth is the use of having a frontal view of the actors if they are so far away that their faces are mere blobs unless viewed through binoculars?

'On this point, it is interesting to compare the view of the late Stephen Joseph—"Actors, like the rest of us, have backs, and what goes on behind a person's back may be fascinating to watch". My own opinion is, I hope, perfectly clear. I am all for thrust stages, open stages and anything which breaks down the barriers between artist and audience in the theatre.'[113]

Next came a letter to *The Guardian* from a Mr John Hodgson, Head of Drama Studies, and Audrey Coldron, Senior Lecturer in Drama, both from Bretton Hall College of Education, which turned Sir Bernard's criticism of the thrust stage back on him. They wrote: "Acting," he says, "is a frontal business, an actor's chief means of expression, eyes and mouth being in the front of his face". The actor's voice, however, carries to all sides and his total movement is trained to be expressive. We certainly rely on voice and movement at the Mermaid, Sir Bernard's tunnel theatre, where over two thirds of the audience are so removed from the actors that their eyes can communicate little even if they were permanently glued on the audience. A close link between actor and audience seems to be most important, and the Sheffield design brings all 1,000 members of its audience to within 14 rows of the acting area.

Twenty years ago, in a book called *The British Theatre*, Sir Bernard was writing: "We need many new theatres built and owned by the State [...] and designed on more flexible lines than the present pattern. [...] thus releasing the drama from its present slavery to the two-dimensional." Reaction seems to have set in. How else can one account for such a radical change of heart and such confusion of priorities?'[114]

Next, it was time for Peter Cheeseman to give his views: 'The whole validity of Sir Bernard's argument must be challenged by those of us who have substantial professional experience of working in other forms. Sir Bernard is quite right in one respect only—that any theatre form in which the actor is partially or totally surrounded by the audience is not a "frontal form". Where he is just plain wrong is to say, therefore you can't act in it satisfactorily. He confuses the issue by imagining actors trying to make it work frontally and failing (quite naturally) to give as good measure to the people on either side and behind him as those in front.

'I have now worked for seven years with a permanent Company in a theatre-in-the-round. In its complete absence of any directional

---

[113] *The Evening Sentinel*, 10 October 1969.
[114] *The Guardian*, 11 October 1969.

axis along which a performance is projected, it is the opposite to the frontal or unidirectional form claimed by Sir Bernard as the exclusive formula for effective theatre. Like the thrust stage, its performance is projected multi-directionally. Its techniques are not based on facing one section of the audience and charging less for the other seats or on gyrating and rushing around in a desperate attempt to conceal the backside. They are based on an inward concentration of the action in which the audience participates. It is as simple as that.

'In unidirectional theatre, the performance is based on a confrontation between actor and audience. The actor is in a kind of position of authority of command. It would never occur to me to use that word to describe any part of the actor's relationship with the audience in a theatre-in-the-round, and it implies a significant difference in the quality of the event. Forms of theatre differ in their techniques of performance, but also philosophically, and even politically in the relationships implied in the human structure of the event they create. People form the total or partial background to the action presented in a thrust or round stage, each spectator can see almost the entire audience, the drama is played out in a space cleared in the middle of a community.

'There are many different forms in which what we call theatre can take place. The development of any one of them into a versatile and subtle instrument for communicating is a lengthy and careful process that can really only take place over a number of years. Unfortunately, Sir Bernard has an easy job in making his case for the exclusive validity of his own favourite form look good on paper. Anyone trying to argue that in non-frontal theatres you don't notice actor's backs has the same problem as the inventor of the iron ship or the aeroplane. But, fortunately, there are now plenty of distinguished artists and critics who have seen our thrust stages and theatres in the round provide theatre just as exciting as the other forms of open and enclosed stage. I hope they will now come forward and say so.'

The playwright Henry Livings, who had previously responded to Mr L. du Garde Peach's criticism in the press, then re-entered the fray: 'Sir Bernard is well known as an amiable eccentric, so it's a pity that Sheffield citizens have taken him so seriously as to damage a rethink of the new Playhouse's shape. I've worked in, watched and

David Campton and Henry Livings

had my plays on, many different kinds of staging, and truly feel myself lucky to be in a theatre of any kind, in whatever capacity.

'However, there are one or two things I don't like; for instance, those theatres whose sightlines are so acute that either the actor spends his working life Down Stage Centre, or part of the audience has to talk among themselves every so often; and the class-dominated theatre where the Gods are the only ones to know how bald the juvenile is, and the front stalls have a deep impression of his cobbler's skill. Things I do like are, I suppose, the reverse of the above: being on a level with the actor so that he has no grandeur that he hasn't earned, and I like it when I can see and hear him.

'The technique for worried theatre workers, of projection in any but the hugest theatres, is to think your voice to the furthest listener; where the audience is on more than one side of the actor, the listener is nearer for the same number of seats, but the technique remains the same. Also, the performer has to show his face to everybody as soon as possible for the same reason; thereafter, they can hear you. We have conversations in my local from snug to taproom, because we know what our friends look like; and when I do a radio job with Bernard Cribbins, they give me a separate mike so that I shan't giggle, but I still do, because I still remember that face.

'This is not an argument for bricking in the fourth wall, all I'm saying is the technical job remains the same, whatever the relationship between stage and auditorium; it really is a bit unnatural in a picture-frame setting to keep your face in view of the spectator most of the time, but you'd be an obstructive ass not to do it. Ditto for thrust, circus, amphitheatre, and television studios for that matter.

'The time it takes to get on or off an open-sided stage could, I suppose, be seen as a problem; but I've never heard of Charlie Cairoli, Sir Laurence Olivier or their audiences complaining about the length of their entrances and exits. Personally, when I've worked in the round, I've been inclined to complain about the time the other actors take about getting on and off. Egocentric stage-hogs!'

Next up, playwright and screenwriter Alan Plater: 'I hesitate to battle with Knights (even theatrical ones), because in terms of influence they still have lances while we commoners are stuck with our fists: but the reaction of Sir Bernard and others to the proposed Sheffield Playhouse seems fair justification to prod out with a left and a right and risk being skewered in retaliation.

'The gist of the objections is the familiar one that in non-frontal theatres, Hamlet has to act with the back of his legs. Having worked a good deal in such theatres at Stoke-on-Trent, Bolton and Scarborough, my own observation is that this objection is totally unfounded. In my professional capacity as a playwright, I have seen the grandeur of my vision dimmed by many factors—notably my own limitations—but never the backs of legs. Drama is a spatial, rather than a linear activity, and if only the eyes can speak effectively to the beholder why didn't Michelangelo fit David with a head on a pivot?

'The frontal/non-frontal debate is obviously about conflicting ideologies, but they are not mutually exclusive: a good show will work at Drury Lane, at Wembley Stadium or on the back of a wagon. The knights are taking up a more dogmatic stance (maybe because of the armour) saying that because Colin George and the city of Sheffield have made a decision that differs from what they, the Knights, would have done, it must be a wrong decision. Oddly enough, it is possible for everybody in the debate to be right; daft, in a way, but theatre is a pretty daft business.

'Ultimately, it is up to Sheffield, in a collective sense, and Colin George, because he'll run the damn thing. Already, they have taken

Alan Plater and David Rudkin

a bold and radical decision, and notwithstanding the distinguished backlash, they might like to know that a good number of us artisans applaud their adventure and guts. It's generally a sign you're on to something good when important people try to stop you.'

Next, it was the turn of the prolific playwright and translator of Classical Greek drama, David Rudkin, who brilliantly took apart Sir Bernard's arguments against the thrust stage:

'Charismatic though the Trinity that be Sir Bernard, Sir Laurence and Sir John compose, their "frontalist" thesis must be challenged. Valid in itself, it is yet no more than a fraction off the total truth. The picture stage, however modified or sophisticated, is essentially a deep-focus two-dimensional plane, from which dramatic actions need to be "turned outwards" upon the audience.

'In terms of the history of world drama as a whole, it is a recent innovation. It could indeed be argued that it is an aberration; certainly, the picture stage comes into its peculiar own with the atrophy of drama's old quasi-religious moral-hygienic function and, therewith, the mutation of theatre into a commercial enterprise. Open staging, on the other hand, far from being a trendy or "freakish" modernism, represents part of a genuine cultural effort to rediscover the old, more mysterious dynamic of which the primal community drama was once possessed.

'Communal experience is enhanced by placing the participants around a focus, rather than massing them in one dense block out front. It is the difference, if you like, between a séance and a sermon. Indeed, one should provide single arm rests rather than double ones, so that the spectators elbow touch: thus creating currents within the audience itself. This type of current is no meaner thing than that more familiar voltage the actor causes to run, impalpably, between the spectators and himself.

'Frontal acting is not the only sort of acting there is. At its best, it tends to that magnificent and dangerous electricality of which Sir Laurence is our prime exponent. At worst it can be ham, such as to raise bad laughs on a more open stage. The eyes of an actor are, I agree, of prime importance—upon the frontal stage. An actor with small or unremarkable eyes cannot succeed there. But there exist, alongside us, powerful theatrical traditions in which the actors are deprived of their face altogether, whether by stylised make-up or by masks.

'Here, the spectator is forced to work so much harder, in projecting his responses outward upon the action, rather than vice versa. Here, surely, we come nearer to the *katharsis* of which Aristotle wrote. While the actor, masked or otherwise, who is encircled by his audience, in their midst, literally on the spot among them, is driven back and ever back if he is not to fail, upon textual and gestural truths richer and deeper than mere effect.

'In the frontal theatre, there will always remain the anomaly of greater or lesser distance from the stage. *Pace* Sir Bernard, this is a divisive factor; one is always aware that people in front of one can see better, possibly hear better, and have very likely paid more for their seats. There is also the uncomfortable fact that the stage picture progressively distorts the further from the centre of the row one sits. When Sir Bernard objects that the thrust stage treats two thirds of the house as grade B spectators, privileged, to coin a phrase, to no more than a view of Hamlet's arse from the sidelines, he is assuming that a triple-fronted stage is being used as though it were a single-fronted one. This would constitute a criticism of the director, not the stage. As for democracy, I know of no atmosphere more austerely egalitarian than that at Stoke-on-Trent, enwrapping the four-deck audience at the Victoria Theatre there—the only sort of theatre I willingly go to now.

'My concern as a writer is that a frontal tradition breeds only a frontal type of play. This will not necessarily always be a bad play. A play that enshrines real truth, frontal or otherwise conceived, will body that truth forth on any sort of stage irrespective of the architectural geometry the author had in mind. But were we to go exclusively frontal, how might our future drama be impoverished? So many extensions, enrichments and ennoblements of our dramatic idiom and experience would be for ever rendered unattainable.

'This future, of course, rests in the hands of the theatrical professionals themselves. They have to accept that other geometries call for other disciplines. An Ibsen, a Chekhov, a Brecht make new approaches to impersonation necessary; the actor can either extend his technique or turn his back upon the challenges to him these dramatists present. A writer, likewise, whose plays might seem all sawdust and cardboard once removed from the illuding frame of the proscenium arch, may either take defensive refuge in the mechanics that have served him well so far, or else commit himself to the lonely search for a wider range of creative principles. A director can choose whether to go on deceiving himself that the projecting tableau is the only viable or valid form of presentation, or else get down to the hard and miserable business of rethinking his compositional procedures from scratch. I speak as someone whose failures and successes as a writer, director and actor in these matters, just about balance out.'

CHAPTER SIXTEEN

Let there be gall enough in thy ink...[†]

Next, it was the turn of Alan Ayckbourn, who was emerging as one of Britain's most important new playwrights. He wrote: 'It is perhaps worth noting that the three theatrical knights who oppose the open staging at Sheffield are all actors-turned-directors. I would suggest that their opinions are based, not unnaturally, on their experience as actors. Their criticism of this form of staging is justifiable only in so far as it is true that many proscenium arch acting techniques are not feasible within it. But then, technical expertise has seldom transferred from one medium to another without considerable modifications. Thus, in my experience, it's the younger actor who's happiest to adapt to these new forms of theatre. Once over the initial panic at the proximity of the audience, he relishes the contact he has with them.

'During the eight or nine years I have worked in open stage theatre, only the theatregoers with the hardest of playgoing arteries have ever complained, and these can be counted on the fingers of one hand. The commonest concern expressed is that 'I could see perfectly, but I was terribly worried about the people on the other side'. It's a typical picture, too, at matinee performances in Scarborough (where seats are not numbered) to see elderly ladies all but coming to blows, determined to sit in what they consider the best seats in the theatre, even though these are positioned all around the auditorium. On investigation, it transpires that these so-called "best" seats were just the first they ever sat in.

'Writing for the open stage can present the author with a freedom which he will rarely find outside radio. If he believes, as I do, that his brief is to create an experience to be shared between one actor and

---

[†] William Shakespeare, *Twelfth Night*, Act III, Scene 2.

an audience, he will happily accept a form of theatre that lays such emphasis on these ingredients.

'It's important that the theatre sticks to its priorities. Films, television, radio, those new-fangled upstarts, can do a lot of things better than the theatre. But the things they do are not what the theatre was intended for in the first place. To compete with the cinema, physically, with elaborate scenery is to reveal oneself, however ingenious, as the poor relation. To compete with television, the medium of the raised eyebrow, with box-set naturalism is merely to show how unnatural the theatre is by comparison. To lay emphasis purely upon the spoken word, with static conversation pieces, is simply radio with distracting pictures.

'Theatre is a human medium, and the eyes, the voice, the hands, are only ingredients of that creature, the actor. What the open stage does for him is to give opportunity for total involvement with his whole range of physical resources.'

And, finally, the playwright Peter Terson contributed to the debate: 'When I started writing plays, the biggest obstacle in the creative bit was linking what was going on in my mind with what I knew of the

Alan Ayckbourn and Peter Terson

theatres. I couldn't, for example, dream of any words of mine coming from the gold and gilt of Cheltenham Rep, or the fire curtain with its adverts in the Theatre Royal Newcastle. I couldn't really imagine those actors who seem to sidle on sideways, crabwise, saying my words; it all seemed so phoney to me, so false: I was always a realist and hated walls that shook and rippled when somebody slammed the door. I couldn't bear to see people supposed to be knocking whiskies back when it was coloured water; and pretending to be drunk. It might be a great acting triumph, but to me it was a pain in the neck.

'However, I continued to write plays blindly; but still aware of this insuperable obstacle. Then I went to the Theatre in the Round at Stoke-on-Trent and suddenly the whole thing clicked. There was no pretence here; no sidling about like crabs; no make-up that ended at the ear; what was going on on the stage seemed to match what was going on in my head. It was as easy as that. All right. I had to make concessions to the drink and let them substitute Ribena for Damson Wine in *The Mighty Reservoy*. But apart from that, there has never been any concession at all. I really cannot sum up all that stuff about theatre-in-the-round and proscenium arch: but to me it is the difference between watching a pavement artist at work and turning up at the Royal Academy after Varnishing Day.[115] (Long after.)'

Among the many letters sent to *The Observer* about the thrust stage was one from Alfred Emmet, Director of the Questors Theatre in Ealing, London. He was not quoted in the newspaper, perhaps because the Questors was an amateur theatre, but his letter (which I saw later) repeated many of the points of an earlier article he had written in *TABS* in March 1967, just as we were starting to design the new Playhouse. This article was, in my view, one of the clearest and most lucid outlines of the ethos and practical demands of the thrust stage.

Emmet got straight to the point: 'My testimony is purely practical and pragmatic—the thrust stage *works*, and this over a wide range of plays of all periods and all types. Our marked preference for this form

---

[115] Varnishing Day is a longstanding tradition at the Royal Academy and refers to when artists put the finishing touches to their works and varnished them before the opening of the Summer Exhibition. It was also a private viewing of the exhibition, where artists, journalists and celebrities could meet and discuss the paintings before the exhibition opened to the public.

of staging in a theatre designed equally for a single-view form is not due to dogmatic theory, but as a result of practical experience. Our many producers, free to choose the stage arrangement, have opted this way. Since the Questors opened in 1964, forty-two productions have been presented on a thrust stage arrangement and eight in the round, while, excluding an annual melodrama which by tradition is presented on a picture-frame stage, only fourteen have been presented on some kind of end-stage with a single-view concept.

'The first and greatest difficulty that we experienced has been to get directors and designers to think sculpturally—three-dimensionally instead of picture-wise two-dimensionally. Most directors and virtually all designers think in terms of visual images. Such images are almost inevitably seen from one viewpoint, and that viewpoint is practically always centre-front. The first attempt to overcome this usually substitutes some other fixed viewpoint, say from the side instead of the front; or an effort to run around the perimeter

Alfred Emmet (left) along with architect Norman Branson, actor Marius Goring, and Questors designer Graham Heywood, examining plans for the Questors Theatre, 1955

either in imagination or in fact, to see that it 'looks all right' from all sides.

'The difficulty does not exist for the actor who usually, once he has surrendered himself to the feeling of being surrounded or nearly surrounded by his audience, finds great imaginative stimulus from the freedom to play directly to his fellows instead of having to present a false continuous face to the audience as in proscenium stage convention. This gives a clue to the director's escape from his dilemma: he can start directing the play from the viewpoint of the actor, internally, as it were, from the middle of the acting area instead of from the point of view of the audience, which implies one section of the audience. A director working on a proscenium stage would plot every move before a "blocking" rehearsal, but will find on an open stage the moves have to come much more from the actors themselves in the course of rehearsal, or from his own subjective association of himself with the actor's state.

'The designer's problem is more difficult. In the case of a free-standing sculpture, its totality may be achieved by the viewer walking all the way round it and adding up the impressions received from this experience. In the theatre, the viewpoint of any individual member of the audience remains fixed. The problem is one of a multiplicity of viewpoints simultaneously existing, not of a changing viewpoint. The totality has to be realised from many different viewpoints at the same time. Representational scenery placed on the stage for the purpose of making a visual statement is not appropriate to the open stage. At the Questors, scenery in the accepted sense is reduced to an absolute minimum. The spatial relationship between a number of well-chosen carefully placed items of furniture can be most evocative, provided the audience can see the whole of the stage floor, and is therefore aware of such a relationship.

'In regard to the acting space itself, our experience has led me to three tentative conclusions; the acting space should not be too large, it should be well-defined in itself, and it should be apart—not confused with the audience space. In terms of open stage work, one often hears bandied about such words as "intimacy", "audience participation" and "involvement", and it is tempting, once the barrier of the old proscenium arch has been removed, to go further and try to spill over any boundary line that remains between audience and actor. It is important to maintain a clear line of demarcation, and when the actor oversteps it, the results tend to be one of embarrassment and unease among the audience. The effect is to alienate rather than involve.'[116]

Mr Emmet conceded that the open stage had some limitations: the quick aside is particularly difficult, as is direct contact with the audience at once, or 'playing out' to the audience. He suggested a number of techniques to address these challenges: to minimise masking, he would position two actors opposite each other but in line with the 'tunnels'; actors would use a slightly curved line of advance towards another character instead of a straight line; and he would allow small movements by the actors in order to avoid being too static.

Although this affected the acting style, he insisted that '[t]here is nothing inherently more difficult or artificial about such techniques than there is about corresponding techniques to enable actors to be seen on a proscenium stage. It would be absurd to pretend that an open stage has no limitations. At the Questors, such limitations seem far less hampering than those met with on a proscenium stage—however well-equipped and well-designed.'[117]

Later, Peter Cheeseman arranged for *Plays and Players* to carry an article including the remarks by the playwrights just quoted. Sir Bernard wrote back to Cheeseman: 'Dramatists are not judges of stages. My experience is that all new dramatists are only too happy to have their plays produced anywhere, "unlooked-for success in a barn" being preferable to no production at all.' Peter replied: 'The dramatists you describe have long got over being frantic for unlooked-for success in a barn. All have considerable experience in working in several kinds of theatre and in television, and I don't think you can dismiss their views so summarily.' He also took a jab at Sir Bernard's repeated references to Benoît-Constant Coquelin, pointing out that Cheeseman and the other playwrights were 'speaking from real experience of a kind which M. Coquelin, however much he knew

---

[116] This echoes the feelings of my father and David Brayshaw after seeing *The Visit* at the Guthrie Theater, when they felt the director had gone too far by spilling the performance into the audience.
[117] Article in *TABS*, March 1967.

about frontal acting, never had. It is a pity we can't consult Roscius, or, even better, Richard Burbage.'

As well as the big guns firing in our defence, there were local advocates in our favour every bit as committed as those from Sheffield who opposed what we were planning. Looking back through my cuttings of that time, three examples stand out.

First, Mr Paul Wilcot of Greenland, Sheffield: 'I am getting extremely bored by all the people who are pouring cold water on the Sheffield Playhouse scheme. It is in my opinion, very narrow-minded and a grave underestimation of the talents of Colin George and the other Playhouse directors, to suggest that the new thrust stage is a mere toy which we'll soon grow tired of.

'It is also very wrong to suggest that this sort of stage is not theatrically viable; on the contrary, this stage will bring the actor in much closer contact with the audience, which is much more theatrical than the conventional stage [...] To me, and to many other of the younger theatregoers, the new scheme is immensely challenging and exciting. It is sheer nonsense to suggest that plays written for a conventional stage will not be able to be performed on a thrust stage. They will simply have to be staged differently, which will be challenging for the director and the actors, and stimulating for the audience because of the re-thinking of familiar plays.

'I was astounded at the impudence of Sir Bernard in criticising the scheme: his links with the city are tenuous. (He was, I believe, with the Playhouse Company in the 1920s.) I am sure that had he been living at the onset of the Restoration, he would have bitterly attacked the proscenium stage, which was just beginning to come into use, pointing out that the old thrust-type stage was responsible for inspiring such geniuses as Shakespeare, Ben Jonson and Christopher Marlowe, and that this new type of stage would be out of date in ten years. As well as hearing the opinions of Miles, Olivier and Clements, I should also like to know what Peter Hall, Trevor Nunn, Peter Brook and John Barton think of Sheffield's new theatre.'

Second, Mr Ivan Morris of Norton, Sheffield: 'Amidst all the condemnation descending upon the promoters of the wonderful new theatre planned for this city, and upon Colin George in particular, I feel it is time those who do support this centre gave some encouragement to those in the fore. Of course, there always is contention, disagreement and argument—with the most famous people on both sides whenever something appears which differs from our cosy surroundings. If there were not invention and experiment, no one would have thought of the proscenium stage, and we should all be sitting happily around the open, projecting stage devised by the Greeks (who had none of the technical sophistications by which we can improve even their proven method of theatre production).

'I was present at the Playhouse open forum and am enthralled at the exciting prospects this new theatre offers. As a piece of architecture, it will be superb, both in appearance and function. It will be a wonderful addition to what is already an exciting and lively city. One criticism levelled against the thrust stage is its inability to allow the production of pantomime; I suggest this is utter nonsense. The chorus girls may have to have geometry lessons, on chords, radii, etc.—but imagine a *Treasure Island*, or a *Jack and the Beanstalk* on such a stage.[118] Stupendous.

'In my opinion the "thrust" (unhappy word) stage offers a much greater scope for a whole range of art forms from our new writers, producers, musicians and actors, than ever can be achieved with the proscenium stage, with its problems of acoustics, lighting, limiting of vision, etc. Let us leave our proscenium viewing to the telly box, the source of so many of our prejudices, and welcome the new theatre. Carry on Colin.'

And third, the briefest letter sent to me personally at the Playhouse from a P J Short of Whalley Range, Manchester: 'Dear Mr George, Stick to the thrust stage. I'm not a theatre fan, but I was at University in Sheffield and I have visited the Playhouse several times. The best of luck with your appeal, and here's a quid towards it.' Well, every little helps.

---

[118] Mr Morris's remark was prescient: my father's first Christmas show at the Crucible in 1971 was his production of *Treasure Island*, adapted by Alan Cullen, which was a rip-roaring success.

xix. David Brayshaw, Tony Hampton and Sir Tyrone Guthrie inspecting the Crucible auditorium under construction, January 1971.

xx. *The engineers take a break in the half-built Crucible auditorium. The steel structure over the under stage, on top of which the thrust stage will be built, is clearly visible behind them.*

xxi. *Tanya Moiseiwitsch and Colin George view the Crucible auditorium as construction nears completion, 1971.*

xxii. *The Company and staff of the Sheffield Playhouse at the start of the last season (1970-71) before moving into the Crucible Theatre.*

xxiii. *Above: The Crucible auditorium, 1971; Below: The ground floor bar.*

xxiv. *The foyers and upper floor bar show Tony Corbett's stunning architectural lighting (designed and installed on a shoestring budget) and Clare Ferraby's vibrant carpets and coloured arrows indicating the auditorium entrances.*

xxv. *Douglas Campbell chairing the Music Hall in* Fanfare *at the Crucible Theatre, November 1971.*

xxvi. *Ian McKellen as Hamlet, 1971. Ian was performing this role in London when he appeared in* Swan Song *at the Crucible's opening.*

xxvii. *Niall Buggy & Fanny Carby in* The Birthday Party *at the Crucible Theatre, May 1972.*

xxviii. *Ann Casson as Kate & Paul Angelis as Petruchio in* The Taming of the Shrew *at the Crucible Theatre, October 1972.*

xxix. Lynda Marchal & Paul Angelis in Alpha Beta at the Crucible, February 1973.

xxx. Colin George playing the title roles in Dr Jekyll & Mr Hyde during his final season at the Crucible, February 1974. It would be nearly 40 years before he would perform again on the Crucible's thrust stage.

xxxi. Scene from Calamity Jane, Colin George's valedictory production at the Crucible, with Lynda Marchal playing the lead, July 1974.

xxxii. *Tanya Moiseiwitsch and Colin George in her home, May 2001.*

xxxiii. *Colin George with the Company and stage crew of Othello on the Crucible thrust stage on his 82nd birthday, 20th September 2011.*

Part V

Fighting for the Crucible

The Crucible Theatre under construction, with the Victoria Hall visible behind, February 1970.

CHAPTER SEVENTEEN

*And if there is still one hellish, truly accursed thing in our
time, it is our artistic dallying with forms, instead of being like
victims burnt at the stake, signalling through the flames.*[†]

Following my formal appointment as Artistic Director of the new theatre on 4th December 1969, I was imprisoned in my office for much of the time, dillying and dallying with the pile of papers on my desk. The interminable minutes of meetings, letters, memoranda, press cuttings, photographs and designs—all of these paraphernalia arrive on your shoulders when you are running the last lap of a marathon to build a new theatre.

I was only too aware of Antonin Artaud's passionate cry (quoted above). Sometimes it did feel like we were all signalling though the flames of criticism. But as I came to realise, building a theatre is very different from putting on a theatrical production. The latter can be altered at will, even at the last minute, and in any case has a limited life, whereas a theatre is there for a generation at least, and decisions about its shape, form and personality are for a time irrevocable.

In October 1969, the architects finally broke ground on the site of the new theatre, and in January 1970 they shared with us the complete technical drawings of the new theatre building. They were impressive and showed all the work everyone had put in over the previous two years (see next page).

As the floorplan of the ground floor shows, the Studio's octagonal shape mirrored the main auditorium, but it was only outlined as a shell as there was no budget for fitting it out. Despite the lack of funds, I did not want to give up on the Studio because I knew that it would perform a crucial role—for experimental theatre, work by Theatre Vanguard and televisual productions. However, the Trustees had approved only a basic scheme for conference and exhibition use with a budget of

---

[†] Antonin Artaud, *The Theatre and Its Double*.

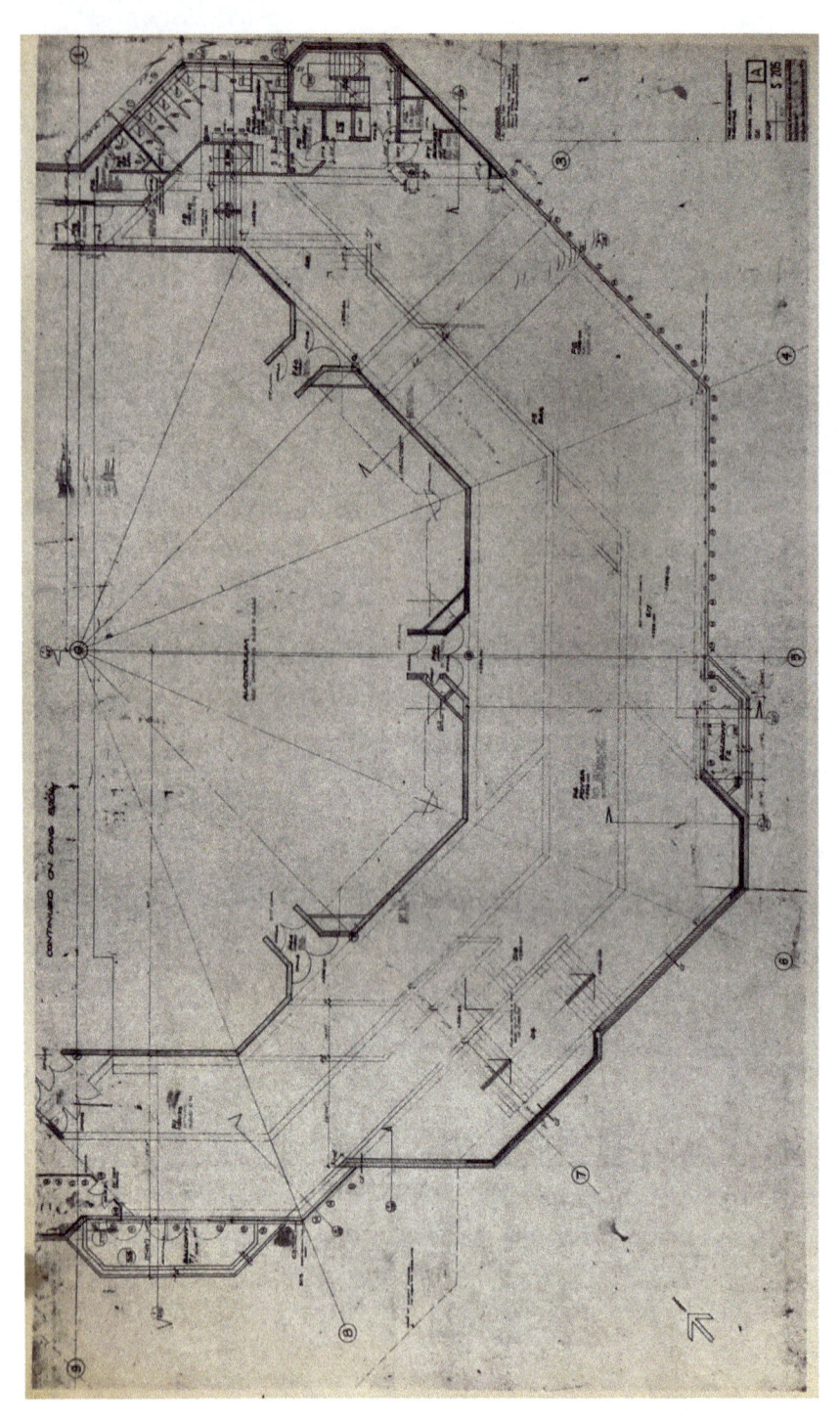

This view of the auditorium and surrounding foyer (above) shows how the octagonal shape of the building emanates from the 'Magic Circle' in the middle of the stage. At the start of construction, the builders placed a pin at the centre of this circle as a visual guide to the geometry of the auditorium.

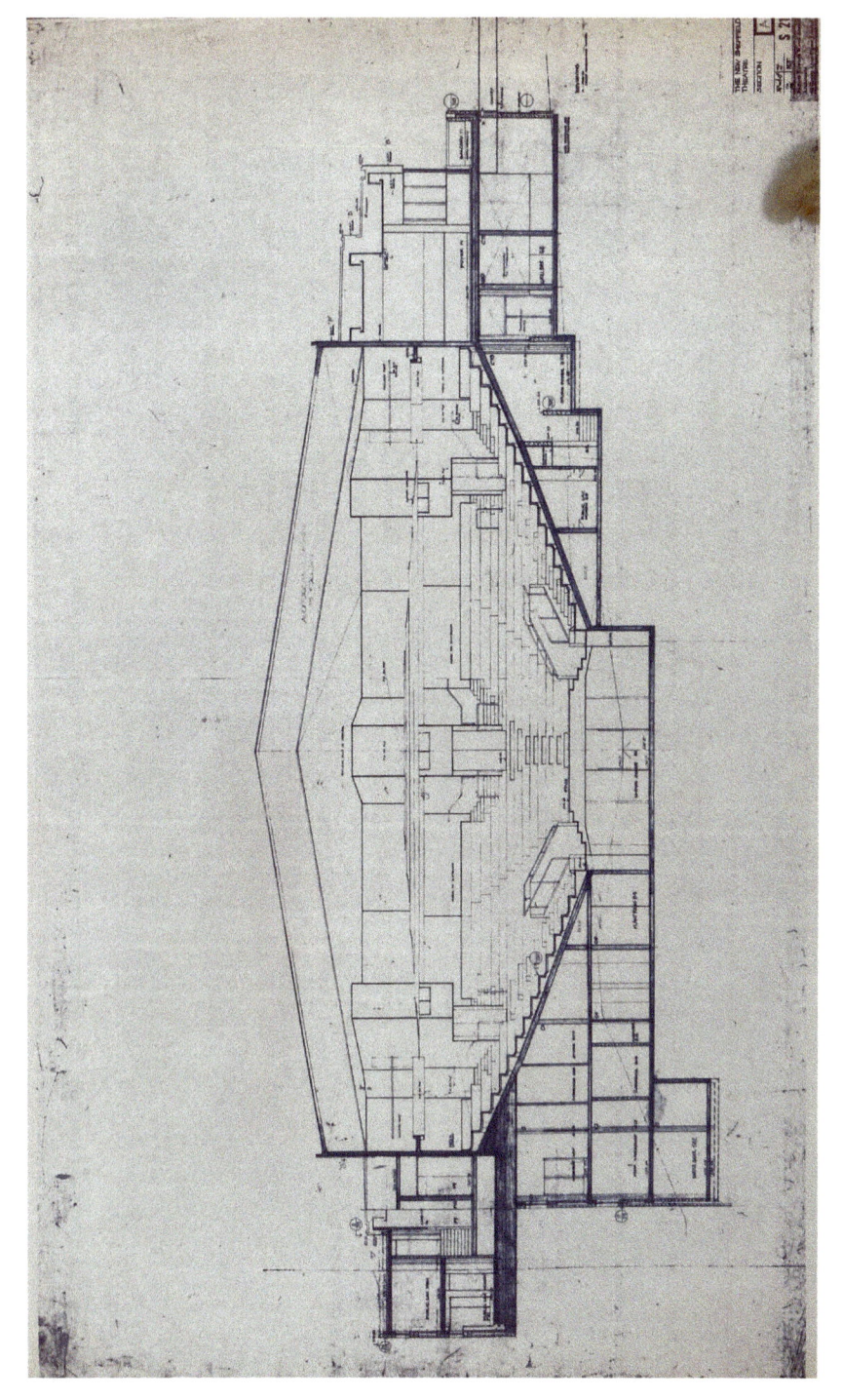

This cut-through shows the hidden warren of passages and rooms underneath the stage where the actors, designers and stage crew would work.

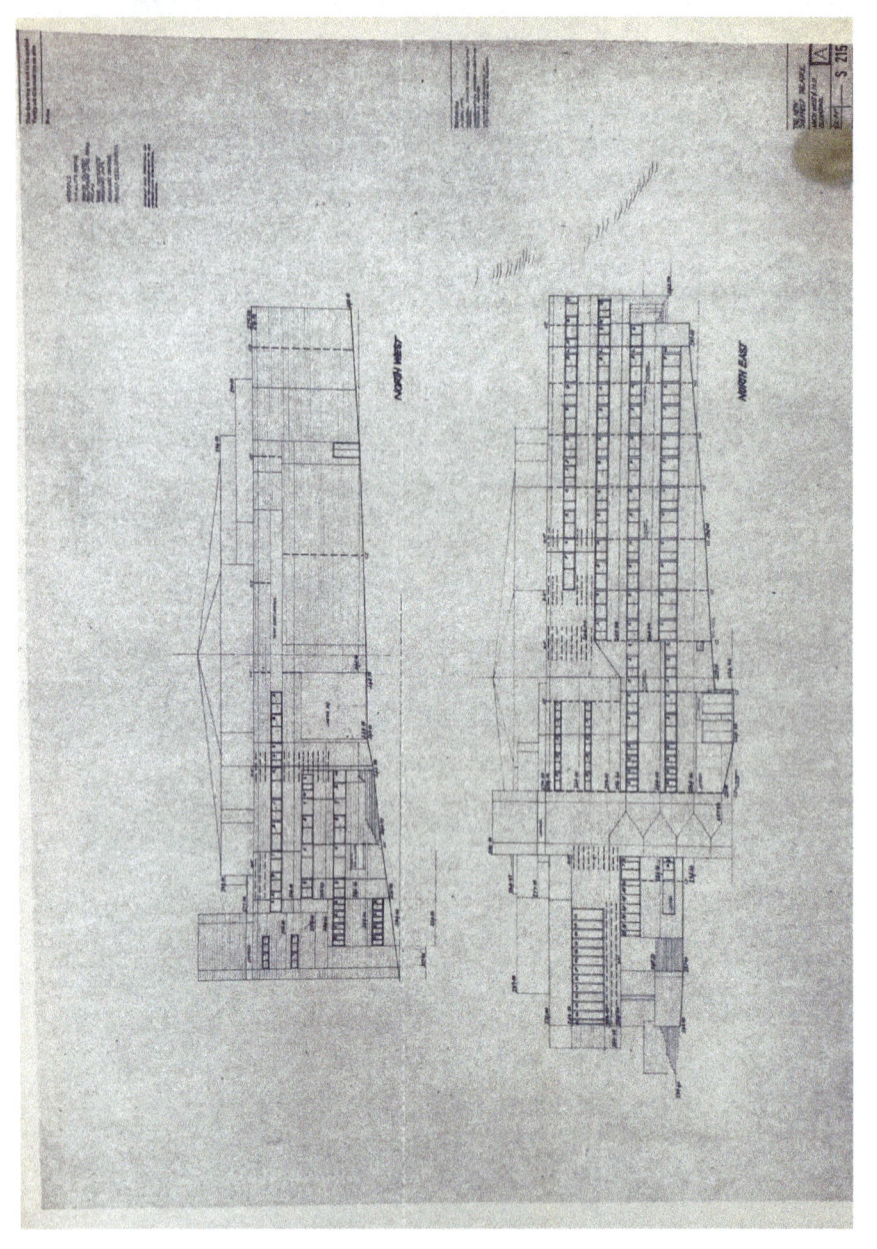

This elevation shows how the architects made use of the sloping land to give the maximum number of windows on the lower floors.

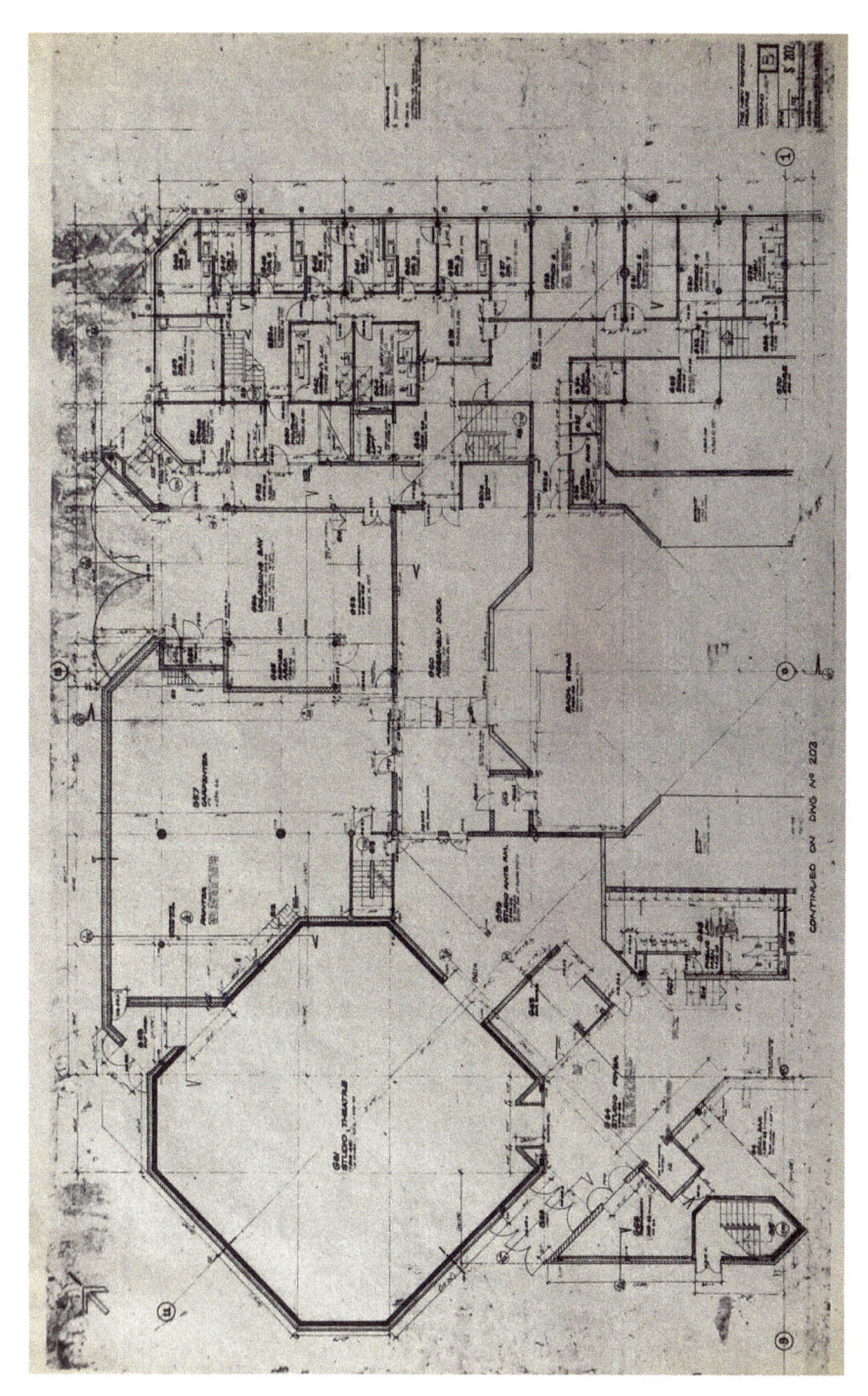

This view shows the Studio, the 'get-in' and loading bay (top middle) and the many rooms for the administration & production teams.

£25,000. To equip the Studio for theatre and television use, as well as full air-conditioning, would cost a further £67,000.[119]

I decided to follow up on Pat Ide's suggestion that special funding sources might be available for the Studio if I were to emphasise the children's theatre connection. In March 1970, I wrote to Alexander Dunbar, London Director of the Gulbenkian Foundation, asking for their support. He wrote back regretting that he doubted the Foundation would help as they had declined similar requests in recent years. But he promised to approach the Gulbenkian Trustees and agreed to meet David Brayshaw and me in London. I brought along the architects' brochures about the Studio and pleaded our case that it was a centre for our children's theatre company. We had a warm and friendly meeting, but there was no promise of money yet.

With the necessary funding unforthcoming, we decided to split the problem in two. First, we would seek funding from the New Sheffield Theatre Trust to build the basic shell and amenities of the Studio. Then, we would seek external funding to fully equip it for use. If that meant we had to wait longer to have a functional Studio Theatre, then so be it. Far better than abandoning the idea altogether.

So, in February 1971, we submitted to the Building Committee an extension to the original contract to build the main theatre, requesting an additional £29,894 to be spent on the Studio, which would include the floor finish, entrance doors and lighting board. Work to complete the Studio and make it fully functional would require a further £24,000. At a meeting on 22nd June, the Building Committee authorised £35,000 of work to fit out the Studio, noting that a further £24,500 would be needed to complete the work. After much back and forth, the Building Committee finally approved this additional amount, setting a ceiling of £61,000 on the total contribution towards the Studio.[120] So we had the shell—but no seats or stage.

I went back to Alexander Dunbar, asking if the Gulbenkian Foundation might help us equip the Studio. On 9th March 1971 he

---

[119] In the architects' report on the Studio Theatre, produced in July 1969, Gleeds estimated the total cost of fitting it out at £87,923, plus an additional £4,000 for full air-conditioning. This is the equivalent of £1.3 million in 2021.
[120] In 2021 this would be the equivalent of £768,000.

wrote back with wonderful news: 'Dear Colin, I am glad to confirm that the Trustees have agreed to offer a grant of £50,000 towards the cost of equipping the Studio Theatre.[121] £35,000 can be made available immediately to meet the cost of ventilation equipment, electricity supply, and essential services. The balance of £15,000 is offered on condition that an additional sum of £11,000 sufficient to meet the remainder of the cost estimated for equipping the Studio in full, is raised from other sources.' It was, I believe, the Foundation's first grant to a professional theatre company—up till that time they had only supported educational institutions. So we had our Studio!

With the key decisions on the theatre's design having been made, I realised there was another glaring problem to address—which had nothing to do with the building itself. This was my total inexperience of working on a thrust stage. I had worked on open stages before and had seen thrust stage productions, but I had never directed a production on a Guthrie thrust stage. Now I would be exposed to its challenges in a very personal way, and I would rightly be judged on my ability to master the stage format I had so fiercely championed.

It was Guthrie who came to my rescue. I realised later, looking at our correspondence over five years, that he had become my mentor. Although I never got the opportunity to work with him and he saw only one of my productions, *The Caucasian Chalk Circle* designed by Tanya, he could not have been more helpful and involved in what we were doing in Sheffield. He was highly supportive of my first mask production of *Oedipus* in April 1968, which had been inspired by his *House of Atreus* in Minneapolis. And over the years he wrote many times recommending actors he knew, some of them at the beginning of their careers, who he felt would contribute to the Sheffield Company.

So, on 3rd November 1969, I wrote to him, suggesting it would be helpful if I could direct on a thrust stage, possibly at a Canadian University. He made another suggestion: 'If it can be arranged Stratford (Ont) is where you should go. I'll "say a word" in the right quarters, but fear it may be late for next season, but there's always the year after. I'll write to Jean Gascon who is Artistic Director and you write to him as well.' Guthrie's influence was, as always, invaluable. As he suspected, I

---

[121] In 2021 this grant would be the equivalent of £630,000.

could not be fitted into the main programme on the thrust stage, but they suggested I direct a production in their proscenium theatre and use my presence in Stratford, Ontario to study the thrust stage.

So, in April 1970, I went to Stratford to direct the world premiere of *Vatslav* by Polish playwright Sławomir Mrożek. Mrożek's *Tango* (1965), an attack on Communist totalitarianism, had established his international reputation. I already knew Mrożek's work as, while I was building links with the theatre in Belgrade, my Assistant Director, Wilfred Harrison, was nurturing them in Poland. He visited theatres in the country in 1968 and in the summer of 1969, shortly after I directed *Romeo and Juliet* at the Boško Buha in Belgrade, the Playhouse hosted a Polish festival programme. This included music, films, art, a three-day visit by the Wroclaw Mime Theatre and a production of *Tango* directed by Wilfred.[122]

Although my production of *Vatslav* was performed not on the Stratford thrust stage but in their proscenium theatre, the experience was to prove hugely useful for two reasons. First, the leading role was played by Douglas Campbell, who had worked in the Stratford Company with Tyrone Guthrie from the very first season. He was able to share a wealth of experience of working on the thrust stage and would be an invaluable help when he joined us for the opening of our new theatre the following year. Second, I was able to see the season's productions on the main house thrust stage several times and familiarise myself with the different requirements for rehearsing, blocking and lighting.

Later that year, the Playhouse's strong connection with Polish theatre gave me the opportunity to work with one of most extraordinary theatre designers of the 20th century, Jozef Szajna. Szajna was born in southern Poland in 1922 and spent the war years in the Nazi death camps at Auschwitz and Buchenwald. The experience, he later said, 'made me interested only in man, and in the basic problems of the contemporary world. Using the language of the visual arts, I try to answer the questions and give my comments on the events which appear on the front—and not the back—pages of daily papers.'

---

[122] This was to be the last production that Wilfred directed at the Playhouse. He resigned as Associate Director in January 1970 and was succeeded by Frank Hatherley, who became Director of Productions for the Playhouse's final season (1970-71). Wilfred returned to play the lead in Geoffrey Ost's production of *The Father* shortly before the Playhouse closed, after which he became the Artistic Director of the Octagon Theatre in Bolton.

Jozef Szajna in his studio, early 1960s

I had seen examples of his work in articles shared with me by the Polish cultural attaché and they made a deep impression on me. One of the articles explored the motivation behind Szajna's work, which stemmed from his traumatic childhood: 'Szajna's sets express the things that every Pole who lived through the last war carries hidden deep within himself, things that are hidden, revealed only in nightmares or in the fumes of alcohol—the indelible memory of past horror. No matter what Szajna does or what medium he uses, his imagination is haunted by the nightmare of Auschwitz.' His designs were 'visions of annihilation'. 'Under the cover of surrealism or "informal surrealism", of toying with varied assemblage of techniques, textures and colour combinations, sometimes erotic motifs and jests, there appear above all tortured, ruined, crumbling, decaying bodies, a world suspended ominously above the men (actors), menacing, sometimes steel-hard, but most often torn, broken, as formless as mud or a man's mangled face.'[123]

---

[123] Tedd's note: I found this article among my father's Crucible papers but have been unable to establish which publication it came from.

I was planning to direct a production of *Macbeth* in the first half of the Playhouse's last season, 1970-71, and I felt that Szajna's disturbing and modern design could enable a very different kind of Shakespeare production. So I invited him to design the show at the Playhouse, which he graciously accepted. He arrived in Sheffield in September 1970 and during the month he spent with us, his presence and imagination were a huge benefit to the Company.

Jozef produced a series of stunning, some might say shocking, designs for *Macbeth*. His central image of a man suspended by his ankles being driven through with swords is particularly gruesome and became the programme cover. But there was much about Szajna's design that was deliberately hidden from view. He believed that 'what is happening on stage should be for the spectator a visualisation of the things that are suppressed within himself'. Some critics—notably from *The Stage*—failed to grasp this and took the production literally (and negatively). But many were swept up by the uneasy subconscious feelings that Szajna's disturbing imagery conjured up within them.

Szajna's work was run through with a determination to expose fascism in all its forms. Thus, in his design for *Macbeth*, the protagonists were divided into three groups: the old generation, represented by Duncan in a wheelchair; the fascist generation (ours), represented by the skinhead Macbeth and Lady Macbeth; and Malcolm, the new generation. *The Guardian* praised Szajna's designs: 'This is a truly masterful presentation of rich barbarism and dark villainy [...] With all due credit to all the good things that are happening on English stages today, it is a revelation to see his work in action.'[124]

This production of *Macbeth* also brought to the attention of the Sheffield public a rising young actor: Nigel Hawthorne. Nigel had joined the Company for the 1969-70 Season and, in the spring of 1970, I directed him in *Strip Jack Naked*, a visceral piece by Company member Christopher Wilkinson which divided the critics. But Nigel's performance as Macbeth took them by storm.

The *Morning Telegraph* reported: 'You will watch in vain for conventional heroics and thunderous speech-making, but [Hawthorne's Macbeth] is an articulate hero who makes sense of his appointment

---

[124] *The Guardian*, September 1970.

Scene from Macbeth *at the Sheffield Playhouse, September 1970*

Szajna's central design & Nigel Hawthorne's skinhead Macbeth

with doom and whose gradual decline into madness is more believable and finally sympathetic than any I have ever seen.' Radio Sheffield's reporter called it 'one of the most stimulating and original productions I've seen for a long time', while the critic from *The Star* described it as: 'The most magnificent *Macbeth* I have ever seen.'

After Jozef had returned to Poland and *Macbeth* was playing to good houses, I wrote to him: 'Life here doesn't seem the same without you! The theatre is not quite so "total" in its intensity as it was when your personality was sparking off those of us fortunate enough to be involved in working on *Macbeth*.' I expressed hope that I would be able to arrange funding to visit Poland and see some Polish theatre, signing off: 'I do sincerely intend not to let our association wither—we must work together again soon.' It would take me three years to achieve that ambition.

The same month we opened *Macbeth*, our new theatre finally got a name. By then the project was more than four years old, and as an un-christened baby the theatre lacked the personality to impress itself on the public's imagination. The Trustees had first invited submissions of names for the new theatre back in March 1968, but they had made little headway. So, after our first press conference in June 1969, the *Morning Telegraph* launched a competition for its readers, offering a £10 prize for the best name—and it was overwhelmed with suggestions.

A Mr Tony Greenwood, member of the Metallurgy Division of

Jozef Szajna chatting with me and the wardrobe mistress, Madge d'Alroy, during rehearsals for Macbeth

British Steel, suggested a list of steel-related names: The Bath and Ladle, The Bessemer, The Casting Pit (actors would have been wary of that!), The Forge, The Hopper, The Hearth and Spoon, The Pig, The Puddle Shop and The Run-Out Table. Other suggestions: The Ace of Hearts, The Colossus, The Dramarama, The Futurist, The Prince of Wales (it was the year of Prince Charles's investiture), The Jennie Lee (after the first Arts Minister), The Sheaf, The Arundel Gate, The New Elizabethan, The New Playhouse, The Stirrings, and rather cheekily—The White Elephant.

The winner was The Adelphi. There was a local reason for this choice as the new theatre would sit on the site of the Adelphi Hotel, in which the Yorkshire County Cricket Club and both Sheffield football clubs had been founded.[125] But the Adelphi was not the name we chose for our new theatre. Why not? Because we felt it could be confused with other Adelphi theatres in England and we needed something distinctive for Sheffield. It was the publicity manager at the old Playhouse, Hilary Young, who came up with the winning suggestion: The Crucible. Mr Bennet-Keenan, the head of fundraising, proposed this name to the Board, who accepted it.

In October 1970, Tony Hampton announced the new theatre's name at a luncheon in the Town Hall given by the Lord Mayor in honour of James Mason, who was in Sheffield to visit the new theatre's construction site. Anthony explained the Trustees' choice: 'What we liked about "The Crucible" was, first and foremost, its obvious connection with the traditional Sheffield trades; secondly its undoubted association with fine quality; and, last but not least, because the new theatre will be a melting pot of ideas. As a theatre name it will be unique. Whenever and wherever it is mentioned, it will immediately call to mind the theatre in Sheffield, England.' Anthony might also have added that the dictionary gives 'crucible' another definition: 'severe trial'. Considering what we had been through to get to this point, it seemed an apt definition. And our severe trial was not over yet.

---

[125] On 30 January 1854, the Bramall Lane Cricket Ground was founded (this later became the home of Sheffield United Football Club); on 8 January 1863, the Yorkshire County Cricket Club was founded; and on 4 September 1867, Sheffield Wednesday Football Club was founded.

For the event, the fundraising committee had come up with novel ways for the public to contribute to the appeal. You could buy a brick for 10 shillings (one of 32,000), have your name inscribed on a theatre seat for £25 or benefit from priority bookings for life for £50. Corporate donors giving £50 or more would have their trademark displayed on a stainless-steel clad wall in the busy grill bar. You could also contribute to the fund by Deed of Covenant for a fixed amount each year over seven years, with the Trust receiving in addition a rebate on the tax paid on this amount.[126] But these were difficult economic times for Sheffielders, and although the appeal eventually raised £118,000 towards to the new theatre, it would fall well short of the ambitious target of £260,000.[127]

Scepticism about our new theatre remained, and in late December, a veteran variety agent, Stan Farrell, offered odds of 100-1 to any

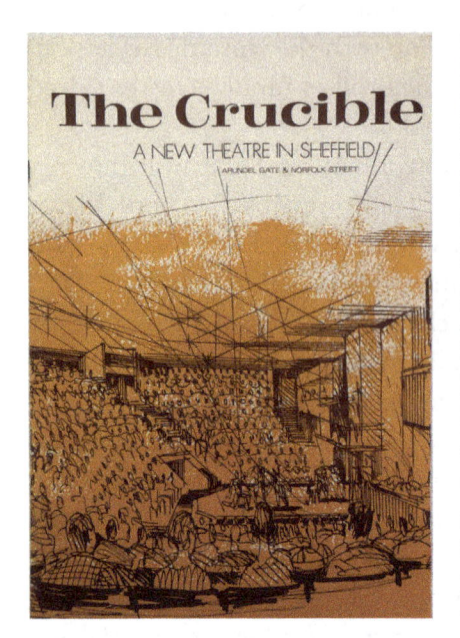

Brochures for the newly named Crucible Theatre, October 1970

---

[126] Given the high rate of tax in 1969, the rebate was considerable: a net annual payment of £5,000 over seven years would not only give the Trust £35,000, but an additional tax rebate of £24,574.

[127] In 2021 terms, the appeal raised £1.5 million out of a target of £3.3 million.

takers that the Crucible would 'show a terrific loss in its first year and be a standing joke'. Frank Hatherley, the Playhouse's Director of Productions, retorted that those odds were too good to miss and claimed there was 'a queue of people here waiting to take him on'.[128] And so, on New Year's Day 1971, a bet was struck live on-air in the studio of Sheffield Radio, Frank wagering one pound against Mr Farrell's prediction. The editor of the *Morning Telegraph* and Michael Barton, station manager of Radio Sheffield, would hold the stakes and adjudicate the outcome, with the winnings to be donated to the Telegraph and Star Old Folks Fund.[129]

Later that month, I was invited back to Canada by the Stratford Company to direct Brendan Behan's *The Hostage* at the new National Arts Centre in Ottawa. The theatre's new thrust stage was a direct imitation of the thrust stage theatre at Stratford, Ontario. The experience of working on a thrust stage, not only with actors but also with the stage management, lighting and sound designers, was the sort of crash course in handling this new space I could not have dreamt about when the new Sheffield theatre was being designed.

I returned to Sheffield to be greeted by a fresh attack on the Crucible. On 20th January, *The Star* carried the headline: 'Theatre Group fight Crucible finance plan'. The newspaper reported that the 'Keep The Lyceum Live' committee had written to the Secretary of State for the Environment, objecting to Sheffield Corporation's application for a £350,000 loan sanction for the new Crucible Theatre. They argued that the Lyceum could be bought for about £150,000: 'a fleabite compared with the money required for the new Playhouse'. They also repeated the claim that the thrust stage would limit visiting attractions, insisting that Sheffield's priority should be a 'civic theatre' for touring plays and amateur dramatics groups.

By April 1971, the headline was more menacing: 'Government bombshell on new theatre'. The newspaper reported that the Department of the Environment had announced it would hold a public

---

[128] *Morning Telegraph*, 1 January 1971.

[129] Tedd's note: I have been unable to confirm whether the bet was paid out. Frank Hatherley shared newspaper cuttings of the wager with me, but no longer remembers placing the bet. As Frank left Sheffield when the Playhouse closed in June 1971 and the bet was not due until November 1972, he probably lost his £1 stake. As it turned out, the Crucible did make a large loss in its first year, but it was far from being 'a standing joke'.

meeting to discuss Sheffield Corporation's plan to grant £350,000 to the Crucible Theatre project. The meeting was scheduled for 3rd June, fourteen weeks before we were due to start rehearsing the first season in the new theatre.

The prospect that the Corporation's funding for the project might be withdrawn at the last moment was disastrous. Tony Hampton insisted that the theatre building contract had been entered into on the basis that the £350,000 would be forthcoming. If the result of the enquiry went against the Corporation and they had to withdraw their support, someone else would have to pay. Alderman Ironmonger said he did not know what would happen if the ministry's decision went against them. Either the theatre would remain an empty shell, or an alternative method of financing would have to be found. The Trust would have until 3rd June to come up with a response.

CHAPTER EIGHTEEN

The valiant never taste of death but once.†

Those of us in the theatre Company had to put the public inquiry out of our minds. It was time to focus on preparing for the Crucible's opening season. I had exchanged ideas with Tyrone Guthrie as early as April 1970 when he was directing *Oedipus* in Australia and I was in Stratford, Ontario directing *Vatslav*. What plays would impress the sceptic and delight the supporter? One adventurous suggestion I made was Shakespeare's *Pericles*.

He replied: 'I love "Pericles" and would love to have a go. But in my opinion, it is not a good idea for one of the early plays at Sheffield. I don't think people will be sophisticated enough to appreciate the extreme naïveté of the storytelling and total absence of "characterisation". I feel strongly that it should be presented in a Shakespearean rep. alongside other specimens of the Bard's handywork.

'Would you consider me doing a Chekhov or a Greek Tragedy? We might do *Oresteia*, if Douglas [Campbell] felt inclined to repeat his Clytemnestra. I have "sort of" (but very "sort of") agreed to do it for Bernard de Mermaid. But only on condition that Campbell and Moiseiwitsch were available. So if you liked the idea and they liked the idea...'[130]

Guthrie asked me to confirm the Crucible's opening date (planned for October 1971), as he had been asked to do two productions in California that autumn but felt he would rather do Sheffield. I replied: 'We should know about the Crucible opening within the next ten weeks. By then the roof should be on. Already the concrete bowl of the auditorium is complete. Could you put off California just a little

---

† William Shakespeare, *Julius Caesar*, Act II, Scene 2.
[130] As it turned out, Douglas wrote to my father that November to confirm that *The House of Atreus* would not be going to the Mermaid owing to lack of funding and visa issues.

longer? I feel certain the theatre is going to be completed in time for our start next year.' As for the opening plays, I suggested we meet and mull this over at leisure.

The following month, having just returned from directing *Vatslav* in Stratford, Ontario, I wrote to Guthrie and formally invited him to direct one of the Crucible's opening productions. He replied 'Yes, I should like very much to be part of the 1972 ongoings in Sheffield.' Having written this, with typical modesty he inserted 'THANK YOU!' in capitals after the 'Yes'. In fact, I should have been the one thanking him for committing himself to the Crucible before other offers.

Guthrie continued: 'Let me know what, and when as soon as you can. I should warn you that I'm having heart strain and have been told to rest for several months and then DO LESS. Oh, well, I am just going to be 70. All best, love to your wife, T.G.' At the time I read his comments as a typically defiant Guthrie attitude to ageing and ill health, but their significance soon became apparent.

In October 1970, Guthrie wrote again from Melbourne to say 'I am cancelling all my American plans for next year—doctor's injunction. So am free any time next fall and at your service. Would you like to consider *The House of Atreus*? I think Minneapolis would make the masks and dresses available at a very reasonable rate. Don't know how Tanya feels nor whether Douglas Campbell could be free. Feel the co-op of Tanya and Douglas would be essential. Warmest wishes. T.G.'

Three months later, on 28th January 1971, Guthrie came to Sheffield to inspect progress on the Crucible building site and to be interviewed by the press. Photos were taken in the auditorium shell, Radio Sheffield interviewed him and he held forth at a buffet lunch in the Playhouse. He was on board and would open *House of Atreus* at the Crucible in October 1971. Or so we thought.

In March, with the Crucible opening only six months away, the Stage Manager, David Marchment, and Designer, Rodney Ford, prepared a staff breakdown for the new theatre. This was based on their experience of working in theatres of comparative size running repertoire on open stages—such as Stratford, Ontario and the Nottingham Playhouse. Total backstage staff, not counting the actors or those working in administration and front of house, came

Two views of the main auditorium & the Studio Theatre under construction

to 37, comprising Stage Management (6), Stage Crew (7), Electrics (4), Wardrobe (11), and Design (9). This was a daunting total after having run the Playhouse with a much smaller staff and, after further discussion, it was whittled down to 21. But we were to discover that, if anything, their first estimate had been too low for a theatre of the complexity and size of the Crucible.

On 10th June, this breakdown was accepted by the Trustees, who made a number of appointments. Rodney Ford became Head of Design, responsible for the execution of design briefs, and David Marchment became Stage Director, overseeing the physical running of rehearsals and performances, and coordinating the stage management teams. It was also agreed to create a new role, Production Manager, who would be responsible to the Artistic Director for the overall functioning of the entire Company: both actors and production staff.

This was a crucial role and we needed someone who was familiar with the thrust stage. We found our man in Stratford, Ontario: Keith Green, whom I had met when he was working in that capacity there. He immediately made useful suggestions: for example, laying rubber matting in the vomitories (which were good for grip and deadened sound) and covering the walls with protective green board (which is soft to bump into).

We also needed a Head of Wardrobe. Given the importance of costume on a thrust stage, where the actors are not removed behind a

Rodney Ford (Head of Design), Keith Green (Production Manager) and David Harvey Jones (Head of Wardrobe)

proscenium arch but so much nearer the audience, the quality of the cutting and making of the costumes had to be first class. And as with the furniture and props, the costumes needed to be fireproof. The perfect recommendation came from Ivan Alderman of the National Theatre: David Harvey Jones, who was filling in at the National's costume department at the time. So we approached him for the job and he accepted.

In March, casting began in earnest. Following Guthrie's suggestion, I wrote to Douglas Campbell, inviting him to join the Crucible Company to play Clytemnestra in Guthrie's production of *The House of Atreus*. He replied: 'I have unfortunately had to commit myself to an engagement in Los Angeles as the lolly was absolutely staggering—however—the engagement ends on October 16th, which means I am free from that time. I am of course anxious and willing to join your coming enterprise.' (In fact, shortly after writing that letter Douglas called to say he was free to join us.)

But Douglas expressed doubts about my choice of *Atreus* to open the Crucible: 'I think you would be well advised to open your theatre with something uniquely your own. Save *Atreus* till later. Tony G is an enormous force and influences everything around him. This, you understand, is not a criticism, just a note.'[131]

I next heard from Guthrie in late March when I was in Dublin directing a short run of *Playboy of the Western World* at the Abbey Theatre. He wrote to me from his home in Annaghmakerrig to tell me about a young actor in the Minneapolis Company who had impressed him: Charles Keating. 'I have taken the liberty of suggesting that I might be able (no commitment) to influence you to let him play Orestes and, maybe, other things in the season. He'd be terrific as Charles Surface (in "School for Scandal"). He's over six foot, very sturdy and handsome and, in my view, very gifted—"star quality" [...] Ring up when/if you can nip up here. Can fetch you if desired—about 2 hours drive. Ever T.G.'

I was able to take him up on his offer and spent Palm Sunday weekend at Annaghmakerrig along with John Goetz and his wife Margaret, whom I had met during my first visit to Minneapolis in

---

[131] Sir Tyrone Guthrie was known as 'Tony' to his closest friends and confidants.

1967. I recall helping trim rhododendrons in the huge garden, Guthrie reading us a Brian Friel story and spending some time chatting with him about *The House of Atreus* and the Crucible opening. He gave me a play by Brian Friel to take to bed and read. I was not overly impressed and told Guthrie in the morning, adding: 'Perhaps I was tired?' 'Yes', he replied smartly, taking back the script, 'I think you were tired'. There was no arguing with Sir Tyrone.

Back in Dublin, the next day I sent a cassette recording to David Brayshaw with my suggestion that we should open with Ibsen's *Peer Gynt*. I had directed *Peer* early in my career for the Arts Council, touring the north of England and Wales. We played all sorts of venues, from city and school halls to a miner's club. A young designer working with Joan Littlewood called John Bury invented a set to adapt to all occasions, with a raked stage and long wooden poles defining the acting areas, leaving the impact of the play very much to the actors. I realised that Ibsen's play had thrust stage potential. So I approached Norman Ginsbury, who had translated the text for Guthrie when he directed it in London with Ralph Richardson and Laurence Olivier, to consider updating it for the Crucible's opening production. He agreed, and as things turned out, it was a happy collaboration.

David Brayshaw wrote back to me in Dublin, where I was rehearsing. 'There's a lot to be said for "Peer". I hope Tony doesn't take umbrage that *he* doesn't open. All sorts of factors seem to be pushing "Atreus" back to the end of November and I'm really very anxious to get open before then if we can.' A major concern was the hire of the costumes which, given fixed costs for freight, would cost £4,600.[132] But if we decided to make our own costumes, the time factor would push back the opening date back. However, there was good news about the theatre's construction: 'The huge crane is out of the site and the roof is practically finished.'

Parties were already being shown around the interior of the theatre and a rota was set up so that the stage door could inform the public when tours were to take place. The centre doors were also left open at lunchtime to let the public view the stage from a roped-off area at the top of the steps. We did all we could to counter the impression

---

[132] This is the equivalent of £58,000 in 2021.

some critics had given the public that the thrust stage was a 'freak' (to use Sir Bernard Miles's epithet). Even seeing the empty structure was reassuring, with a guide to explain what the eventual theatre would look like.

In April 1971, Guthrie began directing *The Barber of Seville* for the Phoenix Opera in Brighton. I had just finished reading the Australian writer Richard Neville's book '*Playpower*' and thought it summed up the 1960s culture of protest by the young: mocking the status quo with 'play' rather than violence. So I sent it to Guthrie. He wrote back, thanking me for the book, which he was looking forward to reading, and adding: 'The high spirits of the *Barber of S* are KILLING me, but not so rapidly as the sense of humour of the singers. If someone says a spoonerism by mistake they laugh for minutes on end, and then keep "going into kinks" for hours after. If someone says something really funny, they don't understand. Ever T.G.'

On April 30th, one week before *The Barber of Seville* opened, I received another letter: 'Dear Colin, *Playpower* was very interesting

The roof of the Crucible under construction, February 1971

and I thought rather wittily written. But its 'philosophy' seems to me very immature and very selfish. But there *is* a justification for young people to reject the materialism which has dominated European thinking since the split in the Christian church circa 1550. But the answer *isn't* a childish anarchy. I think we (i.e. old people) make *far* too much fuss about "drugs" and they (i.e. young people) ditto ditto about "the generation gap". Twenty year olds forget (and *always* have) that in another 20 years they will be fat and forty; and that in another twenty, THEY will be OLD and *two* subsequent generations will be thudding on THEIR door! Time like an ever rolling…

'The unrelenting high spirits of *Barber of S* are killing me—and I've (literally) lost my voice—third recurrence of a sort of bronchial cold. Tanya is grappling with great self-control with A Situation. Last Thursday was to have been a Dress Parade with all costumes complete except for "minor alterations"! One costume (out of 28) was ready (and rather poorly made) and the little lady-gentleman-round-the-corner (an ill-judged economy by the management) didn't seem adequately penitent. "Don't worry", he said, "It'll be all right on the night"—his very words. If Tanya had been Jehovah, he would have shrivelled that second into white ash. Ever T.G.'

After giving further thought to Guthrie's suggestion to open the Crucible with a Chekhov piece, I wrote to him on 12th May: 'Although we may well think it is an excellent thing to do for the warm-up week, our plans are still fluid, and it would have been rash to prevent it from being performed elsewhere. Incidentally, I am hoping we can settle the hiring of the *Atreus* costumes from Minneapolis shortly. With all good wishes, Colin.' But I was not to receive a reply.

Three days later, it was the dress rehearsal of my final production at the old Playhouse, the musical *Britannia's Boys* written by Alan Cullen. I was giving notes to the Company and I noticed the Stage Manager hovering around significantly; I recognised the look on his face and knew straight away that something was wrong. He waited shrewdly for the Company to clear and then came up to me. "You needn't tell me,' I said, 'the wigs haven't arrived from London.' 'No,' he replied, 'I have just heard on the news that Sir Tyrone Guthrie died this morning.'

Even many years later, it is hard to put down in words how news of Guthrie's sudden death affected me. I had no idea that in his last months he was so ill and appeared to sense his end was coming. When I read his comment—made in both of his last two letters to me—that the 'high spirits of *Barber of S* are killing me!', I had taken this to be his usual and enviable literary flamboyance. And now he was gone. I had lost a mentor, a good friend, and a steadfast ally of the Crucible only months before we were due to open. His absence would leave a huge hole.

Charles Keating, who on Guthrie's suggestion I had offered a place in the Crucible's first season, captured how we all felt in his letter to me shortly after Guthrie died: 'The death of a man like Guthrie means so much more than with most people, it seems, not really because of his talent but rather his humanity, far more rare than talent, I think. You selfishly feel yourself cheated, not having spent enough hours talking with him. It's ironic that he didn't get to see the "thrust" develop and find acceptance in England. There's little point in talking about it. I think we share the same feeling. We leave here... and prepare for the new adventure.'

As if to harden the blow, the day of reckoning for the Crucible had come too. Three weeks later, on 5th June 1971, the inquiry into the City's funding of the Crucible was held in the City Hall, chaired by Mr K A Blacker, an Inspector from the Department of the Environment. After all the anticipation of this final showdown, the opposition fizzled out. Only three protesters turned up and the principal objector—a Mr Roger Bingham—was prevented from attending by ill health. A former manager of the Lyceum, Hedley Morton, called for a civic theatre and suggested putting the Crucible up for sale if the Playhouse could not find the money. Yet again the phrase was used that the theatre would become a 'white elephant'.

After a four-hour meeting, Mr Blacker visited the Crucible site, which was nearing completion, and returned to London to report to the Secretary of State, Peter Walker. The result? The City Council had indeed acted in accordance with the terms of the Local Government Act of 1948. The Crucible would be completed.

Two weeks later, on 16th June 1971, a memorial service was held for Sir Tyrone Guthrie in the actors' church, St Paul's Covent Garden. David Brayshaw and I attended and the pews were crowded with members of the profession. The choir was composed of friends from

Sadler's Wells, the Phoenix Opera and the English Opera Group. I remember Dame Sybil Thorndike reading Shakespeare's Sonnet 116: 'Let me not to the marriage of true minds admit impediments.'

When Sir Laurence Olivier's moment came, he told the story of when Guthrie saw Olivier perform Sergius in *Arms and the Man* at the Edinburgh Festival. Olivier, who was about to establish himself as one of the great actors of his time as Richard III, said to Guthrie that he felt the role of Sergius was a foolish one; he couldn't sympathise with the man at all. Guthrie replied: 'If you don't like the character, then the audience certainly won't.' Olivier continued: 'I was so put in my place that I felt like hitting him, but he was so tall you couldn't reach him,' and Olivier gestured upwards. 'Of course, he was right,' he added dryly. He concluded by reading from John Bunyan's *The Pilgrim's Progress*: '...and the trumpets sounded for him on the other side.

The final tribute was paid by Sir Alec Guinness. He described how Guthrie died as he was opening his morning mail. The doctor came and, confirming his death, said, He was a great man,' adding after a pause, 'and tiresome.' The most moving moment came, and it was not rehearsed, after Guinness had finished. He had closed his notes and looked up and said—'William Tyrone Guthrie' and paused. You could tell that the image of his friend was in front of him, and he fought back the tears. So did we. He took a breath and concluded—'Rest in Peace.'

CHAPTER NINETEEN

*You take my house when you do take the prop
That doth sustain my house...*†

Well, there is nothing like being thrown in the deep end. And again I was rescued, this time by the Crucible Company, and especially by those actors who had agreed to join the Crucible for Guthrie's production. The thrust stage in Stratford, Ontario had been thrilling its audiences for eighteen years and Douglas Campbell, his wife Ann Casson, Charles Keating, and Robin Gammell, had all performed there and would bring their experience with them. Douglas and Ann were also seasoned directors and would direct several plays in the Crucible's first two seasons.[133]

With Guthrie gone, we needed to change the opening plays. I would stick with *Peer Gynt* as planned, and at Douglas Campbell's suggestion he would direct and play the lead in *The Shoemaker's Holiday* by Thomas Dekker. I knew the play, having directed it in my first season at the Playhouse, and it had been performed successfully in a semi-operatic version on the thrust stage in Stratford, Ontario. Tanya would design it and rehearsals would start in late September. But there was something missing. After discussing with the Company, we felt that, rather than open immediately with *Peer Gynt*, we should first warm up the building, so to speak, with a week's entertainment. This would eventually become *Fanfare*.

On 26th June 1971, the Sheffield Playhouse played its final performance, a production of *I Was Hitler's Maid* by Sheffield playwright Christopher Wilkinson, which was presented as part of the Sheffield Festival. The production caused a stir and more walkouts.

---

† William Shakespeare, *The Merchant of Venice*, Act IV, Scene 1.
[133] Douglas Campbell directed *The Shoemaker's Holiday* (November 1971), *A Man for all Seasons* (February 1972), *The Taming of the Shrew* (October 1972), and *The National Health* (February 1973), and Ann Casson directed *A Taste of Honey* (January 1972).

The Star reported that the lead—another up-and-coming actor, Alun Armstrong—would appear on stage 'full frontal nude', when, in reality, he wore a long nightshirt throughout the performance.[134] I should point out that this was not a repertory production and would normally be performed in a studio theatre.[135]

After the show ended, I gave a short speech and Wilfred Harrison read Prospero's speech from *The Tempest* (which he had played in his first season in 1965): 'Our revels now are ended...' Then I threw a large switch and the neon 'PLAYHOUSE' sign in Townhead Street went out for the last time.[136] Sheffield would be without a professional playhouse for the next four months as we moved into our new building and got it ready for opening.

The closed Sheffield Playhouse announcing its successor, The Crucible

---

[134] *The Star*, 23 June 1971.
[135] In his interview with Sue Fulton in 2003, Christopher Wilkinson recounted: '[The play] was tagged onto the official season and that was a great risk on [Colin's] part, it was a marvellous chance to do a play like that in a proper theatre, and very tense. I remember hearing the Theatre Manager literally turning people away and saying: "Well, I don't think you should come in" and a middle-aged lady replying: "Don't you tell me what I can do!" So there was a nice sort of tension because normally you would present a play like that in a studio or fringe theatre.'
[136] The Playhouse stood unoccupied until it was sold in April 1973 to property developers for £65,000, which helped fund the Crucible. The site of the old Playhouse is today a block of student flats.

Following the closure of the Playhouse, our Publicity Manager moved on and, given our history of tangles with the press over the thrust stage design, we urgently needed a replacement. We chose David Kay, who had been working in the business world in London, believing his experience would help boost the Crucible's status. What we failed to realise was that he came from a world whose values and expectations were totally removed from those of a provincial theatre. Mr Kay was not to blame. Appointing him was one of the worst decisions we made.

I remember being irked by his first press release. Describing the Company's move from Townhead Street into the new Crucible building, it finished cheekily: 'But does anyone know the whereabouts of forty skips, five actors, the stage carpenter and Colin George's matched Purdeys?' I confess I had no idea what 'matched Purdeys' were. I discovered they were a famous brand of shotgun, and expensive too: a twelve-bore pair was priced then at over £1,600.[137] The image of me as a 'huntin', shootin' and fishin' squire' was not only far from the truth, but counterproductive. Although written tongue-in-cheek, this sort of image played into the hands of our Sheffield critics who depicted those of us involved in the design of the thrust stage as elitist toffs with more money than sense.

Mr Kay also dropped the ball when it came to publicity around the town and outside the theatre. As Publicity Manager, he made it a matter of policy that there would be no poster advertising, as he considered the return to be out of proportion to the cost involved. The Company and staff also volunteered to deliver hanging cards to shops and libraries—but this idea was never taken up.

Mr Kay's press release announcing the opening night of the Crucible was also wide of the mark: 'The New Crucible Theatre, Sheffield, which is costing £1 million, will open on November 9th. Seating 1,000, the theatre will be one of the finest in Europe. The theatre is planned as a Mecca for theatregoers, like Chichester Festival Theatre, and as an Arts Centre open around the clock. Negotiations are at present in hand with transport organisations, hotels and tour operators to set up special travel services and "packaged deal" visits.'

---

[137] This is the equivalent of £20,000 in 2021.

This was very much a Londoner's vision and sent the wrong message. Those of us who had worked in Sheffield for years emphasised that the Crucible's appeal was to Sheffield and the North of England, with a special emphasis on schools and Studio work. Chichester was an unhappy comparison, as unlike the Crucible it was a festival theatre operating initially for a nine-week season. We were replacing the Playhouse, a theatre which operated all year round, and not for an audience slipping down from London. Our audience was local–local meaning Yorkshire.

With opening day approaching, David Brayshaw prepared a memorandum on seat prices and potential takings at the Crucible. I had advocated raising seat prices, arguing that they were so low that it would be better if the theatre were free rather than a charge be made which undervalues what the theatre offers. The public do not value what they buy too cheaply. If seat prices are put up for a particular production, they conclude that the show is better. I noted that a high proportion of our subsidy was being spent on keeping seat prices low. Our top price was just 8/6d; a similar seat in London

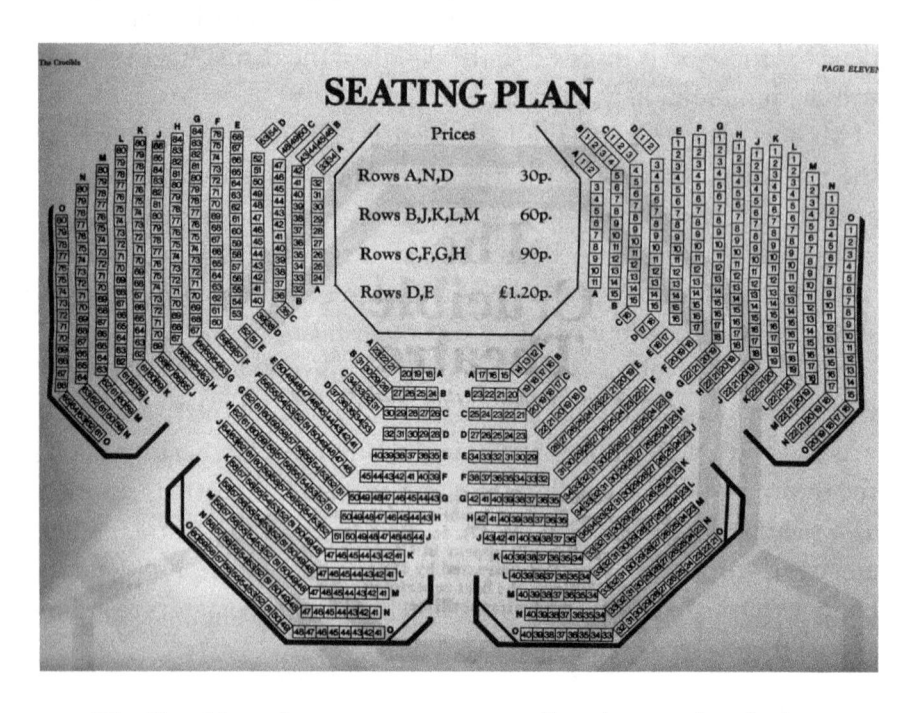

The Crucible auditorium seating costs reflected our earlier thinking

was £1.15d.[138] Although it was cheaper to mount productions out of London, the difference was out of all proportion.

The other question was how to price each seat differently. The main auditorium had 982 seats in 14 rows (this total increased to 1,013 seats if the boxes were included). As we had previously agreed, seat prices would apply all the way round the auditorium—seats on the side were not cheaper, as this fed into Sir Bernard Miles's claim that those members of the audience were second-class citizens. Seat prices would be based on distance from the action on stage.

This meant the very front row had the cheapest seats at 30p. It was hoped this would attract students and was a nod to the groundlings of Shakespeare's Globe. The second row was priced at 60p, the third row at 90p. Then came the most expensive seats: two rows at £1.20. Behind these rows, the seats steadily reduced in price, with three rows at 90p, four rows at 60p and the back two rows at 30p. At these prices a full house would bring in £693.[139]

David's assessment of likely income from the auditorium was encouraging. Assuming that on any attendance, half of the seats were at full price and half at reduced price, a full house would bring in £640.15. Assuming seven shows a week and productions playing for forty-eight weeks of the year, this produced an income range from £140,000 (65% full) to £183,000 (85% full).[140] This dwarfed anything we had been able to achieve at the Playhouse.

When the seat prices became public, *The Star* was predictably outraged that the price of the best seats had more than doubled from 50p in the old Playhouse to £1.20 in the Crucible. But David was unrepentant, insisting our prices were comparable to other new theatres when they opened, and pointing out that at every performance more than half the seats would cost 60p or less and one fifth of them were priced at 30p, which was less than the main cinemas were charging at the time.

It was also around this time that the salaries of the actors were decided. Given the criticism in the press over the 'lavish' expenditure

---

[138] In 2021 this would be the equivalent of £5.35 and £14.50, respectively.
[139] These seat prices in 2021 values would be the equivalent of £3.77, £7.55, £11.32 & £15.10. The takings of a full house would be worth £8,720.
[140] In 2021 terms this would represent a range of £1.8 million to £2.3 million.

made on the Crucible, the actors' salaries were surprisingly meagre. The highest paid members of the Company were Douglas Campbell, who directed and starred in *The Shoemaker's Holiday*, with a weekly salary of £60, and Robin Gammell, who played the lead in *Peer Gynt*, on £50 per week. Salaries then went in a sliding scale from £30 per week for mid-range actors to £18 per week for student actors. To put these salaries in context, a leading actor in the West End in 1971 would have earned at least twice what Douglas Campbell was being paid. Moreover, when compared with today, all the other actors' salaries were below the Equity Minimum![141] Clearly, the actors were not joining the Crucible Company just for the money.

Another example of how money was not the determining factor was the involvement of our lighting consultant, Richard Pilbrow, who I asked to light our first production of *Peer Gynt*. As the leading actors were getting around £50 per week I offered him the same fee. He

Contemplating our new theatre weeks before its completion

---

[141] In 2021 the Equity Minimum Wage was £675.85 per week for theatres of 800-1,099 seats. This is equivalent to £53.72 per week in 1971. Back then the Equity Minimum was just £18 per week.

replied: "OK, I will do this first show at the Crucible for the princely sum of £50, particularly if you don't tell anybody. No, seriously I would be delighted and since I'll be up there anyway in my consultative capacity, I might as well chip in and give a hand with the lighting.' He suggested that we might, as at the theatres in Oxford, Cambridge and Manchester, employ younger lighting designers from Theatre Projects. He tactfully added: 'I have to admit we charge more than this special Gala rate.'

Fearing I had made a misstep, I checked with David Brayshaw and realised I had not been thinking straight to suggest £50—this was based on the long-term weekly wages of the actors. We agreed that we would pay a guest lighting designer a fee of not less than 100 guineas, plus travel and reasonable expenses. Even at this increased rate Richard's total fee would be worth just £1,300 today—some lighting designers would charge more than that for a single day's work!

As we prepared to move into the new building, I wrote a statement of policy that we could all work to. The work of the Crucible would fall into four areas:

- The main auditorium: presenting classical, contemporary and new plays;
- The Studio Theatre: fostering new talent (writers, directors, actors), presenting work by Theatre Vanguard and hosting recitals of music and poetry, and exhibitions;
- Theatre Vanguard: working directly in schools, connecting with the local community and promoting a livelier 'awareness' of Sheffield; and
- Presenting work by other theatre companies, including opera and ballet both in the main house and the Studio.

Regarding our programme, I argued that 'the Director should provide a "balanced diet", recognising that light entertainment is very much provided by television now. As a subsidised theatre, we should provide every growing citizen in the region with an opportunity to see most of the great classics during the twelve or more years of his or her education.' When choosing plays to put on, we should consider plays that cast well within the Company, topical events, plays studied for examination and plays offered by a commercial management. Plays of direct local interest like *Stirrings* also warranted inclusion.

I also listed the daunting challenges we needed to address if we wanted to get the most out of our new theatre and thrust stage:

- To evolve a style of design, directing and acting that exploits and relates to the thrust stage. This would require a continuity of activity by directors, designers and actors;
- To run the Studio effectively (this would require a dedicated director);
- To ensure a high standard of work by Theatre Vanguard and exploit that work in the Studio and main theatre;
- To achieve a longer and adequate rehearsal time for our productions, which could involve running plays for longer;
- To find new work to present in the main theatre; we would need to evolve an effective play reading service, probably by employing professional readers;
- To work towards employing a regular voice and movement coach;
- To evolve a housing policy, especially for actors joining the Company for short periods;[142]
- To sub-let both auditoria for other activities, such as television shows.

Given its high cost, the public assumed we were given the Crucible Theatre ready to wind up and go. In fact, the staff worked as hard—if not harder—to complete the theatre as they did when it was presenting plays. A considerable amount of money was saved by stripping the Playhouse of all fixtures and fittings, furniture, apparatus and appliances, mostly for use backstage. This included a dozen full-length mirrors from the Playhouse bar which were distributed to the new dressing rooms. We also sourced furniture and fittings second-hand, including tables and chairs from the Grand Hotel (which had just closed), seating from a school in Batemoor (for the Studio) and anglepoise lamps from a closed hospital.

On 19th July, several major appointments were made to the Crucible

---

[142] For visiting actors, the Crucible managed to secure some bed and breakfast 'digs' that had been used by artists visiting the Lyceum before it closed.

staff. The design team would comprise Tanya Moiseiwitsch as Design Consultant (or 'Queen of Design', as I designated her), Rodney Ford as Head of Design, and a brilliant former student at the Playhouse, Elaine Garrard, as the third designer. Several members of the Playhouse staff moved to the new theatre in new roles. One was the wardrobe mistress, Madge D'Alroy, 'the grandmother' of the Company, who took responsibility for costume maintenance.[143] Electrician Bry Ferguson (who had served the Playhouse for 25 years) took on responsibility for the building's electrical installations. Some job titles were simply tweaked—for example, Master Carpenter Robin Cave became Production Carpenter, while crew men became 'stage staff'.

September 1971 came and we moved into the Crucible at last. Seeing the brand-new building and the breath-taking auditorium was exhilarating and we set to work preparing for our opening night in just two months' time. There was furious activity as telephones and a switchboard were installed while the office furniture and papers were moved from the Playhouse. Now we were in the building, we could see what working there demanded. One of our first jobs was to install Fablon frosted window film on the wardrobe and rehearsal room windows to prevent people looking in from outside. For acoustic purposes, the rehearsal room also needed drapes fitted on the walls and over the window area as the space was far too resonant.[144] We also realised that we needed to get a sign made reading 'No Admittance—Rehearsal in Progress'. You forget you need these things!

And so it came—the first rehearsal of *Peer Gynt* on 27th September. I remembered a phrase Guthrie used when contemplating a new production: 'Directing is about filling everyone with a desire to come back at ten o'clock tomorrow morning.' As the Crucible Company was a mix of familiar and new faces, I decided we needed to bond as a group before assailing the text. On the first day, the actors and new staff were given a tour of the building and shown the set and costumes for the production. They spent the afternoon being measured for costumes, finding dressing rooms and getting to know the theatre.

---

[143] Tedd's note: Madge was also godmother to my sister Caroline, and she continued to work at the Crucible until shortly before her death in 1975.

[144] The rehearsal room was one of the few design elements that did not work. The ceiling is too low, the dimensions are not right for laying out the thrust stage and there is a large strut right in the middle of the rehearsal area! Even 50 years later it is an unsatisfactory space.

West view of the Crucible with the entrance to the Studio Theatre (left) and the main entrance to the theatre (right)

The next morning at 10.15am, there was a warm-up on stage and then a surprise! A bus was waiting outside to take the Company to Castleton on the Moors, where those who wished could visit the local tourist attraction: the caves. I knew there would be little opportunity for those new to Sheffield to enjoy the Derbyshire countryside over the many busy weeks ahead. A sandwich lunch was provided and everyone explored where the spirit led them, some to the top of one of the peaks, before returning to Sheffield in the late afternoon. Now we were ready for the first read-through of *Peer Gynt*.

Peer Gynt had been cast before Guthrie died and remained unchanged with the Stratford, Ontario actors in the lead roles—Robin Gammell as Peer, Douglas Campbell as the Button Moulder, Ann Casson as Åse and Charles Keating as the Troll King. The rest of the cast comprised 21 English and Irish actors. The leading actors doubled or trebled parts as the text demanded, and the outstanding Irish actor Niall Buggy played four parts, including the Strange Passenger and the Devil.

The week before we started rehearsing *Peer*, I wrote to Douglas Campbell (who was in Hollywood at the time) regarding casting *The Shoemaker's Holiday*. As he would join us in Sheffield on October 18th, I had planned to delay announcing the cast till then, but we needed to start making the costumes. I asked him to approve himself and Ann Casson as Simon Eyre and Margery. I suggested Niall Buggy as Firk (he has just done a superb *Playboy* at the Abbey Theatre), Charles Keating as Ralph and a number of actors Douglas had seen in action at the old Playhouse Company when he was over in England for Guthrie's funeral. I even suggested a middle-aged belly dancer who I planned to cast as Anitra in *Peer* and as Cecily Bumtrinket in *The Shoemaker's Holiday*. For a moment, the demands of Ibsen and Dekker seemed magically to combine. Alas, our belly dancer was only available for *Peer*.

From the time Douglas Campbell arrived on October 18th, we had three weeks to put the first part of the season together. *Fanfare* would open the theatre, then I would have a week rehearsing around *Fanfare* performances to put the finishing touches to *Peer Gynt*. Once I had opened, Douglas Campbell would have three weeks to rehearse *The Shoemaker's Holiday* for a December opening.

By now we had the full staff of the Crucible, from switchboard operator and stage door man to Heads of Departments and all their backstage staff. The army had grown in size and was now comparable with similar theatre personnel in North America. When Rodney Ford and David Marchment had prepared a staff breakdown for the new theatre in March, they came up with a total of 37 staff, later whittled down to 21. But as the opening night in November loomed and work on the productions began in earnest, the Crucible backstage was suddenly alive and buzzing with excited and dedicated people. And the number of backstage staff? 48 in all!

CHAPTER TWENTY

I'm gonna raise the roof
I'm gonna to carry on
Give me an old trombone
Give me an old baton...[†]

In early October, as we were rehearsing *Peer Gynt*, we started to put together the opening show: *Fanfare*. Since June, I had been working on the idea of inaugurating the Crucible with an evening of entertainment designed to show off the potential of the thrust stage and warm up the audience to this new theatrical experience. In August, I outlined my ideas for the 'Fanfare Evening' in a confidential memo to staff. The evening would be divided into three parts:

- Part 1 (40 minutes): Children's theatre devised and directed by myself, involving 34 children sitting in the front row;
- Part 2 (30 minutes): Play performed by a well-known actor, with a well-known director;
- Part 3 (30 minutes): Music Hall & Finale.

Part 1 drew on the strong foundations of children's theatre we had built at the Playhouse, from Saturday morning sessions with the Pegasus Theatre Club to our work with Theatre Vanguard in local schools. Given the success of our work with children, it seemed a good idea to display their talent. Moreover, the idea of Sheffield children being the first performers to stand on the new thrust stage emphasised the sense of rebirth and the city's involvement in the new theatre.

For Part 2, we needed a name actor and I thought of James Mason. As a Yorkshireman, he had been a champion of the Crucible since our first press launch. More important, he had worked on the thrust stage in Canada, performing Oedipus for Guthrie in Stratford, Ontario. When he visited Sheffield to see how the building was progressing, I

[†] From the song *'Before the Parade Passes By'* by Jerry Herman.

suggested he take part in *Fanfare* by performing a short play in Part 2. He was keen on the idea and in August he started reading performing pieces sent to him by myself and his agent. But he couldn't find one that worked for him, so I suggested he act as Chairman of the Music Hall grand finale. He accepted this with enthusiasm, warning that 'the only thing that could possibly interfere with this now would be a threat of an important job which would take me away.'

Which of course is what happened. He wrote in September: 'Suddenly as so often happens, I have an embarrassment of sensible film propositions all at once of which two are positively desirable. At this moment of writing, I shall be bustling off to the United States to earn some money and more important reinstate myself among the upper crust. So there it is. You took a traitor to your bosom. At least you took one who was not yet ready to make the ultimate sacrifice. Though it is not the same thing as actually showing up and being of some use, I am transmitting much affection and encouragement. All the best, James Mason.' Back to square one.

Looking back, it was as if fate had made a space for someone to take advantage of the thrust stage James Mason had left empty. And that someone was an actor at the beginning of his career—Ian McKellen. Ian was playing *Hamlet* in London that August and came to see me there one weekend to offer his services for *Fanfare*. His involvement related directly to Tyrone Guthrie. One of Ian's very first engagements in the theatre had been at the Nottingham Playhouse in *Coriolanus*. His agent had informed him that, as he was starting out in his career, he was to play a soldier. However, on arriving at the theatre he saw the cast list on the notice board and realised he was down to play a leading role, General Tullus Aufidius—the antagonist of Coriolanus, who was played by John Neville.

As rehearsals progressed, Guthrie realised that McKellen was talented but inexperienced and he suggested they work together on the big speeches on their own away from the other members of the cast. In this way, Guthrie gave Ian the confidence he needed to measure up to the challenges of the role and feel at ease in an experienced Company. Ian had not forgotten this.

Regarding Part 2 of *Fanfare*, Ian suggested he performed Chekhov's one-act play *Swan Song*, in which a 68-year-old actor, Vasily Svetlovidov, and an elderly prompter, Nikita Ivanich, alone on the stage one night long after a performance, discuss a life in the theatre. Ian suggested another actor, Edward Petherbridge, for the prompter and the experienced director David William to work with them. Ian and Edward had both been in the National Theatre Company and had experience of performing on Chichester's thrust stage. The piece would last 30-40 minutes and neatly fitted with the evening's schedule. I snatched at Ian's suggestion and sent him material about the theatre and its design. He wrote back, thanking me for the materials and adding: 'It's good to feel Sir T. has a worthy memorial. I'll be up to Sheffield whenever the call comes.'

But there was more drama before the first rehearsal. One week after our meeting, Ian's agent Elspeth Cochrane rang me to say the American producer Sol Hurok was enticing Ian to Broadway with his *Hamlet*. A sleepless night. But in the end the transfer never took place and they soon started rehearsing *Swan Song*. Then there was another complication. A decision was made to open the theatre to the public one day earlier than planned, on Saturday November 6th, for a cut-price preview. This was intended to serve as a 'dress rehearsal' for the front of house staff, letting them get used to managing a full audience in this new space.

I wrote at once to David William, who was rehearsing in London: 'I realise I might have misled you when I said the preview on Saturday 6th November was a performance in which you need not necessarily take part. We are charging minimum prices and the audience will undoubtedly be anticipating a performance of *Swan Song*. I thought the sooner you knew, the better!'

Ian, Edward and David took it well, concluding that if the performance had been announced, then they had no choice but to do it. However, they were concerned that bringing the date forward shortened their rehearsal time on the Crucible thrust stage to just one three-hour session. I discussed this with Keith Green and David Marchment and we rearranged the schedule, giving Ian, Edward and David eleven hours on stage, including two dress rehearsals, before their first performance.

As it happened, given the frantic activity in the Crucible and on the thrust stage, Ian and Edward chose to have their last rehearsal, the night before the opening, in the Playhouse. The auditorium seats had been partially removed or covered in dust sheets, there were just working lights on the empty stage and the atmosphere was perfect for the meeting of an old actor and prompter in the middle of the night in a provincial theatre. They would bring this with them onto the Crucible stage.[145]

Then there was Part 3—the Music Hall Finale. We needed a chairman and Douglas Campbell stepped in, doing a wonderful job in the role. We also needed a lead singer, and for this I turned to one of Sheffield's most popular homegrown talents, my wife Dorothy Vernon. Dorothy had moved to London with our children the previous year to pursue her career in the West End, and I had been commuting between Sheffield and our home in London. She was at the time starring in *Dominoes*, a musical directed by Topol, but she was able to arrange time off to perform in *Fanfare*. Well-known in Sheffield for her singing and acting in *Stirrings* and *The Caucasian Chalk Circle*, Dorothy was also a regular at the Players' Theatre in the Embankment, so was a seasoned Music Hall pro.

I also proposed a couple of *coups de théâtre* to delight the audience. First, we would drive a car out of one of the vomitories onto the stage for a musical number, although I did not know how we could safely achieve this. Someone suggested we use the popular Music Hall song by Billy Murray:

'He had to get under, get out and get under

To fix his little machine—BEEP! BEEP!

He was just dying to cuddle his queen—BEEP! BEEP!...'

Perfect—but which car should we use? The only car small enough to hide in a vomitory and emerge without damaging the structure was a vintage Austin Seven. We got in touch with the Austin works, but as the vehicle was by then an antique, they couldn't help. Then our stage manager David Marchment was driving through Sheffield and he saw the very car. He pursued it to the University of Sheffield and discovered the driver, David Horsman, was a student with an interest

---

[145] Inspired by the eery atmosphere of the abandoned Playhouse, Edward suggested holding the first performance of *Swan Song* in the Playhouse auditorium and following it with a candle-lit procession from the Playhouse to the new Crucible Theatre. Sadly, given health and safety concerns (the theatre had had most of its fittings removed by then), this idea was not taken up. Tedd George's interview with Edward Petherbridge, March 2021.

in old cars. So we made him a deal—free comps to every show for him and his friends if the car was ours to borrow. We had to see the Fire and Safety officer, of course, as the petrol in the car was a fire hazard on the thrust. But we were allowed to put the minimum petrol in the car to get it on and off stage.

The actor who sang the number and drove the Austin was Charles Keating, who had a splendid singing voice and a daredevil attitude. He had no difficulty in driving the Austin up onto the stage, but at the final dress rehearsal the car stalled on the ramp and he had to start it again to get on stage. I was concerned that it might happen during the performance and afterwards asked him what had gone wrong. 'Nothing,' he replied, 'I just thought I'd stall it to see if it might be a useful effect.'

The other piece of showmanship was my idea to bring on a brass band to play a selection of North Country melodies and accompany the Full Company for the Finale. Unfortunately, local brass bands were unavailable, but we were able to secure the Sheffield Steel Band to march on stage and lift the spirits. As it turned out, this was a most fortunate choice, as the players were under the lively direction of their band master (whose name, sadly, I don't remember), a true performer who would put on a show for the people of Sheffield.

The Austin Seven on stage during rehearsal

In the weeks before opening, we ran a flamboyant leaflet campaign across Sheffield: 'Help make history—theatre history. Be a member of the first-ever audience at the new Crucible Theatre. A few seats are still available for the first ever preview of FANFARE on Saturday November 6th at the special price of 20p!'

Given that the Crucible—five years in the building—was about to open, the national press took a renewed interest. I was interviewed by Ronald Hastings of *The Daily Telegraph*, whose article—'Communion in the melting pot'—focused on our outreach to the Sheffield community, especially younger people. I declared that 'every young person growing up in the area should have a chance to see every great play from the past and the present' and noted that the average age of the Playhouse audience had dropped by ten years since I became Artistic Director.

Bill poster for Fanfare, *November 1971*

'I don't believe in the 'regular audience' or the 'Rep audience'; all that disappeared five or more years ago. The situation now is much more fluid.'[146] I also emphasised how the thrust stage gave the actors more contact with the audience—one fifth of the Playhouse audience was farther away from the stage than anyone in the Crucible.

I was also interviewed by Robin Thornber of *The Guardian*, who was keen to contrast the work of the Crucible with that of Peter Cheeseman at Stoke-on-Trent's Theatre in the Round.[147] I defended the thrust stage as 'a timeless classic theatre form, from which the box set itself was a deviation, a passing fad of Victorian England. The Greeks, Shakespeare, Chekhov go very well on the thrust stage, and children—now the next generation—are going back to a theatre of ritual to which it is ideally suited. I've been more relaxed working in the new theatre than in the ten years at the old Playhouse—it's like being released from prison.'

Thornber questioned whether we could fill a thousand-seat theatre without adopting a more commercial policy. I was adamant this wouldn't happen. 'At the old Playhouse, the classics and challenging modern works were always better box office than light comedies.' I also emphasised the importance of the Studio Theatre to the Crucible's work: 'The Studio is not just a shed at the bottom of the garden where we can scribble rude words on the wall. It affects the work in the main auditorium. There's already been some cross-fertilisation from the exciting things the Vanguard, our school's company, are doing.'

Two days before our cut-price preview, *The Star* published a photograph of the complete Company and staff on stage: 72 people in total.[148] It was an impressive sight, and all the more remarkable that we were able to drag everyone from their various duties and rehearsals to pose on stage for the camera. Company photographs are never easy to arrange. It had been a long journey from my Damascene moment in Minneapolis to Norfolk Street, Sheffield, but we had arrived.

---

[146] *The Daily Telegraph*, November 1971.
[147] Richard Thornber, 'Open house', *The Guardian*, 9 November 1971.
[148] The only member of the Crucible team missing from this photo was the Publicity Manager, David Kay, who was out of town that day.

The full Company and staff of the Crucible Theatre, November 1971

1. David Marchment, Stage Director
2. Howard Duckworth, Electrical Dept.
3. Mark Satchell, Electrical Dept.
4. John Watson, Electrical Dept.
5. Rosie Hoare, Stage Manager
6. Billie Williams, Assistant Manager (Accounts)
7. Mrs Quartley, Box Office
8. David Brayshaw, Administrator
9. Arnold Elliman, General Manager
10. David Jones, Catering Dept.
11. Peter Neale, Catering Dept.
12. June Hovers, Telephonist
13. Pat Meek, Cleaner
14. Elaine Chadwick, Telephonist

15. Mrs Marie Butler, Housekeeper
16. Jean Rusling, Accounts
17. Kay Smith, Production Manager's Secretary
18. Jean Broad, General Manager's Secretary
19. Gwen Ellis, Catering
20. Bill Jones, Cleaner
21. Robin Gammell, Actor
22. Roy Brown, Property Master
23. Gwenda Watkin, Box Office
24. Colin George, Artistic Director
25. Peter Ashfore, Electrical Dept.
26. Tanya Moiseiwitsch, Consultant Designer
27. John Pitt, Assistant Stage Manager
28. Gary Williamson, Trainee Designer
29. Peter Gore, Carpenter
30. Chris Miles, Stage Manager
31. Bry Ferguson, Chief Electrician
32. Astrid Rode, Assistant Stage Manager
33. Sheila Turnbull, Box Office
34. Victoria Unwin, Box Office
35. Rona Fineman, Assistant to Director
36. Madge d'Alroy, Head of Wardrobe Maintenance
37. Barbara Osborne, Catering Dept.
38. Margery Wild, Wardrobe Maintenance
39. Elaine Wainwright, Theatre Vanguard Secretary
40. Rodney Ford, Head of Design
41. Keith Green, Production Manager
42. Stephen Wheldon, Actor
43. Charles Keating, Actor
44. Paul Steinberg, Design Dept.
45. Douglas Campbell, Director and Actor
46. Elaine Garrard, Design
47. Richard Appleyard, Property Dept.
48. Ken Jones, Property Dept.
49. Michael Steer, Pianist
50. Ann Windsor, Actress
51. Andrew Branch, Actor
52. Russell Falconer, Actor
53. James Smith, Actor
54. Charles Madge, Deputy Stage Manager
55. Ann Casson, Actress
56. Stephen Marsh, Actor
57. Susan Woolridge, Actress
58. Michael Carter, Actor
59. James Tomlinson, Actor
60. David Grayson, Actor
61. Oliver Smith, Actor
62. Mike Jackson, Actor
63. John Byron, Actor
64. Lynn Smith, Actress
65. Sandra Walsh, Actress
66. John Halstead, Actor
67. Geraldine Wright, Actress
68. Paul Lally, Actor
69. Kay Barlow, Actor
70. Gwen Taylor, Actress
71. Sylvia Howard, Deputy Stage Manager
72. Niall Buggy, Actor

Part VI

Lights Up

CHAPTER TWENTY-ONE

If we wait for the moment when everything, absolutely everything, is ready, we shall never begin.†

With two days until opening, we had three productions in rehearsal simultaneously. *Peer Gynt* was the first to use the thrust stage; I remember directing the opening scene while workmen installed cables on the lighting gantry overhead. At this time, Douglas Campbell was also directing *The Shoemaker's Holiday* and I used to sit in at rehearsals

First rehearsal on the thrust stage, 13ᵗʰ October 1971

---
† Ivan Turgenev.

and watch someone who had for years directed and acted on the thrust stage. I still had so much to learn.

Then, on November 6th, the first members of the public made their way through the foyers—only minutes after the carpets had been laid—to see *Fanfare*. The colours and size of the large foyer were such that the audience gazed around with wonder, as if they were exploring ancient carvings discovered in some foreign subterranean cave. One forgets that at that time only an Opera House could boast of such lengthy and high-ceilinged space—the cost of such elegance denied this to most West End Theatres in the crowded city of London. Desmond Heeley had designed an Enchanter figure for the occasion, which we hung on the staircase wall going up into the foyer, conjuring up the spirits of the theatre.

The previews of *Fanfare* went well and the much-anticipated Gala Performance came on Tuesday 9th November 1971. Merete Bates in *The Guardian* captured the electric atmosphere of that evening: 'The new Crucible Theatre is a glitter of studying lights, silver balls and pipes, glass reflecting and radiating scarlet, cyclamen, and gold within. Colour has been used dramatically in chevrons, diamonds,

The ground floor foyer with the 'Enchanter' watching over

The audience gathers by the monumental entrance doors to the auditorium

stripes. It bombards the crowd, already thronging dazed and smiling, through the shaft doors. Silver hair flies away from a bronzed bald pate; a plum velvet suit escorts a lilac coat; plump tails adjust a white rosebud on a lapel; ribbons and stars plunge with gold chains, like necklines. No one cared if you gawped, because everyone else did, too.'

A flourish of live trumpets shattered the atmosphere and silenced everyone (our nod to the Guthrie Theater), followed by: 'Please take your seats, the performance is about to begin.' Thirty-four schoolchildren had been waiting patiently in the front rows of the auditorium, and with the audience assembled, there was no curtain to rise, the house lights dimmed and the Crucible was born.

For our young actors, we had prepared the clash between the Aztecs under Montezuma and the invading Spanish army led by Hernán Cortés. Colourful cloaks were provided for the Aztecs and primitive armour and wooden swords for the Spaniards. We had rehearsed with the children and had performed at the two previews. But amidst the dazzle of the Gala Night, with the local dignitaries and critics sitting there in their evening dress, the relaxed atmosphere of our Saturday

Young actors take the Crucible stage on opening night

mornings at the Playhouse with the Pegasus Theatre Club felt a world away.

It was then Ian McKellen and Edward Petherbridge's turn to perform *Swan Song*. I remember Ian—fresh from his Hamlet—giving a virtuoso display of a clutch of Shakespearean speeches. He even delivered a very poetic speech from Alexander Pushkin's *Eugene Onegin* which he had learnt in the original Russian. As they exited after the curtain call, they applauded not the audience but the stage and the auditorium above—their tribute to Guthrie and Tanya's thrust stage.[149]

Then came the Music Hall. We had a wonderful Chairman in Douglas Campbell, who opened the proceedings with a flourish: 'It is

---

[149] *Swan Song* would mark the start of a powerful artistic collaboration. Ian McKellen later recalled: 'During rehearsals for *Swan Song*, Edward Petherbridge and I fantasised about a theatre company whose actors would be their own managers, sharing out the parts as a group of equals. David William, our director, challenged us to turn the dream into reality, so we wrote to likely colleagues for their input. One by one, others joined in, and eight months later The Actors' Company was in rehearsal for its opening season.' Ian performed for The Actors' Company in 1972-74, before leaving to join the RSC. Interview with Ian McKellen in October 1999, quoted on www.mckellen.com.

Ian McKellen and Edward Petherbridge in Swan Song

with monumental pride and most egregious gratification that I appear before you in this incomparably innovatory edifice as your *genius loci* for this evening, and that it falls to my lot to welcome you to this, the newest and most stimulating cradle of the Thespian art, the Crucible Theatre.'

All the Company took part in *Fanfare*. Several offered their party pieces, with items such as *Paradise for Two*, *Going There Every Night* (a bawdy duet for two charladies) and *The Loch Ness Monster*. The vintage Austin made a huge impact, introduced theatrically by our Chairman: 'And now with not inconsiderable self-congratulation at our own engineering audacity, we introduce for the first time into this particular amphitheatrical ambience, the central symbol of our era, the epitome of our century—a horseless carriage!' Thankfully, Charles Keating chose not to stall the Austin as it came onto the stage.

Then it was time for the Chairman to welcome back Dorothy Vernon 'to her generative soil to display her galactically glittering personality and unparalleled laryngeal potency.' Dorothy's first song—*'Bird in a Gilded Cage'*—enraptured the audience and showed her star quality. Forty years later, when I took part in a discussion about the Crucible, we were all asked to name our most memorable theatrical moment there. Without hesitation my fellow panellist replied: 'Oh, it would be Dorothy Vernon singing "*Bird in a Gilded Cage*". When I heard her sing, it was like being transported to another world.' Dorothy then sang *'Polly Parker'*, a Yorkshire folk song, and started *'Before the Parade Passes By'* from the musical *Hello, Dolly!* Now it was time for the surprise.

At the end of the first chorus, the air was shattered by the sound of a drum pounding from the back of the empty stage. Up went the drapes and the Sheffield Steel Band made a loud and thrilling entrance onto the stage, led by their outrageous conductor. Sir Laurence Olivier could not have made a more impressive entrance than he did facing the audience and flourishing his baton. After one booming chorus, the band gently accompanied Dorothy in the verse and only climaxed at the end of the number.

The band accompanied Dorothy as she sang *'Sally'*, and then played *'Souza on Parade'*. Then they were joined on stage by the whole Company for a rousing rendition of *'Consider Yourself at Home'* from *Oliver!* As the applause died down, Douglas Campbell raised a glass to toast the new Crucible Theatre. We had arrived!

The Gala Opening got great reviews in the press, with Merete Bates writing in *The Guardian*: 'The night proved the stage was a release, an unleashing of variety and energy that could be at will remote or familiar.' One critic was appalled that I chose to wear denims for a gala opening—a reminder of the conservative attitudes of the time. But my favourite remark was made by a local man who had intensely disliked all the changes I had made at the Playhouse since arriving in Sheffield, and who confidentially said to Bry Ferguson, our electrician: 'The bastard's done it again.'

Fanfare ran for another week and enabled me to develop the children's theatre piece which opened it. Even by the second night, I realised that we were getting stale and were falling somewhere

Dorothy Vernon sings the Finale with the full Company on Gala Night

The Aztecs and the Conquistadors come to blows on the Crucible stage

between a rehearsed play and a free improvisation. So I decided to try something new. I would ask the audience to suggest three words and then we would improvise a short play, sharing all our ideas, based on these words.

Suddenly, the whole thing came to life. We still used the props, but in different ways. Sometimes, the audience tried to catch us out. One night, someone suggested 'football match', another 'rain' and the final word was 'elephant'. I sent a group off into one of the vomitories with some Aztec cloaks and some swords to be an elephant. After getting the football match underway in the rain the moment came when I shouted 'elephant' into the vomitory and out lumbered four boys crouching and hanging onto each other, covered in Aztec cloaks and using two swords for tusks, prompting an immediate round of applause.

A couple of weeks later, a Manchester schoolteacher wrote to me, saying she had tried a similar experiment with her five-year-olds, who had only been in school for three months. 'With incredibly little guidance they wove a good situation around the words water, hippopotamus and witch, which they had suggested, and when coming to a slight stop, they were able to suggest what might happen

Directing our young actors on the thrust stage, November 1971

Bill from the Crucible's opening season, 1971

next. As we have no hall, all this work had to be done in the limited space of the classroom.'

After a week of *Fanfare*, on 17th November *Peer Gynt* opened. I remember the vitality of the Company who used the thrust stage to engage the whole house. One moment in particular grabbed me: in the second act, Robin Gammell 'dried' (forgot his lines). He paused, looked up to the ceiling and said 'Yes?' The voice of the prompter boomed out the line over the speakers and Robin unhesitatingly took up the play again. No tension lost. What a contrast with the actor sidling to the wings to hear an almost inaudible whisper. The Crucible prompt seemed to sum up the style of the thrust stage—the audience really shares the performance, even the prompts!

The production showcased the array of creative and technical talent we had assembled at the Crucible. Rodney Ford's designs were extraordinary, Richard Pilbrow provided the most imaginative lighting and composer Jeremy Barlow—with whom I had worked at

Rodney Ford's design for the Button Maker in Peer Gynt

the old Playhouse—composed music and electronic effects.

The reviews for *Peer Gynt* were mixed, if encouraging. John Peter in *The Sunday Times* wrote: 'The director uses his controversial thrust stage with meticulous care for the text, and some of his imaginative touches stay rooted in the mind, for example the closing moments of the play, with the weather-beaten Peer, stunned and whimpering, curling up like a child at Solveig's feet.'[150] Paul Allen in the *Morning Telegraph* recognised that *Peer Gynt* might not be to every theatregoer's taste, warning: 'Only go if you want to make the effort to come to terms with the most complex dramatic writing of its age, but if you do, I don't think you will be let down. The thrust stage releases all the dramatic imagination Ibsen himself thought could only find free reign between the covers of a printed book.'[151]

Merete Bates in *The Guardian* was more critical of the production but conceded that she had to admire 'the possibly foolhardy and straight

Scene from Peer Gynt *with our scene-stealing belly dancer*

---

[150] *The Sunday Times*, 21 November 1971.
[151] *Morning Telegraph*, November 1971.

dive for the breakers which has followed up other uncompromising decisions in the creation of this theatre. You feel something of the breadth of Ibsen's feeling in *Peer Gynt*—if you take me, take the lot.'[152] But Irving Wardle in *The Times* found the show 'a mediocre piece of work [...] a basic misunderstanding in the preference of pictorial tableaux to the sinewy choreography of thrust stage technique.'[153]

For me, the most satisfying review came from John Bertram in *Theatre Parade*, who recognised the versatility of the thrust stage: '[The play] is an ideal vehicle for exploiting the thrust stage, where scenes can dissolve into each other with lightning speed, and where multiple lifts and a couple of traps can be deployed in an imaginative way. Richard Pilbrow's masterly lighting highlights the varied movement patterns and creates atmosphere where once painted scenery might have been used.

'There seems little doubt that the company are moving towards a fine sort of ensemble playing that demands a new audience involvement. One such incident—a crowd of wedding guests watched with amazement while Peer climbed up and across some high, rocky terrain. Both Peer and the rocks are imaginatively out front and the whole effect depends on concentration by the players and acceptance by the audience. Another telling moment is during a storm at sea. The sailors below, and the look-out high above, sway in unison. There is a rending crash, the ship founders, and the sailors seem to be catapulted across the stage.'

In December, *The Shoemaker's Holiday* opened and received good notices. *The Star* called it 'a good wholesome show for a good wholesome Sheffield audience', while the *Morning Telegraph* delighted in the 'songs, knockabout, anarchic working-class wit, and a bit of pageantry'. Desmond Pratt of *The Yorkshire Post* praised 'a good-natured, jolly, and an excellent evening in the theatre. The production on this thrust stage flashes with colour, movement and music, under the skilful direction of Douglas Campbell.' But B A Young in the *Financial Times* complained that the production had a 'pantomime feeling' which obscured the play's real character.

Tanya's designs were singled out by Paul Allen in the *Morning Telegraph*: 'It is rare that one feels moved to mention the designer first,

---

[152] *The Guardian*, November 1971.
[153] *The Times*, November 1971.

Tanya's designs for the Lord Mayor & Hans Meulter in The Shoemaker's Holiday

but Tanya Moiseiwitsch's costumes, set, props, were so full of life, so colourful, and so very atmospheric, that every scene change was like the dismantling and reassembling of a Flemish painting.' He did feel, however, that the play was not a good choice 'under such critical circumstances as the opening season of a new theatre'.[154]

Paul's comment echoed grumbles in the local press that our choice of opening plays was not 'the working man's cup of tea' (to quote *The Star*). So there could be no such complaints about our choice for the Crucible's first Christmas show, Alan Cullen's adaptation of Robert Louis Stevenson's *Treasure Island*.

Once again, *The Star* was sceptical, feeling that the script would be more appreciated by adults than children. But it praised Douglas Campbell's 'snarling Long John Silver and his crew harassing the good guys stage left, right and centre'. Denys Corrigan, who had reviewed our productions at the old Playhouse for years, wrote: 'Mr

---
[154] *Morning Telegraph*, December 1971.

Cullen's script extracts its material from the original with laudable clarity.' He thought Douglas Campbell's Long John Silver had 'a carefully husbanded strength, guileful strategy, and lurking menace—not overindulged.' Denys concluded: 'The Crucible should be starting to get through to a hesitant and wary public.'[155]

Letters in the press from the public seemed to confirm this view. Here's one from *The Star* under the heading 'Don't be put off this Crucible show!': 'I feel after hearing about the remarks made by your critic on *Treasure Island* that I ought to speak up on behalf of 16 of us—13 of us being children. All occupying the whole front row on Christmas Eve, all at a cost of 30p each. The children were aged between four and 14 and all agreed that it was a marvellous performance. The three adults accompanying us said it had been remarkable value for money. So please, those of you who were thinking of going to see *Treasure Island*, don't be put off by that which you may read.'

Another *Star* reader wrote: 'In answer to your reviewer's criticisms of *Treasure Island* I should like to say that having just returned from the production with my two sons aged 10 and 11 years, your critic obviously underestimates the age at which children are able to appreciate the production. Both my sons enjoyed it immensely, and on being asked what they particularly liked, said they felt nearer to the actors and a part of it. The whole point of the production is that, unlike television, you are no longer looking at a series of pictures, but at real people in a real happening. One hundred cowboys firing guns on the "box" cannot have the smallest impact compared with the first musket fired at the Crucible Theatre.'[156]

My own recollection of the production was of the proximity of the audience and their sense of involvement in the action. In the last scene, the pirates discover the treasure in a huge chest buried in the middle of the stage, filled with doubloons. But what to use for the coins? We needed a hundred or more which would be piled on a golden cloth and lit with special yellow lights secreted in the lid of the chest. I suggested metal washers painted gold, but the Props Department discovered these were too expensive. Then someone suggested using the gold chocolate coins sold at Christmas time. So

---

[155] *The Star*, December 1971.
[156] *The Star*, December 1971.

the Props Department went out and bought these prop 'doubloons' from the local shops.

The first preview was a matinee, which went well. As I was backstage afterwards, giving the actors notes, I heard over the Tannoy: 'Mr George to the stage immediately! Mr George on stage, please!' There was considerable urgency in the voice and I feared someone had been taken ill. I rushed on stage to discover a couple of stage managers trying to hold off an excited group of children from the front rows who, as soon as the 'curtain call' was over and the actors had left the stage, had climbed onto the thrust stage and started stealing the doubloons. They knew, of course, that they were chocolates. We persuaded them to leave the stage, though we had lost a good number

Elain Garrard's poster design for Treasure Island, *December 1971*

of our 'doubloons.' So the stage managers were sent out immediately to scour the shops of Sheffield to replenish our stock of Long John Silver's treasure.

From then on, I arranged for two of the pirates—Black Dog, fearsome in his make-up, and Blind Pew, who had miraculously recovered his sight since the curtain call—to return immediately afterwards with two drawn cutlasses to protect our treasure. Sometimes, the children enjoyed trying to leap on stage to provoke the two guardians of the doubloons. It made a jolly end to the performance, and one I could never have anticipated.

CHAPTER TWENTY-TWO

Any idiot can face a crisis; it's this day-to-day living that wears you out.[†]

We had barely opened the Crucible before the knives came out. Despite strong support for the new theatre from a large part of the Sheffield community, there was still a group who felt cheated of their 'civic theatre' and who viewed the Crucible as the expensive folly of a distant intellectual elite. They had failed to stop the Crucible being built—now they were determined to see it fail.

In the opening weeks, there had been teething problems with running the new theatre complex. The air-conditioning (which had only just been installed) needed reconfiguring after some areas of the auditorium were uncomfortably cool, the lights in the women's toilets needed changing and the showers for the actors backstage did not work properly. Most of the Company and staff were new to working on the thrust stage and we had to learn as we went along.

But the main criticism during our opening weeks was our choice of plays. Looking back after fifty years, one can understand that opening with *Peer Gynt* and *The Shoemaker's Holiday*, plays that today are considered commonplace at the Crucible, was an ambitious gamble in the Sheffield of that time. The Playhouse had been a small compact venture: by comparison, the Crucible in terms of the building, organisation and staff was gargantuan. Much was understandably expected of us.

Right away, the press sensed a division between the Crucible staff and the City Council, and sought to exploit it. Even before *The Shoemaker's Holiday* opened, *The Star* published two lengthy interviews with the Crucible's Administrator, David Brayshaw, and the City Council Leader, Sir Ron Ironmonger.[157] When it came to the theatre itself, they both sang from the same song sheet.

[†] Anton Chekhov.
[157] *The Star*, November 1971.

David was insistent that the Crucible belonged to the people of Sheffield but was not a civic theatre—and had no intention of being one. 'We are a repertory company operating in a regional theatre, we don't want to degenerate into a system where big stars are backed by a second-rate company.' To the question of why we didn't throw open the theatre for free during the first week so that everyone could see the new theatre, he replied: 'Why the hell should we? It is almost immoral to tempt people down for free and then expect them to pay the next week. We are worth money to see.'

Alderman Ironmonger was also steadfast in his support for the Crucible. He insisted that he had never had second thoughts about the project and confirmed that he would consider increasing the annual subsidy the next season 'within reason'. But there was a muffled threat too: 'Public money is invested in the Crucible and so we are obviously going to keep an eye on it. It is only common sense that if the Crucible is not a success, then the Corporation will step in.'

However, when it came to our choice for the opening productions, there was clear division between the two. David insisted that we had been right to open with *Peer Gynt*: 'It is a major classic and one in which the Artistic and Administrative Directors believed. Next season we are delving into every field and will be offering as wide a variety of productions as we possibly can. The Ballet Rambert and Phoenix Opera are coming next June and July.'

But Alderman Ironmonger was not convinced, and he was not afraid to say so: 'In my opinion *Peer Gynt* is far too avant-garde. I wanted to see something more popular for the launching. Why not a good old fashioned Whodunnit, the sort of thing the British public love? Agatha Christie and suchlike have been filling the London theatres for years. What's wrong with having the same here?' When asked if he had seen *Peer Gynt*, he replied: 'No, I haven't seen it at all, but I know enough of the story to know what it is all about, and I've listened to what other people have had to say about it.'[158]

'The Crucible directors MUST—and I want that in capitals—take into account the local people's taste. Speaking as a man with the same ideas as approximately seven tenths of the Sheffield public, I

---

[158] This was exactly the sort of reply that Guthrie had mocked in his letter to my father when dismissing Sir Bernard Miles's criticism of the thrust stage (see page 178).

am certain that the underlying policy of the Crucible must be first and foremost the entertainment of the Sheffield people. I know that if a man has flogged eight hours in a rolling-mill he generally doesn't want his mind stretched at night as well. He wants to be entertained without making too much effort himself.

'There is always a danger when there are purists living in their own little world. This isn't going to happen at the Crucible if I can help it. Public money is involved and the Crucible must not be allowed to become an "in place" for a select few. The City Council went into this with their faith in three or four men who they had to trust. I'm still in it, and proud of it, but I'm sufficiently down to earth to realise that this has got to be kept a going concern.'

The Star then said its piece. Conceding that the Crucible was 'a splendid addition to the centre of Sheffield and one of which we can all feel justly proud', the newspaper continued to insist that we were elitist: 'The recent decision not to renew the contract of Mr Bill Hays, Artistic Director of the Leeds Playhouse, is a warning that it is not for the director alone to draw up policy. Though we think the theatre's Artistic Director and trustees should have a free hand in the choice of plays, we would like to see them banish the feeling which still hangs over the theatre in this country that it is catering for a minority audience.'

In her review of *The Shoemaker's Holiday* in *The Guardian*, Merete Bates sprang to the defence of the Artistic Director: 'It's not too early to question sharply a new, unnerving development in the newly-built theatres of the North. Possibly because more money is invested, more notice and interference is attracted. It's hard to detect the exact motive for the latter: a genuine fear of political irresponsibility or a lurking desire for more power? If the director of one theatre is abruptly asked to leave, if the following day the leader of a city council condemns another director for not opening with Agatha Christie, it is being argued that not only arbitrary but destructive power is at work. What man can build anything on the fear of his name condemned and plastered on the local hoardings? This is, of course, to speak of Leeds and Sheffield.'[159]

---

[159] *The Guardian*, December 1971.

Part of the problem lay in the deep-seated prejudices held by many in the local community. The Minneapolis theatre critic, Peter Altman—who flew over to England to see *Treasure Island* and report on the new theatre—gave an interesting perspective on this problem from someone who had seen years of thrust stage work:

'It appears likely that conservative community attitudes will considerably restrict the Crucible's enterprise. Sheffield, which has a population of 500,000 but is the centre of a densely inhabited region of 2.5 million, is felt to be a town with fairly unadventurous audiences. The city's closest cousin in America might be Pittsburgh, also a steel manufacturing centre. Its most important population groups are union loyal factory workers and conservative, defiantly provincial country gentry more interested in sport than culture. There is not the large middle class of professionals which makes Minneapolis a relatively good city for the arts. If the Crucible's daring may be curbed by local attitudes, it is attracting considerable national attention. It is only England's second thrust stage theatre, and it is incomparably better than its predecessor the Chichester Festival theatre. It should benefit by much support from non-Sheffielders.'

But it was not just a question of whether the opening plays had been the right choice; our critics questioned our belief that all seats in the main auditorium were equally good. The *Morning Telegraph* decided to carry out its own research into this issue, giving two seats to members of the Sheffield public to see *Peer Gynt*: one in the cheapest 30p seat at the very back of the auditorium, and the other in a 60p seat nearer the front. They published the results on 6th December 1971.

The first test subject, Edwina Tarpley, reported: 'Perched at the back of the theatre, the worst seat, the effect was just as startling as sitting in the front row. Colin George's direction of *Peer Gynt* was superb, and he had actors moving around the stage in an ever-changing kaleidoscope. The staging was exuberant, with a life and vitality that was aimed at every section of the audience. *Peer Gynt* was a chance for us to share in a positive orgy of expression, movement and imagery which encompassed every facility the stage had to offer. There was no awareness of being on the sidelines, the actors were playing to my side, your side, and every side.

'*Peer Gynt* is a long, tiring play—for both actors and audience, but after seeing this production with its exciting ideas and imaginative staging, it is impossible to even visualise a watered-down version on a stage with less scope. At last, I can see why the Greeks loved the amphitheatre so much.'

The second test subject, Susan Dewar, focused more on the production of *Peer Gynt* itself, praising the 'bewitching and beautiful sequence of alternating comedy and tragedy' and especially Rodney Ford's designs. But when it came to the issue of whether some seats were better than others, she was unequivocal: 'The promise of an unhindered view from every part of the audience was fulfilled as far as G43 was concerned.'

One week later, Sir Ron Ironmonger and the former Conservative Councillor Michael Swain aired their criticisms of the Crucible on television. This prompted a Mr Ron Rose to write to the *Morning Telegraph*, demolishing their arguments and insisting the thrust stage could house everything from period drama to clog dancing.[160] But

Left: Councillor Michael Swain; Right: Alderman Ron Ironmonger

---

[160] *Morning Telegraph*, December 1971.

rather than galvanise support for the Crucible, Mr Rose's opinions provoked an outpouring of anger from what Minneapolis theatre critic, Peter Altman, had described as 'conservative community attitudes'. The newspaper jumped on the opportunity and published a full page of readers' letters which repeated the familiar criticism of the Crucible and its work. Here is a brief selection:

'Not only was *Peer Gynt* the wrong play to start with, it would have been wrong at any time. Admittedly, it was cleverly contrived and acted, but it was boring in the extreme [...] The players were having an exciting time, but not so the audience.'

'It is unfortunate that the Crucible seems to pander towards those theatrical aficionados whose judgement of any innovation seems to be the reverse of contemporary public opinion. The impression is that, provided the "common herd" think a thing odd or singularly weird, this esoteric intellectual elite must take it as being perfectly acceptable.'

'What we don't want is to be told what we ought to like. We can be led quite a bit. But don't push us. Offer what you've got and leave the rest to us and our sort—unless you have a brand-new set of paying supporters.'

'Frankly, to some of us, Colin George isn't yet as God-like, nor the Crucible Theatre the absolute last word in theatre design that he would have us believe [...] Will he stride forth as a high priest of culture with a capital C and a small but highly intellectual following—and frequent appeals for more public money? Or will he do something for the majority in these parts, for whom stage drama is not the be-all-and-end-all of life, but just one of its trimmings which can at times elevate and comfort in the harsher reality of everyday life that is not a play.'

'It is not necessary to have a thrust stage in order that the performer may give a three-dimensional performance. Furthermore, not every artist wishes to ingratiate himself with the audience to the extent of a cabaret act. Therefore, there is bound to be a gulf between audience and performers which can largely be remedied by previous education of the audience in what they are about to see and hear. Never mind what Colin George thinks. What does Colin Davies, the international orchestral conductor, think? What do international singers like Jon Vickers or Peter Glossop think of Sheffield's thrust stage? It would be hard to imagine epic productions of *Die Meistersinger* or *Aida* being produced at the Crucible Theatre'.

'Like all true ballet lovers, I consider the scenic effects and orchestra pit play an important part in such presentations [...] The scenery is an important factor in taking one away for a few minutes from this mad world of materialism.'

In fairness to those who enjoyed opera and ballet, the closing of the Lyceum led to an understandable frustration at being denied a stage on which such works could be performed in the traditional way. But it was also misplaced. Late in our first season, both the Ballet Rambert and the Phoenix Opera performed at the Crucible, and since then there have been numerous performances of music and ballet by visiting companies.

But we had to swallow this criticism and forge ahead. One of most important decisions to make was the appointment of a director for the Studio Theatre, and we had the ideal candidate in Caroline Smith. Caroline had written to me in November 1971, just before we opened *Peer Gynt*, to express her interest in being involved in our Studio Theatre work. She had been resident director at the Salisbury

Caroline Smith, Director of the Studio Theatre, January 1972

Playhouse and had just finished running the theatre-in-the-round in Scarborough. We met to discuss our Studio policy and we were clearly aligned in our thinking. The job was offered to her, and on 14th February 1972 she took up the post.

Shortly after her arrival, Caroline and the first four actors of the Studio Company were interviewed by the *Morning Telegraph*'s Paul Allen, and they took the opportunity to emphasise how the Studio's role was different from the main auditorium. Paul wrote: 'They want direct and regular contact with their audiences—through the intimacy of the small Studio and a determination to go out into the streets and grab the audience if they won't come of their own accord. They want a certain kind of "truth" which doesn't need the massive make-believe of the big theatres. They want to get at audiences who don't go to posh theatres—because they can't afford it, they're frightened by all the dressing up or they are bored by the prospect of a formal evening.

'The object, says Caroline Smith, is to have so much going on, either in the Studio, or in the main theatre, or out in the street at lunchtime, evening or late-night hours and at cheap rates, that people

The Studio in performance, c.1971

will drift in without knowing particularly what was on—as they would to their local pubs.' New to Sheffield, Caroline vowed to 'absorb the atmosphere and get to know the people and the places. I intend to shut up my own soul for a bit and really concentrate on finding out what is needed for Sheffield. I've got this bee in my bonnet about working for a community.'[161]

Caroline's proactive and energetic approach did much to counteract local opinion that the Crucible was not for the average citizen. She opened with her first play in February 1972, *Camilla*, an adaptation by David Campton of the vampire tale by Sheridan Le Fanu, and in the Studio's first short season there were over 100 performances seen by 4,500 people. Around this time, we also had the good fortune to be joined by the talented actor and director, Job Stewart, who became my Assistant Director. The team was in place.

The main auditorium started 1972 strongly, with two productions which appealed to the Sheffield public. The first was *A Taste of Honey* by Shelagh Delaney which was our first copper-bottomed success, playing for two weeks to 69% capacity. 'Something finally clicked last night,' wrote the *Morning Telegraph*. 'It is with an honest, sensitive and moving performance of an unashamedly middlebrow play that the Crucible Company has finally found its feet, and, one hopes, its audience.' *The Star* was also won over: 'The play is right at last, the acting superb and wonderfully sensitive, and with Shelagh Delaney's funny but moving play the Crucible Theatre company have really produced something to be proud of.'

The second play was Robert Bolt's *A Man for All Seasons*. Denys Corrigan wrote in the *Barnsley Chronicle*: 'Occasionally, one comes across a theatrical experience which seems to defy the traditional critical approach, if not disarming criticism altogether; and for me Wednesday evening at the Crucible was such an occasion. What a pleasure it was to hear fine language on the wing again, to find oneself attentive throughout, unwilling to miss a word.' The attendance was even better, 77.4% over 23 performances, which was somewhat supported by the fact that the play was a set text for secondary schools that year.

---

[161] *Morning Telegraph*, February 1972.

With the popularity of *A Taste of Honey* and *A Man for All Seasons*, *The Star* softened its tone. Still critical of our decision to open with *Peer Gynt*, it conceded: 'No one was more sceptical about the thrust stage and general plans for the Crucible than we were. Yet the Crucible has been successful in all it set out to do—in showing just what the thrust stage can achieve and demonstrating just how creative and exciting this kind of theatre can be. Let's make no mistake. Sheffield has the finest and most up-to-date theatre in Europe and its management is obviously applying many of the lessons it learned from teething troubles.'

Towards the end of the first season, the Ballet Rambert appeared at the Crucible and *The Guardian* review was music to our ears, suggesting that not only could ballet be done successfully on a thrust stage, but that the theatrical experience was enhanced: 'It is in large measure the thrust stage itself which determines the feel of the evening rather than the individual ballets. The fact that the audience and performers share a common space, that there exists a sensed possibility of touch contact with the performers (even though no member of the audience is likely to step on stage to shake a performer by the hand) somehow makes all the difference in an art concerned with movement, dance and physical contact.'[162]

Not long after *A Taste of Honey* opened, *The Guardian's* Merete Bates interviewed me. At the time I was office-bound and feeling overwhelmed by the demands of running such a large organisation—all the letters and phone calls, files and memoranda, big decisions and indeed interviews like the one I was giving. But when she suggested that I might have been better off in the Playhouse, I replied:

'Yes, but I've fallen in love with the Crucible stage. It's the success of the stage that's heartened me all the way through. To seat a thousand people within 59 feet of the actor—that's what the man in the street wants to see and to hear, not all your artistic waffle—is a considerable achievement worth hanging onto. And the space, exploring the space: we've not yet begun. There's no doubt it demands more, far more, from any director or actor.'[163]

Someone who refused to be seduced by the charms of the thrust stage was the Crucible's arch enemy—Sir Bernard Miles. In March

---

[162] *The Guardian*, June 1972.
[163] *The Guardian*, February 1972.

1972, he arrived at the theatre unannounced with his wife on the way to their Yorkshire cottage. I was not in the theatre that day, but the front of house staff quickly recognised Sir Bernard and gave him the run of the auditorium for 45 minutes. He sat at the back of the auditorium and also went on stage to give a few impromptu speeches.

Afterwards, Sir Bernard was interviewed by the *Morning Telegraph*'s Paul Allen to get his verdict on the Crucible. About the building and auditorium Sir Bernard was glowing: 'The architecture is a work of genius: it is the loveliest theatre ever built, and by far the most impressive achievement of any local authority since the war.' But he remained steadfastly opposed to the thrust stage, which he said was 'the most difficult to handle of any I have ever seen in a long and industrious career in the theatre, and I think it may possibly be too big.'

He again concluded that people seated at the sides and towards the rear were second-class citizens and declared: 'When I see the Lord Mayor and civic dignitaries sitting there for a show, I shall donate a large sum to charity.'[164] He predicted that the seating at the sides would be scrapped to reduce the auditorium to 500 seats which, in his view, would make it 'the greatest theatre in England'.[165]

It's a pity I wasn't at the theatre that day, as I could have given Sir Bernard a copy of the reports by the two members of the audience who had sat at the back and the front for *Peer Gynt* and who both insisted that everyone in the auditorium got the same unhindered view and theatrical experience. But Sir Bernard went on his way and, alas, he never did see a production on the Crucible's thrust stage.

We closed the first season in June 1972 with Job Stewart's production of Pinter's *The Birthday Party*, with the brilliant Niall Buggy in the lead role. The title of the play was fitting, as that month my son Edward was born (today known as Tedd). Hearing my wife had gone into labour, I rushed to get the train to London, leaving two hastily-scribbled notes for the Company Manager to put up on the staff notice board—one read 'It's a Boy!' and the other 'It's a Girl!' Later that day, I sent a telegram confirming it was the former.

---

[164] After Sir Bernard left, the Company discussed whether they could arrange this for a production, but it was decided that such a petty response would have been uncharitable.
[165] *Morning Telegraph*, March 1972.

When my wife brought our baby son and daughters up to Sheffield two months later, we were able to carry out a long-standing theatre tradition. The well-known actor Wilfrid Brambell was in town touring a production of *The Late Christopher Bean* and was being interviewed on the Crucible stage when my wife arrived with our children. He asked if we were going to give our baby a theatre christening. I confessed that I didn't know what that was, so he helped us set it up. Baby Edward was put in a basket and dragged over the stage by his family. This would guarantee him success on the stage. The local press took a photo of the moment—now the Crucible stage could be said to have been well and truly christened!

Baby Edward's theatre christening on the Crucible stage, August 1972

CHAPTER TWENTY-THREE

When you start earning you can start moaning! [†]

Criticism of our choice of drama was one thing. More pressing were the Crucible's finances. To put our situation in context, the early 1970s in England were traumatic, with frequent power cuts, industrial unrest and Ted Heath's Three-Day Week. 1972 was a tough year: That January, unemployment reached 1 million, the highest in three decades, and a coal miners' strike caused a month of power cuts. At the time, I was directing *A Taste of Honey* and, without mains power in the auditorium, David Marchment and Keith Green scoured Sheffield looking for a solution, and ended up buying half a dozen lorry batteries which they attached to the arc lights.

The impact on the profitability of our new theatre was huge. The Crucible opened during one of highest periods of inflation in Britain's history, compounded by the switch to decimal currency nine months before the theatre opened.[166] Our seat prices had gone up, but not as fast as our costs. And the heyday of the 1960s, of generous local and national government funding, was long over. It was time for a hard dose of economic reality. At the end of the first season, we were £128,000 in the red.[167]

In late June 1972, David Brayshaw shared with me a confidential report prepared by the City Treasurer, Mr F G Jones, on the Crucible's spending and administration. Reading it back years later, one is immediately aware that it was composed by someone who had a

---

[†] From *A Taste of Honey* by Shelagh Delaney.
[166] Consumer Price Inflation (CPI) averaged 6.1% in 1970, 9.5% in 1971 and 6.6% in 1972.
[167] This is the equivalent of £1.6 million in 2021, which is not far above what had been predicted. In September 1971, David estimated that ticket sales at 65% box office would generate £140,000, leaving an annual deficit of around £100,000 which would need to be funded by grants.

sharp eye for numbers but absolutely no hands-on experience of the complexities of administering a theatre such as the Crucible.

The report tracked how the cost of the new theatre had risen from its initial budget of £700,000 in September 1966 to £910,000 at the appeal launch in October 1969. However, the public appeal fell well short of its target and, as the Trust could not afford to purchase the site on Norfolk Street, the Corporation agreed to lease it to the Crucible for an annual rent of £16,000. This reduced the cost for the theatre to £884,000. Set against the multiple sources of funding for the theatre and Studio (see table opposite), this meant that we were £12,500 over budget—or just 1.5%.[168] Considering the size and complexity of the project and the difficult financial situation of the time (which hurt our fundraising efforts), this was a remarkable achievement.

When it came to the theatre's finances, Mr Jones lamented that the financial consequences of the Crucible project 'were never considered in sufficient detail; were always over-optimistic; and any criticisms were pushed to one side with the thought that in the end somebody would provide'. Despite the commitment of the Corporation to pay £34,400 towards the theatre's running costs in 1972, plus a £4,500 contribution to Theatre Vanguard, a shortfall of £218,100 was forecast. This would be partly reduced by a grant of £88,500 from the Arts Council and £2,000 from the Corporation, but it left a yawning deficit of £127,600.[169]

There was no disputing these numbers—and economies would have to be made. But Mr Jones's recommendations for cost cuts betrayed his total lack of understanding of how a theatre works. He recommended swingeing cuts across the staff, even abolishing David Brayshaw's post of Administrator and combining it with my role as Artistic Director. But it was his comments about the design team—and in particular Tanya's role as Design Consultant—which were to prove the most damaging. Overall, he recommended cuts totalling £19,300 in 1972-73. This

---

[168] As it turned out, the project may have come in under budget. The Playhouse site was eventually sold for £65,000, all of which went to fund the Crucible's cost, producing a small surplus. Moreover, Nick Thompson recalls that around six months before the Crucible opened, the architects were informed by the Building Committee that there was an additional contingency of £85,000 that needed spending! This was used to upgrade the rather basic fittings and finishes of the auditorium and foyers.

[169] In 2021 terms this deficit would be the equivalent of £1.6 million.

Final cost of Crucible Theatre project

Source of funds	Amount (£)
Sheffield Corporation	350,000
Arts Council	300,000
Contributions from Scottish & Newcastle Breweries Ltd	4,500
Appeal Fund (after costs)	118,000
Gulbenkian Foundation	50,000
Studio Appeal*	16,000
Estimated proceeds from sale of Playhouse Theatre	33,000
Total available funds	**871,500**
Cost of Crucible project	(884,000)
Deficit	**(12,500)**

Source: 'Review of the finances and administration of the Crucible Theatre by the City Treasurer of Sheffield', F G Jones, 23rd June 1972.
* Includes £7,000 from the Education Committee of Sheffield Corporation.

would still leave a deficit of £108,300, which he recommended the Arts Council and Sheffield Corporation should fund, as well as deferring payment of the lease rent for at least one year.[170]

Shocked at the recommendations in the report, on 23rd June David and I both wrote lengthy letters to the Trust Chairman, Tony Hampton, responding from different angles, mine as Artistic Director and David as Administrator. David summed up our viewpoint: 'The Report takes an accountant's—and a layman's—view of the organisation of the Crucible; this is essential and has revealed some matters which should, and can, be tightened up. But it also reveals a basic lack of understanding of how a theatre works and what it exists for, which leads to an overall impression of inefficiency and extravagance which must be challenged.'

---

[170] In 2021 terms this would be the equivalent of reducing the deficit by £223,000 to £1.25 million.

In my letter, I conceded that economies had to be made and I agreed that a 60% box office was a reasonable target, albeit not easy to achieve.[171] Although the box office had been disappointing in our first season, at an average of 53%, it was still better than the takings at Coventry (40%) and Nottingham (37%). I also conceded that running repertoire was costly, but I pointed out that it gave us the flexibility to extend popular shows and close money-losers after their initial run.

For me, his recommendations that we put on more 'popular shows' (whatever that meant) and avoid 'obvious loss-making shows' were clumsy phrases that betrayed ignorance of what a subsidised theatre is built for.[172] I enlightened him: 'It is providing a service to the community and enriching the quality of life of those who live within striking distance of it. I think everyone accepts that this has got to be a subsidised concern; what they do not accept is the amount of subsidy that it requires if it is really to do its job properly.'

When it came to staff cuts, I made it clear that Mr Jones's recommendations were nothing short of absurd. His most contentious suggestion of abolishing the post of Administrator, combining it with my role of Artistic Director and giving me an assistant, would achieve a saving of £436 per year. How I was expected to take on this additional responsibility was a mystery, as I explained:

'As Artistic Director, I am responsible for too many things. I plan the policy, not only of the main theatre, but I oversee the work of Vanguard and the Studio Theatre. I programme and arrange tours for the main theatre. I am a Literary Manager and read new plays—with help, of course. I am a Casting Director for the main Company and in consultation with Vanguard and the Studio. I direct four plays a year as a minimum. I also have my public relations work, opening Frecheville Carnival, etc., which is a part of my job.[173]

'At other major theatres in which I have worked, such as Stratford, Ontario and Ottawa, I have had, as a matter of course, an assistant attached to me. When I did *Peer Gynt* I had one. This is no luxury

---

[171] In fact, the Crucible achieved this target in the following season.
[172] It is worth noting that the last two shows in the first season at the Crucible, Harold Pinter's avant-garde *The Birthday Party* and Noel Coward's popular *Tonight at 8.30*, both achieved a similar audience per performance.
[173] Frecheville is a Sheffield suburb which held an annual carnival through its streets.

when managing a major production.' If they went ahead and dissolved David's post, I would have no choice but to ask whoever they hired as my Assistant Director to do the very job David was doing at the time.

As a seasoned theatre administrator, David had no hesitation in saying that abolishing his role and expecting the Artistic Director to do it was utterly unrealistic. 'There is no human being capable of combining both jobs in the first few years of the life of a new theatre—different in size, concept and design from anything the City has known before.' And he rejected suggestions that there had been no control of expenditure, noting that the total deficit for first eight months was only £10,000 (out of a budget of £248,000). Besides, expenditure had been underbudgeted and 'it [was] doubtful if anyone could have done better with so few facts to go on.'

Mr Jones's recommendations regarding the box office and publicity were, as I put it in my letter to Anthony, 'howlers'. Mr Jones questioned the need for an advanced bookings office 'in view of the anticipated average attendances of approximately 65% of the house' and recommended its closure for a saving of £2,500 per year. How he expected to build audiences for future shows without an advance booking office (there was no online booking, those days), I don't know.

Mr Jones also judged that employing a Publicity Officer at £2,000 per year was 'a luxury which cannot be afforded' and recommended abolishing the role, engaging someone part-time and advertising only on certain days and in only one of the local papers. I wrote: 'I find it genuinely puzzling that anyone can suggest that this post is anything but vital to an organisation like the Crucible. As I am sure you agree, we have been undersold as a project right from the opening, both in the city and throughout the country.'

David spelt it out in commercial terms: 'As well as service, the theatre sells a product, and the public will not buy unless it knows what the product is. When that product is constantly changing, the job of keeping the public (which is spread over the whole north of England) informed is complicated and demanding. The Publicity Officer for a theatre of the Crucible's complexity, size and standing is indispensable.'

But our key area of disagreement regarded the design team and budget, both of which Mr Jones regarded as excessive. David questioned his maths: 'To assume that thirteen productions per annum will require ten costumes each and to divide the Wardrobe bill of £11,000 by 130 to give a labour cost of £85 per costume is so unrealistic as to be ludicrous.' David noted that the Production Team made 500 'costumes' in the first twelve months of the Crucible (including hats, boots and shoes), giving an average cost of just £22 per costume.[174] Moreover, 'every one of these is the equal of, if not better than, anything that can be seen on the stages of the West End, the National Theatre or the Royal Shakespeare Company, Stratford-upon-Avon—*because* they are designed and made by top-ranked artists.'

I also pointed out that even a play like *Mister* with the smallest cast that season had around ten costumes, as characters in small cast plays change often—to get some visual variety into the evening, apart from anything else. I also hit back at his idea that you could simply reuse costumes for other shows. We had done this for our children's play *Inside the Mountain* in the Studio Theatre. But buying costumes second-hand from other theatres for shows in our main auditorium would not work, as by the time you had altered and repaired them, you would have spent more than starting from scratch. Not only were our costumes good value for money, but we were booked to open a new theatre with *The Shoemaker's Holiday* and *A Man for All Seasons* using the same costumes (with no refurbishment cost).[175]

When it came to the wig makers, Mr Jones showed his total ignorance of the profession, writing: 'It is doubtful if a wigs assistant is really necessary, for this is probably another description for a hairdresser.' Mr Jones based this conclusion on a remark made by a visiting actress to the Crucible who praised the facilities compared with the West End where 'there was no one to do your hair', which led him to conclude that Sheffield didn't need this service, either. I set him straight on this issue: 'A wig assistant is fully employed

---

[174] In fact, the Crucible used 235 'costumes' for *Peer Gynt!*

[175] That summer, my father had arranged for the Crucible Company to perform the two shows as part of the inaugural season of Sam Wanamaker's Globe Theatre in Southwark. The reimagined Globe Theatre had yet to be built (it opened in 1997), so performances were held in an open-sided tent. Unfortunately, it rained almost every afternoon and the Company often had to stop the show to push water from the bulging tent structure before it burst over the audience.

looking after productions in both theatres, and also making wigs for us—particularly at Christmas time, when hire charges are prohibitive. At the old Playhouse, wigs were sent to be dressed during the run, the work was often inadequately done, the cost for piecework high and one was aware too often of the show looking ragged after a few performances.'

But what really angered me was Mr Jones's suggestion that the Design Team was too large. I reminded him that their work was not solely to produce costumes: 'At the moment Elaine [Garrard] is full-time making masks for *The Persians*, Rodney [Ford] is part-engineer, part-designer and on most productions, as Head of Design, is responsible for work ranging from the mechanics of the boat in *Treasure Island* to the display out front for *Oh! What a Lovely War* And Tanya Moiseiwitsch is perhaps our greatest asset. Only last week, Hal Prince phoned her from New York to lure her to Broadway in the autumn. I hope, in fact, that she will occasionally go away to do a guest production, but her presence at the Crucible is a continual inspiration both to me and the staff, and her work individually last season has done more than anything else to help set a standard for us all.'

David was even more direct. 'This is the comment of the layman who does not appreciate the amount of preparation and effort needed to achieve "first-class stage design"; it is no more possible for one person to design all the shows in a year than it is for one person to direct them all. To achieve first-class design (particularly on the thrust stage) one must have first-class designers—either on the staff or as visitors. There is no question that to dispense with Tanya Moiseiwitsch's services and engage visiting designers would cost more than her salary, not only in the fee paid but also in decreased efficiency resulting from repeatedly accommodating visitors who do not know our routines, the loss of her counsel in establishing a Design Department of this standard and her help in making costumes and properties.'[176]

I summarised my response in three broad points:

---

[176] David included a comparison of costs with the theatres in Nottingham, Birmingham and Bristol. The Crucible's cost of scenery and costumes for 12 productions was one of the cheapest at £12,700, half of Bristol's and one third of Birmingham's. When it came to stage and production staff salaries, Sheffield's budget of £52,813 was on a par with Birmingham and 20% lower than Bristol.

'a) Too much of the thinking behind the analysis of the organisation at the Crucible reflects an opinion that is geared to the running of a small provincial theatre presenting plays for a regular public. We are running a regional theatre with several companies, involved in a variety of activities reaching the widest audience possible both in Sheffield itself and in the north of England. It's sad that so many suggestions seem to be constricting and paring down our activity when I think our outlook at the moment should be expansionist. Of course, this must be geared to the realities of the finance available to us. What we should be looking for, however, is increased revenue and help from educational authorities with regard to our work in the Studio and with Vanguard.

'b) I feel strongly that we have been open for so short a time that it is very misleading to extrapolate on our present experience. Our work is beginning to register with the public and my aim would be in the next two years to strive to achieve a 70% box office, which would alleviate our ever-present lack of money.[177]

'c) I think the Arts Council should be consulted at once to pass their opinion, based on the experience of other theatres similar to ours, on suggestions made by a report which is understandably parochial in outlook.'

David concluded his contribution with a clear-headed assessment: 'It is proper to query whether high standards of design, of costume and scenery and of acting are necessary; would the public really notice and be adversely affected by a lowering (and cheapening) of quality? Without question, the public can tell the difference between first and second class, although it may not be able to put a finger on matters of detail; it will be aware of the second-rate whether in design or acting, will reject it and ultimately refuse to pay to see it.

'Equal in importance to the reaction of the public is the attitude of the profession. In the last years of the Playhouse, it was almost impossible to interest actors, agents, designers, directors and writers in our programme because we were dismissed, in the pejorative phrase, as "provincial rep". The new building and thrust stage have certainly

---

[177] As it turned out, the Crucible achieved an average box office of 67% in 1972-73 and 76% in 1973-74.

caught the theatrical imagination, but the gratifying response we are now getting to our approaches to actors, writers and agents is directly linked to the artistic standards we have set.'

Following further discussions between myself, Tony Hampton and the Board, David presented a 12-page response to the Treasurer's report which condensed our thinking. After making his own assessment, David reckoned it might be possible to find savings of £6,800 for the current year, which if added to optimistic projections of increased catering and box office revenue would reduce the shortfall by £14,100. But this still left a hefty deficit for the year, and he warned that these economies would lower artistic standards.

Following our responses to the report, we attended a Trustee meeting where the ball was placed in my court to offer a way out of our financial difficulties. I had been passionately defending the design of the theatre and our programme, but on this occasion I needed to show the Trust a new face. I was very restrained and appreciative of how the Crucible Company had been supported by the Trust and the City Council throughout all the criticism and attacks. The nub of my speech was that it was going to take time to establish both an administrative plan for the building and to win over a big enough audience to make the Crucible financially viable. David said after the meeting that he felt it was the best speech I had made about the Crucible.

Perhaps losing my restraint, I finished by stating that any new artistic movement suffers extreme criticism before becoming accepted by society, giving the example of the Impressionist painters. The name their critics gave them—'Impressionist'—was actually an insult, insinuating that the artist offered the public not a picture but only an impression of one. I noted that one of the most famous impressionists—Vincent Van Gogh—sold only one painting in his life, for what would then have been £10, which now fetches many thousands of pounds at auction.[178] After a somewhat lengthy pause the Chairman said dispassionately: 'For the Crucible to be a success, Colin, we cannot wait until you die.' Fair point.

---

[178] The painting in question was *The Red Vineyard* which sold for 400 Belgian Francs in 1890, the year of his death. To date, the most expensive Van Gogh painting ever sold at auction is *Portrait of Dr Gachet*, which went for $82.5 million in 1990.

But there was no questioning Anthony's support for the Crucible and its staff. After our meeting, he produced a confidential memo outlining the Trust's response to the report. In it, he rejected the recommendations regarding the box office, reducing the design team and moving away from repertoire, which would be a fundamental change of policy for the theatre. But he recognised the need for a review of our programme policy.

'It had not been fully appreciated that the progression from a 550-seat provincial repertory to a regional repertory theatre of metropolitan standard seating 1,000 required an entirely new approach, nor that patterns in theatre going in the country as a whole had been changing over the last five years. The day has gone when a provincial repertory theatre with a resident Company performed its own programme for eleven months of the year.' Instead, we would run a shortened resident season from October to May, a summer season of touring productions or lighter entertainment, as well as short tours for the resident Company during the summer and touring seasons.

Anthony doubted that many of the promised savings could be made and forecast a deficit of £164,420 in 1972-73. After a contribution of £80,630 from the Arts Council, this would leave a hole of £83,790 in our finances. Reconfirming his belief in the Crucible's long-term future, he called on the Council to pay off the deficit for 1971-72, help fund the gap in 1972-73 and support efforts to secure long-term funding from the Arts Council. In order to achieve this, the Arts Council was invited to inspect the new theatre and meet the team in November.[179]

But then the drama took another twist. The report was leaked to *The Star*, which on 13th September 1972 published excerpts from it, detailing Mr Jones's criticism of what he viewed as excessive costs. No space was given to our detailed rebuttal of his arguments or our counter proposals. The headline that the theatre was '£130,000 in the red' was all the public remembered. Then, on 1st November, *The Star* twisted the knife under the banner headline: 'Crucible chiefs seek

---

[179] The Trust also appointed Roger Heath, a management accountant (rather like a modern-day finance director) to work alongside David. When David retired in October 1975, my father's successor Peter James was re-designated 'The Director' and Roger became 'Administrative Director', a role which he described as 'my old job as accountant plus half of David Brayshaw's!'

£117,000 to avert crisis'. The newspaper reported a plunge in the box office, lamented our failure to make any of the savings demanded by the Treasurer and incorrectly claimed that we were demanding £117,000 from the City Council to pay off our losses.

What was especially damaging about this second report were the comments by the City Council Leader, Alderman Sir Ron Ironmonger, who raised serious doubts about the running of the Crucible: 'To put it bluntly, I am not satisfied they are doing enough to make themselves more efficient. I think the whole control structure should be examined. There are too many Chiefs and not enough Indians.' He was, of course, referring to David's and my roles as Administrator and Artistic Director. Although Alderman Ironmonger accepted that the poor box office reflected a broader national trend of falling theatre attendance, he insisted that the Council would not pay off all the Crucible's debts and that any renewal of the annual subsidy would have conditions attached.

Alderman Ironmonger's comment that there were 'too many Chiefs and not enough Indians' was a clever turn of phrase which

The Star

No. 26,729 SHEFFIELD, WEDNESDAY, NOVEMBER 1, 1972. 4p

Theatre management faced with crunch decision: No 'rescue on the rates' without strings!

CRUCIBLE CHIEFS SEEK £117,000 TO AVERT CRISIS

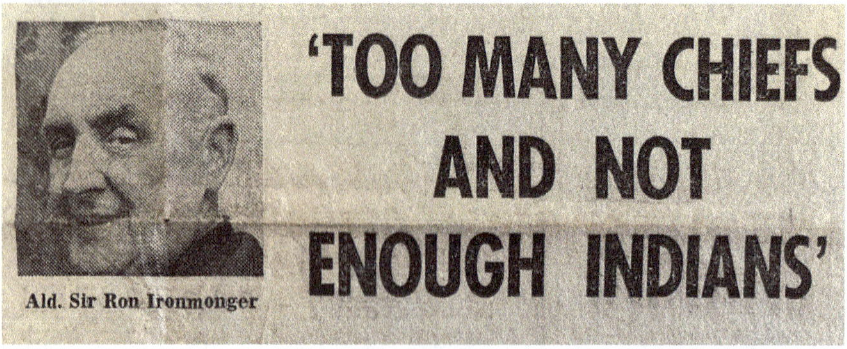

'TOO MANY CHIEFS AND NOT ENOUGH INDIANS'

Ald. Sir Ron Ironmonger

was endlessly repeated in the press over the coming months. It never crossed his mind that for every 'Indian' acting on stage there are at least half a dozen 'Chiefs' directing him, costuming him, making his props and lighting him, and in a building three or four times the size of the old Playhouse, an army of workers was needed to maintain it and service its amenities. But that phrase resonated with a section of the Sheffield public who were opposed to our new theatre, and for me it was to prove the last straw.

CHAPTER TWENTY-FOUR

No more in vice or error to engage,
Or play the fool at large, on life's great stage.[†]

And so we come to the final act, and here I must tread on eggshells. I offer the facts—as I remember them—which led to my resignation as Artistic Director of the Crucible after eleven remarkable years in Sheffield. I have press cuttings and releases about my resignation and departure, but no vital letter or memorandum minute that led to the decision. And David Brayshaw—the one person who could elucidate on this matter—has long since made his exit.

But what I do remember is that the leaking of the report over the Crucible's finances reopened the toxic debate over the theatre and its purpose, emboldening those who wished to see it fail. Headlines of poor box office, rising debts and inefficiency fuelled the belief that the Crucible was the expensive folly of a distant intellectual elite who were squandering ratepayers' money for their own avant-garde fantasies. And after three years of battles over the thrust stage and our vision for the theatre, I was reaching breaking point.

What particularly angered me about the Treasurer's report was the suggestion that Tanya's services as Design Consultant were superfluous. This ignored the fact that from the very start David and I had made it an absolute condition that if a thrust stage were to be built, then the designer must be Tanya Moiseiwitsch. It was her talent—genius, rather—that shaped the Crucible stage and auditorium and influenced the design of the whole building.

Now that the Crucible was at last up and running, I thought it would be a disaster to lose not only her skill as one of the best international and contemporary designers for the thrust stage, but also her influence on members of the creative staff. Given her experience,

---

[†] From Lady Teazle's closing speech in Richard Brinsley Sheridan's *The School for Scandal*.

particular with the thrust stage, she was passing on her knowledge to the young designers, the costume and prop makers, the workshop staff and scene painters. Indeed, as often happens in companies working together for a length of time, she became the grandmother of the theatre—to be referred to when problems arose and whose approval and encouragement was regularly sought.

The timing of the leaked report was unfortunate, as Tanya and I were working together for the first time on her thrust stage: a production of Aeschylus's *The Persians* which was to open our second season. *The Persians* is one of the great anti-war plays, demonstrating great sympathy for the losing Persians (the audience would all have been Greek). Feeling that such a big play needed an open sky to let it breathe, on the first day of rehearsal (14th August), I took the Company up to the Peak District, near Mam Tor, and rehearsed them in the open air.

Although I was the play's director, the hand of Guthrie—whose productions of Aeschylus had brought their tragic grandeur to immediate life—was visible everywhere. The translator and adaptor of *The Persians*, John Lewin of Minneapolis, had translated all of Sir Tyrone's later Greek productions.[180] Tanya—who had designed the setting, costumes and properties for Guthrie's Greek work—was designing, and she produced a stunning array of masks and costumes, with the lead actors on 10-foot-high stilts. And two of the leads playing King Darius and Queen Atossa were Douglas Campbell and Ann Casson, who had been acting with Guthrie since the early Stratford days. They instinctively contributed to the *mise-en-scène* and in rehearsals offered advice on the chorus work.

Perhaps my most cherished memory of that production came one night early in our run, when I watched an old, white-haired and magnificent lady, sitting or rather leaning forward, watching her daughter, Ann Casson, perform on stage. Her eyes shone with wonder and delight. After the performance, the old lady was fêted in the bar. Then it came time to go. Crippled with arthritis, she could not descend the stairs to the taxi waiting below. So, four actors picked up

---

[180] On opening night, John Lewin and his wife Hazel sent my father the following telegram: 'One cone of incense to Zeus, one to Ahuramazda', referring to the most powerful deities in Greek and Persian mythology.

the chair in which she was sitting and, hoisted shoulder high, Dame Sybil Thorndike made a royal exit from the Crucible. Her first remark on seeing the auditorium remained with me. 'If only we had had a theatre like this to work in when we were young!'

The Persians was well received by the critics, who felt the stage admirably suited the play. Robin Thornber's review in *The Guardian* revealed Guthrie's deep influence: '[The production] totally rejects realism, which would reduce the tragedy to the logistic differences of a Middle Eastern megalomaniac. It chooses instead a supernaturalism which makes these blown-up pains and passions the problems of all people at all times. And it is the technical accomplishment of this production—making everything larger than life—which makes it true to life. It is the grotesque costumes, designed by Tanya Moiseiwitsch, with their fixed masks of agony, the luxurious folds of their robes, and the foot-high raised clogs which turn the whole thing into a psychedelic dream. And it is then that you can accept the histrionic posturing as not only natural but inevitable.'[181]

However, the Sheffield public did not share this view and box office was disappointing—the show's 15 performances played to 36% capacity. Perhaps they were not quite ready for Guthrie-style Greek drama. But there could be no questioning our choice for the second half of the season. After much clamouring from the public, we announced that *The Stirrings in Sheffield on Saturday Night* would be revived, opening in April 1973. We would bring back several of the original cast— Barrie Smith, Anthony Naylor and Neil Boorman—as well as newer *Stirrings*-ites like Richard Wordsworth and Fanny Carby. I asked Tanya to design it and she agreed we would start planning in the New Year.

On 17th November, shortly after *The Persians* closed, a team from the Arts Council visited the Crucible, comprising Mr Field and Mr Collins from the Finance Department and Mr Mair from the Drama Department. They spent a day in the theatre, viewing the facilities and talking with the staff. I had just opened a new play by John Spurling— ironically entitled *Peace in Our Time*, about the events leading up to the Second World War—and this visit cast a pall over the production,

---

[181] *The Guardian*, 5 October 1972.

Tanya's design for The Persians, *September 1972*

which did not do well at the box office. The conversations that day were positive, but it was clear that the Arts Council would back a number of staff cuts, including in the Design Department. They promised to report their findings in January.

It was, I think, around this time that David Brayshaw told me Tanya was leaving. Alas, I have no written record of him telling me this or more importantly why this had come about. It may be that as often happens at a particularly painful time in life, Shakespeare's 'warder of the brain' (memory) slammed the cell door shut on what we prefer to forget. I am not aware there was any meeting where Tanya was told her services were superfluous. She may, as it were, have taken the hint.

Many years later, I asked Tanya what had led to her leaving the Crucible. She was by then an old lady, and as it was more than 30 years previous, she couldn't remember the exact chain of events. But the account she gave of her time at the Crucible had her characteristic enthusiasm and good humour, without a hint of rancour:

'I got into a very high state of excitement that there was going to be a theatre. You and David Brayshaw had been to America and Canada and decided that the kind of stage you wanted was the open stage and not another proscenium stage—which may or may not have overexcited Bernard Miles! He dashed into print to say terrible things, which was enough to make you want it all the more. You were sold on the idea—you'd seen it work. So, I enjoyed being in Sheffield and being part of all that. But once the stage was ready to be acted on, you and David said: "Now we have built the theatre, you've got to prove that you can work in it, so will you stay?" And I said: "Ooohhh! Why not? I'd love to!" And you said: "Do a couple of shows and then we'll talk about it again." Three months later, it was like: "I don't think we can afford to pay you anymore, so you'd better leave now!"'[182]

To be fair, Tanya had a career to pursue herself. She had already turned down an offer from the American theatre director Hal Prince to design the latest Stephen Sondheim Broadway musical, *Company*. And when she did leave Sheffield at the end of March 1973, she went to design at the National Theatre. Whatever her reasons, I believed that her leaving, which she did during the *Stirrings* run, to be the direct result of Mr Jones's criticism that a consultant was one too many in the design department. All I can remember is that David, a person of the utmost integrity, gave me the news that Tanya was leaving as if it was our joint defeat.

I had shrugged off the interminable attacks on the Crucible. I was not so naive as to think the controversial thrust stage design coupled with the closing of the Lyceum theatre would not provoke considerable antagonism. However, Tanya being pushed out against my wishes was the tipping point. I had spent eleven years of my life in Sheffield and very rewarding ones they were, but I felt that my time was coming to an end, too.

---

[182] Colin George's interview with Tanya Moiseiwitsch, May 2001.

Two weeks after the Arts Council inspection, I made a short visit to Poland. I had been invited by Jozef Szajna to direct in Warsaw and—after seeing Szajna during his visit to England that August—I flew to Warsaw on 24th November to discuss our production for the following summer. I believe that it was while I was in Poland—away from the Sheffield press and the whirligig of running the Crucible—that I made the decision to resign as Artistic Director.

Shortly after my return to Sheffield, I learned that the Trustees had managed to persuade the City Council to renew the £50,000 grant for the Crucible and pay off the deficit from our first season. The theatre's critics predictably accused the Council of being overgenerous, but what alternative did they have? The only option being offered by extremists in the city was to demolish the Crucible complex and use the site for a profit-making car park, supermarket or bingo hall!

With the Crucible's immediate financial future secure, I felt I could resign without leaving the theatre to an uncertain fate. But I would not leave in a huff, shaking the dust of the city from my shoes as I left. Rather, I wanted to leave the new theatre in a strong position and as established as it could be in the uncertain world of the theatre. So I agreed to stay for a transition period to enable the box office to improve and give the Trust adequate time to find a successor for me. After nine years at the Playhouse and two at the Crucible, my shoes would not be easy to fill.

I informed David and the Trustees of my decision and it was agreed that I would announce my resignation at a press conference. Before this took place, I called the Company together and informed them of my decision to resign, letting them know that I intended to stay until the end of the 1973-74 season to ensure a smooth handover. Tanya was there and I asked her afterwards what her reaction was, and she said: 'Well, it is always a shock when the captain says he is leaving the ship.'

On 1st March 1973, David sent a letter to the Crucible management, enclosing a copy of the Arts Council's report of its visit to the Crucible the previous November. David's summary was remarkably upbeat:

'The Arts Council gained a first impression "of a sense of purpose, hard work and enthusiasm which is very encouraging" and went on to state the view that "on the evidence available, the financial problems of the theatre stem from a lack of income rather than over expenditure against budget". They say that "it is difficult to assess what major cuts could be made in expenditure which would not seriously damage the Crucible's artistic standard", that production expenditure is being kept under control and that no other area is excessively above budget.' They even recommended expanding, not reducing, the Publicity budget.

But there was a sting in the tail. 'The report underlines the need to increase income at the same time as recommending one or two economies.' Among these economies was the proposal to restructure the design team, removing the role of Design Consultant. On this issue, the report included this ominous line: 'The situation may solve itself soon by the departure of Miss Moiseiwitsch.' Tanya did indeed leave the Crucible at the end of March.

The following month, on 19th April 1973, I announced to gathered press that I was resigning as Artistic Director of the Crucible and would be leaving at the end of the 1973-74 season. I made no mention of Mr Jones's report or the ousting of Tanya, instead saying I believed that after three seasons 'the immediate goal of my appointment will have been reached'. But I acknowledged that the experience of getting the Crucible built had been 'probably the toughest assault course anyone outside London has ever had to survive'.[183]

After my announcement I was interviewed by the *Morning Telegraph*'s Paul Allen, a long-time supporter of the Crucible, although not without criticism, and his article published on April 24th captures the fierce opinions that my tenure as Artistic Director of the Crucible had stirred up. He wrote:

'There are certainly quite a few people who would have liked to see [Colin George] sacked; in the days surrounding the announcement last week I heard him criticised in separate conversations for being too arrogant, too loyal, too concerned with "the intellectual few", too ready to rely on old work he had done successfully in the past, too remote, too trendy, too far from what was happening in the modern theatre and heaven knows what else.

'What no one can take away from him, however, is the simple fact that he has opened a spanking new theatre—which Joan Littlewood

---

[183] *Morning Telegraph*, 19 April 1973.

With the Company of The Duchess of Malfi *and Jozef Szajna on stage in Warsaw, June 1973*

said the other day was the finest in Europe. Not many directors have done that; fewer still have been able to make the announcement of impending departure in the knowledge that the theatre is now running relatively smoothly to audiences which are probably as good as any comparable in the country; and better than most.'

Speaking of my decision to resign, I said to Paul: 'Obviously, it still has a long way to go—I'd be a fool to think otherwise—but the theatre is *working* now; it's a good time for it and me to look for new directions. I felt that either I had to commit myself to another five or ten years working in a single community, a life which inevitably is time- and soul-consuming, or look around.

'I have quite enjoyed seeing the "Crucible Shock" headlines and lived through it. I grew up in the Midlands in a family where the idea of being at the centre of controversy and continually provoking comment was quite common. My father was a free church minister who actually went into pubs if that was there his people were. And later on, I went through the same kind of atmosphere at Nottingham. But it can affect your judgement, and it can certainly sap the creative effort.'

However, I noted that Sheffield 'is not at all like London, which can be much worse, sharp and vicious. Here one of the problems is that you can suffer from a lot of hostility which is largely ill-informed rather than malicious, or you get out-and-out adulation.' I finished with an upbeat, if rather ironic, comment: 'What'll happen now, of course, is that in a couple of years' time, the Crucible will really take off, and I shall regret like hell not being here.'

Among the letters I received after my resignation was one from Colin Brannigan, editor of *The Star*, musing that 'it seems to be a week for shock resignations in the entertainment world. First Bobby Charlton, and now Colin George!' But *The Star* couldn't resist twisting one of my comments at the press conference to suggest I had rejected a new five-year contract from the Trust (no such offer was made or even considered).

The same month, *Stirrings* opened for its final revival and was a hit. It played to packed houses for 47 performances and a combined audience of 39,000 people. This made it our most successful show up to that point.[184] But my memories of the production are tinged with sadness, as it coincided with Tanya's departure and my resignation as Artistic Director. One can understand criticism that we should have opened the Crucible with *Stirrings* in November 1971—David Brayshaw was among those who felt that strongly. But alongside Guthrie's Aeschylus Trilogy, it would have been an ill-matched bedfellow. Moreover, Canadian actors had already been engaged for the Greek classics and *Stirrings* was always cast with Northern actors to whom the accent was second nature.[185]

At the end of April, we lost another member of the team, Caroline Smith, who resigned as Director of the Studio Theatre. Her assistant, Ed Thomason, stepped into her shoes and went on to direct shows in both the Studio and the main auditorium. He was joined in July

---

[184] *Stirrings* was just ahead of *Treasure Island* in December 1971 (38,000) and *Rumpelstiltskin* in December 1973 (37,000).

[185] Many in the Company were against opening the Crucible with *Stirrings*, among them Christopher Wilkinson who said in his interview with Sue Fulton in 2003: 'I am not saying *Peer Gynt* was the right play to open with, but I think it would have been a disastrous mistake to open a new theatre, a revolutionary theatre, with something which had been done three times before.'

1973 by Rex Doyle, who became Associate Studio Director with responsibility for Theatre Vanguard. A changing of the guard was underway.[186]

In June, I visited Poland to direct *The Duchess of Malfi* at the Warsaw Palace of Culture. I had directed the play at the Playhouse in 1966, with Edward Furby's claustrophobic settings and a grinding operatic score by Gilbert Kennedy. But with Jozef Szajna designing the costumes and props, the prolific Andrzej Sadowski designing the scenery, and a Company of talented Polish actors playing the roles, this was a very different production. Some of the costumes were outrageous, to say the least. But it was a wonderful experience working with Szajna in his own country, and the sense of being part of one theatrical family was completed when my wife and our three children joined me in Warsaw one week before the show opened.

I returned to Sheffield ready to plan my final season as Artistic Director and for once was greeted by positive news in the press. On 12th July, we released our box office figures for the 1972-73 season and they showed a marked improvement. Total audiences were up by 40% and we had reached an average box office of 61.6%, meeting the target laid down in F G Jones's infamous report. Moreover, in the six months since our Christmas 1972 shows, average attendance had risen to 71.5%, well above comparable theatres in Birmingham, Bristol and Nottingham. During one purple week (11-17 March 1973), there were 21 performances of eight different productions which were seen by 11,071 people.[187] In total, 189,820 people saw shows at the Crucible that season, equivalent to nearly one third of Sheffield's population at the time. Now we could genuinely say we were serving the Sheffield community.

Under the headline 'Figures bring sweetness and light to the Crucible', Paul Allen wrote: 'These figures reflect a growing rapport between the theatre and a general public which for various reasons was formerly suspicious if not downright hostile.' He noted that the Crucible had found a steady audience for its range of productions:

---

[186] Ed Thomason ended up leaving the Crucible the following year to become Director of the Belgrade Theatre, Coventry, and Rex Doyle took over his role as Studio Director.
[187] To give some comparison, in a good week the Playhouse would perform two to three different productions to a total house of no more than 3,000.

around 6,000 for 'high-brow' shows like *Peer Gynt* or *The Persians*, around 15,000 for 'solid middlebrow' works like *The Taming of the Shrew* and *The National Health*, and over 30,000 for Christmas shows and hits like *Stirrings*.[188]

Even *The Star* grudgingly admitted: 'You can't please all the people all the time, but you can make some happy enough to come back for more.' A long-term opponent of the thrust stage, the newspaper printed in the same edition an article entitled 'A stage that has won over the top professionals', with comments from leading actors—among them Tom Courtenay, James Bolam and Derek Bond—who had played on the Crucible's thrust stage during its first two seasons and had been won over to its charms.[189]

Buoyed by this news, we opened my last season in late August 1973 with the final run of *Stirrings*, which again played to packed houses. I then directed a Japanese-inspired version of *Macbeth*, designed by husband-and-wife team Ann Beverley and John Bloomfield, with

Playing Astrov in Uncle Vanya, *November 1973*

---

[188] *Morning Telegraph*, 11 July 1973.
[189] *The Star*, 12 July 1973.

silent Aikido-inspired fight scenes arranged by Anthony Naylor. It played for 23 performances to an impressive 74% house. That year's Christmas show—*Rumpelstiltskin*, directed by Rex Doyle—was the hit of the season, running for 38 performances at 96.6% capacity, and it was followed by Roderick Horn's production of *Irma La Douce*, which ran for 40 performances.

I also used the opportunity of being at the Crucible to act in a couple of productions, as I was planning to return to acting after my contract ended in July 1974. In November 1973, I played Astrov in Job Stewart's production of *Uncle Vanya*, and in February 1974, I played the title roles in Ed Thomason's production of *Dr Jekyll and Mr Hyde*, which had a foreboding 'soundscape' created by Mark Wing-Davey and Tim Foster. This was the first time my daughter Lucy saw me act on the stage—perhaps not the wisest choice for a five-year-old!

On 10 March 1974, my successor was announced—Peter James, Artistic Director of the Shaw Theatre in London. Peter had a long history in experimental theatre. In 1964, he co-founded Liverpool's Everyman Theatre, and he had been Associate Director at the Young Vic. Peter also had a history with the Sheffield Company, having brought his production of *Rosencrantz and Guildenstern Are Dead* to the Playhouse in March 1971 during our last season there. He had also directed *Oh! What a Lovely War* on the Crucible stage in April 1972, so he knew what kind of a challenge he was taking on as Artistic Director.

In April 1974, there was more good news. Figures for the 1973-74 season showed that our box office had risen to 72%, exceeding not only the former City Treasurer's target of 60% but also the Arts Council benchmark of 65%. Including the Studio Theatre, over 250,000 people had seen 482 separate performances, ranging from pop concerts and brass bands, to West End comedies, opera, ballet, Shakespeare and musicals. Our 'freak' was winning a genuine body of supporters for whom the Crucible was their theatre, and of which they were justly proud.

And so it was time to wrap up my directing duties with a run of three shows to close out the season. First, in April 1974, was Richard Brinsley Sheridan's *The School for Scandal* with the talented Northern actress Lynda Marchal as Lady Teazle.[190] The show was well received by the critics and ran for 20 performances with an impressive 72% box office. Then, after directing a short run of Noel Coward's *Private Lives*, it was time for our summer musical—*Calamity Jane*, which would be performed on stage in the UK for the first time.

The choice for my valedictory production of a light-hearted musical rather than a meaty tragedy surprised some. I explained it thus: 'After 14 years spent in the city, years which have seen such change in the theatrical scene amid much lively controversy, it seemed appropriate to exit with a bang. We opened the Crucible with Cowboys and Indians (with local school children during the *Fanfare* week) and I am happy to ride out of town in similar fashion.'[191]

While I was rehearsing *Calamity Jane*, I gave an interview for the Crucible Club newsletter, in which they asked me to explain the difference between working in film/television and working in the theatre. My response, I think, summed up my experience of working with the Playhouse and Crucible Companies and why we were all committed to working in theatre:

'What the theatre has not got—in fact, this is part of its quality—is a permanent record of the performance. Each night is a little different; it can often be enlivened by something technical going wrong with which the actor has to cope. Looking back on twelve years in Sheffield, I have newspaper cuttings which, on the whole, are quite misleading; I have photographs which look very dramatic; but the feeling and atmosphere of the first night of *The Stirrings in Sheffield*, or the last night of *Britannia's Boys* at the old Playhouse, or again the first night of the Crucible—not the strange and intimidating night of the official opening, but the sneak preview on Saturday, when, for the very first time in the Crucible, a thousand people sat in front of a performance, and we were able to say with certainty that they were listening and laughing and applauding and that theatre was going to work, are experiences recorded now only in the memory, and for those of us who are deeply involved have already been embroidered beyond belief.

---

[190] At that time, Lynda Titchmarsh used the stage name Lynda Marchal. Today, she is better known as a prolific writer of novels and screenplays under her pen name, Lynda La Plante.
[191] *Morning Telegraph*, 26 June 1974.

'Film and television are mediums in which one's work is permanent and can be viewed in retrospect years later. Neither of them seems to me the medium in which the actor is supreme. The editor of a film can "create" a star and destroy a good actor. What the actor has in the theatre is that *live* communication with his audience and he (rather than the director, or the lighting man, or the designer, or even the author), is in command.

'I like to feel that the Crucible stage is very much the actor's stage, for on it he is in as close a proximity as one can engineer with a thousand people. Having now twice appeared myself at the Crucible, I can appreciate the excitement, and indeed the terror, that so many of our visiting performers have when they first look at the stage; it is gratifying to note how soon they respond to its challenges when they stand on it. I like to feel that in the future the theatre in Sheffield will flourish, principally, because it offers such a wonderful and indeed literal platform for the actor and author.'[192]

On 27th June 1974, we opened *Calamity Jane* and it ran for three weeks, playing to 76% box office. Lynda Marchal gave a gutsy performance in the title role which caught the critics' and the public's attention. She went on to reprise the role later that year at the Belgrade Theatre in Coventry.

As I approached my leaving date, there was surprise for me in the press, and not at all what I had been expecting. *The Star* had had a change of heart and published a lengthy and unreserved apology: 'Colin George, the man behind Sheffield's Crucible Theatre, a role which brought him into frequent and sometimes heated conflict with traditionalists and with those reluctant to engage in experiment, bows out with characteristic assurance and grace. He leaves, having established himself as something of a legend. And what is more to the point, his departure can be seen as a chapter in which the concepts which he fervently believed have been proved not only correct, but highly successful.

'The Star never concealed its dislike of the thrust stage, which it saw as an aspect of experimentation unsuited to the city. Nor were we impressed by the design of the theatre, which appeared to us too

---

[192] Crucible Club Newsletter, June 1974.

much of departure from the familiar shapes. In making clear our point of view, we believed that we were expressing the views of many of our readers.

'Success and acclaim for the Crucible were not instantaneous, but when they came, they were on a scale which we are now happy to admit proved the extent to which Mr George was right in his firmly-held beliefs and to which we, conditioned by traditional ideas of the shape of a theatre and its aspirations, were wrong. Today, we are happy to congratulate Mr George on the success that marked his bold endeavours. For what he has done has been far more than the scoring of a personal victory. He has endowed Sheffield with a modern theatre, as venturesome in its productions as in its design. He has given Sheffield something of lasting value.'

It was perhaps too little, too late, but for the staff and Company of the Crucible who had endured years of criticism from *The Star*, it was viewed as a victory and a vindication of all our years of hard work.

Two nights before we closed the Crucible, the staff threw me a farewell party in the Studio, 'Col's Last Round-Up', and after the last performance on 20th July 1974, Tony Hampton presided over a ceremony on stage. As I was invited on stage, a fanfare was played which was suspiciously like the theme tune to *Coronation Street*—a joke from the Company, who knew I was going off to play Jimmy Graham on 'the Street' that August. Anthony presented me with a tape recorder and a canteen of Sheffield-made cutlery, and I gave a short speech, ending with the final words of William Broadhead at the end of *Stirrings*: 'I know that to the end of my days, whatever my fellow citizens think of me, I shall always feel a very lively interest in the welfare and the future prosperity of the good old town of Sheffield.'

In my programme notes for *Calamity Jane*, I paid tribute to my colleagues: 'It is stating the obvious that being involved in planning and running the Crucible has been for me a unique opportunity; just as it is to add that without the active support of innumerable people in the city and the unhesitatingly-offered "hard graft" of a passionate, unswervingly loyal, and highly professional Company of actors, technicians, and front of house staff, I would have sunk without trace long ago.

'Our critics have often shrugged off the idealism that has informed the thinking behind this building, and which incidentally has generated

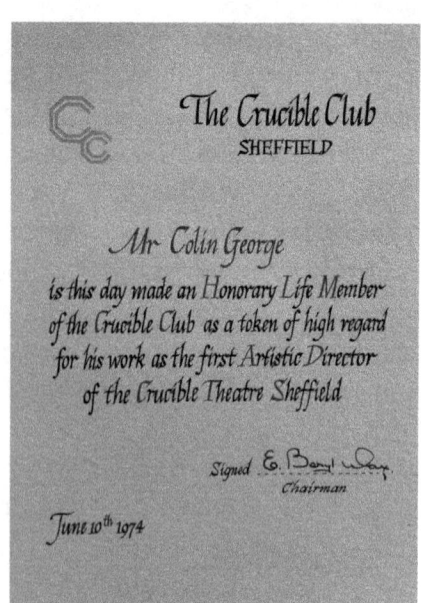

A flier for 'Col's Last Round-Up' and a certificate granting me Honorary Life Membership of the Crucible Club

the adrenaline to keep it going, as a posh sort of group salesmanship—remote, self-centred and with its "head in the clouds". If I had to come down to the footlights of this city to answer this, I could find no better words than Arthur Miller's [from *Death of a Salesman*]:

"He had the wrong dreams you say—you don't understand. For a salesman, there is no rock bottom to the life. He don't put a nut on a bolt [...] He's a man way out there in the blue, riding on a smile and a shoeshine. And when they start not smiling back, that's an earthquake [...] But a salesman has got to dream, boy, it comes with the territory.'"

And my territory fifty years ago was Sheffield, where I shared the adventure of building a controversial new theatre with a small but talented army of committed companions, who never doubted that our joint vision—the thrust stage—would prevail. It is a remarkable performance space. It has tempted the public with an extraordinary variety of offerings—from Shakespeare to snooker. And the theatre's very name, the Crucible, has become linked both nationally and internationally to this northern city, where I joined a fortnightly rep in 1962 without the slightest idea of what the future held for all of us working there.

For me personally, two moments in time influenced its singular design. The first was when I walked down a tunnel in a Minneapolis theatre and suddenly saw a stage in front of me, thrusting itself into the light and offering the actor and director 'the brightest heaven of invention'. And the other moment? Many years before, when the 'onlie begetter' himself, Sir Tyrone Guthrie, was forced by a thunderstorm to move his production into a ballroom and thrust *Hamlet* at the surrounding audience. When life offers itself to your imagination in this way, well, 'the readiness is all'.

The opportunity to be involved in building a new theatre may come the way of a director once in a generation. Sheffield gave me that chance. The City Council and Theatre Trust could have easily lured a director of distinction from London. They chose me—as an acknowledgment of the commitment I had already shown to the City of Steel. So, finally, let me say, with real sincerity—thank you, Sheffield.

David Brayshaw and I watch the Crucible rise out of the ground, July '70

EPILOGUE by Tedd George

What wound did ever heal but by degrees?[†]

In July 1974 my father and the Crucible went their separate ways, and it would be 37 years before he was to return to the thrust stage he helped create, this time as an actor. His departure signalled a changing of the guard, and within a few years many of the protagonists in the battle to build the Crucible had also moved on. These included David Brayshaw, who retired in October 1975, the Crucible Trust Chairman Tony Hampton, and several long-serving Board members who had championed the new theatre.

The new Artistic Director, Peter James, started strongly with a string of hits, but within a couple of years the Crucible was under severe financial strain as recession bit and public finances dried up. A number of options were considered to boost revenues, but the master stroke came with the decision to host the 1977 World Snooker Championship in the main auditorium. The story goes that snooker legend Mike Watterson was approached to find a new venue for the championship. His wife had seen a show at the Crucible and told her husband it would make a perfect venue for snooker. So he called the Crucible's Manager, Arnold Elliman, a deal was struck and the event went ahead. It proved so successful that the World Snooker Championship has been held at the Crucible every year since.

In truth, my father and many theatre professionals were initially aghast at the idea of the Crucible Theatre being used for snooker. But they soon recognised that snooker put the Crucible on the international map and secured the theatre's financial stability. Over time, my father would come to see snooker as another feather in the Crucible's cap, proving that its unique performing area could be used

---

[†] William Shakespeare, *Othello*, Act II, Scene 3.

in ways the designers had never imagined. From the start, he had insisted that the Crucible should be a public space, regularly visited by Sheffielders even if they only came in for a drink; in his view, they would eventually buy a ticket for a show. Little did he realise that the opposite might happen and that a theatregoer would be inspired by a theatrical show to host snooker in the auditorium!

Over the following years, a series of Artistic Directors left their mark on the Crucible, pushing the boundaries of what could be achieved on the thrust stage and in the Studio Theatre. An entire generation of actors, singers, dancers, musicians, designers, and technicians performed and worked on both stages and it would almost be easier to list those who did not work at the Crucible than those who did.

One person who left a lasting legacy was Clare Venables, Artistic Director of the Crucible throughout the 1980s. During her tenure, Clare not only established the Crucible Youth Theatre (continuing the tradition of Theatre Vanguard), but she was the driving force in saving the adjacent Lyceum Theatre from ruin. Determined to bring the theatre into the Crucible fold, Clare persuaded the City Council to buy the Lyceum and invest £13 million in its refurbishment. The work was carried out by the Crucible's architect, Nick Thompson, and his team, who completely redesigned the foyers and backstage areas and restored the magnificent auditorium.

On its reopening in December 1990, the Lyceum joined the Crucible and the Studio in a single theatre complex—Sheffield Theatres—which became the largest in Britain alongside the National Theatre and larger than Stratford-upon-Avon. This was a truly extraordinary turn of events and offered the opportunity to create productions for all kinds of theatrical space, from the Lyceum's traditional proscenium, to the Crucible's thrust stage auditorium, to the experimental box of the Studio. The creators of the Crucible would never have dared to dream of such an outcome.

Over the past 50 years, the Crucible Theatre complex has also changed. In 1984, it underwent its first full refurbishment, by which time many of the carpets and fittings had become very worn. Clare Ferraby redesigned the carpets and the colour scheme for the bar, restaurant, shop and stairs, and there was new lettering for the foyer. Then, in 1991, Nick Thompson was asked by the chairman of Thorntons to increase the seating capacity of the Studio Theatre. Thorntons was at that time sponsoring the world-famous Lindsay Quartet to perform there and needed more paying spectators to help offset the costs. By adjusting the circulation, increasing seating in the gallery and by adding an external staircase, Nick and his team increased the audience capacity from 250 to 400.

By the mid-2000s, all three theatres were again in need of refurbishment, not only to replace worn fittings but also to meet modern health, safety and public access standards. So, in 2007, the architects Burrell Foley Fischer (BFF) were appointed to carry out a £15 million refurbishment, and over the next two years they made substantial changes to the building. Prior to the refurb, only 10% of the building was accessible to wheelchairs, and to address this a lift was added to the south-west corner of the building, along with a large ramp into the main foyer. Modern fire regulations also required the installation of additional fire doors and screens, which somewhat broke up the feeling of an unimpeded thoroughfare.

Backstage facilities, including the offices, workshops, dressing rooms, and rehearsal space, were significantly expanded, the auditorium's air-conditioning system was redesigned, and vast amounts of wiring and obsolete equipment were replaced.[193] But the famous auditorium was mostly left untouched, preserving its acoustics, with minor adjustments to the seating to incorporate wheelchair places and the replacement of 1,000 light bulbs with LEDs.

The most notable change was the addition of a distinctive box on stilts on the front of the main entrance, with iconic lettering announcing the Crucible. However, owing to budget cuts the complete design—which was to have included an enlarged restaurant and rehearsal room—was not fully realised. Nonetheless, the importance of the Crucible was recognised during the refurbishment when the building was awarded

---

[193] Sadly, the auditorium's innovative air-circulation system had to be redesigned. The system delivered fresh air, heating and cooling through the gaps under the seating and extracted air from the ducting in the roof above the seats. But it was discovered that there were small quantities of asbestos under the modular slabs, and to remove these would have required dismantling the entire structure—effectively rebuilding the theatre. So instead, the vents were closed off and an alternative was introduced to reverse the original system, delivering air from the roof and extracting it through the back wall of the stage. However, I am told that it does not work as effectively as the old system. Tedd George's interview with John Bates, June 2021.

The Crucible Theatre, with its new entrance, and the restored Lyceum

The Crucible auditorium during a technical rehearsal of Victoria Wood's Talent, *June 2021*

The Studio Theatre, June 2021

The Lyceum Theatre auditorium, 2014

Grade II listing. The revitalised Sheffield Theatres complex reopened in February 2010, at which point my father re-enters the story.

In the years after leaving the Crucible my father had directed, acted and written prolifically. In August 1974, one month after leaving Sheffield, he appeared in ten episodes of *Coronation Street* as Jimmy Graham, Rita Littlewood's love interest. The story of a married man having an affair with one of the show's stars stirred up so much interest in the press that he was one of the first actors in England to be harassed by Corrie fans who were outraged by his on-screen behaviour (some also winkingly approved).

In 1975, my father took up the post of Head of Drama at the University of New England in Armidale, New South Wales, and the following year was offered the artistic directorship of the Adelaide State Theatre Company, which he ran from 1976-80. While at Adelaide, he was finally able to direct a production of *Oedipus* with Tanya Moiseiwitsch designing—a fitting tribute to the great Guthrie.

Playing his final scene with Rita Littlewood (Barbara Knox) in the Rovers Return, Coronation Street, *August 1974*

After a short spell as Artistic Director of the Leicester Haymarket Theatre (1980-81), my father went to Hong Kong to act for the Anglo-Chinese Chung Ying Theatre Company, at the time under the direction of his former Sheffield colleague, Glen Walford. He eventually took over as Artistic Director of the Company until in 1985 he was appointed Head of Drama at the brand-new Hong Kong Academy for Performing Arts. He spent eight years at the Academy and was influential in the development of many of the current generation of Hong Kong actors and directors. While at the Academy, he toured his Chinese-language production of Euripides' *The Bacchae* to Beijing and Shanghai.

By this time, my father had become a Quaker. He was taken to his first meeting by David Brayshaw, who came from a Quaker family, around the time of the opening of the Crucible in late 1971, and he became a Quaker while in Australia. His involvement with the Quakers in Hong Kong led to him volunteering in the Vietnamese refugee camps, where he ran a drama club for children there, just as he had with the Pegasus Theatre Club at the Sheffield Playhouse. It was through the Quakers that my father met his third wife, Sue, whom he married in 1992.

Playing the Porter in Macbeth, *Chung Ying Theatre Company, Hong Kong, March 1982*

The following year, they returned to England so that he could resume his original passion: acting. In 1994, he joined the Royal Shakespeare Company where he spent two seasons (1994-96 and 1997-99). His roles included Aragon in *The Merchant of Venice* and Alonso in *The Tempest*, as well as understudying the leads in both plays, and Angelo in *Measure for Measure*. His other productions included *Peer Gynt* at the Young Vic and Simon Callow's production of *Les Enfants du Paradis* at the Barbican.

During his time at the RSC, my father started developing one-man shows, which he performed at the RSC Fringe Festival. After leaving the Company, he toured a number of shows around the country, most of which premiered at the Edinburgh Fringe Festival, including *Me and Shakespeare*, *Image of an Actor*, *The Black Monk*, *Lying for a Living*, *Shakespeare's London* and *My Son—Will!* (the latter co-written and directed by former Playhouse and Crucible colleague, Anthony Naylor). The shows my father saw by the Trestle Theatre at the Edinburgh Festival rekindled his interest in working with masks, and most of his later shows used masks designed by his former Crucible colleague and good friend, Elaine Garrard.

My father also acted in touring shows, playing the roles of Polonius

Left: Colin George next to a photograph of himself playing Begriffenfeldt in the RSC production of Peer Gynt *at The Young Vic, 1995; Right: As John Shakespeare in his one-man show* My Son Will!*, 1999*

and the Gravedigger in *Hamlet* with the Oxford Stage Company in 1996 and Underwood in Alan Bennett's *The Lady and the Van* at the Birmingham Rep in 2000-01. In 2002, he was awarded a Joseph Rowntree Fellowship to write and tour a show about the life of George Fox, founder of the Quakers.

But in all the years since leaving Sheffield, my father kept his distance from the Crucible. Although he had publicly departed on good terms, there was bitterness left from the ousting of Tanya and the beating he had taken in the local press. The breakthrough came in May 2010, when the Crucible's new Artistic Director, Daniel Evans—whom Colin had become friends with when they were both working at the RSC—invited him to take part in an on-stage discussion about the Crucible as part of the 'bedding in' of the refurbished theatre. Sitting on the stage of the Lyceum and recalling the battle to build the Crucible lifted a major mental block for my father.

Two passionate and visionary Welshmen—Colin George & Daniel Evans on the opening night of Othello, *September 2011*

Shortly afterwards, Daniel persuaded my father to join the Company for the 40th anniversary production of *Othello*, and in late 2011 he returned to the Crucible to play the roles of Brabantio and Gratiano. As fate had it, opening night was on 20th September 2011— his 82nd birthday. Sitting in the auditorium and watching my father playing on the thrust stage he had fought to create was one of the proudest moments of my life—and it was a star-studded production, with Dominic West, Clarke Peters, and Lily James in the lead roles.

It was while at the Crucible that my father resumed writing the book about the theatre's creation that he had been working on almost since the day he left in 1974. Coloured by the positive experience of acting what would be his last role on the Crucible's thrust stage, he produced a manuscript that was full of positivity and genuine gratitude to the City of Sheffield for the opportunity it had given him.

Although the onset of Alzheimer's prevented him from completing the manuscript, he had done enough to ignite my own passion for the Crucible and inspire me to complete his book. The Crucible was one of the great unresolved periods of my father's life—one full of passion and inspiration, but also bitter struggle and regret. However, in his final years I believe he was able to make peace with the remarkable beast he had created in Sheffield.

DRAMATIS PERSONAE

1. Crucible Theatre Trust (formerly New Sheffield Theatre Trust)

Tony Hampton (Chairman)
Peter Bennett-Keenan
Dr H P Brody
David R Brayshaw
Richard Doncaster
Mrs A B Hampton
Alderman H Hebblethwaite
Alderman Sir Ronald Ironmonger
Alderman I Lewis

Alderman A E McVie
Councillor W Owen
Dr W D Pugh
Brian Pye-Smith
Professor H N Robson
Mr F A Ross
Councillor G Wragg
Dr Gerard Young

Hon. Secretary: Mr D B Harrison
Joint Hon. Treasurers: Mr J M Beard / Mr F G Jones

2. Theatrical Advisers

Sir Tyrone Guthrie
Colin George, Artistic Director, Sheffield Playhouse
Wilfred Harrison, Associate Director, Sheffield Playhouse
Patrick Ide, Consultant to Sheffield Playhouse
Geoffrey Ost, General Adviser

3. Architects: Renton Howard Wood Associates

Nick Thompson, Lead Architect
Robin Beynon, Job Architect
Peter Howard, Supervising Partner

4. Consultants

Stage Area: Tanya Moiseiwitsch
Structural Engineers: Ove Arup & Partners
Mechanical Engineers: Dale and Benham
Stage Lighting and Equipment: Theatre Projects Ltd
Architectural Lighting: Light Ltd
Acoustics: Hugh Creighton
Quantity Surveyors: Gleeds
Building Contractors: Gleeson (Sheffield) Ltd
Carpet Design: Clare Ferraby Designs, Brintons Ltd
Graphic Designers: Stringer Sutton Paddock
Appeal Organiser: Peter Bennett-Keenan

5. Crucible Theatre (1971-72)

Artistic Director: Colin George
Assistant Director: Job Stewart
Director of the Studio Theatre: Caroline Smith
Administrator: David Brayshaw
General Manager: Arnold Elliman
Production Manager: Keith Green
Stage Director: David Marchment
Stage Managers: Rosie Hoare and Chris Miles
Chief Electrician: Bry Ferguson
Production Carpenter: Robin Cave
Design Consultant ('Queen of Design'): Tanya Moiseiwitsch
Head of Design: Rodney Ford
Consultant Designer: Elaine Garrard
Wardrobe Manager: David Harvey-Jones
Wardrobe Maintenance: Madge D'Alroy
Property Manager: Roy Brown

BIBLIOGRAPHY

Books & academic studies

Barrault, Jean-Louis, *Reflections on the Theatre*, Rockliff Publishing, 1951

Collison, David, *The Sound of Theatre*, Entertainment Technology Press, 2020

Corrigan, Denys, *The Stirrings in Sheffield*, The Sheffield Repertory Company, 1971

Cullen, Alan, *The Stirrings in Sheffield on Saturday Night*, Methuen Press, 1974

Evershed-Martin, Leslie, *The Impossible Theatre*, Phillimore, 1971

Forsyth, James, *Tyrone Guthrie (The Authorised Biography)*, Hamish Hamilton, 1976

Fulton, Sue, 'Before the Green Baize', Masters dissertation, University of Sheffield, December 2003

Guthrie, Tyrone, *A Life in the Theatre*, Hamish Hamilton, 1959

Guthrie, Tyrone, *Tyrone Guthrie on Acting*, Studio Vista, 1971

Guthrie, Tyrone, Moiseiwitsch, Tanya et al., *Thrice the Brinded Cat Hath Mewed*, Clarke, Irwin & Co., 1955

Hayman, Ronald, *The First Thrust: The Chichester Festival Theatre*, Davis-Poynter, 1975

Joseph, Stephen (ed.), *Actor and Architect*, Manchester University Press, 1964

Landstone, Charles (ed.), *The Repertory Movement in Great Britain*, Council of Repertory Theatres, 1968

Mackintosh, Iain, *The Guthrie Thrust Stage: A Living Legacy*, Association of British Theatre Technicians (ABTT), 2011

Marshall, Norman, *The Other Theatre*, John Lehmann, 1947

Mulryne, Ronnie and Shewring, Margaret, *Making Space for Theatre: British Architecture and Theatre since 1958*, Mulryne & Shewring Ltd, 1995

Ost, Geoffrey, *Stage Lighting*, Herbert Jenkins, 1954
Pilbrow, Richard, *A Theatre Project*, PLASA Media, 2011
Scholes, H Kevan, 'The Crucible Theatre, Sheffield, report for workshop', Sheffield City Polytechnic, 1976
Seed, Alec, *The Sheffield Repertory Theatre: A History*, The Sheffield Repertory Company, 1959
Sheffield Theatres, *Crucible 40*, Boco Publishing, 2011
Ziegler, Philip, *Olivier*, MacLehose Press, 2013

Articles & interviews

Blundell Jones, Peter, 'Staging a comeback', *BD Reviews*, September 2010
Carr, Martin, 'A Year at Nottingham', interview with John Neville, TABS, March 1965
George, Colin, interview with Tanya Moiseiwitsch, May 2001
George, Tedd, interviews with Nick Thompson, October 2020 and February 2021
Kerr, Walter, 'The theater breaks out of Belasco's Box', *Horizon Magazine*, July 1959
Harris, Kate, *Theatre Archive Project* interview with Colin George, 21 November 2005
Joseph, Stephen, 'Planning for new forms of theatre', TABS, 1966
Thompson, Nick, 'Crucible Theatre, Sheffield', *Theatres Magazine*, Spring 2008
Various authors, 'The Crucible Theatre, Sheffield', *The Architectural Review*, February 1972 (reprint)
Various authors, A4 pamphlet on the Crucible Theatre, 1977

Reports & meeting minutes

Arts Council of Great Britain, 'Report on the Crucible Theatre Trust Limited', 5 January 1973
Brayshaw, David, 'Notes to accompany the City Treasurer's Review and Mr Brayshaw's comments thereon', 23 October 1972
Brayshaw, David, 'Notes on Arts Council Report on the Crucible Theatre', 1 March 1973
Collison, David, 'Sheffield Theatre: Sound Reproduction, Intercommunication and Stage Manager Control System', 20 January 1969

Crucible Theatre Trust, 'Minutes of the Meeting of the Building Committee', 24 August 1971

Crucible Theatre Trust, 'Minutes of the Meeting of the Crucible Theatre Trust Limited', 20 October 1971

George, Colin, 'Notes on the new Sheffield Playhouse', Autumn 1966

George, Colin, 'A study of professional children's theatre in Yugoslavia and Czechoslovakia with reference to the work of the Boško Buha Theatre (Belgrade) and the Jiří Wolker Theatre, Prague', Sheffield Playhouse, May 1967

George, Colin, 'Memo on dressings rooms at the new theatre', 11 June 1968

George, Colin, 'Report by Colin George on his visit to Yugoslavia, October 14-26 1968', November 1968

George, Colin & Brayshaw, David, reports to the Sheffield Playhouse Trust on their visit to North America to study thrust stage theatres, November 1967

George, Colin & Brayshaw, David, responses to the Review of the Finances and Administration of the Crucible Theatre by the City Treasurer, June 1972

Ide, Patrick, 'Plans for the New Sheffield Theatre: Comments by Patrick Ide', 17 July 1968

Ide, Patrick, 'Draft brief on the Studio Theatre', Spring 1969

Jones, F G, 'Review of the finances and administration of the Crucible Theatre by the City Treasurer of Sheffield', 23rd June 1972

Mann, Dr Peter H, 'The Sheffield Playhouse Survey', University of Sheffield, March 1965

New Sheffield Theatre Trust, 'Report from the Building Committee to the Trust', February 1967

New Sheffield Theatre Trust, 'Minutes of the Sheffield Playhouse Trust', 15 March 1968

New Sheffield Theatre Trust, 'Catering Brief', no date [c. early 1969]

New Sheffield Theatre Trust, 'Notes on the public appeal for the new theatre', August 1969

Renton Howard Wood, 'Revised Draft Programme', 14 December 1967

Renton Howard Wood, 'Sheffield Playhouse, preliminary investigation for thrust stage', 19 January 1968

Renton Howard Wood, 'Minutes of Meeting to discuss preliminary sketch design', 9 February 1968

Renton Howard Wood, 'Revised Outline Schedule of Accommodation', 1 March 1968

Renton Howard Wood, 'Minutes of meeting on stage lighting & equipment with the New Sheffield Theatre Building Committee', 17 January 1969

Renton Howard Wood, 'Minutes of meeting on Mechanical and Electrical Services Installations and Stage lighting and Equipment with the New Sheffield Theatre Building Committee', 23 January 1969

Renton Howard Wood, 'Minutes of meeting on stage lighting & equipment with The New Sheffield Theatre Building Committee', 24 January 1969

Sheffield Playhouse, 'Record of discussions between representatives of The Arts Council of Great Britain, the Sheffield Repertory Co. Ltd. and the Sheffield City Council', no date [c. late 1965]

Young, Dr Gerard, 'G. Y.'s summary of advice by Sir Tyrone Guthrie on Sunday, 15th October 1967 on plans for Sheffield's new Playhouse', October 1967

Young, Dr Gerard, 'Random notes by G.Y. following first visit to Tyrone Guthrie Theater, Minneapolis', 18 May 1968

Newspapers
Morning Telegraph (Sheffield)
The Star (Sheffield)
The Guardian
The Observer
The Daily Telegraph
The Financial Times
The Sunday Times
The Evening Sentinel
Barnsley Chronicle
The Stage
Plays and Players

1948 Assembly Hall

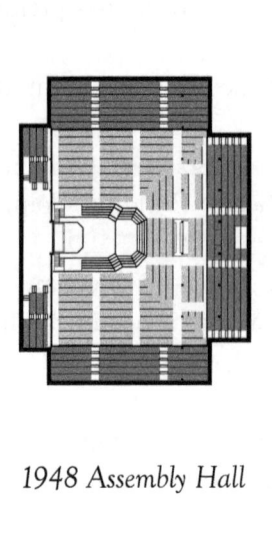

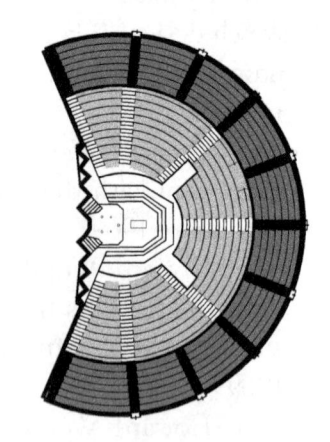

1957 Stratford, Ontario

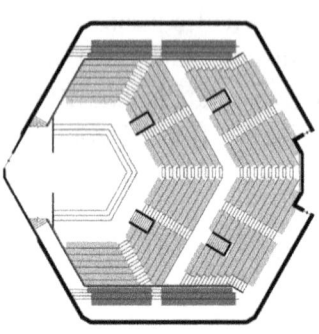

1962 Chichester

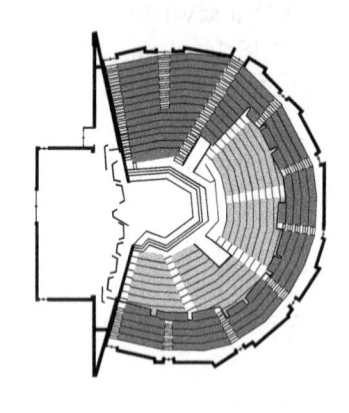

1963 Minneapolis

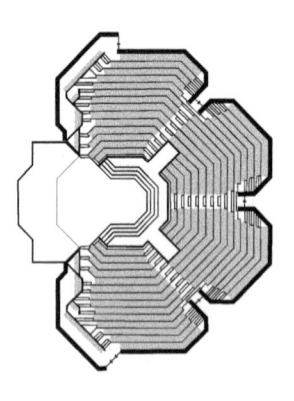

1971 Crucible

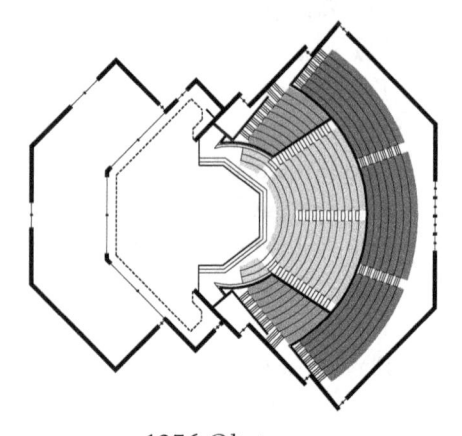

1976 Olivier

Six Thrust Theatres: 1948 to 1976, by Iain Mackintosh

The *Assembly Hall* of the Church of Scotland was built in 1859 and was chosen by Tyrone Guthrie as the perfect place to stage a forgotten 16th century Scots play, *The Thrie Estaits*, for the second Edinburgh International Festival in 1948. The *Assembly Hall*, which held 1,350, then became the inspiration for the first purpose-built thrust stage theatre, created by the formidable combination of Guthrie and Tanya Moiseiwitsch. The Festival Theatre *Stratford, Ontario* opened under a tented roof in 1953 and was completed as a finished building in 1957 as shown here, with a balcony taking the capacity up to 2,250.

The *Olivier* at the National Theatre opened in 1976. The auditorium holds a little over 1,100 in a 90% fan. It is described as a 'scenic end stage', but in the endless debates between 1964 and 1967 of the Building Committee, who were advising an architect who had never built a theatre (Denys Lasdun), the problems of a thrust stage were discussed. This was because Laurence Olivier was both Chairman of the Committee and the actor manager who had opened the *Chichester* Festival Theatre in 1962. On that stage, he had had unhappy experiences, chiefly because he disliked the fact that the audience on one side could see past him to those on the other. Olivier himself preferred a stage where he could see most of the audience with both eyes, which is what he got at the National. Guthrie was not a member of the Committee. Moiseiwitsch did join later in 1966, but too late to influence the form of the *Olivier*.

Chichester had opened in 1962 shortly before Colin came to Sheffield. He saw, as I did, the revival of *Uncle Vanya* in 1963, which converted me to the thrust stage and which hitherto had seemed magnificent for Shakespeare, but not so much for Chekhov and the like. Colin's account of what was wrong with that theatre and the lessons he learnt with the guidance of Guthrie is masterly, in particular, the central issue of the need for the actor to be able to stand on the stage in the very centre of the room. Another problem, which the *Crucible* also solved, was getting the rake of the front rows precisely right—not too steep, but also not too shallow as at *Chichester*.

I never visited the Guthrie Theatre, *Minneapolis* of 1963, which held

1,440, but reports are uniformly good. There had been creative tension over the introduction by the local young architect of asymmetry in the auditorium, to which Guthrie and Moiseiwitsch were opposed at the outset. But it contributed to that theatre's success. When, after a little over 40 years, the Board of the Guthrie acquired a much better site, plus the distinguished French architect Jean Nouvel, one vital condition was imposed. This was that the entire original theatre space was to be reproduced in the new building without any changes, save for a few minor matters specifically requested by the director and his staff and a little more comfort which reduced capacity to 1,100.

Of the *Olivier* and *Chichester*, it must be added that today, such are the inferior acoustics of both, every actor in every show, whether spoken drama or sung musical, wears an individual microphone all the time. I would have loved to hear Colin's views on this!

Lastly, please note that all the stages in the comparative same-scale drawings on the previous page show the original steps surrounding the thrust stages. These were never intended to be permanent and indeed are now rarely seen complete as drawn. Today the repertoire is broader and the acting area wider.

I got to know Colin after he left the RSC as an actor in 1999. We bonded on Guthrie: I was able to boast that I saw the *Thrie Estaits* in the *Assembly Hall* in 1948. In 2011, for the Association of British Theatre Technicians (ABTT), a group was formed to create an entry for the Prague Quadrennial in the theatre architecture section. I edited an accompanying publication, *The Guthrie Thrust Stage: A Living Legacy*. The six comparative drawings on the previous page were researched and drawn for this publication by Anne Minors and Susanne Bochmann of Sound Space Vision. Both the ABTT and they have kindly given permission for their reproduction here.

ARCHITECTURAL PLAN OF THE CRUCIBLE THEATRE, 1971

Ground floor

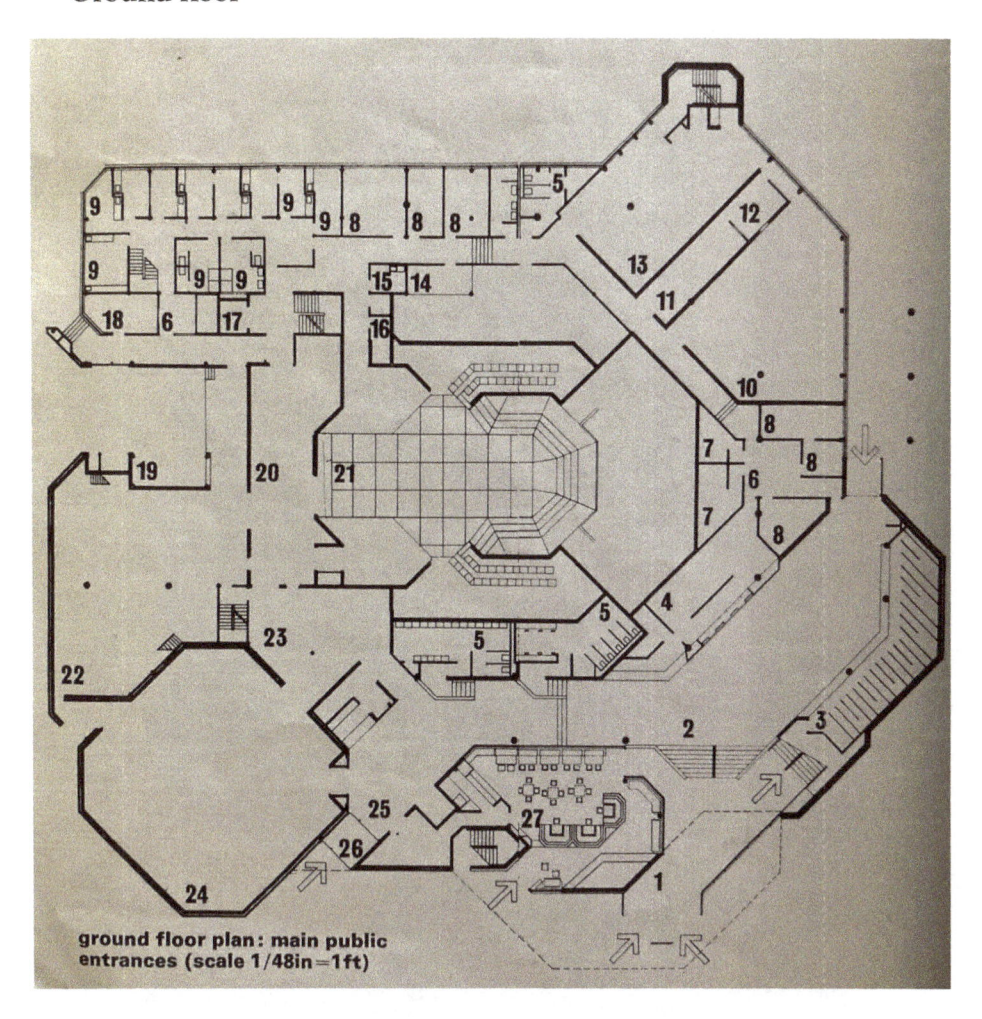

ground floor plan: main public entrances (scale 1/48in = 1ft)

Upper foyer

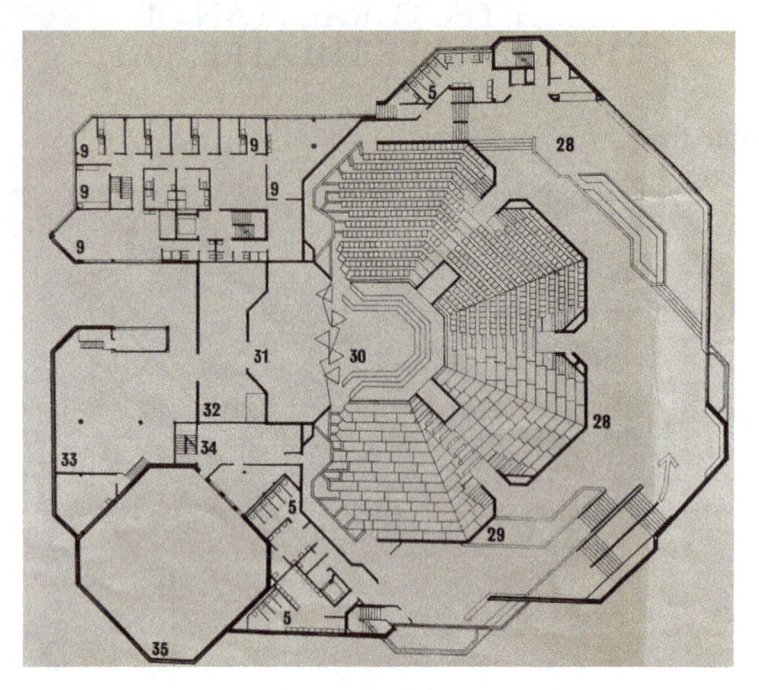

Upper level

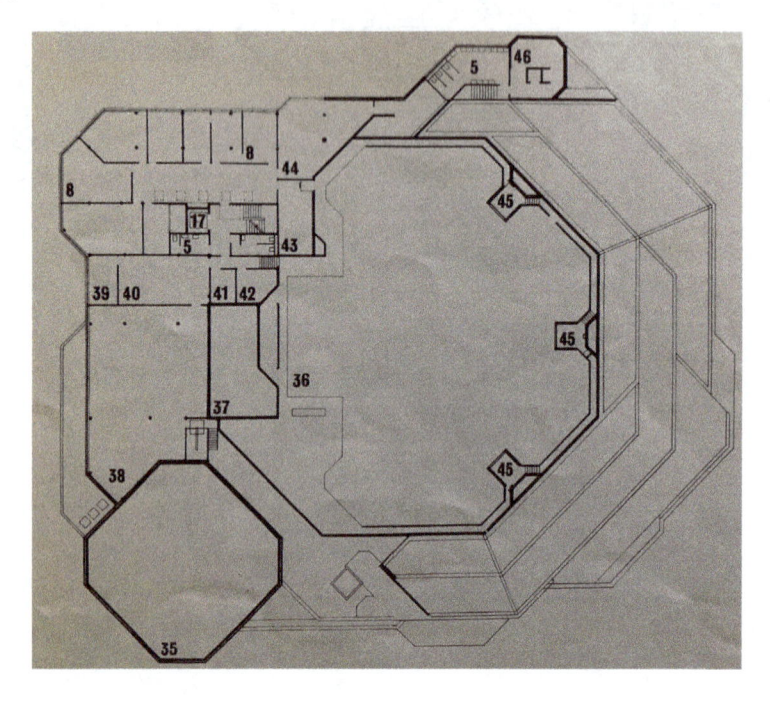

Key

1. Main theatre entrance
2. Lower entrance foyer
3. Cloakroom
4. Box office
5. Lavatories
6. Waiting area
7. Lockers
8. Office
9. Dressing room
10. Rehearsal room
11. Band room
12. Recording room
13. Green room
14. Store
15. Kitchen
16. Quick change room
17. Goods lift
18. Stage door
19. Unloading area
20. Assembly dock
21. Backstage
22. Carpenters' shop
23. Studio anteroom
24. Studio Theatre
25. Foyer
26. Studio entrance
27. Grill bar
28. Foyer
29. Void
30. Auditorium
31. Upper part backstage
32. Upper part assembly docks
33. Upper part carpenters' and painters' shop
34. Future studio dressing rooms
35. Upper part studio
36. Upper part auditorium
37. Upper part assembly dock
38. Plant room
39. Electricians' office
40. Electricians' workshop
41. Switch room
42. Battery room
43. Dimmers
44. Board room
45. Lighting and sound control room
46. Tank

Source: *The Architectural Review*, February 1972

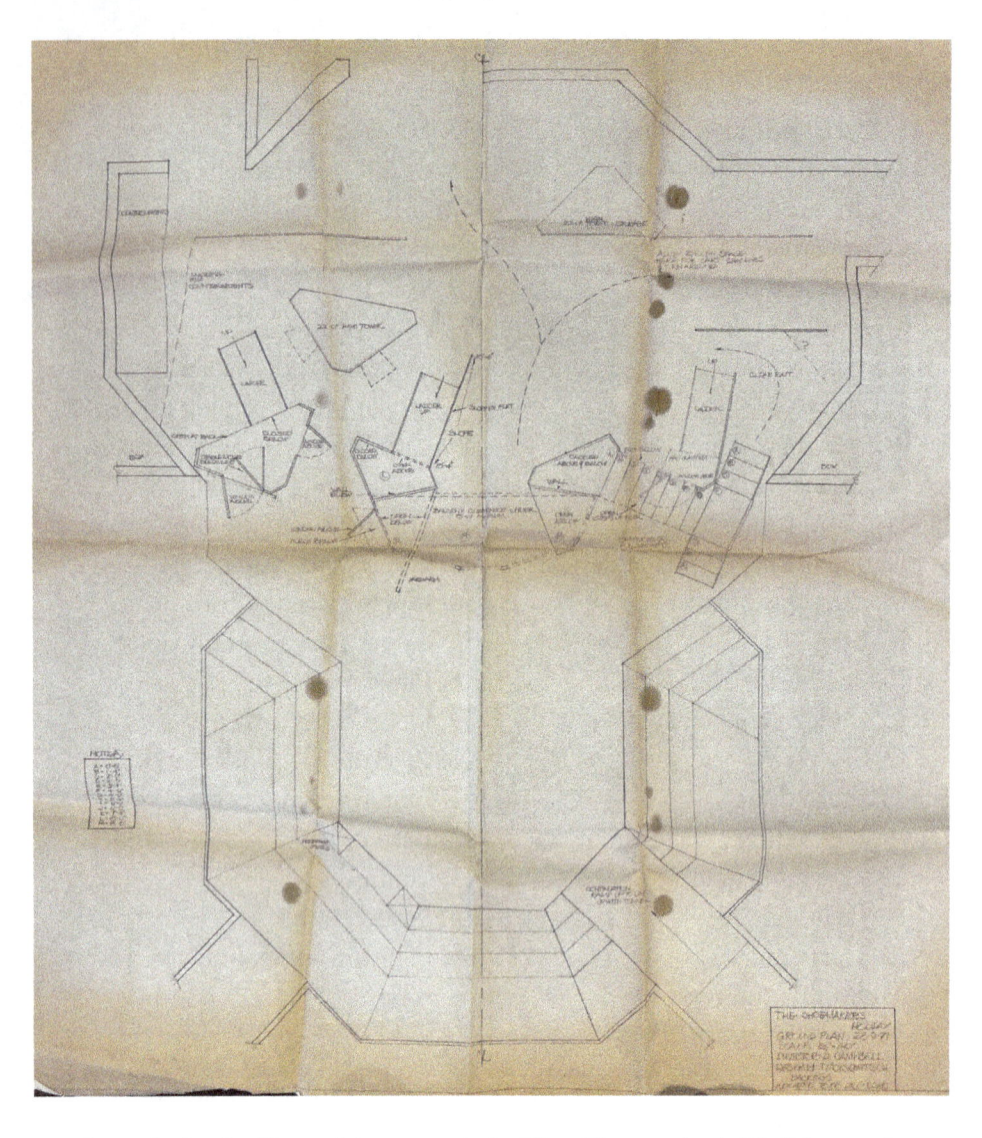

Ground plan by Tanya Moiseiwitsch for The Shoemaker's Holiday *at the Crucible Theatre, December 1971. This design, Tanya's first for the thrust stage she designed in Sheffield, is a good example of what she and the seasoned actors from Stratford, Ontario (among them the show's director, Douglas Campbell) envisioned the thrust stage should or could be used for. The design includes Tanya's trademark thrust stage, with steps leading down at its corners to the vomitories, and an adaptable back wall where four periactoids are deployed to create an arched entrance, two towers and a balcony above.*

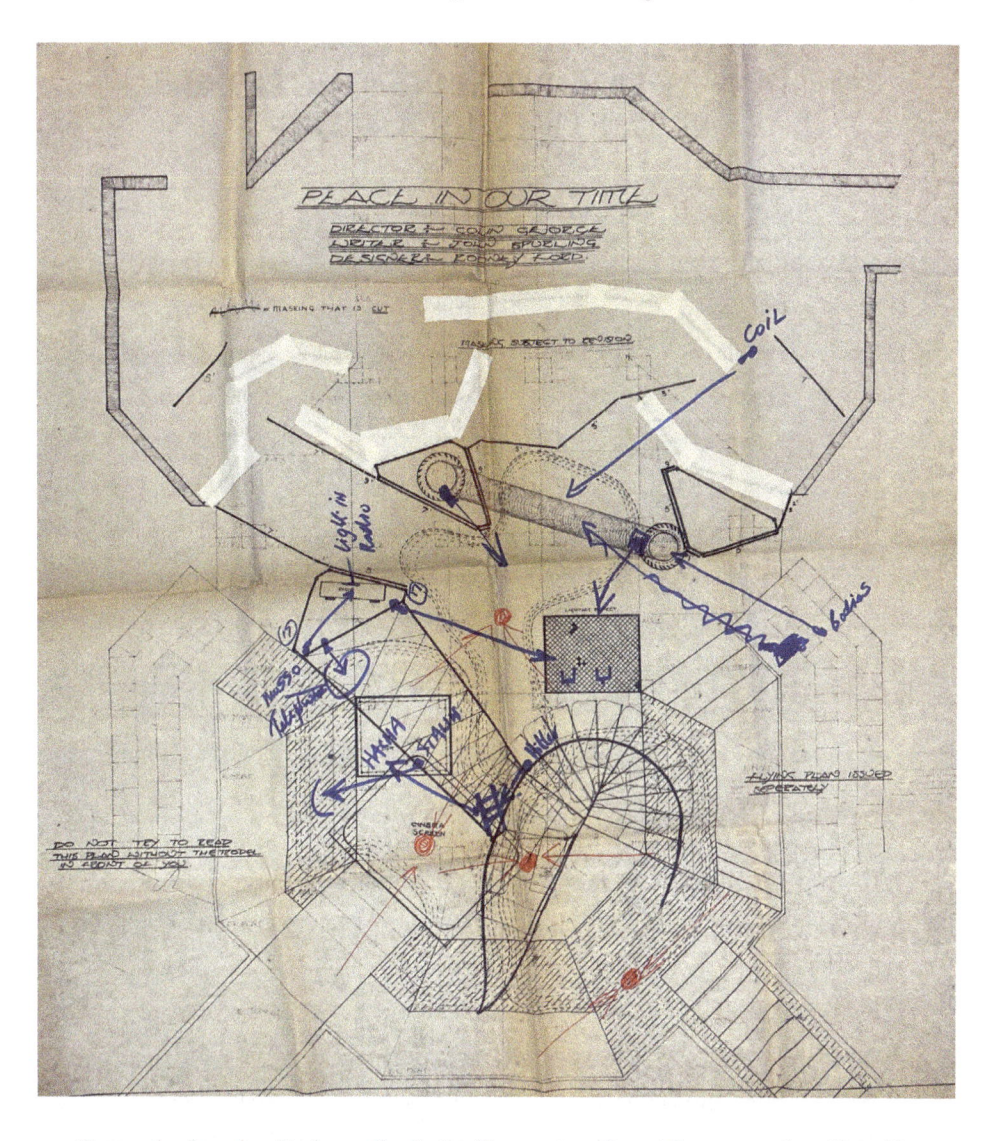

Ground plan by Rodney Ford for Peace in Our Time at the Crucible Theatre, November 1972. This design uses the thrust stage very differently, with complex scenery dominating the 'Sacred Circle', including a spiral staircase made of plexiglass. Tanya, I am told, did not approve of this use of the thrust stage and some of the cast referred to the rickety staircase as 'the Leaning Tower of Pisa'. Nonetheless, it is a striking example of how directors and designers experimented with the thrust stage during the Crucible's opening seasons, and this process has continued ever since.

MAIN AUDITORIUM PRODUCTIONS AT THE CRUCIBLE, 1971-74

Opening	Production	Director	Designer
09-Nov-71	Fanfare	Colin George	Elaine Garrard
14-Nov-71	Peer Gynt	Colin George	Rodney Ford
30-Nov-71	The Shoemaker's Holiday	Douglas Campbell	Tanya Moiseiwitsch
24-Dec-71	Treasure Island	Colin George	Elaine Garrard
31-Jan-72	A Taste of Honey	Ann Casson	Paul Steinberg
25-Feb-72	Mister	Colin George	Elaine Garrard
29-Feb-72	A Man for all Seasons	Douglas Campbell	Tanya Moiseiwitsch
06-Apr-72	Oh! What A Lovely War	Peter James	Rodney Ford
10-May-72	Tonight at 8.30	Charles Keating	Paul Steinberg
16-May-72	The Birthday Party	Job Stewart	Elaine Garrard
02-Oct-72	The Persians	Colin George	Tanya Moiseiwitsch
05-Oct-72	The Taming of the Shrew	Douglas Campbell	Bronwen Casson
16-Oct-72	Under Milk Wood	Job Stewart	Elaine Garrard
15-Nov-72	Peace in Our Time	Colin George	Rodney Ford
23-Dec-72	Pinocchio	Caroline Smith	Elaine Garrard
23-Dec-72	The Boy Friend	Job Stewart	John Pascoe
14-Feb-73	The National Health	Douglas Campbell	Rodney Ford
21-Feb-73	Alpha Beta	Job Stewart	Elaine Garrard
04-Apr-73	The Stirrings in Sheffield	Colin George	Tanya Moiseiwitsch
01-May-73	Facets on a Golden Image	Colin George	Rodney Ford
25-Aug-73	The Stirrings in Sheffield	Colin George	Tanya Moiseiwitsch
24-Sep-73	Getting On	Job Stewart	Rodney Ford
09-Oct-73	Macbeth	Colin George	John Bloomfield & Ann Beverley
13-Nov-73	Free for All	Ed Thomason	Rodney Ford
27-Nov-73	Uncle Vanya	Job Stewart	David Harvey-Jones
22-Dec-73	Rumpelstiltskin	Rex Doyle	Elaine Garrard
22-Dec-73	Irma La Douce	Rodney Horn	Rodney Ford

Opening	Production	Director	Designer
13-Feb-74	Dr Jekyll & Mr Hyde	Ed Thomason	Rodney Ford & Elaine Garrard
03-Apr-74	School for Scandal	Colin George	Rodney Ford
30-Apr-74	Private Lives	Colin George	David Harvey-Jones
29-May-74	Twelfth Night	Ed Thomason	Art Penson
27-Jun-74	Calamity Jane	Colin George	Rodney Ford & Elaine Garrard

CONTEMPORARY & INFLUENTIAL THEATRES

Name	City	Country	Capacity	Opened
Municipal Theatre	Malmö	Sweden	1,595	1944
Assembly Hall	Edinburgh	UK	1,350	1948
Sheffield Playhouse	Sheffield	UK	541	1954[†]
Studio Theatre Company	Scarborough	UK	250	1955
Festival Theatre	Stratford	Canada	2,262	1957
Mermaid	London	UK	600	1959
Festival Theatre	Chichester	UK	1,206	1962
Victoria Theatre	Stoke-on-Trent	UK	250	1962
Guthrie Theater	Minneapolis	USA	1,400	1963
Nottingham Playhouse	Nottingham	UK	770	1963
Georgian Theatre	Richmond	UK	214	1963
ANTA Theater	New York	USA	1,130	1964
Questors	London	UK	355	1964
Vivian Beaumont Theater	New York	USA	1,100	1965
Forum Theater (VBT)	New York	USA	399	1965
Octagon Theatre	Bolton	UK	400	1967
Octagon Theatre	Perth	Australia	685	1969
Babs Asper Theatre	Ottawa	Canada	900	1969
Young Vic	London	UK	420	1970
Cockpit Theatre	London	UK	240	1970
Crucible	Sheffield	UK	980	1971
Olivier Theatre	London	UK	1,127	1976
Royal Exchange	Manchester	UK	800	1976

[†] Date of full refurbishment.

INDEX

'A Bird in a Gilded Cage', by Arthur J Lamb & Harry Von Tilzer 262
Abbeydale (Sheffield school) 186
Actors' Company xi, 260
acoustics 42, 75, 94, 124-125, 138, 142, 143, 149, 167, 206, 243, 316, 325, 333
Adams, Bob 42
Adelphi Hotel (Sheffield) 32, 221
Adrian, Max 68
Aeschylus 82, 187, 298, 305
Agamemnon, by Aeschylus 82, 115
Agamemnon's Tomb (Mycenae) 131-132
Ahura Mazdā 298
Aida, by Guiseppe Verdi 279
aikido 308
air conditioning 42, 143-144, 214, 273, 316
air circulation (cooling & heating) 69, 120, 142, 273, 316
Albee, Edward 78
Alderman, Ivan 229
Allen, Paul 96, 154-155, 164-165, 169, 267-269, 280-281, 283
Almond, Paul xix
Altman, Peter 276, 278
amateur theatre xix, 3, 11, 12, 14, 33, 39, 166, 171, 186, 191, 201, 223
Ancient Greek Theatre 52, 60-61, 82, 84-86, 88, 118, 123, 155, 164, 187, 188-189, 196, 206, 225, 252, 277, 298-299, 305

Angelis, Paul Plate xxviii, Plate xxix
Annaghmakerrig 229
Anouilh, Jean 77
Apollo 83-84, Plate xv
Arbuzov, Aleksei 47
architects xiv, xviii, xxxii, 40-45, 47, 51, 56, 66, 69-71, 73, 75, 88, 100-103, 105-106, 108-110, 112, 115, 120-124, 127, 130, 133-135, 141-142, 144-147, 153-154, 165, 172, 186, 202, 209, 212, 214, 286, 315-316, 316, 324, 326, 331-332
architectural lighting, see *Light Ltd*
Aristophanes 168
Aristotle 197
Armidale (Australia) 319
Armstrong, Alun 23, 236
Artaud, Antonin 209
Arts Council of Great Britain xiv, xvi, xxi, xxiii, 5, 7-8, 15, 16, 21, 23, 30, 31, 33, 38, 73, 230, 286, 287, 292, 294, 299, 300, 302, 308, 327, 329
Arts Council Panel for Young People's Theatre 24
Arundel Gate (Sheffield) 32, 130, 131, 137, 139, 221
Association of British Theatre Technicians (ABTT) 326, 332
Athens 52, 82, 118
Atkinson, Martyn 170-173, 177
Auschwitz 216-217
Austin Healey 3000 110
Austin Seven 249-250, 261

Australia 41, 186, 225, 231, 320, 340
avant-garde 44, 274, 288, 297
Avocet Typeset iv, xviii
Ayckbourn, Alan 199-200
Aztec 259, 263-264

Baker, Charlie 74
Bakewell 159
ballet 19, 44, 155, 173, 176, 179, 241, 274, 279, 282, 308
Ballet Rambert 173, 274, 279, 282
Barkworth, Peter 153
Barlow, Jeremy 266-267
Baron, David, see *Harold Pinter*
Barrault, Jean-Louis 326
Barron, Keith 153
Barstow, Stan 20
Barton, Jill 186
Barton, John xix, 205
Barton, Michael 223
Bass Charrington (caterers) 152
Batemoor (Sheffield) 242
Bates, John xviii, 147, 316
Bates, Merete 258-259, 262, 267-268, 275, 282
Bean, Richard xi
'Before the Parade Passes By', from Hello, Dolly! 246, 262
Beard, J M 324
Beaubourg project, see *Pompidou Centre*
Belasco, David 57, 60, 327
Behan, Brendan 223
Belgrade 24, 145, 216, 328
Bell, Alfred 88
belly dancer 245, 267
Bennett, Alan 322
Bennett-Keenan, Peter 152, 324, 325
Bensley, John 42
Benson, Frank xix

Bergman, Ingmar 44
Bertram, John 268
Beverley, Ann 307, 338
Beynon, Robin xviii, Plate xvii, 110, 122, 123, 324
Bingham, Madeleine 14
Bingham, Roger 233
Bingo 32, 101, 171, 187, 302
Black and White Minstrel 173, 178
Blacker, K A 233
Bloomfield, John 307, 338
Blundell Jones, Peter 327
Bochmann, Susanne iv, xviii, 333
Bolam, James 307
Bolt, Robert 281
Bolton 186, 195, 216, 331
Bond, Derek 307
Boorman, Neil 299
Bournemouth 171
Bradley, David Plate x
Bramall Lane Cricket Ground 221
Brambell, Wilfrid 284
Brannan, Inspector 136
Brannigan, Colin 305
Branson, Norman 105, 202
Brayshaw, David vii, 7, 28, 30, 39-40, 71, 73, 96, 99-101, 152, 160-161, 164, 166, 168, 171, 204, Plate xix, 214, 230, 233, 238, 241, 253, 273-274, 285-286, 289-294, 297, 300, 301, 305, 313, 314, 320, 324, 325, 327, 328
Brecht, Bertolt 10, 62, Plate iv, 115, 162-163, 198
Brett, Dick 111
Bretton Hall College of Education 192
Brighton 69, 231
Brintons (Kidderminster) 132, 325
Bristol v, 10, 35, 291, 306
British Broadcasting Corporation (BBC) xx, 148

British Council 145
British Steel 221
Broadhead, William 26-29, 311
Broadway (Manhattan) 62, 94, 248, 291, 301
Brody, Dr H P 324
Brook, Peter 205
Brown, John 81-82
Brown, Roy 253, 325
Bryden, Ronald 188
Buchenwald 216
Buggy, Niall Plate xxvii, 245, 253, 256, 283
Building Committee, see *Crucible Theatre design*
building contractors, see *Gleeson*
Bull, Polly xviii
Bunyan, John 234
Burbage, Richard 187, 205
Bury, John 183, 230
Burrell Foley Fischer (BFF) 316
Butler, Bill 7, 30, 32

Cairoli, Charlie 195
Cambridge 146, 241
Cambridge Circus (London) 105
Campbell, Douglas 57, 79, 80, 82, 84, 85, 87, Plate xxv, 216, 225, 226, 229, 235, 240, 244, 245, 249, 253, 257, 260, 262, 268-270, 298, 336, 338
Campton, David 190-191, 194, 281
Canada 54, 59, 69, 165, 215, 223, 246, 301, 305, 340
Capezzani, Mariano xviii
Carby, Fanny Plate xxvii, 299
Carli, Carlo de 62
carpenter 9, 237, 243, 253, 325, 335
carpet design, see *Clare Ferraby*
Carnegie Hall 92
Carr, Martin 327

Casson, Ann 79, Plate xxviii, 235, 244, 245, 253, 298, 338
Cassandra 83
Castleton 244
Caterham xix
Cave, Robin xviii, 9, 22, 243, 325
Celje (Yugoslavia) 145
Chamberlain, Peter 105
Charlton, Bobby 305
Chaucer (Sheffield school) 186
Cheeseman, Peter 25, 64, 165, 188, 189, 190, 191, 192-193, 204, 252
Chekhov, Anton xi, 17, 169, 198, 225, 232, 247, 252, 273, 332
Chelsea (London) 105
Chichester, see *Theatres: Festival Theatre, Chichester*
Chichester Players 68
children's theatre 11-12, 21-24, 26, 30-31, 51, 58, 81, 96, 100, 118, 131, 138, 145, 155, 214, 246, 252, 259-260, 262, 269-272, 290, 309, 320, 328
Chinese v, 320
chorus (Ancient Greek drama) 82-85, 119, 188-189, 298
Chorus (theatre company) 44, 51, 114, 134-135, 142, 206, 262
Christie, Agatha 274, 275
Christmas shows 7, 8, 25, 206, 269, 270, 291, 306-308
Church, Tony xxi
Church of Scotland 53
cinema 62, 137, 164, 200, 239
City Engineer (Sheffield) 40, 43, 74
City Surveyor (Sheffield) 40, 74, 143
City Treasurer (Sheffield) 285, 287, 293, 295, 297, 308, 324, 327, 328
Civic Circle (Sheffield ring-road project) 32-33
civic theatre 33, 171, 223, 233, 273-274

Classics 6, 19, 23, 34, 52, 58, 82, 85, 196, 241, 252, 274, 305
Clements, John 175, 177, 180, 182, 205
Clytemnestra 82-83, 85, 115, 225, 229
coal xix, 143, 285
Cochrane, Elspeth 248
Coldron, Audrey 192
Collaboration, The 186
Collison, David 149-150, 326, 327
Communism 216
Company, by Stephen Sondheim 301
Compton, Fay 68
Computer Memory Control (CMC) system 128-129, 147-148
Conan Doyle, Arthur 17
Concrete Society 147
Conductor (musical) 67, 262, 278
conquistador 263
Conservative Party 33, 38, 170, 172-173, 277
'Consider Yourself at Home', from *Oliver!* 262
Consumers' Gas Company 27
Coquelin, Benoît-Constant 181, 204
Corbett, Tony 147, Plate xxiv
Corneille, Pierre 181
Cornelia Street Café, New York 23
Coronation Street 311, 319
Corrigan, Denys 8, 10, 28-29, 120, 269-270, 281, 326
Cortés, Hernán 259
costumes 44, 47, 66, 77, 80, 83, 85, 90-91, 104, 163, 228-230, 232, 243, 245, 269, 290-292, 298-300, 306
Cotton, L W 159-161, 166, 173-174
Court Masque 61
Courtenay, Tom 307
Coward, Noel 146, 168, 170, 288, 309

cowboys 270, 309
Creighton, Hugh 42, 143, 325
Cribbins, Bernard 194
Crucible Club 186, 309-310, 312
Crucible Theatre
  budget 38, 40, 43, 46, 69, 132, 144, 147, 152, Plate xxiv, 209, 286-287, 289, 291, 303, 316
  children's theatre 12, 58, 100, 131, 138, 145, 155, 214, 246, 252, 259-266, 269-272, 290, 309
  Company xvi, Plate xxii, Plate xxxiii, 214-215, 225, 228-229, 235, 237, 240-244, 250, 252-253, 261-263, 266, 268, 273-274, 280-281, 283, 288, 290, 293-294, 298, 302, 305, 306, 311, 323
  naming of theatre 155, 220-221
  Open Forum (September 1969) 166, 170-174, 206
  public appeal 38, 137, 152-153, 177-178, 180, 185-187, 206, 222, 286-287, 325, 328
  salaries 239-241, 291
  seat pricing policy 150-151, 238-239, 285
  vision & programming policy 241-242
Crucible Theatre design
  architects' models & architectural drawings 108, 109, 123, 139-142, 153-154, 172, 210-213, 333-335
  auditorium Plate xxiii, 317
    concrete bowl 120-121, 225
    entrance doors 131-132, 134, 259
    heating & air circulation 120, 142, 316
    lighting 127-129, 147-149, 240-241, 266, 268

Red Dot 110, 139
revolve 45, 105, 110, 115-117
seating 35-36, 38, 45, 73, 99, 109, 111-112, 120-123, 137, 138, 141, 143-144, 150-151, 154, 164, 173, 176, 180-181, 185, 222, 237, 238-240, 252, 276-277, 282-283, 285, 294, 316
sound 94, 120, 129, 142-144, 149-150, 228, 308, 326, 327, 335
stage 35, 40, 41, 43-47, 51-52, 58, 99-111, 114-117, 120-128, 138-139, 141-142, 148-151, 154-155, 159-165, 172-185, 187-206, Plate xx, Plate xxx, Plate xxxiii, 210-211, 223, 228, 231, 237, 242-243, 246-250, 252-253, 257-274, 276-279, 283-284, 291-292, 298-299, 301, 307, 310-315, 323, 325, 326, 328, 333-335
Building Committee 38-43, 99, 103, 105-106, 112, 114, 125-126, 127, 129, 134, 146-147, 161, 214, 286, 328-329
foyers 66, 130-135, 137, 139, 141, 147, Plate xxiv, 258, 286
  carpet design 103, 131-133, Plate xxiv, 258, 315, 325
  colour design 35, 122, 124, 132-133, 146, Plate xxiv, 258-259, 315
  grill bar & catering 130, 137, 141, 144, 151-152, Plate xxiii, 222, 253, 293, 328, 335
backstage & front of house
  box office 141, 252-253, 285, 288-289, 292-295, 297, 299-300, 302, 306, 308-310, 335
  dressing rooms 44-45, 124, 126, 134-135, 142, 242, 243, 316, 328, 335
  loading bay 139, 172, 213, 335
  offices & administration 131, 316
  workshops 36, 124, 142, 144, 298, 316, 335
building materials xxiii, 78-79, 111, 121-122, 125, 130, 132-133, 137, 141, 146-147, 243, 250, 308, 316
  cladding 133, 143, 222
  concrete & forticrete 75, 90, 111, 120-122, 133, 143, 146-147, 225
fire, health & safety regulations 121, 124, 135-137, 229, 249, 250, 270, 316
Studio Theatre, see separate entry
Crucible Theatre Trust 38, 40, 43, 72-74, 80, 96, 99-102, 104-106, 113, 114, 124-126, 137, 146, 152-153, 155, 161, 166, 172-173, 176, 185, 209, 214, 220-222, 224, 228, 275, 286-287, 293-294, 302, 305, 313, 314, 324, 327, 328
Crucible Youth Theatre 315
Cullen, Alan 8, 17, 23, 25, 28, 47, Plate vii, Plate xi, 145, 206, 232, 269-270, 326

D'Alroy, Madge 220, 243, 253, 325
Dale & Benham 42, 120, 129, 143, 325
Damascus 96, 252
Daneman, Paul xxi
Davies, Colin 278
Death of a Salesman, by Arthur Miller 312
deficit 126, 285-287, 289, 293-294, 302
Dekker, Thomas 235, 245

Delaney, Shelagh 281, 285
Denmark 52-53, 182-183
Department of the Environment 223, 233
Derbyshire 101, 166, 244
Dewar, Susan 277
Diehl, Fin 88
Die Meistersinger, by Richard Wagner 279
Doncaster, Richard 324
Douglas Home, Wiiliam 169
Doyle, Rex 306, 308, 338
dramatist 167-169, 190, 198, 204
dressing rooms 30, 44-45, 66, 71, 124, 126, 134-135, 142, 242, 243, 316, 328, 335
Dronfield 133
Dublin 229, 230
Dunbar, Alexander 214-215
Dürrenmatt, Friedrich 78

Ealing (London) 201
Eames, Charles 114
Eastern Europe 24, 145
eccyclema 83
Eddington, Paul 153
education 21, 24, 34, 35, 192, 215, 241, 278, 287, 292
Edinburgh Festival xx, 53, 234, 321, 331-332
Edinburgh Fringe Festival 321
Edwardian 56
El Greco 162
elite 5, 164, 237, 273, 275, 278, 297
Elizabethan Theatre Company xx
Elliman, Arnold 152, 253, 314, 325
Elliot, Michael 110, 122-123, 127, 149, 188-189, 190
Emmet, Alfred 201-204
Enchanter, The 258
England xiv, xx, xxi, 30, 61, 69, 155-156, 186, 221, 230, 233, 238, 245, 252, 276, 283, 285, 289, 292, 302, 319, 321
Ensler, Eve 23
Equity 21, 240
Euripides 320
Europe 24, 73, 145, 232, 237, 282, 304
Evangelist 96
Evans, Daniel xv, xvi, xviii, 322
Evershed-Martin, Leslie 68-69, 326
Eyam (Yorkshire) 47, Plate xi

Fahy, Sean 43, 133
Falstaff 82
farce 78, 155, 169
Farrell, Stan 222-223
Feast of Fools 24
Ferguson, Bry 243, 253, 262, 325
Ferraby, Clare xviii, Plate xvi, 132-133, Plate xxiv, 315, 325
Festival of Britain (1951) 69
Fiesta (Sheffield nightclub) 186
films 14, 19, 34, 36, 57, 82, 124, 164, 166, 177, 200, 216, 243, 247, 309-310
Finney, Albert xx, 10, 185-186
Firth Park (Sheffield) 186
First World War 3
Fitzallan Square (Sheffield) 32
Flemish 269
Fletcher, John 67,
Florence 62
fly tower 45, 66, 173
football 30, 32, 35, 164, 186, 221, 264
Forbes, Julian 162
Ford, John 67
Ford, Rodney xv, xviii, 226, 228, 243, 245, 253, 266, 277, 291, 325, 337-339
forestage, see *Theatre design*
Forsyth, James 326

Foster, Tim 308
Fox, George 322
Frances, Myra Plate viii, Plate ix, 145
Frecheville Carnival 288
Friel, Brian 230
frontral acting 176, 181, 190-193, 195-198, 205
Frost, Robert 51
Fry, Christopher 77
Fulton, Sue xv, 236, 305, 326
Furby, Edward 20, 119, 306

gala 186, 241, 258-259, 262-263
Galsworthy, John 3
Gammell, Robin 79-80, 235, 240, 244, 253, 266
Garde Peach, L. du 8, 166-168, 169, 193
Gardner Merchant Caterers 152
Garrard, Elaine 163, 243, 253, 271, 291, 321, 325, 338-339
Gascon, Jean 89-90, 215
Geering, Ben xviii, 71
geometry 111-112, 139, 146, 198, 206, 210
George, Caroline xv, 47, 243, 284, 306
George, Colin
    early life & career (pre-1962) xix-xxi
    Assistant Director of the Sheffield Playhouse (1962-1965) xxi, 3, 7-15, 62, Plate ii, Plate iii, Plate iv, 235
    Artistic Director of the Sheffield Playhouse (1965-1971) 15-32, 46-47, Plate v, Plate vii, 103, 105, 117-120, 127, 145, 151, 162-163, 216-220, 232, 302, 306
    at the Ludlow Festival (1964-66) 4, 13, 30, 63-65
    at the Nottingham Rep v, xx-xxi, 3, 7, 13, 51-52, 57, 62, 64, 68, 117
    at the Birmingham Rep v, xx, 7, 10, 186, 322
    and Tyrone Guthrie 43-44, 57-59, 72-74, 99, 101-102, 163, 177-179, 215, 225-226, 229-234,
    and Tanya Moiseiwitsch 54, 103-120, 125, 162-163, Plate xxi, Plate xxxii, 215, 235, 243, 253, 291, 297-303, 305, 319
    and Douglas Campbell 79-80, 82, 84, 87, 216, 225-226, 229, 235, 240, 244-245, 249, 257-258, 260-262, 298, 338
    acting xvi, xix-xxi, 10, 51-52, 67, 307-308, 319-323, 332
    directing xx-xxi, 9-10, 12-14, 19-21, 25-29, 47, 51, 84, 117-120, 127, 145-146, 162-163, 215-220, 223, 225, 229-230, 232, 235, 243-244, 246, 249-250, 257-258, 262-266, 270-272, 276, 298-299, 305-310, 338-339
    children's theatre 11-12, 21-24, 34-36, 145, 246, 259-266, 320
    Eastern Europe 24, 145, 216, 302, 306, 328
    studying theatre design 60-71
    trip to North America (October 1967) 74-96
    influence on Crucible Theatre design
        dressing rooms 44-45, 134-135
        fire safety 135-137
        lighting 127-129
        revolve 115-117
        seat prices 150, 238-239

stage 35, 43-47, 51-52, 75-76, 96, 99-100, 108-110, 114-115, 164-165
Studio Theatre 32, 34-36, 38, 214-215, 241-242, 252, 279-280, 288
vision for theatre 33-37, 99-100, 155, 172, 241-242, 251-252
response to City Treasurer's report (June 1972) 287-293
resignation as Artistic Director of the Crucible 296-305
post-Crucible years (1974-2016) 319-323
photographs xx, xxi, 9, 12, 13, 16, 26, 72, Plates i-v, Plate vii, Plate xi, Plate xxi, Plate xxx, Plate xxxii, Plate xxxiii, 220, 240, 253, 264, 284, 304, 307, 313, 319-322
sketches & designs 62, 65, 81, 91, 93
view on best place to sit in auditorium 150-151
views on thrust stage 164-165, 179-181, 184-185, 282 309-310, 313
views on what theatre is for 24, 179-180, 251-252, 309-310
George, Gwendolyn xv, xviii, 7
George, Lucy Tertia xv, xviii, 40, 284, 306, 308
George, Sue xv, xvii, xviii, 320
George, Tedd (Edward) xv, xvi-xxiv, 283-284, 314-323
Gide, André 72
Ginsbury, Norman 230
Glass, Masie 30
Gleeds 42, 144, 214, 325
Gleeson (Sheffield) Ltd 43, 103, 133, 325
Glossop, Peter 278

Glyndebourne 101
Gods (theatre) 35, 67
Goetz, John & Margaret 229-230
Goldfinger, Ernö 42
Goldfinger, Peter 42, 120, 129
Goring, Marius 202
Grand Hotel (Sheffield) 242
graphic design, see *Stringer Sutton Paddock*
Gray, Terence 179
Greek Theatre, see *Ancient Greek Theatre*
Green, Keith 228, 248, 253, 285, 325
green room 131, 142, 152, 335
Greenwood, Tony 220-221
Greg, Hubert 169
Griffith, Kenneth xiv, 4, 13
groundling 239
Guinness, Alec 56, 114, 183-184, 234
Guinness's Yard 114
Gulbenkian Foundation 138, 214-215, 287
Guthrie, Tyrone xiv, Plate xiii, Plate xv, 184, Plate xix, 243, 324, 326, 329, 331-332
and the thrust stage xi, xiv xxiii, 52-57, 63, 69-70, 104, 110, 122-123, 182-183, 215
at the Assembly Hall, Edinburgh 53-55, 179, 331-332
at the Festival Theatre, Stratford, Ontario 54-57, 117-119, 185, 215-216, 246
at the Guthrie Theater 57, 81-86, Plate xv, 115, 117
at the Nottingham Playhouse (1963) 64
at the Old Vic 149
at the Sheffield Playhouse 57-58, 162-163

influence on Chichester Festival Theatre 68-70
influence on Crucible Theatre 43, 58-59, 70, 72-74, 99, 101-102, 113, 124, 127, 162-163, 167, 177-179, 226, 274
plans for Crucible's opening season 225-226, 229-235
influence on *The Persians* (1971) 298-299
directs Ian McKellen 247-248, 260
death & memorial service 232-234, 244-245
productions
  Coriolanus, Nottingham Playhouse (1963) 64, 247
  Hamlet, Kronborg Castle (1937) 52-53, 313
  Harpers Ferry, Guthrie Theater (1967) 81-82, 88
  Oedipus Rex, Stratford, Ontario (1954) 57, 117-120, 246, 319
  Oedipus (film), 1957 82
  Oedipus, UNSW (1970) 225
  The Barber of Seville, Phoenix Opera, Brighton (1971) 231-233
  The House of Atreus, Guthrie Theater (1967) 82-86, Plate xv, 104, 115, 117, 124, 215, 225, 226, 229, 230, 232, 305
Guthrie thrust stage, see *Theatre design*

Hadfield Cawkwell Davidson 42
Hainsworth, John 26
Hall, Peter xix, 205
Hall, Willis xxi
Hallé Orchestra 19
Hampton, Antony 'Tony' vii, 7, 30, 32, 35, 39, 153, 155, 171, 172, 185, Plate xix, 221, 224, 287, 293, 311, 314, 324
Hare, David 169
Harley, Michael (Mike) xviii, 119
Harris, Kate 327
Harrison, D B 40, 324
Harrison, Wilfred 20, 28, 30, 40, 52, 72, 114, 119, 127, 162, 216, 236, 324
Harvey-Jones, David 228-229, 325, 338-339
Hastings, Ronald 251
Hatherley, Frank iv, xviii, 127, 216, 223
Hathersage (Sheffield) 18
Hastie, Rob xviii
Haworth Tompkins 71
Hawthorne, Nigel 218, 219
Hayman, Ronald 326
Hays, Bill 275
Heath, Roger 179
Heath, Ted 285
Heath Robinson (contraption) 79
Hebblethwaite, Alderman H 73, 172, 173, 324
Heeley, Desmond 88, 91, 92, 110, 258
Hello, Dolly! 262
Herman, Jerry 246
hexagon (shape) 111
Heywood, Graham 202
High Storrs (Sheffield school) 186
Hirsch, Robin 22, 23
Hoare, Rosie 325
Hodgson, John 192, 253
Hodkin & Jones (Dronfield) 133
Hong Kong Academy for Performing Arts v, 320
Hook, Geoff 23
Horace (Quintus Horatius Flaccus) 30

Horn, Roderick 8, 21, 25-26, 28, Plate vii, Plate xi, 308
Horsman, David 249-250
Howard, Peter 41, 47, 110, 144, 172, 324
Hurok, Sol 248

Ibsen, Henrik 198, 230, 245, 267, 268
ICI 122
Ide, Patrick 104, 105, 114, 124-125, 130, 134, 137-138, 146, 152, 153, 214, 324, 328
Iles, Paul xv
Impressionism 293
improvisation 21, 23, 53, 58, 60, 264
inflation xxiii, 69, 144, 285
International Theatre Association 62
in-the-round, see *Theatre design*
Ionesco, Eugène 16, 20
Ironmonger, Alderman Ronald 33, 73, 172, 224, 273, 274-275, 277, 295-296, 324
Ironside, Isaac 27-28
Italian hill towns 134
Italy 61-63, 178
Ithaca (New York) 87, 91

Jack and the Beanstalk 52, 206
James, Lily 323
James, Peter 135, 294, 308, 314, 338
Japan 35, 85, 183-184, 307
jazz 24
Jeffery, Kath xv
Jonson, Ben 205
Johnson, Roy 40, 41, 46, 74, 147
Jones, Emrys 13
Jones, F G 285-291, 294, 301, 303, 306, 324, 328
Jones, Inigo 61

Joseph, Stephen 191, 326-327
Joseph Rowntree Fellowship 322
Jovanovic, Arsenio 145

kabuki 183
kaleidoscope xiv, 276
katharsis (Ancient Greek theatre) 197
Kay, David 237-238, 252
Keating, Charles 229, 233, 235, 244-245, 250, 253, 261, 338
Kennedy, Gilbert 306
Kerr, Walter 7, 56-57, 60-62, 327
King Edward (Sheffield school) 186
King Ecgbert (Sheffield school) 186
Kleos Advisory Ltd v
Knox, Barbara 319
Kronborg Castle 52

Labour Party 33, 38, 173
La Plante, Lynda 309
Lancashire 4, 185
Landstone, Charles 326
Lang, Robert 68
Lang, Veronica 27
Lasdun, Denys 41, 105, 165-166, 175, 331
Leaning Tower of Pisa 337
Lee, Jenny 221
LEGO 120
Leicester 191, 320
Le Fanu, Sheridan 281
Leigh, Vivien 52
Lessac, Michael 93-94
Lewin, John 82, 298
Lewis, Alderman Isador 32, 73, 324
lighting xiv, 9, 12, 35, 47, 51, 63, 67, 68, 76, 82, 84-85, 89, 92, 94, Plate xviii, 100, 104, 115, 122, 124-126, 127-130, 135, 141-144, 145, 147-150, 165, 167, 170, 172, 181, 185, 206, Plate xxiv, 214,

216, 223, 240-241, 249, 257, 266, 268, 270, 285, 296, 310, 312, 316, 325, 327, 329, 335
Light Ltd 147, 325
limbo dancing 186
Lincoln Center 92, 94
Lindsay Quartet 316
Lindsay, David 53
Linklater, N V 7-8
Littlewood, Joan 230, 303
Livings, Henry 170, 193-195
Ljubljana 145
Local Government Act (1948) 233
London xii, xxi, 8, 33, 40, 41, 52, 64, 101, 105, 131, 138, 146, 175, 176, 180, 201, Plate xxvi, 214, 230, 232, 233, 237-239, 247-249, 258, 274, 283, 303, 305, 308, 313, 321, 340
Longfield, Gary xviii
'Long John Silver' 176, 269-270, 272
Lord Mayor 31-32, 165, 185, 221, 269, 283
Lord Mayor's Show 165
Los Angeles (CA) 225, 229
Loving-Richardson gunfight 23
Ludlow Festival 4, 13, 30, 63-65
Lyceum Theatre (Sheffield), see *Theatres*

Malmö (Sweden) 44, 340
Mackintosh, Iain xv, xviii, xxii, 326, 331-332
Mac Liammóir, Micheál 24
MacNaughtan, Alan 153
Magic Circle 45, 60, 71, 106, 110, 115, 189, 210
Maginot Line 179
Mam Tor 298
Manchester 3, 127, 186, 188, 206, 241, 264, 326, 340
Mann, Dr Peter 16, 328

Marchal, Lynda Plate xxix, Plate xxxi, 309, 310
Marchment, David 226, 228, 245, 248, 249, 253, 285, 325
Margate 35
Marlowe, Christopher 23, 205
Marsden's (caterers) 152
Marshall, Norman 326
masks 83, 84-85, 118-119, 163, 187, 197, 215, 226, 291, 298, 299, 321
Mason, James 57, 185-186, 221, 246-247
Master Cutler 39, 185
Matcham, Frank 146
Maugham, Somerset 168
May, Val v, xx, xxi
McGoohan, Patrick 153
McGovern, Will xviii, 71
McKellen, Ian xi-xii, xv, xvii, Plate xxvi, 247-249, 260, 261
McVie, Alderman A E 324
Mecca 237
Meccano 172
mechanical engineers, see *Dale & Benham*
Medcalf, Paul iv, xviii
Messel, Oliver 77
Michelangelo 195
Midlands 304
Milan (Italy) 62-63, 78
Miles, Chris 253, 325
Miles, Bernard xvii, 4, 64, 175-181, 182, 184, 188, 190, 205, 225, 231, 239, 274, 282-283, 301
Miller, Arthur 312
Minneapolis xi, 36, 57, 73, 74, 78, 82, 87, 88, 89, 90, 91, 94, 96, Plate xv, 100-101, 104-105, 107, 117, 125-127, 130, 178-180, 215, 226, 229, 232, 252, 276, 278, 298, 313, 329, 300-332
Minors, Anne iv, xvii, 332

Mitchell, Robert 88
moat 45, 106, 109, 110-111, 115, 122, 126, 141
Moiseiwitsch, Tanya xiv, Plate xiv, Plate xxi, Plate xxxii
  early career (pre-1952) 54, 127
  at the Festival Theatre, Stratford, Ontario 54-57, 326-237, 331
  at the Guthrie Theater xi, 57, 85, 332
  designing the Crucible (1968-1971) xi, xiv, xxii, 59, 99, 103-117, 120, 122-125, 129, 138, 167, 260, 297, 325
  sketches of Crucible stage & revolve 106-107, 116-117
  designs for *The Shoemaker's Holiday* (1971) 269
  ground plan for *The Shoemaker's Holiday* (1971) 336
  at the Sheffield Playhouse (1969) 162-163, 215
  at the Phoenix Opera (1971) 232
  at the Crucible (1971-73) xi, 225-226, 235, 243, 253, 268-269, 286, 291, 297-303, 322, 327, 338-339
  at the National Theatre 301, 331
  at the Adelaide State Theatre Company (1978) 319
modernism 42, 62, 196
money, value of xxiii-xxiv
Montezuma 259
Moors, The 102, 244
Morris, Ivan 205-206
Morton, Hedley 233
Moya, Hidalgo 69
Mrożek, Sławomir 216
Mulryne, Ronnie 183, 326
Munn, Councillor Reg 173
Murray, Bill 249

Music Hall 29, 79, 88, 164, 212, 246, 247, 249, 260
musicals 10, 23, 25, 92, 173, 176, 186, 232, 249, 262, 301, 308, 309, 332
musicians 23, 36, 68, 77, 123, 124, 206, 315
Mycenae 131-132

Naples (Italy) 62
National Theatre xi, 34, 41, 73, 100, 105, 107, 108, 127, 128, 129, 141, 155, 160, 165, 177, 181, 183, 184, 185, 229, 248, 290, 301, 315, 331
Naylor, Anthony xviii, 299, 308, 321
Nazism 216, 218
Nether Edge (Sheffield) 18
Neville, John xvxi, 13, 51, 64-66, 117, 247, 327
Neville, Richard 231
New Sheffield Theatre Trust, see *Crucible Theatre Trust*
newspapers
  Barnsley Chronicle 281, 329
  Morning Telegraph (Sheffield) 58, 120, 153, 154-155, 159, 161, 164, 166, 169, 171, 173, 174, 180, 219, 220, 223, 267, 268, 269, 276, 277, 280, 281, 283, 303, 307, 309, 329
  The Daily Telegraph 7, 251-252, 329
  The Evening Sentinel 191-192, 329
  The Financial Times 268
  The Guardian 192, 218, 252, 258-259, 262, 267-268, 275, 282, 299, 329
  The Observer 67, 180, 182, 188, 189, 201, 329
  The Stage 10, 154, 218
  The Star (Sheffield) 34, 153-154,

159-161, 170-176, 220, 223, 236, 239, 252, 268-270, 273-275, 281-282, 294-296, 305, 307, 310-311, 329
The Sun 155-156
The Sunday Times 180, 267, 329
The Yorkshire Post 268, 329
New South Wales 319
New York 23, 60, 73, 74, 87, 92, 100, 165, 291, 340
Noh theatre 35, 85, 183-184
Noise Rating (NR) 143
Norfolk Street (Sheffield) 32, 40, 43, 102, 124, 130, 137, 139, 186, 252, 286
North America 32, 34, 69, 73, 74-96, 101, 102, 108, 115, 116, 125, 164-166, 179, 226, 245, 276, 301, 328
Norton (Sheffield) 206
Nottingham xx, xxi, 3, 7, 13, 19, 32, 33, 36, 41, 43, 51-52, 57, 62, 64, 68, 73, 75, 117, 143, 144, 159,
Nouvel, Jean 333
Nunn, Trevor 205

O2 Academy 152
O'Casey, Sean 181
octagon (shape) 63, 111, 138-139, 141, 209, 210
Octagon Theatre, see *Theatres*
Oedipus 13, 51, 57, 64, 82, 117-119, 127, 215, 225, 246, 319
Oh! What a Lovely War 12
Oliver! 262
Olivier, Laurence xix, 52, 66-68, Plate v, 127, 129, 141, 160, 161, 175, 177, 179, 181-183, 195, 205, 230, 234, 262
open stage, see *Theatre design*
opera xix, 19, 41, 42, 44, 67, 75, 129, 155, 171, 173, 176, 178, 179, 191, 231, 234, 235, 241, 258, 274, 279, 306, 308
orchestra 19, 35, 43, 67, 92, 136, 189, 278, 279
Oresteia, by Aeschylus 82, 88, 225
Orestes 83-84, 229
Osborne, John xx, 23
Ost, Geoffrey 4-7, 9, 14, 30, Plate ii, 153, 216, 324, 327
Osterholzer, Katie xv
Ottawa 223, 288, 340
Over Arup Associates 41, 42
Ove Arup & Partners 120, 143, 325
Oxford & Cambridge Players v, xix, xx, 60,
Owen, Councillor W 324

pantomime 172-173, 206, 268
Park Hill (Sheffield) 141, 152
Parthenon 85
Partridge, Bernard 162
Pass, Jackie xv, xvi, xviii
Paul, David 7
Peak District 298
Pegasus Theatre Club 11, 21, 23, 246, 260, 320
Pembroke Dock (Wales) v, xix
periactoid 123-124, 336
Perth (Australia) 186, XXX 331
Peter, John 267
Peters, Clarke 323
Petherbridge, Edward xi, xviii, 248-249, 260-261
Pickles, John 23
'picture box' frame, see *Theatre design*
Pilbrow, Richard xviii, Plate xviii, 127-129, 147-149, 182, 240-241, 266, 268, 327
Pinero, Arthur Wing 169
Pinter, Harold xx, 10, 20, 23, 283, 288

Pirandello, Luigi 79, 145
Pittsburgh 276
Plague of 1665 47
Plater, Alan 195-196
Plays and Players 204, 329
playwright xiii, 8, 10, 23, 44, 57, 60, 85, 159, 164, 169-170, 183, 188-189, 193, 195-196, 196, 199-200, 204, 216, 235
Plowright, Joan 68
poetry xix, 23, 24, 34, 141, 241, 260
Poland 216-17, 220, 302, 306
'Polly Parker' 262
Polly, Victor 88-90
Pompidou Centre (Paris) 42
Powell, Philip 69
Prague 24, 145, 328, 332
Pratt, Desmond 268
Prentice, Herbert 'Pip' 3-4
Prince, Hal 291, 301
Prince Charles 221
productions
   A Kind of Loving, Sheffield Playhouse (1965) 20
   A Lily in Little India, Sheffield Playhouse (1968) Plate ix, 127
   A Man for All Seasons, Manoel Theatre (1961) xxi
   A Man for All Seasons, Crucible Theatre (1972) 235, 281-282, 290 338
   A Taste of Honey, Crucible Theatre (1972) 235, 281-282, 285, 338
   All's Well That Ends Well, Stratford, Ontario (1953) 56
   Alpha Beta, Crucible Theatre (1973) Plate xxix
   Arms and the Man, Ebinburgh Festival (1946) 234
   Britannia's Boys, Sheffield Playhouse (1971) Plate xii, 232, 309
   Calamity Jane, Crucible Theatre (1974) Plate xxxi, 309-311, 339
   Camelot, Theatre Royal, Drury Lane (1964) 128
   Camilla, Crucible Studio Theatre (1972) 281
   Celebration, Duchess Theatre (1961) xxi
   Charley's Aunt, Sheffield Playhouse (1965) 19, 21
   Coriolanus, Nottingham Playhouse (1963) 64, 247
   Dominoes, London (1971) 249
   Dr Jekyll & Mr Hyde, Crucible Theatre (1974) Plate xxx, 308, 339
   Facets on a Golden Image, Crucible Theatre (1973) 338
   Fanfare, Crucible Theatre (1971) xi, Plate xxv, 235, 245-251, 258, 259-266, 309, 338
   Free for All, Crucible Theatre (1973) 338
   Getting On, Crucible Theatre (1973) 338
   Hamlet, Kronborg Castle (1937) 52-53, 313
   Hamlet, Nottingham Playhouse (1959) xx, xxi
   Hamlet, Ludlow Festival (1965) 13
   Hamlet, Prospect Theatre Company (1971) 212, 247, 248, 260
   Hamlet, Oxford Stage Company (1996) 322
   Harpers Ferry, Guthrie Theater (1967) 81-82, 88
   Henry V, Edinburgh Festival (1953) xx

Henry, Sweet Henry, Palace Theatre, New York (1967) 95-96
I Was Hitler's Maid, Crucible Theatre (1971) 235
Irma La Douce, Crucible Theatre (1974) 308, 338
It Happened in Irkutsk, Sheffield Playhouse (June 1967) 46-47
John Willy and the Bee People, Sheffield Playhouse (1966) 8, Plate vii, 145
Julius Caesar, Nottingham Playhouse (1962) 3
Juno and the Paycock, Sheffield Lyceum (1966) 181
King Lear, Sheffield Playhouse (1963) 10, Plate ii
Les Enfants du Paradis, RSC (1996) 321
Look Back in Anger, Nottingham Playhouse (1960) xx, 23
Macbeth, Manoel Theatre, Malta (1961) xxi
Macbeth, L. du Garde Peach's production (mid 1960s) 166
Macbeth, Sheffield Playhouse (1970) 218-220
Macbeth, Crucible Theatre (1973) 307-308, 338
Macbeth, Chung Ying Theatre Company, Hong Kong (1982) 320
Man of la Mancha, ANTA Theatre (1967) 92-93
Measure for Measure, RSC (1998) 321
Mister, Royal Lyceum, Edinburgh (1967) 128
Mister, Crucible Theatre (1972) 151, 173, 290, 338
Much Ado About Nothing, Ludlow Festival (1966) 13, 30, 65
My Son Will!, touring one-man show (1999) 321
Oedipus Rex, Stratford, Ontario (1954) 57, 246
Oedipus, film (1957) 82
Oedipus, Nottingham Playhouse (1964) 13, 51, 64
Oedipus, Sheffield Playhouse (1968) 117-120, 127, 215
Oedipus, UNSW (1970) 225
Oedipus, Adelaide State Theatre Company (1978) 319
Oh! What a Lovely War, Crucible Theatre (1972) 291, 308, 338
Othello, Crucible Theatre (2011) xvi, Plate xxxiii, 322-323
Peace in Our Time, Crucible Theatre (1972) 299, 337, 338
Peer Gynt, Arts Council Tour (1959) xxi, 230
Peer Gynt, Crucible Theatre (1971) 230, 235, 240, 243-245, 246, 257, 266-268, 273, 274, 276-279, 283, 288, 290, 305, 307, 338
Peer Gynt, Young Vic (1995) 321
Pinocchio, Crucible Theatre (1972) 338
Playboy of the Western World, Abbey Theatre, Dublin (1971) 229, 245
Private Lives, Crucible Theatre (1974) 309, 339
Reluctant Heroes, Nottingham Playhouse (1959) xx
Racing Demon, Crucible Theatre (2011) 168-169
Richard III, New Theatre (1944) xix

Richard III, Stratford, Ontario (1953) 56-57, 88, 114, 183
Richard III, Old Vic (1962) xxi, 7, 20
Ring o' Roses, Sheffield Playhouse (1967) 47, Plate xi
Rodney Stone, Sheffield Playhouse (1965) 17-18
Romeo and Juliet, Boško Buha (1969) 145, 216
Roots, Notthingam Playhouse (1960) xx
Rosencrantz and Guildenstern Are Dead, Sheffield Playhouse (1971) 308
Sergeant Musgrave's Dance, Sheffield Playhouse (1966) 182
She Stoops to Conquer, Guthrie Theater (1967) 87
Six Characters in Search of an Author, Sheffield Playhouse (1967) 145
Strip Jack Naked, Sheffield Playhouse (1970) 218
Tango, Sheffield Playhouse (1969) 216
Swan Song, Crucible Theatre (November 1971) xi, Plate xxvi, 247-249, 260-261
Talent, Crucible Theatre (2021) 317
The Bacchae, tour of China (1990) 320
The Bald Prima Donna, Sheffield Playhouse (1965) 20
The Barber of Seville, Phoenix Opera, Brighton (1971) 231-233
The Bear Who Liked Geraniums, Theatre Vanguard (1967) 23
The Birthday Party, Sheffield Playhouse (1965) 20, 23, Plate xxvii, 283, 288, 338
The Boy Friend, Sheffield Playhouse (1963) 10
The Boy Friend, Crucible Theatre (1972) 338
The Broken Heart, Chichester Festival Theatre (1962) 67
The Caretaker, Nottingham Playhouse (1961) xx, 10
The Caucasian Chalk Circle, Sheffield Playhouse (1969) 162-163, 215, 249
The Chairs, Sheffield Playhouse (1965) 20, 21
The Chances, Chichester Festival Theatre (1962) 67
The Duchess of Malfi, Sheffield Playhouse (1966) 306
The Duchess of Malfi, Warsaw (1973) 304, 306
The Enchanted Lake, Sheffield Playhouse (1968) 8
The Father, Sheffield Playhouse (1971) 14, 216
The Good Woman of Setzuan, Sheffield Playhouse (1963) 10, Plate iv
The Hostage, National Arts Centre, Ottawa (1971) 223
The House of Atreus, Guthrie Theater (1967) 82-86, Plate xv, 104, 117, 124, 215, 225, 226, 229, 230, 232
The Importance of Being Oscar, Sheffield Playhouse (1966) 24
The Iron Harp, Birmingham Rep (1957) 10
The Jolly Potters, Victoria Theatre, Stoke-on-Trent (1965) 25, 64
The Keep, Sheffield Playhouse (1962) 10, Plate iii
The Lady and the Van, Birmingham Rep (2000) 322

The Late Christopher Bean,
  Crucible Theatre (1972) 284
*The Life and Times of Charlie
  Peace*, Sheffield Playhouse
  (1969) Plate x
The Little Foxes, Vivian Beaumont
  Theater (1967) 94
*The Man with a Flower in his
  Mouth*, Guthrie Theater (1967)
  79
The Merchant of Venice, Ludlow
  Festival (1964) 13
The Merchant of Venice,
  Nottingham Playhouse (1964)
  13, 64
The Merchant of Venice, RSC
  (1998) 321
The Nap, Crucible Theatre (2016)
  xi
The National Health, Crucible
  Theatre (1973) 235, 307, 338
The Persians, Crucible Theatre
  (1972) 291, 298-300, 307, 338
The Real McCoy, Sheffield
  Playhouse (1964) 14
The Room, University of Bristol
  Drama Studio (1957) 10
The Secretary Bird, The Crucible
  (1972) 169
The School for Scandal, Crucible
  Theatre (1974) 297, 308-309,
  339
The Shoemaker's Holiday, Crucible
  Theatre (1971) 124, 235, 240,
  245, 257-258, 268-269, 273,
  275, 290, 336, 338
The Silver Box, Sheffield (1919) 3
*The Stirrings in Sheffield on
  Saturday Night*, Sheffield
  Playhouse (1966 & 1968) 8,
  25-29, 33, 47, 64, 79, 127, 146,
  242, 249, 309, 311
*The Stirrings in Sheffield on
  Saturday Night*, Crucible
  Theatre (1973) 299, 301, 305,
  307, 326, 338
The Taming of the Shrew, Oxford
  & Cambridge Players (1952) xx
The Taming of the Shrew, Crucible
  Theatre (1973) Plate xxviii,
  235, 307, 338
The Tempest, Sheffield Playhouse
  (1965) 20, 236
The Tempest, RSC (1998) 321
The Thieves' Carnival, Guthrie
  Theater (1967) 77, 82
The Thrie Estaits, Assembly Hall,
  Edinburgh (1948) 53, 177,
  331-332
The Visit, Guthrie Theater (1967)
  78-79, 82, 87-88
Tiny Alice, Scott Hall, University
  of Minneapolis (1967) 78
Treasure Island, Mermaid Theatre
  (1961) 176
Treasure Island, Crucible Theatre
  (1971) 8, 173, 206, 269-272,
  276, 291, 305, 338
Trudi and the Minstrel, Sheffield
  Playhouse (1965) 26
Twelfth Night, Guthrie Theater
  (1968) 125
Uncle Vanya, Chicester Festival
  Theatre (1962) 67-68, 181
Uncle Vanya, Sheffield Playhouse
  (1965) 17-18, 20
Uncle Vanya, Guthrie Theater
  (1969) 178
Uncle Vanya, Crucible Theatre
  (1973) 307-308, 332, 338
Under Milk Wood, Crucible
  Theatre (1972) 338
Vatslav, Stratford, Ontario (1970)
  216, 225, 226

Where Love Is, God Is, Sheffield (1919) 3
promontory stage, see *Theatre design*
props 47, 80, 88, 90, 94, 104, 136, 142, 163, 229, 253, 264, 269-271, 291, 296, 298, 306, 325
proscenium arch, see *Theatre design*
Punch 162
Pugh, Dr W D 324
Punshon, John xv
Purdeys 237
Pushkin, Alexander 260
Pye-Smith, Brian 324

Q-File lighting control 148, 150
Quakers (The Society of Friends) xix, 320, 322
Quantity Surveyors, see *Gleeds*

radio 166, 168, 194, 199-200
Radio Brighton 69
Radio Sheffield 220, 223, 226
Race (company) 121
rake, see *Theatre design*
Redgrave, Michael 68
refurbishment
　Chichester Festival Theatre (2012-14) 69, 71
　Crucible Theatre (1984) 315
　Crucible Theatre (2007-10) 133, 147, 316-319, 322
　Lyceum Theatre (1990) 315
　Sheffield Playhouse (1953-54) 6, 340
　Studio Theatre (1991) 315-316
rehearsals xi, xx, 4-5, 13, 19, 26, 45, 53, 55, 56, 66, Plate xv, 101, 103, 117, 125, 135, 146, 150, 152, 203, 216, 220, 224, 228, 230, 232, 235, 242, 245, 246-248, 250, 252, 257, 259, 260, 264, 298, 309, 317

rehearsal room 66, 87, 126, 131, 142-143, 243, 316, 335
Reinhardt, Max 179
Renaissance 61, 189
Renton Howard Wood Associates xxxii, 41-42, 129, 324, 328-239
Renton, Andrew 41-42, 44, 101, 141, 142
repertory (or 'rep') theatre xiii, xxiii, 3-5, 7-8, 17-18, 33, 60, 171-172, 236, 274, 292, 294
repertoire xxiii, 12, 18-21, 24, 25, 34, 66, 226, 288, 294, 333
Restoration (period) 61, 189, 205
Rhondda Valley xix
Rice, Peter 42, Plate xvii, 120, 131
Richardson, Ralph 230
Richmond (England) 35, 340
ritual 24, 53, 85, 118, 151, 179, 252
Robertson, Toby xix
Robson, H N 324
Romans 60-61, 189
Rome (Italy) 62
Roscius (Quintus Roscius Gallus) 205
Rose, Ron 277
Ross, F A 324
Royal Academy 201
Royal Shakespeare Company (RSC), see *Theatres*
RSC Fringe Festival 321
Rudkin, David 196-198
rugby xxi, 58
Russell Brown, John 159-160
Russian xi, 260

Sadowski, Andrzej 306
Saint-Exupéry, Antoine de 127
'*Sally*' 262
scenery 4, 45, 47, 53-55, 57, 65, 66, 77, 79-80, 87-91, 99, 104, 107, 110, 124, 128, 136, 142, 151, 173,

200, 203, 268, 279, 291, 292, 306, 337
Schick, Oliver iv, xviii
Schneider, Alan 87
Scholes, H Kevan 327
sculpture 83, 178, 202, 203
Second World War xi, 4-5, 36, 143, 216-217, 299
Seed, Alec 4, 37, 39, 327
sfumato 88
Shakespeare plays
  All's Well That Ends Well 56
  Coriolanus 64, 247
  Hamlet xx, xxi, 13, 52, 176, 178, 188, 195, 197, Plate xxvi, 247-248, 260, 313, 322
  Henry IV, Part I 159
  Henry IV, Part II 38, 99
  Henry V xix, xx, 51, 75, 114, 175, 188, 313
  Julius Caesar 3, 225
  King Lear 10, Plate ii
  Love's Labour's Lost 60
  Macbeth xxi, 114, 166, 218-220, 307, 320, 338
  Measure for Measure 321
  Much Ado About Nothing 13, 30, 65
  Othello v, xvi, Plate xxxiii, 314, 322-323
  Pericles 225
  Richard III xix, xxi, 7, 20, 23, 56, 88, 114, 183, 234
  Romeo and Juliet xx, 55, 145, 216
  The Merchant of Venice 13, 64, 235, 321
  The Taming of the Shrew xx, Plate xxviii, 235, 307, 338
  The Tempest 20, 87, 236, 321
  Twelfth Night 125, 199, 339
Shakespeare, William xix, xx, 3, 6, 19, 23, 24, 38, 52, 53, 55, 56, 60, 61, 87, 90, 99, 155, 159, 162, 164, 165, 168, 169, 175, 179, 187, 188, 189, 199, 205, 218, 225, 234, 235, 239, 252, 260, 300, 308, 312, 314, 321, 331
Shaw, George Bernard 160
Sheaf Valley (Sheffield) 130, 139, 221
Sheffield City Council xiii, xiv, 25, 30-33, 73, 127, 170-173, 233, 273, 275, 293-295, 302, 313, 315, 329
Sheffield City Hall (1932) 19, 171, 233,
Sheffield Corporation 38, 223-224, 274, 286, 287
Sheffield Festival 235
Sheffield Fire Brigade 136-137
Sheffield Playhouse xiii, 340
  early years (1914-1938) 3-4, 176, 205
  Geoffrey Ost as Artistic Director (1938-1965) 5-14
  Colin George as Assistant Director (1962-1965) xxi, 3, 7-15, 62, Plate ii, Plate iii, Plate iv, 235
  Colin George as Artistic Director (1965-1971) 15-32, 46-47, Plate v, Plate vii, 103, 105, 117-120, 127, 145, 151, 162-163, 216-220, 232, 302, 306
  Arts Council funding xxiii, 5, 7-8, 15-16, 21, 23, 30-31, 33, 329
  audience 4-5, 7, 10-11, 16-20, 25, 28-29, 45-46, 251-252, 292
  children's theatre 11-12, 21-24, 26, 30-31, 51, 58, 100, 105, 138, 145, 214, 260, 320
  Company & staff 21, 30, 32, 36, 44, 79, Plate viii, Plate ix, Plate

x, Plate xi, Plate xii, 134-135,
152-153, 185, 187, Plate xxii,
221, 223, 228, 243, 245, 266-
267, 273, 292, 296, 321,
324
  inadequate facilities 4, 30, 33, 35-
36, 64, 128, 152, 291
  new & experimental work 10-11,
13-14, 20, Plate iv
  refurbishment (1954) 6, 42
  seat prices xxiv, 19, 58, 239
  talk by Tyrone Guthrie (1967) 52,
57-58
  closure (1971) 235-236, 242, 249
  sale of site (1973) 286-287
Sheffield Playhouse Board 6-8, 14-
15, 21, 28, 30, 33, 39, 72, 74, 96,
166, 168, 221
Sheffield Steel Band 250, 262
Sheffield Theatres 315, 319, 327
Sheffield Town Hall (1897) 30-32,
42, 208, 221
Sheffield United 186, 221
Sheffield Wednesday 186, 221
Sheridan, Richard Brinsley 135-136,
297, 308
Sherwood, Harry 70
Sherwood, Rozalia iv, xviii
Shewring, Margaret 183, 326
Shipton Street (Sheffield) 3
Shooters Grove School, Sheffield 22
Short, P J 206
Silkstone 143
Sim, Alasdair 13
Skye Edge (Sheffield) 141
Skylon 69
Slade, Keith 69
Smith, Barrie 8, Plate viii, Plate ix,
199, 127, 299
Smith, Caroline 279-281, 305, 325,
338
Smith, James xviii, xxi, 253

snooker, see *World Snooker
Championship*
Society for Theatre Research (STR)
xv, xvi
solicitor 38, 301
Sondheim, Stephen 301
Sophocles 52, 118, 179
sound xiv, 12, 77, 78, 82, 94, 120,
129, 142, 144, 149-150, 168, 223,
228, 262, 308, 326, 327, 335
sound design 149-150, 223
soundproof xxiv, 44, 125, 138, 142,
143
Sound Space Vision iv, xviii, 332
Southampton 35
Southern, Richard 43
Southport (England) 4
Sprague, William George Robert
121, 146
stage door 21, 131, 139, 230, 245,
335
Stage Lighting (1954), by Geoffrey
Ost 9, 327
stage lighting & equipment, see
Theatre Projects Ltd
Stanworth, Lyndsay 12
Stavis, Barrie 81
steel 4, 29, 38, 44, 111, 120, 143,
144, 188, 208, 217, 221, 222, 250,
262, 276, 313
Stevenson, Robert Louis 269
Stewart, Job 281, 283, 308, 325, 338
St John, Michael 162
St John Wilson, Colin 146
St Paul's Covent Garden (London)
233
Strand Lighting 148
Stratford, Ontario, see *Theatres:
Festival Theatre, Stratford, Ontario*
Stratford-upon-Avon, see *Theatres:
Royal Shakespeare Theatre (RSC)*
Strehler, Giorgio 62, 78

Strick, Peter 191
Strindberg, August 14
Stringer Sutton Paddock 325
structural engineers, see *Ove Arup & Partners*
Studio Theatre (Crucible) 32, 34-36, 38, 94, 95, 105, 124-125, 137-144, 186, 209, 213-215, 227, 236, 238, 241-242, 244, 252, 279-281, 286-288, 290, 292, 305-306, 308, 311, 315-316, 318, 325, 328, 340, 335
Swain, Councillor Michael 170-173, 177, 277
Sydney Opera House 41-42
Szajna, Jozef 216-220, 302, 304, 306

TABS 64, 201, 204, 327
Tarpley, Edwina 276-277
teacher 11, 17, 23, 264
Tebbutt, Alderman Grace 31-32, 138
telegram 112, 283, 298
Telegraph and Star Old Folks Fund 223
television xi, 5, 8, 19, 61, 62, 68, 73, 125, 127, 148, 153, 161, 164, 165, 168, 187, 195, 200, 204, 209, 214, 241, 242, 270, 277, 309-310
Temperance Hall (Sheffield) 3, 6, 30, 36, 42, 47
Tenby (Wales) xix
tennis 58
Terson, Peter 200-201
The Architectural Review 122-123, 327, 335
The Libation Bearers, by Aeschylus 82
The Mighty Reservoy, by Peter Terson 201
The Furies, by Aeschylus 82
The Tent (Festival Theatre Stratford, Ontario) 57
The Three Knights 175-177, 195, 199
Theatre design & terminology
 apron stage xxiii
 forestage xxi, xxiii, 35, 43, 45-46, 51-52, 59-60, 64, 92, 100
 the 'Fourth Wall' 194
 Guthrie thrust stage xi, xiv xxiii, 52-57, 63, 69-70, 104, 110, 122-123, 182-183, 215
 in-the-round xxiii, 25, 36, 60, 62-64, 79, 92, 113, 124, 125-126, 170, 183, 191-193, 195, 201-203, 252, 280
 open stage xvii, xxii-xxiii, 13, 24, 35-36, 43, 46-47, 54, 57, 60, 63-64, 67, 73, 78, 82, 92, 100, 103, 104-105, 115, 117, 124, 128, 138, 150-151, 160-161, 163-166, 168-169, 176-177, 181, 183-184, 191, 193, 195-197, 199-200, 203-204, 206, 215, 298, 301
 'picture box' frame 60-62, 67, Plate iii
 promontory stage xxii-xxiii, 75, 92, 154, 178-181, 187
 proscenium arch xi, xxii-xxiii, 6, 13, 29, 35, 43, 45, 47, 51-53, 56, 58, 60-64, 66-67, 71, 73, 75, 77-78, 80, 85, 87-88, 92-96, 99-100, 104, 106-109, 121, 128, 135-137, 148, 150, 150, 164-166, 168-174, 185, 187, 189-190, 198-199, 201, 203-206, 216, 229, 301, 315
 rake 35, 45, 67, 71, 91, 112, 120-121, 126, 131, 230, 331
 thrust stage v, xi, xiv, xvii, xxii-xxiii, 29, 43, 45, 52-57, 59-60, 63-71, 73-74, 77-82, 84-96, 99-117, 121-122, 125-128, 130, 135-136, 138, 142, 148-150, 154,

159-161, 164-166, 169, 173-197, 201-202, 205-206, Plate xx, Plate xxx, Plate xxxiii, 215-216, 223, 228, 230-231, 233, 235, 237, 242-243, 246-248, 250, 252, 257-258, 260, 264, 266-268, 271, 273-274, 276-278, 282-283, 291-292, 297-298, 301, 307, 310, 312-315, 323, 326, 328, 331-332, 336-337

traverse stage xxiii, 63, 184

vomitory (tunnel) 45, 55, 63, 70-71, 82, 92, 94-95, 99, 106, 109-112, 120, 141, 151, 228, 249, 264, 336

Theatre of the Absurd 190

Theatre In Education (TIE) 21, 24

Theatre Parade (TV programme) 268

Theatre Projects Ltd 111, 127, 129-130, 141-142, 147-150, 241, 325

Theatre Vanguard 22-24, 30, 36, 96, Plate vi, 105, 209, 241-242, 246, 252, 286, 288, 292, 306, 315

Theatres & Theatre Companies

Adelaide State Theatre Company, Australia v, 319

Aldwych Theatre, London 131, 148

ANTA Theatre, New York 92-94, 340

Assembly Hall, Edinburgh 53-55, 64, 179, 330-332

Babs Asper Theatre, Ottawa 223, 288, 340

Barbican Theatre, London 105, 183, 321

Belgrade Theatre, Coventry 21, 24, 32, 41, 288, 306, 310

Birmingham Repertory Theatre ('Birmingham Rep') xx, 4, 7, 10, 33, 186, 291, 306, 322

Boško Buha Theatre, Belgrade 24, 145, 216, 328

Cheltenham Repertory Theatre ('Cheltenham Rep') 201

Chung Ying Theatre Company, Hong Kong v, 320

Cockpit Theatre, London 340

Coventry Repertory Theatre ('Coventry Rep') v, xx, 21

Crucible Theatre, see separate listing

Duchess Theatre, London xxi

Empire Palace Theatre, Edinburgh 136

English Opera Group 234

Everyman Theatre, Liverpool 308

Festival Theatre, Cambridge 179

Festival Theatre, Chichester xviii, 66-71, 100-101, 105-106, 111-112, 127, 148, 154, 155, 160, 169, 175, 177, 178, 180-183, 237-238, 248, 276, 326, 330-332

Festival Theatre, Stratford, Ontario 54-57, 69-70, 73-74, 80, 88-91, 94, 99-100, 105, 112, 114, 127, 135, 155, 178, 179, 180, 183, 185, 215, 216, 223, 225-226, 228, 235, 244, 246, 288, 298, 330-332, 336

Forum Theater, New York 95, 340

Gaiety Theatre, Manchester 3

Georgian Theatre, Richmond 35, 340

Globe Theatre, London 61, 189, 239, 290

Guthrie Theater, Minneapolis 36, 57, 74-89, 91, Plate xv, 105, 107, 110, 115, 125-126, 130, 137, 204, 259, 329, 331-332

Jiří Wolker Theatre, Prague 24, 145, 328
La Fenice, Venice 75
Leeds Playhouse 33, 275
Leicester Haymarket Theatre 320
Little Theatre, Southport 4-5
Lyceum, Sheffield xvi, 7, 32, 100-101, 121, 146, 173, 181, 223, 233, 242, 279, 301, 315, 317-318, 322
Manoel Theatre, Malta xxi
Mermaid, London 64, 105, 175-176, 179-181, 191-192, 225, 340
Minerva Studio Theatre, Chichester 71
Municipal Theatre, Malmö 44, 340
National Arts Centre, Ottawa 223, 288, 340
Nottingham Playhouse xx-xxi, 3, 7, 13, 19, 32-33, 36, 41, 43, 51-52, 57, 62, 64-66, 68, 73, 75, 117, 143, 144, 159, 170, 226, 247, 288, 291, 304, 306, 327, 340
Octagon Theatre, Bolton 186, 216, 340
Octagon Theatre, Perth 186, 340
Old Vic, London xx, xxi, 7, 19, 20, 54, 105, 127, 149
Olivier Theatre, London xxii, 160, 177, 182-183, 330-332
Oxford Stage Company 322
Palace Theatre (Attercliffe), Sheffield 7
Palace Theatre, New York 95
Phoenix Opera, Brighton 173, 231, 234, 274, 279
Piccolo Teatro, Milan 62
Players' Theatre, London 249
Questors, London 105, 201-204, 340
Royal Exchange, Manchester 180, 340
Royal Opera House, Covent Garden 129
Royal Shakespeare Company (RSC), Stratford-upon-Avon v, 19, 54, 100, 107, 260, 290, 315, 321, 322, 332
Sadler's Wells, London 234
Salisbury Playhouse 279-280
Scott Hall, University of Minneapolis 78
Shaw Theatre, London 308
Sheffield Playhouse, see separate listing
69 Theatre Company ('Theatre 69'), Manchester 127, 188, 241, 340
Studio Theatre, Crucible, see separate listing
Studio Theatre Company, Scarborough 195, 199, 280, 340
Teatro Sant'Erasmo, Milan 62-63
Theatre Royal, Drury Lane 54, 128, 135, 195
Theatre Royal, Newcastle 201
Thorndike, Leatherhead 149
Trestle Theatre, St Albans 321
Victoria Theatre, Stoke-on-Trent 25, 64, 165, 188, 191, 195, 197, 201, 252, 331
Vivian Beaumont Theater, New York 73, 92, 94-95, 100, 135, 165, 340
Young Vic, London 308, 321, 340

Thomas, Gwyn 10, Plate iii
Thomason, Ed 305-306, 306, 308, 338-339
Thompson, Nick xviii, xxxi, xxxii, 42, 46-47, 51, Plate xvi, 102, 110-

112, 121-122, 130-134, 143, 146, 286, 315-316, 324, 327
Thorn Lighting 148
Thornber, Robin 252, 299
Thorndike, Sybil 79-80, 234, 298-299
Thorne, Angela 153
Thorntons 316
thrust stage, see *Theatre design*
Tinsley, Vicar of 14
Tolstoy, Leo 3
Top Rank Suite 152, 185
Toronto 91
Totley (Sheffield) 18
Townhead Street (Sheffield) 3, 6, 32-33, 236-237
Trades Union Congress (TUC) 29
tragedy 58, 85, 118-119, 225, 277, 299, 309
traverse stage, see *Theatre design*
Tudor Square (Sheffield) 139
Turgenev, Ivan 257
Turner, Michael 9, Plate ii
Turrell, James 145
Tynan, Kenneth 67-68
Tyzack, Margaret 153

United Gas Company 27
University College, Oxford v, xix
University of Birmingham 160
University of Bristol v, 10
University of Cambridge xix
University of Manchester 186, 326
University of Minneapolis 78
University of New England, Armidale (Australia) 319
University of Oxford v, xix
University of Sheffield 16-17, 26, 30-31, 38-42, 114, 125, 127, 161, 186, 206, 249, 326, 328
University of Warwick 42
University of Waterloo (Canada) 91

Van Gogh, Vincent 293
Vanguard, see *Theatre Vanguard*
Varnishing Day 201
Vega, Suzanne 23
Venables, Clare 315
Venice (Italy) 62, 75
Vernon, Dorothy 8, 11, 22-23, 27, 28, 47, Plate vii, Plate x, 163, 249, 262-263, 283-284, 306
Vickers, Jon 278
Victorian 32, 35, 75, 146, 164, 189, 252
Vietnamese refugee camps 320
Vinci, Leonardo da 88
vomitory (tunnel), see *Theatre design*
Von Blon, Philip 80
Voysey, Patricia 7

Wales v, xix, xxi, 101, 221, 230, 322
Walford, Glen 23, Plate vi, 320
Walker Art Center 74
Walker, Peter 233
Wanamaker, Sam 290
Wardle, Irving 268
wardrobe 36, 142, 220, 228, 243, 253, 290, 325
Warsaw 302, 304, 306
Waterhouse, Keith xxi, 169-170
Watford 24
Watterson, Mike 314
Wembley Stadium 195
Wesker, Arnold xx
West, Dominic 323
West End (London) 6, 19, 23, 105, 137, 141, 149, 169, 240, 249, 258, 290, 308
Whitfield, William 41-42
wigs 232, 290-291
Wilcox, Andrew xviii
Wilcot, Paul 205
Wild West 12

Wilkinson, Christopher 23, Plate viii, 134, 218, 235-236, 305
William, David xi, 248-249, 260
Williams, Emlyn 169-170
Wilson, Sandy 10
Wing-Davey, Mark 308
Wolfit, Donald xix, 4
Wood, Humphrey 41, 47
Wood, Victoria 317
Wolfe, Caroline de xv
Wordsworth, Richard 299
Wordville Press xviii
World Cup (football) 30
World Snooker Championship xi, 111, 312, 314-315
World War 1, see *First World War*
World War 2, see *Second World War*
Wragg, Councillor G 324
Wroclaw Mime Theatre 216

York 129
Yorkshire xi, 32, 147, 185-186, 221, 238, 246, 250, 262, 283
Young, B A 268
Young, Dr Gerard 38-41, 72-74, 101, 121, 125-126, 135, 161-162, 324, 329
Young, Hillary 152, 221
Yugoslavia 145, 328

Zagreb 145
Zeisler, Peter 80
Zeus 298

Lightning Source UK Ltd.
Milton Keynes UK
UKHW020209051222
413327UK00001B/4